D0812049

DATE DUE

Post-Soviet Russia

POST-SOVIET RUSSIA

A Journey Through the Yeltsin Era

Roy Medvedev

Translated and Edited by George Shriver

Columbia University Press   New York

Columbia University Press
Publishers Since 1893

New York   Chichester, West Sussex
Copyright © 2000 Columbia University Press

Library of Congress Cataloging-in-Publication Data
Medvedev, Roy Aleksandrovich, 1925–
Post-Soviet Russia : a journey through the Yeltsin era /
Roy Medvedev ; translated by George Shriver.
p.cm.
Includes bibliographical references and index.
ISBN 0–231–10606–8 (cloth : alk. paper)
ISBN 0–231–10607–6 (pbk : alk. paper)
1. Russia (Federation—Economic policy—1991–.
2. Russia (Federation)—Economic conditions—1991–.
3. Capitalism—Russia (Federation).
I. Title.
HC340.12.M429 2000
338.947'009'049—dc21   00–040443

Printed in the United States of America
Designed by Audrey Smith

c 10 9 8 7 6 5 4 3 2 1
p 10 9 8 7 6 5 4 3 2 1

Contents

PART 3
1998: A YEAR OF UPHEAVAL

POSTSCRIPT
YELTSIN'S LAST YEAR

Translator's Note

Much of this translation derives from a manuscript version of Roy Medvedev's *Kapitalizm v Rossii?* [Capitalism in Russia?] (Moscow: Prava Cheloveka [Human Rights Publishers], 1998. The author's work on the Russian book was completed in January 1998, although much of the text was written in 1995–96. The book investigates in depth the attempt to create a capitalist system in post-Soviet Russia during the 1990s. In this English version some of the chapters have been abridged and some appear in an order different from that followed in the Russian book. A certain part of the Russian manuscript, which we have included in this translation, was published in Russian in the pamphlet by Roy and Zhores Medvedev, *Rossiya i Zapad v kontse XX veka* [Russia and the West at the End of the 20th Century] (Moscow, 1997), but not in *Kapitalizm v Rossii?*

A special feature of this English version is Part 3 (chapters 9 and 10), which covers the critical events of 1998, and the "Postscript" on the further upheavals of 1999 through the December elections to the Duma (parliament) and the resignation of Russian President Boris Yeltsin.. The English version also contains an analysis of the 1995–96 elections that is more detailed than in the Russian book. This analysis pays special attention to Yeltsin's chief opponent in the 1996 elections, Gennady Zyuganov, and his Communist Party of the Russian Federation (CPRF), including excerpts from the writings of Zyuganov and campaign literature and related material of the CPRF.

In effect this book reviews the entire "Yeltsin era" which is now coming to an end—from Boris Yeltsin's rise to dominance in the wake of the unsuccessful coup attempt of August 1991, through "liberal-ization" of prices, "shock therapy," and privatization of state-owned industry to the tank bombardment of the Russian White House and dispersal of the Russian Supreme Soviet in October 1993, the elections of December 1993, then those of 1995–96, and finally, the crises of 1998, which resulted in the premiership of Yevgeny Primakov. The "Postscript," as we have said, takes the story through the end of 1999.

In all this material the author's consistent theme is that imported schemes for creating a particular type of "neoliberal" capitalism in Russia cannot work. In his view, given Russia's specific social, politi-cal, and economic characteristics in the twentieth century, a mix of government planning and market mechanisms seems more likely to be effective.

The book provides telling thumbnail sketches of many new figures who have trod the boards of Russian public life during the 1990s—some only briefly, others for a longer time: among them, Gaidar, Burbulis, Chubais, Chernomyrdin, Rutskoi, Khasbulatov, and more recently, Nemtsov, Kiriyenko, Lebed, Primakov, and Putin.

NOTE ON THE SPELLING OF RUSSIAN NAMES

The more familiar and readable system of Russian transliteration has generally been used, omitting diacritical marks (such as hard signs and soft signs) and in most cases using y rather than i or j, or -ii or -ij. (Thus, Gennady Zyuganov, not Gennadii Ziuganov, and Boris Yeltsin, not Boris El'tsin or El'cin.) Names of tsars are usually Anglicized. Titles of books or periodicals are sometimes given in the Library of Congress form of transliteration as an aid to readers wishing to locate them in a library catalogue.

Introduction

Roy Medvedev

During the twentieth century Russia experienced a great number of political, social, and economic upheavals, accompanied by fundamental changes in property relations and the system of government. At the beginning of the century Russia was an enormous empire without any democratic institutions. As an absolute monarchy, the unifying factor in the system of government was the emperor, or tsar; in relations between nationalities, the unifying factor was the Russian language; and in matters of ideology, the unifying factor was the Russian Orthodox Church, which functioned as part of the government, there being no separation of church and state.

In the Russian empire one's rights were not restricted for reasons of race or ethnic origin, but there were restrictions on non-Russian languages and religions. The Austro-Hungarian empire, in contrast, published its legal code in all the languages of the nationalities included in that empire. The Russian empire published its laws only in Russian.

In Russia the autocracy relied mainly on the army to maintain power. For ideological support it relied on the formula "autocracy, orthodoxy, nationality"—the third item in this formula standing for certain historical traditions of the Russian state.

The main economic conflict in Russia before World War I was not so much the struggle between bourgeoisie and proletariat over the ownership of industry as the struggle between the smallholder peasantry and the large landed proprietors over ownership of the land. The main conflict among nationalities had to do with forced Russification, especially after the decrees of Tsar Alexander III making Russian the only official language for use in government, the courts, and educational institutions from elementary school to the university level.

The Russian empire collapsed as a result of the February 1917 revolution and defeat in World War I. After the downfall of the monarchy a bourgeois-democratic republic arose briefly, but in October 1917 it too was overthrown by the more radical socialist parties. As a result of this revolution there began a radical transformation of property relations, which provoked a lengthy civil war. The Communist Party headed by Vladimir Lenin eventually triumphed in this civil war, and on the territory of the former Russian empire a new state took shape—the Union of Soviet Socialist Republics (USSR).

The Soviet government did not consider itself the "legal heir" of the Russian empire, and it publicly renounced the treaties signed by the former tsarist rulers of Russia, as well as the debts incurred by them. The dictatorship of the proletariat was proclaimed as the basic principle of government in the Soviet Union, but this soon evolved into the dictatorship of the Communist Party, which later developed de facto into a new form of autocratic rule by the general secretary of the party, Joseph Stalin. The ideology of "Marxism-Leninism" (as interpreted by Stalin) became the official ideology of the country, with repressive measures directed against all forms of religion.

The Soviet government ended forced Russification, replacing it with a policy of "free association of nations," a "family of nations" in which it became possible to construct educational systems (elementary, secondary, and higher education) in all the main languages of the nationalities of the USSR. The principle of internationalism replaced that of Russian nationalism, at least officially. The development of the national cultures of the peoples of the USSR, however, was separated from its roots in the particular history and religion of each people. Cultural development was supposed to follow the formula "national in form, socialist in content."

During the time of the New Economic Policy, roughly 1922 to 1929, the Soviet government permitted capitalist elements in the economy to a limited extent. In the 1930s Stalin's repressive totalitarian regime ended most forms of private economic activity. The socioeconomic system that arose in the USSR in the 1930s combined elements of socialism (a system of social protections, a kind of welfare state; free and universal public education; free health care for all; relatively equal distribution of material goods; and central planning of the economy) with elements of state feudalism (the peasants were bound to the land, not allowed to leave the collective farms or state farms to which they were assigned, while industrial workers were tied to their plants or factories, which they, too, were not allowed to leave). There was even an element of slave-owning society in the form of the "corrective labor" camps (the millions of prisoners doing forced labor in the Gulag system). While the development of modern industry accelerated, in agriculture a substantial sector of primitive natural economy, production for bare subsistence, continued in the form of peasants' household plots and the garden plots used by city dwellers for growing fruits and vegetables.

The destruction of the totalitarian system began in 1956 with Nikita Khrushchev's so-called secret speech about the Stalin "cult of personality." A prolonged and contradictory process ensued during which the Soviet Union was opened to Western influence as far as scientific and technological progress was concerned. Meanwhile internal political processes and foreign policy were shaped by the general condition of confrontation with the West, the Cold War. Not until the coming to power of Mikhail Gorbachev did the Soviet Union make a decisive turn toward democratization. The totalitarian political censorship of the press was eliminated in 1987 with the advent of the policy of glasnost, and in 1989 a new electoral system brought with it a genuine parliament (the Congress of People's Deputies) and a multiparty system.

Most of the new political parties, with their many and varied programs, did not emerge from social movements active on the level of the USSR as a whole; they arose mostly within the limits of one or another "national republic" (Ukraine, Armenia, Lithuania, and so on) accompanied by a revival of local nationalism. Meanwhile, economic difficulties in 1989–90 resulted in attempts to establish a mixed economy in the USSR combining elements of both socialism and the capitalist "free market" system.

The attempt by the Soviet Communist Party to reassert its monopoly of power (the attempted coup d'etat of August 1991) ended in a fiasco, followed by the disintegration of the USSR in December 1991. The Soviet Union broke apart into fifteen sovereign states, which quickly received international recognition. These were the Russian Federation, Ukraine, Belarus, Moldavia, Georgia, Armenia, Azerbaijan, Kazakhstan, Turkmenia, Uzbekistan, Kirgizia, Tajikistan, Lithuania, Latvia, and Estonia. In addition, five states proclaimed themselves independent but did not receive international recognition (the Dniester Republic, Abkhazia, Karabakh, Southern Ossetia, and Chechnya).

The Russian Federation, largest of the new countries in the "post-Soviet space," declared itself the legal and historical heir not only to the USSR (assuming the debts and treaty obligations of the USSR, retaining the Soviet Union's seat as a permanent member of the UN Security Council, and maintaining the status of a nuclear power) but to prerevolutionary Russia as well (reviving the tsarist flag, coat of arms, and honorary orders of old Russia, as well as official Russian nationalism). According to its constitution, however, the Russian Federation is not a "national" state but a *multinational* entity, created by many nationalities "united by a common destiny" within a common territory.

During the years 1991–1999 the new rulers of the Russian Federation introduced a political program that amounted to a new "revolution from above," whose aim was to transform the so-called socialist system of former Soviet Russia into a liberal capitalist system. President Boris Yeltsin, together with a cabinet made up of young reform-minded economists, carried out extensive measures to eliminate state-owned industry and privatize the entire economic infrastructure, as well as nearly all real estate (including houses and apartments), and to make Russia an integral part of the worldwide "free market" economic system. In implementing this "reform" program, Yeltsin and his government had no base of support in the form of a political party; they did not even have a publicly stated program. They used exclusively administrative methods, sometimes employing force and violence (the bloody suppression of the Russian Supreme Soviet in October 1993, for example).

The reform scenario was based on recommendations by Western economic experts and advisers, and the financial means for carrying out these reforms were guaranteed by credits and loans from Western banks, governments, and international financial institutions, above all the International Monetary Fund (IMF).

This capitalist "revolution from above" also ended in disaster as of August 1998. It took the quite unusual form of a kind of "self-implosion" without any pressure either from within the country or from the outside, under conditions of complete passivity on the part of the population. The revolution of February 1917 was a truly popular revolution in which masses of people took part. It was not organized by parties or politicians. The October 1917 revolution was an organized insurrection that overthrew the bourgeois Provisional Government. The Bolshevik party worked out the strategy and tactics of that revolution, but in the main it was supported by the masses. The anti-Communist revolution of August–December 1991 also had political leaders, with Boris Yeltsin at their head, and enjoyed the support of a substantial part of the population disillusioned with the sorry results of Gorbachev's perestroika. No one organized the collapse, and effective overthrow, of the capitalist system in August 1998. It collapsed of its own accord, under the weight of its own mistakes and miscalculations, for it ended up in financial bankruptcy.

The last "reform" government—of Sergei Kiriyenko—left a political vacuum in its wake. For nearly a month there was hardly a political party in Russia willing to declare its readiness to take the leadership of the country. Not until the middle of September 1998, and only after great difficulties, did a new government begin to take shape. It consisted of leaders who had a fundamentally new political orientation. Chapter 9 of this book ("1998, A Year of Upheaval") examines some of the programmatic priorities these new leaders adopted.

The events of the past decade have been so complex and contradictory, so full of dramatic encounters and confrontations, and they have ranged over so broad a field, that simply to comment on all the events in their interconnectedness is an extremely difficult task. We find ourselves unable to evaluate the full meaning of many conflicts in which we find interwoven, often in a capricious way, the role of mass movements and personal ambitions, intelligent calculation and banal ignorance, rivalry between political and ethnic elites, and between outlying regions and the central government. We find foreign intervention, both open and covert, pressures exerted by particular social and economic interests, even by criminal organizations, and along with all this, besides the lust for profit, the yearning for social justice.

5

I have tried to outline and analyze the main events that have transpired in the Russian Federation since late August 1991. My primary focus was on the period 1991–1995, but I have also made use of considerable material, including historical documents, from 1996–97 as well as the late 1980s. And separate chapters deal with 1998 and 1999.

This book of course presents my own view of events—what I regard as the most significant aspects. In discussing many of the problems Russia faces, I feel that I am mainly posing the question, not giving the answer. But as one of my mentors at Leningrad University used to say, half the solution to a problem is presenting it correctly.

Undoubtedly a more complete understanding of all the changes that have occurred will come with the passage of time, not only because some historical distance is required but also because there will be more information than we have access to at present.

But our common task—as historians, journalists, scholars, and writers—is to record our impressions of current events in a timely fashion and in a form true to our own point of view, as well as to make some preliminary analysis, no matter how limited our sources might be. The views and opinions of contemporary eyewitnesses are inevitably subjective and admittedly limited. Still, they provide a basis, in fact the *only* basis, for virtually all future historical writing.

PART I

MYTHS AND REALITIES OF

CAPITALISM IN RUSSIA

1

A Capitalist Perestroika: First Steps, 1992–1993

After the failed coup attempt of August 1991 the power of the central government of the Soviet Union faltered. Real power was in the hands of Boris Yeltsin, who only a month before had taken his oath of office as president of Russia. The central ministries of the Soviet government were paralyzed; officials in the central governmental structures did not know what their powers or prerogatives now were, or what their future might be. By September the Russian Federation and other union republics in fact were operating as fully independent states, and they were obliged to deal with problems previously under the jurisdiction of the president and government of the USSR.

Yeltsin and his circle, unprepared for this turn of events, didn't know what to do first. Oleg Poptsov, a writer and Yeltsin confidant, gives this account:

> During those days [August 19–22, 1991] power fell at the democrats' feet. It tumbled down out of the heavens in all its vast dimensions and crushed to the ground the none-too-sturdy administrative organism of the democrats. Yeltsin's whole conception had been geared toward a long, tough struggle with the

central government, steadily pushing it back, denying it any right to administer Russia. That perspective within an hour's time had disappeared. To be sure, it would have been a wearing struggle, but in the conception held by Yeltsin's team, it had its indisputable advantages. First, it allowed the democrats a fair amount of time to get to know their own strength, to smooth out the form and functioning of their government, to maintain the potential, advantageous on all occasions, of speaking from the opposition, of accusing the central government of failure in making economic reforms. Most important, it would have allowed time to form a fundamentally new administrative apparatus, in contrast to the central bureaucratic structures.

(Oleg Poptsov, *Khronika vremen "tsaria Borisa"* [Chronicle of the Times of "Tsar Boris"], Moscow, 1996, pp. 205–206)

The ministries of the Russian Federation were also unsure what to do next; they had no program to follow, nor much understanding of the situation in the country. It seemed that Yeltsin himself didn't know, or didn't want to know, about the growing breakdown and disorder everywhere. Even the apologists Vladimir Solovyov and Yelena Klepikova, who were writing a biography of Yeltsin, were surprised by this. They had quickly flown to Moscow from New York right after the failed coup, in order to add a new chapter to their book. Here is what they reported:

Yeltsin had grown used to being in the opposition. He had made preparations for prolonged trench warfare with the Kremlin. Then suddenly power fell into his hands as a result of the conservatives' failed coup. He had neither a concrete plan nor the habit of rule—hence the kind of stupor the new Russian rulers fell into during the first weeks after the putsch. We found the Moscow "White House" lost in dissension, intrigue, and bickering. Their enemy had disappeared, and the democrats were busy sorting out relations among themselves. Even the "Sverdlovsk mafia" . . . was disunited, its members vying with one another for the attention of their boss, as though fighting over a woman.

(Solovyov and Klepikova, *Boris Yeltsin*, Moscow, 1992, pp. 9–10)

Within a few weeks after their coming to power a reshuffling of the personnel on Yeltsin's team began. In late September his longtime associate Ivan Silaev submitted his resignation from the post of prime minister. During September and October 1991 Yeltsin considered various candidates as a replacement.

Yeltsin rejected quite a few promising candidates—first of all Vice-President Aleksandr Rutskoi, who in the fall of 1991 was very active in various fields of administration, from the consolidation of Russia's new borders and the creation of a new customs service to problems with Chechnya and the fate of the former Soviet armed forces. Yeltsin and those closest to him viewed Rutskoi's initiative and independent activity with disfavor.

Mikhail Bocharov, chairman of the Supreme Economic Council of the Russian Federation, was an experienced economic administrator and legal expert, but from Yeltsin's point of view, he was aiming too high. A prime minister, in Bocharov's opinion, should direct the work of all cabinet ministers and be solely responsible, based on the principle of unified management. In the fall of 1991 he sent Yeltsin a long letter on the situation in Russia and ways to emerge from the crisis. It had been Yeltsin's practice to consult frequently with Bocharov and take his advice to heart, but now Yeltsin refused even to meet with him. Soon Bocharov withdrew his candidacy and resigned.

Grigory Yavlinksy had for several months worked as Silaev's deputy and headed the Government Commission on Economic Reform. But Yeltsin rejected him with the comment, "He's a Gorbachevite."

A more difficult problem was the candidacy of Yuri Skokov, who was part of Yeltsin's inner circle. When the government of the Russian Federation had been formed, this tough, experienced administrator was appointed first deputy premier, and twice during 1991 Yeltsin spoke of his desire to see Skokov in the premiership. Now, however, the only post Yeltsin offered him was that of adviser on security affairs.

Nikolai Petrakov, a distinguished economist, was another rejected candidate, as was Oleg Lobov, who had long worked with Yeltsin in Sverdlovsk. Yeltsin himself had invited Lobov to come work in the government in Moscow, but Lobov had not distinguished himself in his position as one of several vice premiers.

Not until November did Yeltsin make his choice—Gennady

Burbulis, another old associate from Sverdlovsk, but one who had no experience in government or the economy. On Burbulis's advice Yeltsin himself assumed the post of premier, but not the actual responsibilities. He named Burbulis first deputy premier, assigning him to form a cabinet and chair its meetings.

Gennady Burbulis was from a working-class family and as a young man had been a metal worker for about a year. After graduating from Uralsk University he earned a candidate's degree in philosophy and for fifteen years brought edification to students at technical colleges in the field of Marxist philosophy and "scientific communism." His political opponents often reproached him for his many years' work of propagating Marxism-Leninism and Burbulis answered his critics with the cautiously vague and flowery rhetoric so typical of him: "I would refer to that period in this way: a turbulent interweaving of selfless sincerity, professional university-level functioning, and naive self-deception. . . . Yes, I loved educational work. I love it still. There are still powerful homiletic-confessional chords in my soul; sometimes they are manifested more, sometimes less" (*Rossiya*, September 11–17, 1991, p. 3)

In 1988, a time of ideological ferment and widespread challenging of official doctrine, Burbulis had been active in forming party clubs and forums for discussion, and soon became a candidate for the USSR Congress of People's Deputies. He made Yeltsin's acquaintance in March 1989 and immediately proclaimed himself a Yeltsin supporter. This helped him win election. But he also helped Yeltsin, who was then taking his first steps as a leader of the democratic opposition.

Burbulis quickly became part of Yeltsin's inner circle. He was not a good speaker and did not know how to dialogue in a straightforward way with people of competence, but with his vague and pseudo-scientific line of argument he was able to captivate the none-too-well-educated politician, Yeltsin. The latter has acknowledged this influence. "Our intimate communication pleased me," Yeltsin has written:

> I will not hide the fact that my conversations with Gennady Eduardovich [Burbulis] inspired me to new ways of thinking. He knew how to look ahead. How to lend a broader, strategic, global assessment to immediate events. A conception of a new politics, a new economics, a new governmental system and system of daily life for Russia was sketched out ever more vividly, clearly, and distinctly. . . . He made a powerful impression on me with

his erudition as a professional philosopher. And we had common roots. Memories of Sverdlovsk meant a lot in our relationship. Last but not least, he was a serious soccer enthusiast. Like me, he loved sports.

(*Rossiya*, September 11–17, 1991, p. 3)

At the time of Yeltsin's election as chairman of the Supreme Soviet of the RSFSR in 1990 Burbulis was his chief of staff, just as he was when Yeltsin was elected president of the Russian Federation in July 1991. A special post was created for Burbulis, not provided for in the Russian constitution—secretary of state of the Russian Federation. Officially his job was to "oversee" several important ministries, but in the unofficial Table of Ranks he held second place to no one in Russia but President Yeltsin himself.

Burbulis understood the dangers facing the reformers, but he convinced Yeltsin it was necessary to carry through a rapid transformation of the entire social system, not just try to solve particular problems from moment to moment. It was a harsh and utopian program, similar to those of the left-wing Communists of spring 1918 and fall 1920, only heading in the opposite direction. Yeltsin approved this program.

In choosing his first deputy premier, Yeltsin had been guided mainly by concern for preserving his own personal power. Burbulis did the same, choosing his team from among those for whom he would be an indisputable authority. His choice of a chief figure to carry out the "reform" program fell on a young and little-known economist, Yegor Gaidar.

Gaidar had no experience in industry or administration. He was a typical representative of that small cohort which in 1991–92 rose from being heads of research departments to become government ministers. He grew up in a family that was very well provided for under the Soviet system. He never knew poverty or want. His paternal grandfather, Arkady Gaidar, was the author of "classic" works of Soviet children's literature. His maternal grandfather was also a writer well known in Russia, Pavel Bazhov. His father was a naval officer and celebrated journalist, Timur Gaidar. While still a university student, Yegor Gaidar married the daughter of the science fiction writer, Arkady Strugatsky. He joined the CPSU as a student and received a Lenin scholarship to Moscow State University, testimony to his academic achievements and ideological loyalty. Graduating with distinction, he went on to write a dissertation for a candidate's degree on the relatively narrow topic of value indicators in the Soviet system of "self-financed" enterprises. The central idea of this dissertation was the not very profound observation that, whether under capitalism or socialism, an enterprise has to make a profit.

After defending his doctoral dissertation, Gaidar was put in charge of the economic policy department of *Kommunist*, the main theoretical magazine of the CPSU Central Committee. In 1990 Gaidar became head of the economic section of *Pravda*, the CPSU's main newspaper. His prominent posts in the party press made Gaidar an influential figure in party ideological circles. He supported perestroika and called for full utilization of the potential of the socialist economy while freeing it from the mistakes and deformations of the past. He favored a cautious introduction of the principles and mechanisms of a socialist market economy. He openly withheld support for the programs and proposals of the radical marketeers Shatalin and Yavlinsky. In early 1990 Gaidar wrote: "There exists an entire industry for producing pseudo scientific constructs and providing an aura of scientific respectability for these unwise programs. Among professional academics this occupation is not highly regarded; on the other hand, it is quite lucrative" (*Kommunist*, 1990, no. 2, p. 33).

Actually, at the time, Gaidar himself was enthralled with an idea that could hardly be called scientific. Writing in *Pravda* on April 16, 1990, he called for the abolition of government control over prices— arguing that the "liberalization" of prices should be the first and most important market-reform measure. An entire series of transformations would follow in a logical chain. "In economics," he wrote, "everything must be paid for. The time is past when the economy could be stabilized without difficult and unpopular measures. It is a frightening thing to unfreeze prices given the present rates of growth of the total currency in circulation. But it can be done by making a decision once and for all. *We must simply shut our eyes tightly and leap into the unknown.*"

In April 1990 no one either supported or criticized Gaidar's proposal. It just didn't seem serious. In the fall of 1990 the Gorbachev government did make an attempt at unfreezing prices on bread, tobacco products, and beer, but so much protest erupted that Gorbachev and his prime minister of the time, Nikolai Ryzhkov, retreated.

At the end of 1990 Gaidar was given the opportunity to organize a new research center, the Institute of Economic Policy. Among the young economists brought in to work at this new institute were Andrei Nechaev, Vladimir Mashits, Vladimir Mau, Aleksei Ulyukaev, and Aleskandr Shokhin. Some Western analysts have tried to argue that as early as the mid-1980s Gaidar, Chubais, and Shokhin held anti-Communist views and were working within the socialist system to get to know it better, so as to be able to eliminate it more quickly. This is empty conjecture—although it is true that for Gaidar personally it was not a difficult psychological transition to reorient toward capitalist methods and accept the advice of Western experts. He had long been called a "Chicago boy" (referring to the Chicago school of neo-liberal economists).

In 1992 the Russian magazine *Business People* (*Delovye Lyudi*) wrote that Gaidar was "a thoroughly Americanized professional" for whom many terms were easier to pronounce in English than in Russian. The magazine went on: "There is nothing in him that could appeal to the man in the street: he doesn't play tennis or volleyball, like Yeltsin, or fly a plane, like Rutskoi. He has no interest whatsoever in cars, horses, stamps, or playing cards. In this sense Gaidar is said to be something of an outsider in his own country" (*Delovye Lyudi*, July–August 1992, p. 83).

Soon after the failure of the attempted coup of August 1991 Burbulis began putting together a large group of young economists to work out economic policy and a program of economic reform for the Russian Federation. Gaidar was placed at the head of the group. A number of Western experts, headed by Jeffrey Sachs, were also drawn into this work. The standard recommendations of the International Monetary Fund (IMF) and International Bank for Reconstruction and Development (IBRD) were adopted as the basis for this work, even though these recommendations did not take into account the structure of the Russian economy and its particular features. On the contrary, these proposals carefully guarded the interests of the wealthy Western countries, whose contributions of course are the basis for virtually all international financial institutions.

Burbulis introduced Gaidar to Yeltsin in late October 1991. They had a very long talk. Gaidar explained to the Russian president the general outlines of his program, especially its central feature—"liberalization of prices." He assured Yeltsin that prices would rise only by a factor of three, or four at the most, and that liberalization was indispensable if the economy were to be healed and genuine market reforms instituted. The population would, of course, be against this measure and the overall risk was very great, but passivity and a wait-and-see policy were even more dangerous. Moreover, Yeltsin could always demand the resignation of his cabinet, which would take full responsibility for the drastic measures.

Yeltsin took a liking to Gaidar. "He knew how to talk simply," Yeltsin wrote in his memoirs,

> And this was tremendously important. First of all, sooner or later it would be necessary to talk with our opponents, and he could do this, not me. He did not oversimplify his conception, but spoke in simple terms about complex matters. He is able to make his ideas catch on, and the person he is talking to begins to see clearly the road ahead. Finally, there were two other decisive factors. Gaidar's scientific conception coincided with my own inner determination to get through the most painful part of the journey quickly. I couldn't make people keep waiting, postponing the main events and most important processes for years to come. Gaidar let me know that an entire team of very young and highly varied specialists stood behind him . . . independent, eager to go, and free of psychological complexes. I understood that, in addition to the hidebound old Russian wheeler-dealers, this kind of "brazen youth," if you will, were bound to enter the Russian business scene. And I very much wanted to give them a try-out, to see them in practice . . . In addition to that, you know, it's a curious thing, but I couldn't help being affected by the magic of his name. After all, Arkady Gaidar—entire generations of Soviet people had grown up with that name. Including myself. And my daughters. And so I had faith in the inherited talent of Yegor, son of Timur, grandson of Arkady Gaidar.

> (*Zapiski Prezidenta*, Moscow, 1994, pp. 164–165)

A few years later, reminiscing about his first meetings with Yeltsin, Gaidar wrote about the Russian president's personal qualities as follows:

> His is a complex and contradictory character. In my view, his greatest strength is his ability to intuitively sense the public

mood, and to take that into account before making decisions full of the greatest consequence. In matters of fundamental importance he trusts his own political instinct far more than any advisers. Sometimes in this way he makes the absolutely right decision, but sometimes he is seriously mistaken. As a rule, what is to blame in such cases is his mood, which changes fairly often and leads him astray. One of his great strengths is his ability to listen. A personal appeal to him, one that echoes with him convincingly, can influence him more than the finest, most carefully written document. But a danger is concealed here: whoever gains his confidence and manages to persuade him also has a chance to abuse this confidence, something that has happened more than once, including in the making of extremely important decisions. I have often caught myself thinking about the similarity between Yeltsin and that hero of medieval Russian epics, Ilya of Murom, who at one moment was bravely slaying Russia's foes and the next, was sleeping on the stove.

(Gaidar, *Dni porazhenii i pobed* [Days of Defeats and Victories], Moscow, 1996, pp. 105–106)

Gaidar managed to win Yeltsin's confidence quite quickly. While everyone else was suggesting a period of three to five years for their economic plans or programs to be carried out, Gaidar convinced Yeltsin that a fundamental change for the better could be accomplished in just one year. Within a few days of meeting Yeltsin, Gaidar and his team were occupying offices on Old Square and New Square, the main locations of Russian government agencies at the end of 1991. The new vice-premier's official title was "deputy to the chairman of the government of the RSFSR on questions of economic policy, minister of finance and the economy." Enormous power, and a key role in government, were in his hands. Burbulis remained nominally the first vice premier and was considered the head of the cabinet, but people immediately began to speak in terms of a "Yeltsin-Gaidar government."

The Fifth Congress of People's Deputies of the RSFSR, convened on October 28, 1991. It was an extremely important event in deciding Russia's destiny. The Congress accepted Yeltsin's decision to assume the post of "chairman of the government." Also, the members of the first Constitutional Court of the RSFSR were elected, headed by Valery Zorkin. After several rounds of voting Ruslan Khasbulatov was elected chairman of the Supreme Soviet of the RSFSR. The most significant event at the congress, however, was Yeltsin's announcement of a new program of economic reforms and the Congress's decision to grant him additional powers in order to carry through this program.

Aleksandr Shokhin, the minister of labor, sought to explain the concept "liberalization of prices," which many failed to understand. It would take place without a preliminary demonopolization of production, he said, and with an unstable financial system and a major budget deficit. This was contrary, he admitted, to all the recommendations of "classical" economics, and there was a danger that prices would start to rise too quickly. He expressed confidence, however, that any inflationary upsurge would not be very big, because a system of price monitoring would be introduced. Moreover, he said, market mechanisms would start to operate full force once the reforms began, and Russia would soon have a stable currency. It was the conviction of the new government that *within a year* Russia would have a budget without a deficit and a system of maximum social protection for its population (*Rossiyskaya Gazeta*, October 30, 1991).

The new reform program was presented only in general outline. Yeltsin and Gaidar preferred not to make it fully known at the Congress of People's Deputies. A more detailed presentation was given in a confidential memorandum addressed to the IMF. Gaidar hoped to receive more than just the IMF's approval; he hoped for substantial inputs of foreign currency, without which the most important aspects of the program could not be implemented. There were other reasons, too, for the secrecy of the program. This had to do with very painful measures of "shock therapy," which the authors of the program did not wish to make public. Besides that, many aspects of the program had not yet been worked out; it was proposed that the government deal with problems as they arose.

The Fifth Congress approved the new program of radical economic reforms without any serious objections. It granted Yeltsin emergency powers, but only until December 1, 1992. The president was given the right to unilaterally decide questions having to do with the structure and reorganizations of the highest bodies of the executive branch, including the composition of the cabinet. Yeltsin sought to reassure the deputies at the Congress and the citizens of Russia in general, who were alarmed by the rise in prices that had begun even before "liberalization."

"The time has come," he said,

> to act decisively, with toughness and without hesitation. Everyone knows what our starting point is. The situation is a very tense one. There are difficulties with food and other prime necessities. Our financial base is on the verge of collapse. Inflation has reached a critical point. Fifty-five percent of our families are living below the poverty line. And the situation is not getting any better . . . A one-time transition to market prices—that is the difficult but necessary measure we are forced to take . . . *Things will be worse for everyone for about half a year, then [there will come] a lowering of prices, and the filling up of the consumer market with goods. By the fall of 1992, as I promised before the elections, [there will be] stabilization of the economy, and gradual improvement in people's lives.* [Emphasis added.—R.M.] To defend everyone's standard of living in the first stage of the reforms is something we cannot do.

(*Rossiyskaya Gazeta*, October 29, 1991)

The people's deputies of the Russian Federation and the citizens of Russia were willing to be patient for another half year, or in the worst case, for another year. They never imagined what difficult times and cruel disappointments lay in store for them.

LIBERALIZATION OF PRICES

In December 1991 hardly anyone blamed the Russian government for the difficult, if not desperate, economic situation. It had to its credit the confidence of the population, which was more important than the scanty financial credit being offered by Western governments. The measures taken by the Yeltsin-Gaidar government were not the only possible ones. A system of rationing and price controls, possibly combined with free-market experiments in selected cities or regions, was another option. But instead, as so often in its history, Russia was taken down an untrodden path.

On January 2, 1992, a decree on "liberalization of prices" went into effect. As Yeltsin himself said, Russia plunged into the water without knowing how to swim.

The Russian economy was thrown into the anarchy of the market system with its hands tied. No competitive environment had existed, even among related industries. No legal standards for market relations had been adopted, and the necessary infrastructure was lacking. The realities of January and February 1992 confirmed, not Gaidar's expectations, but the worst predictions of the opponents of "liberalization." Yeltsin and Gaidar kept asserting that during the first quarter the increase in prices would not be greater than 300 percent, that in April inflation would slow down to 10–12 percent, and that by the end of the year it would be down to only a few percent. Gaidar estimated that for the whole year the decline in production would be no more than 10–12 percent.

In a speech on Russian television on February 20 Yeltsin was still saying: "We will obtain real results as early as the fall of 1992. I believe that reform will win out and that the victory will be evident, without question, this year." These promises were to have the same fate as Yeltsin's 1991 promise to "lay his head on the rails" if an increase in prices were to be carried out in Russia.

In the first quarter of 1992 prices, "allowed to float freely," increased by 800–900 percent for most goods and services. Prices for some items that had been extremely cheap before were suddenly 20 to 30 times more expensive. The price of salt rose from 9 kopeks to 9 rubles per kilogram, a hundredfold increase. The price for a box of matches increased 250 times over, from one kopek to 2.5 rubles. In contrast, average wages only doubled during the first quarter.

The leap in prices was not a "one time only" affair: they kept rising all through 1992, now faster, now slower. There were various estimates of the extent of this headlong inflation, based on differing methods. The lowest estimate was that prices rose 2,500–3,000 percent (i.e., 25–30 times over). The highest estimate was a hundredfold increase.

There was no observable financial stabilization. Production declined by more than 20 percent. There was a notable reduction in the productivity of labor and an increase in all production costs. Factory managers kept raising the prices of their goods to try to compensate for their losses. But since all other prices kept rising, production costs rose in turn; and once again management had to seek to compensate at the consumer's expense.

The whole process had nothing to do with "the market." The actual quantity of goods in circulation kept growing smaller. The government's income also grew smaller, but the budget deficit increased quickly despite cutbacks in social welfare and military spending. Enterprises found themselves seriously short of working capital. The rural areas, which had sold their products in the fall at the "old" prices, could not afford to buy machinery or fertilizer. Many factories serving the agricultural sector were simply shut down because their warehouses were overflowing with unsold goods.

The sharp rise in prices meant a greatly increased need for currency, including large-denomination bills worth 200, 500, and 1,000 rubles. But the factories of Gosznak (the government money-printing agency) were not prepared for the increased workload or the changed currency denominations. For some reason Gaidar blamed Khasbulatov for allegedly blocking implementation of government decisions in this area—decisions which, Gaidar claimed, had been issued in a sensible and timely fashion. Whatever the truth of that charge, by March 1992 there was a currency shortage, and tens of millions of people were not paid wages, pensions, scholarships, and other benefits on time. From then on, every spring and every fall a similar "crisis" has arisen—although Gosznak has gotten used to printing 50,000-ruble notes, and even notes for 100,000 or 500,000 rubles.

Some enterprises began paying wages in kind—for example, dishes, bottles of vodka, lumber, coal, candy, fabrics, refrigerators, canned goods. A special decree announced unrestricted freedom of trade: Russian citizens could henceforth sell whatever they wanted wherever they wanted. For several months the streets and squares of downtown Moscow were turned into a giant yard sale or swap meet. It was no longer against the law to engage in speculation, and many restrictions on foreign trade were also lifted.

The Yeltsin-Gaidar government feared a social explosion in response to the skyrocketing inflation, but it did not occur. The number of strikes increased, but not significantly. Among blue-collar and white-collar workers, confusion and disorientation prevailed. Besides, during 1991 many families had stockpiled essential goods.

There was no support for the reform. A poll conducted by the Institute of the Sociology of Parliamentarism showed rising discontent and disruption of the social equilibrium. In January the number of people expressing discontent increased from 61 to 81 percent; 46 percent of those polled, and 67 percent of invalids and pensioners, said the price increases were "impossible to endure." To the question, "Do you believe Yeltsin's economic policy will succeed?" the number who said "Yes" on January 2, 1992, was 53 percent, but on January 30 it was only 38 percent. Only 6 percent believed Yeltsin's promise that the economic crisis would be overcome by the end of 1992. Another 20 percent had hopes that the economic situation would start to improve during 1993–94, and 21 percent were sure life would get better in five years, in 1997. Only 14 percent had no hope for improvement even in ten years, and 13 percent considered it necessary to remove the Yeltsin-Gaidar government, including by "forcible pressure" if necessary. There was nothing to rejoice about in this, however, because the "reforms" continued, creating ever new difficulties.

There also arose the phenomenon of "capital flight" from Russia. A large share of the profits from exports were deposited in Western banks, usually in private foreign-currency holdings that served as a hedge against inflation and a protection for large- and medium-sized operators from the taxation agencies of the Russian government. Part of the dollar earnings from exports were used to expand imports aimed at the consumer market, thus becoming a further negative pressure on domestic manufacturers of consumer goods.

The idea of stealing a railroad car full of copper or an entire train-load of petroleum would hardly have occurred to anyone before these "reforms." The internal prices for raw materials had been fairly low, and the borders closely watched. Now the situation changed. The borders with former Soviet republics became extremely porous.

The earnings from this illegal commerce were shared among officials and wheeler-dealers not only in Russia but in the "near abroad" and the "far abroad." As early as 1992 tens of thousands of tons of nonferrous metals were being exported from Estonia, although there was no mining of such metals in that country

SUMMER AND FALL 1992: A WORSENING SITUATION

A rather dry report from the Government Statistics Committee said the following about the first half of 1992:

The decisive beginning and energetic implementation of economic reforms had a strong impact on all sectors. The most painful aspect for the people and the economy was the liberalization of prices. By June, in comparison with December 1991, consumer prices had risen tenfold. Purchasing activity by the population declined sharply, and commodity circulation fell by 42 percent. In industry there was a fifteenfold increase in wholesale prices, while collective farm market prices were six times higher . . . The national income declined by 18 percent in comparison to the same period the previous year. The number of redundant, or unneeded, enterprises grew. In industry, the indebtedness of enterprises for products delivered came to 2.5 trillion rubles, and in more than half the cases, the payment-due date had expired. The indebtedness of enterprises to their own employees also grew. The lack of wherewithal to pay wages was felt especially sharply in Tyumen province, Yakutia, Krasnoyarsk territory, the provinces of Murmansk, Chelyabinsk, Irkutsk, and Kemerovo, and in several other areas.

(*Ekonomicheskaya Gazeta*, July 30, 1992)

The same report told us that production of consumer goods had declined by 14 percent, and that of food products by 23 percent. Moreover, production of meat fell by 27 percent, of sausages by 37 percent, and of whole milk products by 48 percent. The production of bread and sugar also declined, although prices for those products increased.

From July to September things continued to worsen. Social programs began to be terminated. The financing of health, education, culture, and science was cut back sharply. Many plants in the military-industrial complex stopped working. Because of the dissolution of the USSR, the army and navy began to fall apart, as did the transport, electric power, and airline systems. The former union-wide security and legal systems also disintegrated.

The tender shoots of domestic business found it hard going, burdened as they were not only by taxes and the extortions of corrupt officials but also by the cruel racketeering that kept growing stronger. Comprador groups, those working directly for or with foreign capital, were better protected against taxes, bribes, and racketeering.

Academician Oleg Bogomolov, assessing the results of eight months of economic reform, wrote the following in an article characteristically entitled "Hope Remains."

Falling living standards are outpacing the decline in production. Commodity circulation is half what it was; the real income of the population, it seems, is even less. In comparison to January 1991, the cost of living has risen twenty times over, while wages for those employed in the national economy are only seven or eight times higher . . . . People are trying to adapt to the changing circumstance in order to survive: they are economizing wherever they can, cultivating vegetable gardens, abandoning state-owned enterprises and going into business for themselves, mainly in commerce and services . . . . As the inflation spirals higher and the money famine continues, capital investment in new construction and the upgrading of equipment is cut back . . . Incentives for the development of agriculture are disappearing. Weakened control over foreign trade and the unjustifiably low exchange rate of the ruble are accompanied by an outflow of raw materials and energy resources to the detriment of the Russian economy. A substantial proportion of foreign currency earnings (as much as US$1 billion per month) are being hidden away and deposited abroad, because our tax and foreign-currency policies make it disadvantageous or impossible to use those earnings to import many types of goods. For now, only one thing can be said: the attempt to apply shock therapy in Russia following the Polish model and the advice of the International Monetary Fund and a group of Western experts has turned out to be very painful. Will this attempt have a curative effect? Doubts about that are prevalent. But hope remains.

(*Moskovskie Novosti*, September 6, 1992)

The "Westernizers" among the radical democrats were dissatisfied. They criticized the "managerial" democrats for imitating the "social engineers" of the Soviet Communist Party, who had imposed Communism on Russia by force. Like them, these new "democratic" social engineers were trying to drive Russia by force—but this time into capitalism. The legal expert Viktor Danilenko argued,

Power today should be organized in such a way that there would be a government of property owners, controlled by property owners, oriented toward the interests of property owners, and in all ways effectively open to their influence. The most important government decisions would be made directly by people who have shouldered the burden of property. . . . Only in this way can it be achieved that the interests of the economy stand at the head of politics, and not the other way around. Only in this way can the revolution of words, slogans, and the finest intentions become a revolution of practical deeds.

(*Izvestia*, August 18, 1992)

How could such a recommendation be carried out in the Russia of 1992? There was no social class of property owners formed over the course of decades, or even centuries. There was not even a thin social stratum of such people, let alone a solidly established class. Property owners as a social group were just coming into existence, and among them the same old managerial stratum of the 1970s and 1980s predominated. The groups of independent businessmen that did exist were much less powerful or influential than the great body of government bureaucrats, who were quickly reasserting the might they had enjoyed under the Soviet system.

DOWNFALL OF BURBULIS

As early as May 1992 Yeltsin began making changes, not so much in his policies as in government personnel. By then, the immense dissatisfaction with the reforms felt by a large section of the population and by most people's deputies was focused on the figure of Burbulis. A new phrase was even coined—the "Burbulization of Russia." Yeltsin removed Burbulis as first deputy premier, while leaving him in charge of a group of presidential advisers until November. The widely held negative view of Burbulis was described in an article signed L. Leonidov:

For the man in the street Burbulization refers to the criminal free-for-all (*bespredel*) in the economy, the complete loss of any decency or respect on the part of government bureaucrats, cynicism, and cruel, cold indifference toward the "little people" of this world. . . . Burbulization is when decrees that have no effect are adopted every day, and there is no law dealing with organized crime. No good books or symphonies are being written; the strength and talent of creative people are being used mainly to adapt to the new geographical and socioeconomic circumstances. Judging theoretically, Burbulization is a state of total collapse of society, including in political, economic, and spiritual respects, with a constant increase in destructive processes, conditioned by the unnatural form of the preceding existence and way of thinking. (*Nezavisimaya Gazeta*, May 19, 1992)

A typical time server, able to hold onto power thanks solely to his connection with Yeltsin, Burbulis shocked many people with his arrogant manner, which apparently concealed an inferiority complex, according to one of his former assistants, who wrote:

> Without Yeltsin's authority he could not have expected much. The people have a keen sense for detecting those who really care about them and those who are just titled favorites. . . . A politician on the scale of Burbulis should not have been entrusted with the baubles of privilege accompanying government office. That is another vulnerable area for the present-day secretary of state. If he is going to have an office, it has to be the former office of Suslov or Gorbachev, if an automobile it has to be the kind that the people rightly call "chlenovoz"—member-of-the-top-circle-carrier.

(*Rossiyskaya Gazeta*, November 26, 1992)

Sitting in his office in the Kremlin (formerly Gorbachev's), Burbulis gave an interview to journalists. He was asked: "Do you think that at some point Yeltsin will turn against you?" and he answered: "No." He was asked more pointedly: "Do you mean to say that in Yeltsin's entourage you have no rivals?" Burbulis answered: "I would like to put it more delicately and precisely: I know my own worth. No one else can do what I can do" (*Novoye Vremya*, 1992, No. 34, p. 16).

Nevertheless, Burbulis was obliged to evacuate his Kremlin office and his place by Yeltsin's side. "The posts and offices I hold," Burbulis once said, "are variables, but my relationship with Yeltsin is a constant." Yeltsin, for his part, was saying at the time, "I never give up my people." And yet he had to give up Burbulis, and not only him. In the same way the Russian tsars in olden times would be forced to choose some boyar who was especially hated by the people and throw him to the crowd raging outside the Kremlin, which would tear him to pieces. Burbulis got off more lightly. He became head of the nongovernmental Strategy Foundation. Although he still sought, through informal contacts within Yeltsin's circle, to push one or another policy suggestion, hardly anyone paid attention to him after 1992. In his memoirs Yeltsin explained why he retired Burbulis. The Russian president placed all the blame on Burbulis and on Gaidar's team for the unsatisfactory results of the first year of the reforms.

In the summer of 1992 Yeltsin added to his government several representatives from the corps of experienced factory directors. Georgy Khizha, the vice mayor of St. Petersburg, became vice premier. Not long before that he had been head of a very large electrical engineering complex, the Svetlana group. Khizha would be unable to hold his post for long; within a year he retired from Russian politics. Another vice premier was Vladimir Shumeiko, who not long before had been director of a measuring-instruments plant in Krasnodar. He was also a people's deputy of the RSFSR and deputy chairman of the Supreme Soviet of the Russian Federation. Shumeiko lasted in his post for about a year and a half, and would remain in high politics in Russia until January 1996. A third vice premier—in charge of the fuel and energy sector of the economy—was Viktor Chernomyrdin, chairman of the board of the newly formed Gazprom corporation.

As for Yeltsin himself, he withdrew from the premiership, while Yegor Gaidar assumed the duties of prime minister. From then on sessions of the cabinet proceeded under Gaidar's leadership.

On July 17, 1992, an elaborate program of activities projected by the new cabinet was published in the official government newspaper *Rossiyskaya Gazeta*. The document was entitled "A Program for Deepening the Reforms." Although it did not use the term "capitalism" it spoke of the need for creating at a forced pace "a market economy whose primary motive forces would be entrepreneurship and competition, based on private ownership." The government warned that a certain decline of production would continue but not beyond "a certain level" and in its place there would soon come "the economic revival of Russia, the flourishing of the domestic economy, and the assurance of prosperity and freedom for all citizens on this basis." The government promised the all-round development of trade, stabilization of the financial system, strengthening of the ruble, more privatization and private enterprise, increased competitiveness of Russian goods on the world market, and integration of the Russian economy into the world economy. It undertook the obligation to pursue an active social policy and protect the more vulnerable strata of the population.

Hardly anyone paid much attention to this program, since it had little to do with the economic realities in Russia. Throughout the summer and fall the destruction of the economy continued, and living standards declined further. The idea of reducing inflation to only 3 percent per month remained a pious wish, as did the promises of tax reform and support to agriculture and domestic small business. Plans to attract major foreign investment in the Russian economy also remained only on paper.

THE ROBBING OF SAVINGS BANK DEPOSITORS

In the Russian Federation at the end of 1989 there were 118 million savings bank accounts, totalling 192 billion rubles. The average account was worth 1,626 rubles. The main holders of such accounts were people over fifty, and their savings were intended to provide some security against old age and illness; for many pensioners, this was their "funeral money." (See *Narodnoe khoziaistvo SSSR, 1989: Spravochnik* [USSR National Economy, 1989: Handbook], 1990, p. 92.) Also, many people were saving money for their children or toward the purchase of an apartment or automobile.

Yegor Gaidar later claimed that a large part of the savings in these accounts came from "inflationary money" in 1990–91. But that was not so. Inflation tended to cause more spending, not saving. During 1990–91, only 24 billion rubles were added to total savings, which at the end of that period amounted to 216 billion. That was not a very large sum in terms of Russia's economy, and in fact, when inflation is taken into account, it was a smaller total than had existed in Russia's savings banks in 1989.

For the professional economists on Gaidar's team it was unforgivable to assume that only ordinary citizens would suffer from the devaluation affecting savings accounts and insurance policies. The government, and Gaidar's own cabinet, suffered no less, perhaps even more. Savings were not kept in safety deposit boxes. This was money that circulated in the economy. Western economists, too, have described the wiping out of the population's personal savings as a major strategic error committed by the Russian authorities. By deliberately devaluing the internal debt, the Russian government destroyed the main source of future private investment. According to *Izvestia*

(November 10, 1995), 70 percent of the working capital in the USSR and almost 100 percent of investment "could be accredited to" (i.e., had as its source) the financial surplus deposited by the population in the national savings bank, Sberbank.

According to most thoughtful economists, the ratio between the amount of credit available to an economy and the total sum of savings by the population is one of the main criteria determining the maturity of market relations in any given country. Under normal conditions, the ratio should be 1:1. In other words, the amount of credit permitted in a nation's economy should not be greater than total deposits in savings banks. Yet in Russia by late 1992 the amount of credit in circulation was 5 trillion rubles, whereas savings accounts totaled only 680 billion. Thus, in Russia credit no longer corresponded to its natural base. (The source for these figures is the same issue of *Izvestia* mentioned above, for November 10, 1995.)

The confidence of the population in savings banks and the government was undermined. Given the wild inflationary spiral, no one was interested in putting their savings in the Sberbank. It made more sense to buy foreign currency and squirrel it away at home. But there wasn't much foreign currency in Russia in 1992, and what there was cost dearly. This was the psychological background against which various financial pyramid schemes were able to flourish—such notorious operations as MMM, Vlastelina, Khoperinvest, and Tibet. By advertising massively on all TV channels, these "investment funds" were able—without any interference by the government—to finish the job of robbing most of Russia's small investors.

Throughout the world investments are made with the use of savings, whether those of governments, businesses, corporations, or private individuals. Government savings were greatly reduced during the Gorbachev era and continued to shrink under Yeltsin. What savings, or reserves, the government had went, not for new investment, but to service the foreign debt. The savings of individual enterprises had also shrunk; they were insufficient to provide even for planned repairs or to replace worn-out equipment. Many enterprises, in order to remain above water, were forced to sell off some of their material resources or unused production areas, or the like. The private savings of individuals either disappeared or passed out of government control. As a result, for an extended period the economy was deprived of the means for expanded reproduction, and was often unable to maintain current production.

29

The liberalization of prices and the robbing of investors laid the basis, not for the reestablishment of Russia's financial system on a healthy basis, but for a financial disaster whose consequences had still not been overcome by the end of the decade.

THE FALL OF GAIDAR

As the economic crisis deepened and the material conditions of the population kept growing worse, a political crisis developed and spread. A center of opposition arose in the Kremlin itself. Vice President Aleksandr Rutskoi began to speak out more and more sharply, criticizing the cabinet and eventually Yeltsin himself. Formerly a military pilot, leader of "Communists for Democracy" in 1990–91, and an active defender of the Russian White House in August 1991, his criticism of the cabinet began as early as the fall of 1992 when he denounced Gaidar's team as "boys in pink trousers."

With the intention of neutralizing, perhaps discrediting, the vice president, Yeltsin put Rutskoi in charge of agrarian reform. A man trained for military duty in the air force was obviously not prepared for this kind of assignment. Profound knowledge of agriculture was not necessary, however, to understand the absurdity of the agricultural policy pursued in 1992. As he took his first trips around the country Rutskoi was surprised by the chaos and lack of elementary good management, as well as the enormous losses being suffered at all stages of agricultural production. In Stavropol territory the sunflower crop simply was left unharvested, while the government imported vegetable oil from abroad. In Oryol and other apple-growing provinces a huge crop was lost, while Russia spent $102 million buying apples from Western Europe. In 1992, 45 percent of Russia's sugar beet crop perished, but in the same year $605 million was spent importing sugar. Rutskoi estimated that no fewer than twenty beet-sugar processing plants could have been built with this money.

At the end of 1991 the government announced it would pay $60 per ton for grain produced above the planned quotas. This would have been advantageous to both the government and the peasants. Documents showed that Moscow had earmarked $5 billion to meet these obligations. By the end of 1992, however, the countryside had received only $500 million worth of imported goods. The rest of the money and goods somehow "got lost" on the way to the villages. Rutskoi called such policies criminal and said that instead of talking about reform, legal steps should be taken. In response to Rutskoi's criticisms, Yeltsin stopped meeting with him and would not even talk to him on the phone.

By the fall of 1992 the inhabitants of the "White House," the people's deputies of the Russian Federation, were becoming more and more actively opposed to the policies of Yeltsin and his cabinet, as were most of the political parties and movements in the country. A large number of oppositional parties had been registered in the spring of 1992. On the right wing of the political spectrum were the Russian nationalist and "patriotic" parties. These included the Russian National Assembly (Sobor), the Russian Party of National Revival, the Russian All-People's Alliance, Officers for the Rebirth of the Fatherland, the Union of Officers, the Council of Opposition Forces of Moscow University, the self-styled Permanent Presiding Committee of the USSR Congress of People's Deputies, the Council of Popular and Patriotic Forces of Russia, and the "Dignity" Women's Council. As a rule, these were radical organizations that rejected both Communism and liberal pro-Western ideology.

There were also radical and moderate organizations on the left, usually formed from one or another current in the former CPSU. These included the Russian Communist Workers Party, the Russian Communist Party, Toiling Russia, Toiling Moscow, the Union of Communists, and the Socialist Party of Working People. Early in the fall of 1992 a large number of opposition organizations agreed to coordinate their activity within a common bloc. A "Political Declaration of the Left and Right Opposition" was published in a number of oppositional papers. (See, for example, *Sovetskaya Rossiya*, September 22, 1992.)

A month later came the founding conference of the National Salvation Front (NSF), which demanded the resignation of the president and cabinet. (*Sovetskaya Rossiya*, October 27, 1992.) (For more on the NSF, see chapter 7, on Gennady Zyuganov.) On the eve of this founding conference an impressive demonstration of oppositional forces was held, with approximately 250,000 taking part. A counter-demonstration hastily called in support of the government was able to attract only a few thousand. The swift decline of the "democratic" movement, which in 1990–91 had brought out hundreds of thousands to its demonstrations, was further underlined by the Third Congress of the organization Democratic Russia, held at the end of 1992. The press took hardly any notice of this congress, although this was the organization that in 1990 had brought Yeltsin to power. Yeltsin himself did not appear at the congress, although he had promised to. The only prominent politicians taking part were Gennady Burbulis, Anatoly Chubais, and Galina Starovoitova

There was a mounting sense of uneasiness in Yeltsin's circle. On October 28, he signed a decree banning the "so-called National Salvation Front" on the grounds that it was an extremist organization tending to destabilize society. However, the Constitutional Court quickly ruled his decree unconstitutional.

Given the changed atmosphere in society, the Seventh Congress of People's Deputies of the Russian Federation, scheduled for December 1, 1992, loomed as a threat to Yeltsin. Some of his advisers urged him to dissolve the congress and dispense with the existing constitution, which recognized the congress as the highest governing body in Russia. (See, for example, the article by the then-popular writer Aleksandr Ivanov in *Kuranty*, October 30, 1992.) Article 121 of the constitution stated: "The president of the Russian Federation does not have the right to dissolve or stop the functioning of the Congress of People's Deputies of the Russian Federation. . . . The president's powers cannot be used to change the national-governmental structure of the Russian Federation, or to dissolve or stop the functioning of any legally elected government body."

For two years Yeltsin had had fairly solid support among the people's deputies. It was they who, in their majority, first made him the head of the Russian Federation, and most of them had supported Yeltsin in his struggle against Gorbachev. They had decisively opposed the attempted coup by the so-called State Committee on the State of Emergency. The Supreme Soviet of Russia, elected by these deputies, had ratified the Belovezh agreements dissolving the USSR, and the Fifth Congress of People's Deputies of Russia had approved Yeltsin's program of radical economic reforms, granting him extraordinary powers for carrying them out. These special powers expired, however, on December 1, 1992.

As early as April 1992 the rather idyllic relationship between Yeltsin and the people's deputies had begun to come apart. At the Sixth Congress of People's Deputies of Russia, held that month, there was sharp, and sometimes quite coarse, criticism of Yeltsin's policies. I remember, in particular, the vivid oppositional speeches of Aman Tuleyev, deputy from the Kemerovo region; Nikolai Travkin, leader of the Democratic Party of Russia; and Ivan Rybkin, a deputy from the Volgograd region, one of the leaders of the group called Communists of Russia.

It was at the Sixth Congress that, for the first time, Chairman of the Supreme Soviet Ruslan Khasbulatov spoke out openly and emphatically in opposition to Yeltsin and his government. Two years earlier Khasbulatov had been a virtual unknown. Having a doctoral degree in economic sciences, he headed the economics department at the Plekhanov Institute of the National Economy in Moscow. In 1990 he was elected to the RSFSR Congress of People's Deputies as a representative from the Chechen-Ingush Republic, his original home. At that time, when Yeltsin became chairman of the Supreme Soviet, Khasbulatov was elected deputy chairman, and he actively supported Yeltsin until the end of 1991.

Khasbulatov had not been included in Yeltsin's new government team in the fall of 1991. His disagreement with the new economic policies, his own considerable ambitions, his dislike of Yeltsin's new favorites, Gennady Burbulis and Sergei Shakhrai, plus the changing attitude of the majority of people's deputies all prompted Khasbulatov by the spring of 1992 to forget about his former loyalty to Yeltsin. He quickly became one of the Russian president's strongest and most dangerous opponents.

Yeltsin, too, observed the change of mood in the legislative bodies of the Russian Federation. He began to discuss with his inner circle various possible ways of eliminating both the Congress of People's Deputies and the Supreme Soviet, which acted in behalf of the Congress when the latter was not in session. The scenarios first considered by Yeltsin and his advisers involved trying to destroy these institutions from within, using the numerous supporters that Yeltsin and his cabinet still had in the Congress.

The situation in Russia caused uneasiness among Western politicians, too. In the fall of 1992 George Bush was of course campaigning for the U.S presidency, and any trouble in Russia might adversely affect his chances against Bill Clinton. In October he sent Henry Kissinger to Moscow to look the situation over. At the end of October Robert Gates, director of the CIA, also visited Moscow. He had himself filmed making a one-man "victory march" in Red Square to mark the winning of the Cold War by the West. This incident was not, however, shown on government-controlled Russian television.

The Congress of People's Deputies opened in the Great Hall of the Kremlin on December 1, 1992. Although the same deputies gathered as in 1990 and 1991, the heated passions and clash of opinions between political parties and factions were far more intense than at previous gatherings. The main questions before the body were appraisal of the economic reforms and confirmation of the prime minister. The debates were broadcast over Russian television and radio. Khasbulatov began the proceedings with a powerful and persuasive speech condemning not just particular failings but the overall plan of radical reform carried out along lines advocated by American monetarists. Gaidar's report was superficial and noticeably lacking in self-criticism, although he had to admit failure in the most important area—financial stabilization and strengthening of the ruble. Yet it was precisely Gaidar whom Yeltsin proposed to the Congress for the post of chairman of the Council of Ministers. Voting by secret ballot, the delegates rejected Gaidar's candidacy by a vote of 490–470.

The situation was red hot. All night long the lights stayed on in the president's Kremlin palace. The mood among those in Yeltsin's inner circle favored confrontation. The next morning from the speaker's platform Yeltsin appealed to the deputies and to the population at large to show their support either for himself or for the Congress. He called on his supporters in the Congress to walk out and take no further part in its proceedings. This was a call for the elimination of the Congress of People's Deputies as a governing body.

The total number of deputies was 1,049, but only about 1,000 had come to Moscow. The various votes showed that about 320 were resolutely opposed to Yeltsin and his cabinet. About 300 deputies from the reform coalition consistently voted with Yeltsin and his team. A group of 150 deputies had formed what they called a "centrist bloc of constructive forces." A group of about 250 deputies voted in various ways, depending on the circumstances. In the parliamentary jargon this grouping was called "the swamp."

Yeltsin greatly overestimated his influence on the deputies as a whole. He had assured Gaidar that the vote for him would be between 540 and 560—i.e., well above the 520 he needed to win. It turned out that he could only count on 470. However, if all the reform-coalition deputies walked out, the Congress would be deprived of a quorum and would not be able to function. Here too, however, Yeltsin and his advisers, with Burbulis still playing first violin, miscalculated. People's deputies valued their status quite highly. They had many rights and privileges which they would lose if the Congress ceased to function. Many of them would have to leave Moscow and return to their impoverished home regions. Few of the deputies had yet managed to privatize the Moscow apartments assigned to them. Even some of Yeltsin's closest adherents were reluctant to return to the status of ordinary citizen and "man in the street."

I was present at this session of the Congress and observed that in response to Yeltsin's appeal for a walkout, only a small number of deputies left their seats. Together with Yeltsin they went off into some of the innermost rooms of the building. Several dozen deputies went out into the lobby but did not follow Yeltsin. After half an hour of confusion, a new round of registration of deputies still in attendance showed that Yeltsin had failed. More than 850 deputies still remained in session. This constituted a quorum, and Khasbulatov announced that the Congress would proceed with its work. Among those present were the ministers of defense, internal affairs, and state security, the attorney general, and the chairman of the Constitutional Court.

A demonstration outside the Kremlin walls in support of the president drew only about 50,000, but Yeltsin refused to return to Congress sessions. Difficult negotiations began, ending in a compromise. The opposition factions made the proposal to Yeltsin that of the 17 candidates he should select five, reserving the right to choose among any that received more than 50 percent of the vote. He still hoped for Gaidar to win, but these hopes were in vain. In a straw poll, the voting gave Yuri Skokov 637 and Viktor Chernomyrdin 621, but only 400 for Gaidar, just one vote more than was gained by Vladimir Kadannikov, director of a major auto plant in Togliatti, who had just flown to Moscow. The vice premier Vladimir Shumeiko came in last, with 270 votes. Yeltsin asked for an hour to think things over. He consulted with various people in his inner circle, including Gaidar, who said, "Pick whoever you want—only not Skokov." Yeltsin proposed Chernomyrdin and the Congress immediately approved him by an overwhelming majority. It was late on the evening of December 14, 1992, that the Congress adjourned, having completed its work.

Burbulis's political career ended after the Seventh Congress. Not so with Gaidar. Although he left the government, he remained in politics and repeatedly made his presence felt in the subsequent period.

VIKTOR CHERNOMYRDIN

The selection of Chernomyrdin for the premiership was a surprise to most deputies at the Congress, even though a large number had voted for him. It was a surprise to Yeltsin, too, although he himself had added Chernomyrdin's name for the straw poll. It was a surprise to journalists and political observers at the Great Hall of the Kremlin, including this author, who had been closely following all the ins and outs of that longest and tensest session of the Seventh Congress, not concluded until midnight. But the one most surprised was Chernomyrdin himself, who never suspected on the morning of December 14 that before the day was over he would be chairman of the Council of Ministers of the Russian Federation. He rose to the speaker's platform and thanked the deputies for their vote of confidence, but during the first break he rushed for the exit, refusing to hold a press conference. Surrounded by journalists, he did make a few remarks, which were frequently quoted afterward: "I am for a market, but not for a bazaar." "I am for the development of a market, but not through the impoverishment of the people." "I am for Russia, but not for a Russia of street peddlers."

Chernomyrdin spent that night at the government building on Old Square, as did nearly all the government ministers and vice premiers. Besides inquiring about his views, the journalists began looking into his past career. Viktor Stepanovich Chernomyrdin was born in 1938 in Orenburg province, in the village of Cherny Ostrog. He was not an especially diligent student. School records showed him getting mostly the equivalent of C's and D's. Unlike the exemplary student Gaidar, who went directly from high school to the university, Chernomyrdin at the age of seventeen took a job, first as a metal worker, then as a machinist, at an oil refinery in Orsk. After serving two years in the army, he returned to the Orsk refinery. Not until 1962 did he take up higher education, entering the Kuibyshev Polytechnic Institute, and after graduating he again returned to the Orsk refinery, this time as a supervisor. Next, he completed correspondence courses up to the postgraduate level. He holds a candidate's degree in technical sciences and, by training, is an engineer-economist and an engineer-technologist. He joined the CPSU in 1961 and in 1966 was promoted to head the industry and transport department of the CPSU's municipal committee in Orsk. But he was not drawn to party work, and he soon switched to a job as chief engineer at a natural gas processing plant in Orenburg, becoming the director of that plant in 1973. Twenty years later Chernomyrdin declared at a conference: "I am proud to have come from the ranks of the 'Red directors.' "

From 1983 to 1985 Chernomyrdin headed Tyumengazprom, the association of industrial enterprises engaged in the extraction of natural gas in the Tyumen region of western Siberia. In 1985, the year Gorbachev became head of the Soviet ruling party, Chernomyrdin was made minister of the natural gas industry for all of the USSR. In 1989 the Ministry of the Gas Industry, for the sake of greater efficiency in this sector, was reorganized as a government-owned corporation, Gazprom, with Chernomyrdin remaining as chairman of the board. This was market reform of a far-sighted kind. At a time when oil exports and the export of other commodities were shrinking, the production and export of natural gas had been expanding. In 1992 it accounted for roughly one-third of Russia's foreign currency earnings. On European markets, even the powerful German concern Ruhrgas was being squeezed by Gazprom.

When Yeltsin formed his first cabinet in late 1991 he appointed Vladimir Lopukhin minister for fuel and energy. Lopukhin was a 40-year-old economist and friend of Gaidar's whose experience was limited to work as a researcher at academic institutions in Moscow. Half a year later, without even consulting Gaidar, Yeltsin relieved Lopukhin of his duties and appointed Chernomyrdin in his place, something the "Chicago boys" did not view kindly. Amidst general economic collapse in 1992 Chernomyrdin kept the gas industry working efficiently while transforming the major enterprises in his branch of industry into joint-stock companies and making a smooth transition to free-market prices for sources of energy.

The left-wing press greeted the selection of Chernomyrdin with open approval, while the radical "democrats" made no secret of their disappointment, predicting that market reforms would be stopped or that a total change of course would occur. Yeltsin stated that he and this "Red director," Chernomyrdin, had worked together for decades in the sphere of industrial production, that they knew each other well and got along well together. On Gaidar's team despondency reigned. Yeltsin announced, however, that under Chernomyrdin there would be no retreat from market reforms and no big reshuffling of the government. For his part, Chernomyrdin did not ask for governmental changes—and even suggested Gaidar remain in the cabinet. But Gaidar declined. When asked his view of the new premier Gaidar would say only: "At least he's a decent person."

Most economists and political scientists welcomed Chernomyrdin's appointment. Commentator Leonid Skoptsov made this observation: "To say that Chernomyrdin is less of a free-market supporter than Gaidar only on the grounds that Gazprom earns its foreign currency on the world market while Gaidar coaxes it out of the International Monetary Fund, thus displaying his excellent knowledge of English— that is more than I can do" (*Rossiyskaya Gazeta*, December 17, 1992).

As early as mid-1992, when the first conflicts with the Supreme Soviet had begun, the "Gaidarite" government ministers made a decision: if Gaidar were to leave the government, all the members of his "team" would do so too. But after the Seventh Congress there was no rush to resign. Anatoly Chubais and Vladimir Shumeiko immediately announced their intention to remain in the government, and most of the other "Gaidarites" held onto their posts. With little enthusiasm Chernomyrdin agreed that the new finance minister and vice premier would be Boris Fyodorov, whose views diverged fundamentally from those of the ministers with experience in industry, like Chernomyrdin. Fyodorov had earlier worked on the staff of the European Bank for Reconstruction and Development and had become a director at the World Bank; thus he had the confidence of international financial circles. He immediately began to conduct himself in a completely independent way within the government, and by no means did he always carried out direct orders from the new premier.

All in all, the decisions of the Seventh Congress brought about no fundamental changes in the composition of Yeltsin's cabinet nor any change in Russia's foreign and domestic policies. The people of Russia bade farewell to 1992 without regrets, but without any great hopes for the year to come. It had been the most difficult year in Russia's post-World War II history, but 1993 turned out in many respects to be even worse.

ECONOMIC CRISIS AND DECLINE CONTINUE

There were many circumstances creating difficulties for Chernomyrdin from the outset.

First of all, the force of inertia behind the negative processes in the economy, the social sphere, and in Russia's relations with other countries, both "near" and "far," was so great that they proved impossible to stop. On January 1, 1993, there was a substantial rise in prices on a large number of goods and services, producing once again a chain of dangerous consequences: social protest, nonpayment of wages, increases in wages, benefits, and pensions, increased taxes, continued nonpayment of wages, then another rise in prices. Some sort of program for economic stabilization was needed, but Chernomyrdin had none. Nor did he try to elaborate a new conception for Russia's economic development. With no long-term, overall strategy, he was condemned to trying to cope by stopgap measures and partial solutions.

Second, he took the premiership without having his own team. For the first several months the cabinet continued to consist mainly of "Gaidarites." Only gradually did new names begin to appear—Aleksandr Zaviryukha, Oleg Soskovets, Yuri Yarov, Oleg Davydov, Vladimir Babichev. Even then, people whom Chernomyrdin himself called "market romanticists" predominated. By the decision of President Yeltsin, Gaidar himself was returned to the cabinet as a vice premier, though he had no clearly defined functions. The operations of government were often paralyzed as a result of this disparate composition of the topmost officialdom. There were many instances in which Chernomyrdin, Soskovets, or Viktor Gerashchenko, head of the State Bank, would make a decision to provide financial aid to enterprises whose continued work was essential to the country, but within a short time Fyodorov, Chubais, or Gaidar would stop these subsidies.

The Chernomyrdin group drafted a plan for an economic union within the framework of the Commonwealth of Independent States (CIS) and for a single ruble zone for part of the CIS. The other vice premiers and government ministers worked in the opposite direction. Addressing Chernomyrdin at a session of the Supreme Soviet, Ruslan Khasbulatov exclaimed: "Viktor Stepanovich, who is in charge of this government? I suspect it is not you." Western analysts discussed openly that the chief figures in Yeltsin's cabinet in 1993 were Boris Fyodorov, Anatoly Chubais, Aleksandr Shokhin, and, later in the year,

Yegor Gaidar. Specific negotiations with the IMF or the G-7 were said to be conducted exclusively by these members of Yeltsin's government.

The separate administrative apparatus of the Russian Presidency, which kept growing in size and influence, also impeded the work of the cabinet and of Chernomyrdin personally. The presidential administrative system became a kind of parallel government, more and more obviously playing the kind of role the CPSU Central Committee apparatus had formerly played in running the country. The numerous agencies of presidential authority had long since outgrown the Kremlin and expanded into the thousands of (former Central Committee) offices on Old Square and New Square. The heads of the "power ministries" (armed forces, ministry of internal affairs, state security) and many vice premiers and heads of economic ministries were appointed directly by Yeltsin, not by Chernomyrdin, who also had no influence on the Foreign Ministry or the Ministry of Information. Many cabinet members had direct access to Yeltsin and drafted decrees and orders for him without consulting Chernomyrdin. Although Yeltsin took leave of Burbulis, the system of favoritism in his inner circle persisted. The head of the presidential guard, Aleksandr Korzhakov, acquired influence that extended far afield, even to certain economic areas.

Although Chernomyrdin often felt troubled by this absurd state of affairs, he carefully concealed his dissatisfaction, avoiding conflicts with Yeltsin and with other cabinet members. Things were not going well in Russia, and criticism of the government kept intensifying, but it was hardly ever directed against Chernomyrdin personally. The main blows of the opposition, both the moderates and the intransigents, were aimed at such government figures as Shumeiko and Chubais, Shokhin and Gaidar, Mikhail Poltoranin, and Sergei Shakhrai.

Chernomyrdin was a man who had devoted his working life to one branch of industry. His knowledge in other fields was limited. Unlike such politicians as Khrushchev, Gorbachev, and Yeltsin, who had risen through the party machinery and as party bosses were inclined to issue orders on any and all questions—from agriculture to space research to art and literature—Chernomyrdin had no desire to act like an expert on all questions. As premier during the first months of 1993 he sought to gain some understanding of the problems of the various branches of the economy, traveling a great deal, both near and far, getting to know the situation first-hand. For a while he made no major decisions.

His first decision in the economic sphere was to provide financial support to the fuel and energy industry: in late December 1992, with the approval of the parliament, 200 billion rubles of credit on easy terms were made available. Economists commenting on this measure noted not only that the new premier was supporting "his own" branch of industry but that, unlike Gaidar, he was seeking to promote development in basic industry.

Not until the end of January 1993 did the new premier give his first press interview. He said his main concern was to determine the actually existing state of affairs. He did not hide his critical attitude toward the results achieved in 1992. "We had a certain level of economic development. We *had* it. Why were we obliged to lose the level that we had? After all, the workforce [at the various enterprises] had not changed. They were working just as they always had. Well, then, what changed was the structure, the administration. The forms of property are changing . . . . Let them change! But that does not necessarily have to lead to such a steep decline. Forecasts can be made, results can be estimated in advance, and appropriate measures can be taken." Chernomyrdin cited the natural gas industry, in which there had been no decline.

His chief immediate concern, he said, was to ensure the food supply, and to provide machinery and fertilizer to the rural areas at acceptable prices. Farmers would receive subsidies in return for commitments to sell the government a set amount of food products in the fall. In industry, credit would be granted only to those enterprises capable of using it rationally to increase the wealth. For example, Russia needed thousands of airplane engines, which it bought from Poland, using foreign currency. Meanwhile, the Baranov plant in Omsk, on its own initiative, had begun to produce airplane engines that turned out to be more compact, more reliable, and cheaper than the Polish ones. The government would support plants like the one in Omsk, he said, adding that there were quite a few such plants.

He corrected his earlier remarks about "street peddlers." He was not against them, he said. Let them engage in commerce, but they should be licensed, pay taxes, and clean up after themselves.

"I am for private farming," he said,

But not indiscriminately—just giving out land to anyone. I'm a practical man. For the private farmer to work properly there must be a rural banking system. That doesn't exist yet. There should be a system enabling the farmer to order fertilizer and machinery. I've had occasion to see where people have been given land, but all that's growing there, just like before, is weeds. I am for the market. But as I've said before, without work, without the strictest discipline, nothing will come of it. It just isn't true that we can live like they do in the West while working like we do in Russia. We must work hard. Using our heads. Moochers and idlers should be punished. And not just "by the action of the ruble."

In 1993 production continued to fall. The negative trends in the economy were slowed but not stopped. Social tensions increased, and the conflict between president and parliament developed in new ways, distracting attention from the task of solving economic problems. The government expended its main efforts in trying to solve urgent, but partial, problems, dealing with the consequences of bigger and more frequent industrial accidents, and seeing to it that the weakened economy did not collapse completely under the weight of unsolved problems.

By the end of August 1993 neither economists nor those in charge of production were able to detect any signs of economic stabilization. In practically all regions and sectors of the economy the situation was getting worse. A small number of people were growing rich but millions were slipping down below the poverty line. In order somehow to pay its obligations despite its reduced income, the government increased taxes on the profits of successful enterprises, thus sawing off the branch on which production was barely being maintained. The "reform" elements in the government gave a big build-up to Finance Minister Boris Fyodorov for being able to say "No" to Chernomyrdin himself (in matters involving subsidies for essential industries). But many economists felt that one reason for the continued decline was the clumsy conduct of financial business and the desire to squeeze as much money out of the sick economy as possible without investing in expanded production or in the social sphere.

For the new class of businessmen and for many government-owned and privatized businesses alike, it was to their advantage to take their money out of the country, rather than invest in the Russian economy. Under these circumstances it was unrealistic to count on generous

Western investment. It was hard to find an entrepreneur in Russia who honestly paid all his taxes, which sometimes amounted to 95 percent of profits. Fictitious profit rates were listed in contracts, and huge sums of money circumvented the government agencies overseeing payments. As a result fewer resources flowed into the government budget than might have if the Ministry of Finance had established more reasonable tax rates.

At an all-Russia economic conference the audience responded with the greatest sympathy to a sharply worded speech by Georgy Kostin, director of a large plant in Voronezh. Evaluating the results of the first half of 1993, he complained that there was still no plan to bring the country out of its economic crisis. The heavy engineering sector of the Central Black Earth region, he said, had been paying 35–40 percent of its budget for energy. But in August, with price rises for coal, gas, and electric power, that figure was expected to go up to 57–63 percent. It was impossible to go on in that way (*Rossiyskaya Gazeta*, August 4, 1993).

The overall results for 1993 were not consoling. Over the course of the year, gross domestic product had shrunk by 12.5 percent and national income was 14 percent lower. Industrial production had fallen by 25 percent; agricultural, by 5.5 percent. The average monthly inflation rate was 16 percent. The rate of exchange had worsened: at the end of 1992 it had been 450 rubles to the dollar; at the end of 1993, it was 1,250 rubles to the dollar. The material conditions of the population had also worsened substantially (see *Voprosy Ekonomiki* [Problems of Economics], 1994, No. 1, pp. 86–96).

A report by the economics division of the Russian Academy of Sciences summing up two years of "shock therapy" said the following:

> The income of the 10 percent of Russia's citizens most well-provided-for was ten times higher than that of the least well-provided-for 10 percent. A third of the population has income below the official "subsistence minimum," and 10 percent, or 15 million people, are below the threshold of what is considered necessary for physical survival. This signals the entry of society into a phase of severe social conflict. . . . The moral foundations of society, its social values and ideals, the hopes of families and individuals—all are breaking down. A process of marginalization is going on in the population. The number of beggars,

homeless people, alcoholics, drug addicts, and prostitutes is growing, and more and more children with defects are being born. The society that is actually taking shape in Russia today is far removed from the models existing in countries with highly efficient, socially oriented market economies. It resembles to a greater extent a society based on hypertrophied property differentiation, corruption, organized crime, and foreign dependence. From the socioeconomic point of view, this is not a step forward. Rather, our country has been thrown back two centuries to the "savage era" of capitalism, the era of primitive accumulation. An analysis of the course of the reforms and their results during 1992–93 makes it possible to draw several conclusions.

FIRST. This profound crisis is not the result of unresolved problems accumulated in the past, of particular errors, or of resistance by conservative forces (although all of these have been present). It is the inevitable consequence of the course of reform that was chosen and the methods by which it was carried out. The attempt to solve all problems "at one leap" or by a "cavalry charge" was dictated not by sober scientifically-grounded calculation, but by impatience and political ambition. The course of reform, despite the assertions of its initiators, was and remains driven by ideology to an extreme degree and is being implemented by methods that can be characterized as "neo-Bolshevik."

SECOND. Confronted with the failure of their economic policy, the initiators of "shock therapy" did not draw the appropriate lessons, but stubbornly insisted that their policy must be continued. This only worsened the situation and placed new burdens of the population. In an attempt to cover up the fiasco, the reformers in power sought to misinform pubic opinion, distorting the real situation and the real living conditions of the people.

THIRD. From the very beginning a mistaken orientation was adopted as to the decisive role of foreign aid, and internal sources for the stimulation of business and investment activity were not brought into play. It became clear that this was a major strategic miscalculation. The miserly amounts of the aid that was constantly being promised could not under any circumstances have seriously affected the results of the changes taking place in Russia.

FOURTH. At the root of many of the errors and the refusal to change the course of economic policy lies a claim to infallibility, to possession of the absolute truth. Hence the wish not to listen to criticism, the desire to portray all criticism as coming from "enemies of reform." One idea is stubbornly instilled in the public mind—the absence of any alternative to the "shock therapy" chosen by the authors of this policy and the particular strategy and tactics by which it was carried out. Belief in one's own infallibility serves as a breeding ground for the deliberate refusal to seek a national consensus.

FIFTH. By now the lack of professionalism of the authors of "shock therapy" has become clear. Evidence of this is seen in their ignorance of the realities of Russia's economy and of the mentality of the populations inhabiting Russia, their selection of inadequate reform methods, and their crude miscalculations in forecasting the economic and social consequences of the measures implemented. For a prolonged period the government has declined to discuss fundamental problems of its policies with leading scientifically trained economists and representatives of progressive parties, movements, and civic organizations.

I have quoted at length from this previously unpublished document, a copy of which is in my personal archives. It was distributed to all leading institutions in Moscow, to all public organizations, and to the press, but it was deliberately ignored by the authorities. There were other, similar studies that drew analogous conclusions.

Scientists and scholars in almost every field condemned the policy of "shock therapy" precisely because science and the system of higher education in Russia were being destroyed even faster than industry and agriculture. Tens of thousands of scientists and researchers from all branches of knowledge were leaving the country. At the same time in the cities, tens of thousands of astrologers, fortune tellers, clairvoyants, psychics, specialists of all kinds in magic spells and the spirit world surfaced. None of them, however, could conjure away the "evil eye" effects of faulty economic policy.

2

Obstacles to Capitalist Development in Russia

The failure of Gorbachev's reforms from 1985 to 1990 caused great discontent and disillusion among the people. The reformers themselves were dismayed. Some of them were inclined to abandon the framework of socialism, within which the reforms had remained. Valentin Pavlov, who replaced Nikolai Ryzhkov as premier, admitted later that by 1990 he was firmly convinced that only a bourgeois-democratic revolution could save Russia. (See *Segodnya*, November 29, 1994.)

The attempted coup of August 1991, followed by the removal of the CPSU from power, the disintegration of the USSR, and Gorbachev's departure from the Kremlin, brought new political forces into the leadership—forces opposed to socialism as well as to the former leaders of Soviet society. Many historians, sociologists, and other commentators refer to the events after August 1991 as a "revolution." It is variously called a "liberal revolution," an "anti-Communist revolution," a "democratic revolution," an "anti-totalitarian revolution," even a "national liberation" revolution.

IS IT CAPITALISM THAT'S DEVELOPING IN RUSSIA?

But hardly anyone calls it a "capitalist revolution." Partly this is for tactical reasons, with intent to deceive the public. In 1991 the masses supported demands for freedom and democracy, opposed the privileges and power so long monopolized by the Communist Party bureaucracy, and hoped for an improvement in their material conditions. The mass rallies for Yeltsin featured banners such as "Down with Gorbachev" and "Down with the CPSU," but I never saw a banner saying "Long Live Capitalism" or "All Power to the Bourgeoisie."

In recent years the Polish Social Democrats (former Communists), who have been winning elections in their country, have refrained from using the term "socialism." They have advanced a slogan that seems strange to us, although it has proved popular in Poland: "Build Capitalism for the People, for the Workers." The "reformers" around Yeltsin have been reluctant to use the term "capitalism" openly, and Yeltsin himself has not designated capitalism as the ultimate goal of the "structural reforms" being carried out in Russia.

Nevertheless, economist Aleksei Ulyukaev, a close associate of Yegor Gaidar, considered Yeltsin's victory in the 1996 elections a decisive step "forward" toward capitalism. Those elections, in his opinion, answered the decisive question, "Who will prevail?" in favor of capitalism (*Segodnya*, September 20, 1996).

Prime Minister Viktor Chernomyrdin consistently rejected the term "capitalism." "The main thing I want to say," he declared in 1993, "to those who cry out everywhere that Russia is heading toward capitalism is that we are not leading Russia toward capitalism of any kind. Russia simply does not have the capability for that. It will be neither socialist nor capitalist" (see the newspaper *Argumenty i Fakty*, No. 42 for 1993). Two years later he explained, "We are building a totally new society, without 'isms' " (*Segodnya*, August 9, 1995).

Some authors speak of the "systemic transformation" of the society, but their explanations generally defy comprehension. Gennady Burbulis, the prime ideologist of the new government, defined its aims more candidly. "The socioeconomic goals of reform, from my point of view, can be expressed this way: to establish the institution of private ownership. People must live in a society where they can acquire and freely exercise, without fear, ownership of any form of private property. Historical experience teaches that nothing that corresponds more closely to human nature has been invented in the last ten thousand years. It is not an ideal system, but it is normal" (quoted in V. V. Sogrin, *Politicheskaia istoriia sovremennoi Rossii, 1985–1994* [Political History of Present-Day Russia], Moscow, 1994, p. 118).

Cabinet ministers under Yeltsin and Chernomyrdin were from the beginning more outspoken, disdaining to conceal their intention to work toward establishing capitalism. "Russia has already chosen capitalism," declared Yevgeny Yasin, minister for the economy. "Today we are making a further choice, between an efficient kind of capitalism and an inefficient, oligarchical kind" (*Pravda*, October 5, 1995).

This lack of agreement in defining the aims of the "structural reforms" is noteworthy, but not accidental. It reflects fears and hesitations flowing from the *unpopularity* of the notion of establishing capitalism in Russia. It reveals the uncertainty of the reformers, an uncertainty that has weighty grounds.

One of Gaidar's associates sought to explain away the difficulties and deprivations the population was suffering with the argument that they would not be long lasting. Setting the ship of state on a new course, he argued, required much effort and careful maneuvering. But once the sails were set for the new course any wind would be to the advantage of the ship and its passengers. The greater part of this difficult and painful change of course, be said, had already been accomplished, and the wind of capitalist development was already blowing in the sails of Russia's economy.

Not all the reformers shared this optimism. Some of them warned that the transition to capitalist development might take two or three generations before the fruits of the "glorious capitalist future" could be tasted.

There is a huge difference between a program of carefully thought-out, gradual market reforms in a country with a nonmarket economy and a program aimed at transforming a socialist society into a capitalist one by "shock therapy." Hardly anyone today disputes the fact that "state socialism" led Russia into a dead end, from which no escape was possible without using some forms and methods of a market economy. An intelligent program of privatizing some state-owned enterprises and the gradual creation of a competitive environment, the restoration of many forms of private ownership in small and medium-sized production, in trade, and in service industries, the encouragement of Western investment in the Russian economy, partial liberalization of foreign trade, joint ventures and jointly owned companies, banks, and stock markets, and other elements of a market-oriented infrastructure would all be steps in the right direction.

Moves in this direction were begun under Gorbachev and they should be continued, deepened, speeded up. I will not go into the successful experience of China, which over the last twenty years increased production by 500–600 percent and raised living standards for its 1.3 billion population by 400–500 percent. This success has set a record for the twentieth century, which has had no shortage of "economic miracles." We should also recall the experience of postwar Germany and Japan, which in twenty years managed to overcome destruction and chaos and emerged as economic leaders of the West.

Even Lenin, under the New Economic Policy (begun in 1921), successfully tried to use market methods. Steps in the same direction were taken by Aleksei Kosygin in the 1960s. In the 1970s the Politburo discussed the idea of establishing, on a trial basis in several small cities, a system of private services, including small shops and restaurants. Discussions were held with Henry Ford II about the possibility of his company's participation in construction of the Kama River Auto Plant (Kamaz), and with the Hilton corporation about establishing several hotel complexes in Moscow. Even under Stalin during the war with Germany, when state industry was used entirely for the needs of the army, a revival of private trade and small-scale private production was permitted. Huge goods markets and even commercial stores arose in Soviet cities, as well as semi-legal foreign currency exchanges. The authorities put an end to this unofficial NEP only after the monetary reform of 1947.

In the 1970s and 1980s Soviet society and the Soviet economy were in dire need of radical reform. But the attempt to establish a Western-type capitalist society—to impose full-scale capitalist relations on a society where noncapitalist relations had taken shape over a period of seventy years—was absurd, utopian, and bound to fail.

Gaidar himself wrote at a later time (i.e., after his unsuccessful premiership):

> We began the reforms in a very interesting situation, in which it was possible to list at length everything that we did not have to show why reforms could not be carried out. I myself could have

explained very well why they couldn't be carried out in 1992. There was no stable support in the parliament, there were no normal institutions of government capable of taking action (army, customs personnel, police)—they had been shattered by the crisis of power in 1990–91. There were sixteen central banks instead of one, there was no tradition of private entrepreneurship, and there was no strong private sector, as there was in Poland. There wasn't even a kopeck to spare in the way of foreign currency or gold reserves, and there was no possibility of attracting resources on the free market, the international financial market. But in spite of all that, we did not have the option of waiting and doing nothing while explaining why we couldn't do anything.

(Cited in Yeltsin's memoirs, *Zapiski Prezidenta*, Moscow, 1994, p. 246)

Gaidar in this instance is misleading his readers. In late 1991 the program put forward by him and his team was only one of many anti-crisis programs. Other government leaders and economists were offering Yeltsin their support and their programs. They weren't proposing "to wait and do nothing" or simply explain "why they couldn't do anything." Gaidar, in his articles and books, presents only the secondary factors working against radical capitalist reform in the state of crisis, confusion, and disarray of 1990–91. The obstacles facing any attempt at capitalist revolution were far more serious.

In 1990 Gaidar proposed to the leaders of the USSR that we should "close our eyes tightly and leap into the unknown" (*Pravda*, April 16, 1990). In 1991 the same Gaidar proposed to the leaders of Russia "to extricate ourselves from socialism" and "return to the path of capitalist development" (Gaidar, *Dni porazhenii i pobed*, p. 247). It might have made sense to propose this in some form in the Czech Republic, Hungary, Lithuania, or Poland, which had not diverged from the capitalist road until the late 1940s. Capitalist relations had taken root in those countries much more deeply than in Russia before 1917. But for the Russia of the 1990s a *return* to the capitalist road was a bizarre notion, since that "road" had been torn up long since and even the faintest traces of it were no longer discernible.

There is an unalterable general law of development of socioeconomic formations, or systems—that is, the different forms taken by human civilization. The Bolsheviks disregarded this law after 1917, and the radical reformers did likewise after August 1991. No social system or new form of civilization can be built if it has not already taken shape in the interstices of the previously existing form of civilization, or social system. Socioeconomic formations, as Marx called them, are not dead, inert forms, but living, self-driven systems. Their emergence can be assisted, or speeded along, but only living seeds and shoots can develop roots and stems, trunks, branches, and leaves. Living systems are governed by inner laws of operation, not by the desires or endeavors of legislators and/or reformers.

It is wrong, then, to liken social development to the construction of a building or the sailing of a ship, as we so often do. A less superficial analogy would be the tending of an orchard or forest, neither of which can develop in two months, let alone two years.

TEN FACTORS IMPEDING CAPITALIST REVOLUTION

Below I list ten factors that have doomed the attempt at a capitalist revolution to failure, an attempt that for too many years now has caused the people of our country unjustifiable suffering and required unnecessary sacrifice.

1. The Previously Existing Economic Reality

The plan for a "systemic transformation" worked out by Gaidar and his Western advisers was not applied to conditions of chaos and ruin, like those in Russia in 1920–21, Germany in 1945–46, or China in 1977–78. Since 1929, there had been twelve five-year plans, and a vast system of economic production had been created in the USSR, a system that served the needs of both government and population, sometimes well, sometimes poorly, sometimes "fair to middling." Extreme centralization and administrative-command methods of management were not the only problems. Two dogmas of the Marxist school of political economy were embodied in this system—dogmas that might have seemed true in the nineteenth century but were out of line with the economic realities of the twentieth.

According to the first dogma, free competition under capitalism inevitably leads to economic anarchy and overproduction, consequently to cyclical downturns and unemployment. Moreover, as monopoly replaces competition, the result is higher prices, slower progress in technology, and stagnation. Both monopoly and competition are bad, but a socialist planned economy can eliminate the cycle of boom and bust and transform monopolistic centralization into a positive advantage. Under the Soviet system a strict government monopoly on production and distribution was maintained, with competition ruled out even in the service industries. Auto producers, rather than compete with one another, simply produced machines of different types and sizes. The task of producing various diameters of pipe was divided up among several metallurgical plants. All the paper cups for the entire Soviet Union were produced in one plant in the Baltic region. When all production could not be centralized in one or a few plants—for example, in the production of meat and dairy products—the markets that needed to be supplied were divided up, and each plant worked for a strictly defined region.

According to the second dogma, large or very large production units enjoy significant advantages over small or medium-sized units, especially in the realm of planning and efficiency of organization, as well as in the utilization of resources and application of new methods or new models. Thus, in the USSR gigantic factories predominated, while small businesses, such as barber shops, hairdressing salons, laundries, and bathhouses, were grouped together into huge "trusts" under the direction of the Ministry for Municipal Economies. This "gigantomania" was also reflected in the kind of goods produced. The largest excavating machinery in the world, the largest generators, the largest trucks, tractors, and combines, the world's biggest lathes—all were produced in the USSR. Production of mini tractors or small electric power plants was disregarded. Hundreds of new cities came into existence, each centered on one or two giant plants.

Today we can see that this mistaken policy doomed the USSR to economic and technological backwardness. One cannot help seeing, as well, that the production relations that took shape in the USSR affected the entire superstructure—from the forms of government and administration to our laws and moral values. Each element of the economy became a single cell in the larger system, and the country as a whole was like one huge factory, with the government as the sole employer. This type of production gave rise to solidly entrenched stereotypes of behavior and thought affecting several generations of industrial workers, office workers, and technical intelligentsia (engineers, etc.), not to mention the party and government bureaucracy, the so-called nomenklatura.

It is not hard to show that in the super-centralized Soviet economy there were many excesses and defects that were partially offset or compensated for by administrative rather than economic action. Nevertheless, there were certain advantages in this cumbersome economic system. In a number of areas, the Soviet Union was able to concentrate enormous resources in order to achieve certain major objectives. It was possible and necessary to change and improve the system, eliminating its deformations and inadequacies, modifying or getting rid of excessive centralization and privatizing some publicly owned property. It would have been useful to trim down some of the industrial giants, creating a parallel system of small or medium-sized enterprises based on private or cooperative ownership. Irrational monopolization could give way to rational competition, and economic methods of regulation could have supplemented or partially replaced the purely administrative methods, etc. A slow and careful reform process was required, based on scientific research, discussion, and experimentation. Only in this way could the Soviet economy have been given the flexibility and dynamism characteristic of the market without depriving it of the advantages of centralization and planning.

"Shock therapy" or "radical surgery" could do tremendous harm to the rather unusual economic and social organism existing in Russia, while producing hardly any significant positive results. Radical reforms have been under way in Russia since the beginning of 1992. There have been changes, of course, but the extent to which they have been changes for the better should not be exaggerated. The same giant auto plants, tractor plants, metallurgical complexes, shipyards, mines, ore-enrichment plants, oil fields, petrochemical plants, natural gas pipelines, nuclear power plants, paper plants, and vodka distilleries are in operation now as before 1992. But today all these economic units are functioning much less efficiently than they did ten or twenty years earlier. Things are also much worse on the land, where the former state farms and collective farms have been reorganized as joint-stock companies or distributed to small farmers or medium-sized farming businesses. There are exceptions, of course, but they are very rare.

The reformers' disregard for Russia's existing industrial capacity and infrastructure, and for the tremendous potential of its millions of skilled personnel, is surprising to many Western economists. Alice Amsden, an economics professor at the Massachusetts Institute of Technology, and Lance Taylor, an economics professor at the New School for Social Research in New York City, have written about this as follows:

> although Eastern Europe's overthrow of its ancien regime circa 1989 qualifies as "revolutionary," what it has tried to create in its stead is by historical standards already outdated. True, the transition has been as unique as it has been unprecedented; nowhere in the world has capitalism been created *after* pseudo-socialism. But instead of lurching toward a new economic and political system in order to catch up with the world's richest countries, Eastern Europe's societies have searched for mores, methods, and models to help them catch up in ways congruent with their own highly selective memory and with the mythologized histories of the most advanced capitalist countries. . . .
>
> No revolution is ever completely successful in coming to terms with its own past, but few revolutionary societies have dipped into history so indiscriminately, or abused the past so wastefully, as Eastern Europe's. . . . [A]llowing first-rate firms to go bankrupt and world-scale research and development laboratories to deteriorate has delayed not just catching up with the world's richest countries but recovering pretransition income levels by several years. Most important, the choice of a capitalist model that dates back to the eighteenth century and that represents an extreme, primitive form of market economy has failed in five years to lay the groundwork . . . for modern capitalist development.

[Translator's note: The author cites as his source for the above quotation: *Ekonomicheskaya Gazeta*, October 1995, no. 35–39. Actually, this Russian-language journal was quoting from a book by Amsden, Taylor, and the Polish economist Jacek Kochanowicz, *The Market Meets Its Match: Restructuring the Economies of Eastern Europe* (Cambridge: Harvard University Press, 1994), pp. 2–3.]

These two American economists discuss the negative consequences of mistaken economic policies in such countries as Poland, Hungary,

Bulgaria, and the Czech Republic. They make a direct link between the political instability in those countries and the "insufficient utilization" of the previously created economic potential there. Russians know, from the experience of life since 1992, that the defects of economic policy Amsden and Taylor describe, which have been partly corrected in some countries of Eastern Europe, were much more substantial and much less explicable in Russia. It is not surprising that *Ekonomicheskaya Gazeta* put a more expressive title on its review: "The Task Ahead for Russia—Replacing Learned Foolishness with Good Common Sense."

2. The Military-Industrial Complex—Legacy of the Cold War

For specific historical, political, and ideological reasons the chief sector of the Soviet economy was the so-called military-industrial complex. Total expenditures on arms production, the armed forces, military aid to allies, the space program, and intelligence of all kinds, as well as on the state security apparatus, added up to no less than one-third of the government budget.

To serve military needs, whole new rail lines and airports were built, along with huge new factories, whether on the shores of Lake Baikal or in the suburbs of Moscow. A large share of the research done by the Academy of Sciences was for the military-industrial complex. In the 1970s and 1980s this part of the Soviet economy, having grown to gigantic proportions, became a heavy burden hampering the overall development of the economy. Many superficial Western observers, having discovered that Soviet industry was incapable of producing good typewriters or reliable tape recorders, assumed that the quality of Soviet tanks, helicopters, and ICBMs was equally poor. Serious economists outside the USSR did not share that opinion. Many Western military experts also had no doubt about the effectiveness of Soviet military industry and the Soviet military machine.

Having worked for about twenty years in the field of polytechnical education, I became familiar with many different enterprises in various branches of the economy and all regions of the country. Even to a nonspecialist the discrepancies in the level of technology and production organization were striking. The lowest productivity of course, and the lowest standard of living, was in agriculture, which since the 1920s had served as a donor to the rest of the Soviet economy. The "pumping over" of material and intellectual resources from the countryside to the city, which in the debates of the 1920s was called "a temporary tribute," not only continued but actually increased in the subsequent decades. In light industry and the food industry the productivity level was not very high, although these sectors received a large share of the Soviet budget. Soviet extractive industry also lagged behind world standards, even though the export of raw materials was the main source of foreign currency for the Soviet state. Heavy engineering and the metallurgical industry were more advanced economically and technically. Most of the productive plant in these sectors was built during the first five-year plans and symbolized the industrial might of the Soviet Union. The general level in these sectors was nevertheless lower than in analogous economic sectors in Western Europe and the United States. This becomes evident in any comparison of quality and variety of goods produced.

I was not personally acquainted with the operations of the secret military plants or those in the space industry. But those more familiar with the military-industrial complex have testified that the productivity level and quality of output was quite comparable to, and sometimes better than, analogous operations in the West. Millions of the most highly skilled workers were employed in Soviet military industry, as well as the best technical and engineering personnel. The many research institutes and design offices in those sectors employed hundreds of thousands of specialists from the universities. The enormous material resources and strategic reserves of the Soviet Union were concentrated here.

In the West, production of the most advanced weapons systems and production for the space program are not primarily based on market principles. This is because of the very nature of the goods produced. A new type of missile or a new system used in the space program requires fifteen to twenty years to go from planning and design to production. The same is true for new generations of nuclear submarines, bombers, and aircraft carriers. New types of tanks, armored cars, or helicopters require eight to ten years. The scale of such production and the length of time required mean that these things cannot be accomplished without scientifically based planning, broad cooperation among different branches of industry, and major budget allocations. Besides, governments are the only customers for most types of military output. Competition does exist, but it tends to be between countries more than between companies, and the operation of the laws of the market is therefore quite limited.

The production of nuclear submarines, missiles, and aircraft carriers does not make a country richer. The costs of military production have been a burden on the economies of the United States, Britain, and France for many years. The economic successes of Germany and Japan are largely related to the restrictions imposed on them after World War II, preventing them from having large armies or producing major offensive weapons. Other Western countries also managed to produce both guns and butter. They did not have such a big disparity between sectors of the economy as existed in the USSR previously and in Russia still. Competition required companies to pay serious attention to the production of shoes, food products, perfumes, and passenger cars, not just tanks and bombers. That is one reason why economic reform models applicable in the West cannot be simply transferred to Russian soil. What Russia's economy needed was a separate reform plan for each sector, whether light industry, agriculture, the machine industry, the extractive industries, or the energy industry, each having its own methods and timing. Particular care and caution should have been taken in reforming military industry. These distinctions were ignored, and that is one of the reasons for the difficulties.

Gorbachev, in carrying out perestroika, was advised by a number of prominent economists—Leonid Abalkin, Stanislav Shatalin, Abel Aganbegyan, and Nikolai Petrakov. Yeltsin surrounded himself with younger, but not very competent, economists, who had no experience of working in the government or on the scale of the economy as a whole. There was a third school of economists in Russia, headed by the late Yuri Yaremenko. The Russian press, which touted many other economists, paid little attention to Yaremenko, and only in his obituaries was he referred to as "a classic." Many learned about him only after his death.

Yaremenko engaged in deeply probing research and analysis and came up with the most solidly grounded economic forecasts, but he scorned publicity and did not consider it necessary to fight to promote his work. His book *Structural Changes in the Soviet Economy* is considered the most serious analysis of the post-World War II era, but it is written in a highly specialized language and would be difficult for a nonspecialist to understand—and the leaders of the USSR, CPSU, and Russian Federation can be counted among the nonspecialists.

Yaremenko was not overburdened with official duties and ceremonial titles. He learned a great deal in the research institutions of the State Planning Commission and as early as the 1970s headed an institute for forecasting scientific and technical progress under the Soviet Academy of Sciences. After the dissolution of the USSR Yaremenko became director of the Institute of Economic Forecasting of the Russian Academy of Sciences. I never heard of him taking part in the conferences of economists held by Gorbachev and Ryzhkov—or later by Yeltsin and Chernomyrdin. Yet the findings of Yaremenko and his institute were more thoroughly researched than those of other economists. Between the cautious proposals of Yaremenko's group and the wild schemes of Gaidar, Chubais, and their Western advisers, Jeffrey Sachs and Anders Aslund, there is simply no comparison.

In Yaremenko's opinion, Western economic theories could not be applied to Russia, because of the enormous disparity between the super-modern aeronautics and space industry and military production systems, on the one hand, and civilian industry with its massive reliance on manual labor, on the other. Both the U.S. and the USSR pursued the arms race, but its effects on the two countries were not identical. For the USSR it meant massive diversion of resources from civilian sectors, resulting in social degradation. Although consumption increased in the USSR, the quality of goods remained low, and the shortage of resources was made up for by intensified exploitation of the raw material base, disregard for the environment, and increased production of alcohol. Various means were employed for pressuring or inducing people to work in unattractive locations. The civilian consumer economy was artificially restricted, and this led to the growth of organized crime and other forms of social degradation. For forty years the USSR, with amazing recklessness, exerted almost all its energies on trying to maintain military parity with an economically more powerful opponent. This could not help but end in disaster.

Strange as it may seem, Yaremenko linked the suicidal policies pursued in the "era of stagnation" to a reduction in the leading role of the CPSU. In his opinion, various government agencies escaped from party control and ceased to function as parts of a unified whole. They became more autonomous, and in pursuit of their own goals began to devour the resources of the country at an accelerated pace. The military departments proved to be the most voracious, although others were no slouches. Yaremenko hoped that sooner or later the government would come to its senses and change its policies. The main thing he insisted on was an end to the Cold War. He did not give advice to political leaders and did not wish to prompt the authorities into any hasty decisions. But, he said, the government had to get out of a game that it could only lose. Only by extricating itself from the Cold War could the USSR begin to reform military industry and convert defense production to civilian use on a large scale.

Investment and resources could gradually be shifted from the military sectors to the construction of quality housing, the development of areas with summer cottages and gardens for city dwellers, production of consumer goods, and improvement in the technical level and organization of production in civilian sectors. This would make it possible to develop new incentives for people to work and would stop the process of social degradation. Yaremenko was not opposed to limited market reforms, but he protested emphatically against making the market the chief regulator or the chief instrument for reforming the Soviet economy. That was not the road to prosperity, in his opinion, but to chaos and decline. The country would have to pay too dearly if market relations for which it was not ready were introduced in unwise ways. Defense industry was an ace in the hole, the chief means of encouraging the growth of civilian production and raising its technical level. Such a complicated reorganization could not be carried out, he felt, by the use of market reforms. Planning and government regulation of the economy would have to continue.

Yaremenko considered arguments about the so-called inherent inefficiency of a planned economy to be nonsense. Instead of the Gaidar-Chubais formula "Transform power into property," which he also considered nonsense, Yaremenko proposed another formula—"Transform military might into economic might." A transition to the market and to an "open society," in his opinion, should not be the first step in such a transformation, but the second. He was not opposed to democracy, but he was a realist. He was troubled by many of Gorbachev's initiatives, especially when the entire Soviet press was talking about democratization and transition to a market economy, but no one was paying any attention to the question of conversion.

Yaremenko's forecasts became increasingly gloomy concerning the abrupt turn in 1992 toward the capitalist market system. He predicted mass unemployment and a weakening of the position of those

59

strata of the population with technical skills and other forms of higher culture. The reckless opening of Russia's borders, he believed, would turn Russia into a second-class power for decades to come. "A country must live by some idea," Yaremenko wrote. "In the modern world positive ideals are linked in one way or another with high technology. The elimination of the highly qualified upper stratum would mean the loss of ideals. What would remain in that event? Primitive consumerism, which in its crassest form can be neither an effective stimulus nor a constructive idea" (*Segodnya*, September 20, 1996).

In the years 1992–95, Yaremenko tried to develop a number of scenarios that would prevent, or soften the impact of, the crash that would inevitably result from the capitalist reforms. In his opinion, those reforms had not been chosen by the people but were imposed by Russia's former opponents in the Cold War in alliance with the corrupted upper echelon of the new Russian government and the economists in its service, as well as the oil and gas lobby. But no one was interested in the opinions and suggestions of this outstanding economist.

Not only for a trained economist like Yaremenko, but for many nonspecialists as well, it was evident that the attempt at a hasty capitalist transformation of society was unwise and doomed to failure. Late in the fall of 1992 a major conference was held in the auto-producing city of Togliatti in Samara province on the Volga. Taking part were directors of most of the largest factories and plants in Russia— 80 percent of them belonging to the military-industrial complex. Also participating were nearly all members of the Russian government, including Gaidar, Shokhin, P. Aven, and A. Nechaev. The Italian journalist Giulietto Chiesa also attended the conference and provides an account of it in his recently completed book *Farewell, Russia*. The following passages from his book appeared in Russian in *Novaya Gazeta*, March 17–23, 1997.

> All the "Red directors" were there, at least of the biggest factories that were still state-owned. I remember those "cadres," those stalwarts of the nomenklatura's middle echelons, who embodied the monopolistic principle of the Communist state. They took the microphone one after the other while on the presiding committee there sat young people, almost juveniles, who

had just left the walls of American universities, fully steeped in the Reagan-Thatcher credo, convinced believers in deregulation.

All the "Red directors" said approximately the same thing: we understand that socialism is dead; we know that a good part of our productive capacity must be sacrificed on the altar of competition, efficiency, and the market. But we beg you, we implore you, to consider two key aspects of the situation. First, behind us stand millions of families, who we cannot just abandon to the whims of fate. Second, many of the factories and plants represented here could become competitive on the world market in fairly short order if only the government worked out an investment policy aimed at revitalizing them. We are ready to shut down what must be shut down, but please tell us what we can save, what you want to set your sights on that would contribute to the growth of production in the future.

I remember what boredom was etched on the faces of the young men of the presiding committee. They had not contemplated any government investment program. Still less were they concerned about the families of those who would lose their jobs. Not because of hardness of heart. It simply never entered their minds that reform on such an awesome scale, such an unprecedented, extremely complex operation, might be carried out by enlisting the support of, not the majority of course (that would be practically impossible), but a significant part of the population. I was amazed by the lack of comprehension in their responses. The cabinet that had just been formed by Boris Yeltsin had not the slightest conception of what a conversion of military industry to civilian uses might entail. The youthful government simply never envisioned such a thing.

According to Chiesa, not all international economic agencies agreed with the recommendations of the IMF and the group of experts sent to Russia from the West. A study by the World Bank made in early 1992 argued that the state must play a central role in at least four areas that are of first-rate importance for any transition to a free-market capitalist economy. These are: (1) maintenance of social equality, which guarantees the stability necessary for reform to proceed; (2) support of the private sector through clearly defined programs and antimonopoly action; (3) preservation of an internal market, distinct from the world market, with protection of its weaker structures against the predictable pressures exerted by overly powerful foreign investors; and (4) state control over the key elements of financial policy. "This advice of the World Bank," Chiesa declares, "which cannot be suspected of either foolishness or Marxism, helps to dispel once and for all the notion that any criticism of the Yeltsin model of 'reform' signifies, in the best case, lack of understanding of the laws of the market or, in the worst case, hidden Communist sympathies."

By mechanically reducing government orders for goods produced by the defense industry, the Yeltsin-Gaidar regime dealt a serious blow not only to the plants and factories of the military-industrial complex but to all civilian sectors of the economy as well, denying them the opportunity for modernization based on the resources and skilled personnel of this most advanced part of the former Soviet economy.

The factories and plants of the defense sector are still in operation today. The factories that produced nuclear submarines are now busy eliminating them. To take nuclear warheads apart and find some use for the remaining components has proved to be not much easier or less dangerous than making them in the first place, although the government is barely paying for the labor involved. The Russian defense industry is trying to sell its goods—the world's best tanks and military aircraft—to Third World countries, to India and China. But meanwhile the Russian army does not have the means to pay for military exercises or training flights.

Life goes on in the formerly top-secret towns, about fifteen in number, that are under the direct jurisdiction of the ministries of defense and atomic energy. There is more openness about these towns now. You can read articles on them in the magazine *Sovershenno Otkryto* (whose title means "Absolutely Open"—i.e., the opposite of "Top Secret"). But the standard of living in these places is much lower than before. Apparently today in the towns of Krasnoyarsk-26 or Chelyabinsk-65 there are no killings by orders from on high, but suicides do occur, including some of the most outstanding scientists. The gigantic potential of the military-industrial complex continues to be slowly destroyed. An influential figure in the management of the economy said to me in 1994, "So defense is being destroyed. Let it be. Who needs it?"

3. Geography, Nature, and the Russian Economy

Factors having to do with geography and nature are of course enormously important to the economy of any country. With the dissolution of the USSR all the more southern and western republics separated from Russia. In territory, Russia remains the largest in the world, but this is mostly northern and eastern land with a harsh continental climate.

None of the major capitals of the world has a winter so long and so fierce as Moscow. Spending on capital construction, heating, and lighting is much greater than elsewhere. The big industrial districts of the Urals and Siberia are located in climate zones that are even colder than Moscow's. In such cities as Yekaterinburg, Chelyabinsk, Krasnoyarsk, and Novosibirsk, temperatures may reach as low as -30C or even -40C (-22 to -40F). Russia's vast territory adds to its wealth, but with this vastness comes the added burden of high transportation costs, while the consumption of gas, electricity, oil, and wood is extravagant. Russia does not economize on water usage, and neglects recycling. Yet even if the thriftiest use of resources prevailed, Russia would still have to spend more per unit of output than the United States, Japan, or Western Europe.

By refusing subsidies and keeping rates for power and transportation high, the Yeltsin government made Russian factories noncompetitive on the world market. Much of Russia's oil and gas, for example, comes from above the Arctic Circle, meaning greater cost and less profit in the exporting of these materials.

The Russian Federation has a great deal of land, but the climate of course is not very favorable for the pursuit of agriculture. Butter from Vologda province may be of better quality, but it is not, and cannot be, cheaper than butter from New Zealand. Under conditions similar in some ways to Canada's, a population of 150 million, not 26 million, must be fed.

Despite these special geographical difficulties, the hastily thrown together plans for "structural transformation" on whose basis the Gaidar team began breaking up and rearranging the Russian economy, copied Western models or IMF programs for Southeast Asian and Latin American countries. These programs and models did not provide for any large-scale government aid to industry, agriculture, or transport. Italy or Argentina could do without such subsidies perhaps, but not Russia. In 1990, Finance Minister Valentin Pavlov told me: "Looking at the big picture, we have no need for Vorkuta. The best thing for our country would be to shut down all those mines in the Far North, which were profitable only under Gulag."

What Pavlov said may be true. But in that case the government is obliged to take a hand in relocating the residents of the northern European mining city of Vorkuta to warmer climates and providing jobs for them. The government of Russia, however, is no longer concerned even with such an important part of the economy as the northern Siberian city of Norilsk with its giant nickel mining and processing industry.

4. Spirit of Enterprise and the Russian Soul

There can be no hope of success in making abrupt economic changes if objective factors like the ones discussed above are disregarded. But that is also true of subjective factors—popular traditions, the capabilities of the population, the general cultural level and the quality of the culture, particular national or religious features, the psychological outlook and accepted system of values prevailing in a country. It would be rash to use IMF recommendations worked out for Mexico or Nigeria as a guide for reforming Russia. This was understood in China, where different variants of economic reform were elaborated for different provinces. But the Gaidar team made a conscious choice to reject such an approach. "There are no special countries," Pyotr Aven, one of Gaidar's cabinet members, declared in February 1992. "From an economist's point of view, if economics exists at all, then it is a science with its own laws and, on the level of currency stabilization, all countries are *one and the same*" (emphasis in original; see *Nezavisimaya Gazeta*, February 27, 1992). It is awkward even to argue with such an assertion—or to point out to Aven that there is a difference between economics and mathematics.

One may speak with disdain about Soviet traditions and training and scornfully refer to Soviet citizens as "moochers" who lacked initiative and were content with a state of dependency. One may angrily complain that too many Soviet citizens would have preferred to remain "little cogs" in the vast and powerful machinery of the Soviet state, which, after all, did look after them in many ways. What cannot be done is to simply ignore the particular traits of Russia's population, for it is the only one we have. Only idealists and adventurers, out of touch with reality, could propose that all we need do is break up the totalitarian structures and institute democratic mechanisms and the market, and then the previously shackled creative powers of the Russian people would automatically move the country's economy and culture forward and change life for the better.

The creative potential of the Russian people is indeed great, but releasing these hidden powers is not such an easy task. After being defeated in the 1995 Duma elections, Yegor Gaidar declared that his chief constituency was among the schoolchildren who were earning more than their parents by washing cars in the streets and parking lots. This is not only extremely cynical but indicates an unwise approach toward Russia's long-term prospects. Does Gaidar include among his future constituents those high school girls who display such an enviable "spirit of enterprise" in other forms of street business?

Undoubtedly the totalitarianism of past decades produced forms of consciousness corresponding to the social "being" of those times. But before October 1917, too, Russian conditions and traditions differed substantially from those in the West. That was one of the reasons for the failure of many of the reforms attempted by Pyotr Stolypin, Russia's premier in the aftermath of the 1905 revolution.

Aleksei Kiva, a political scientist loyal to Yeltsin, writing in the government newspaper *Rossiyskaya Gazeta* (September 2, 1995), gave the following advice to the regime he supports:

> For the average Russian the idea of social justice stands higher than the idea of democracy. . . . The interests of the collective and of the state stand higher than those of the individual. Collectivism and solidarity are valued more highly than individualism. The individual in Russia has not won the necessary respect, and the idea of the inherent value and importance of the individual remains an abstraction, without specific content. The idea of wealth or of social inequality is not accepted with any enthusiasm. The idea of patriotism, of a strong state and a strong army, is just as influential as previously. Especially highly valued is the idea of a spiritual foundation, and the role of moral incentives is exceptionally great. . . .
>
> Only those who are far removed from a historical view of things can think that this hierarchy of values was erected acci-

dentally thanks to the influence of bad tsars, evil rulers, and popular delusions. There are certain lawful regularities behind all of this, conditioned by the course of Russian history itself. Any party will inevitably doom itself to defeat if for one reason or another it begins to disregard the popular frame of mind. By disregarding those values that are most highly regarded among the people, the democrats doom themselves to failure. Russia can't be reconstructed on the basis of appeals for the building of capitalism, which does not have the best associations in the minds of most Russians. One may unintentionally construct a new Gulag.

The humorist M. Zhvanetsky once asked, "Why is it that we can't live like they do 'over there' when living like we do here is obviously impossible?" A similar question was raised in an article by Larisa Piyasheva (L. Popkova) entitled "Whose Pies Are Puffier?" (*Novy Mir*, 1987, No. 5). Many thought her article was meant as a parody, but she explained later: "When I think about the ways and means of reviving Russia, nothing comes to mind but to transfer to our territory the experience of the postwar 'German miracle.' My hopes center on the idea that if the 'spirit of enterprise' is unleashed in our land, it will reawaken the will to live and revive the Protestant ethic."

Such naivete is amazing. What lessons Piyasheva, holder of a doctor's degree in economics, has drawn from her own enterprising but unsuccessful ventures in Moscow I do not know. (In 1991–92 she headed the Committee for Economic Reform of the Moscow mayoralty and began the first campaign to privatize state-owned businesses in the capital city.) But I do know that it isn't possible to "revive" a Protestant ethic where it never existed—in Orthodox Russia, Islamic Tatarstan, or Buryat Mongolia with its traditions of Lamaist Buddhism. Marx himself acknowledged that the Western type of capitalist economy was based on a particular cultural and religious foundation. He wrote to Vera Zasulich that his volumes of *Capital* reflected Western realities and were not always applicable to Russia.

The connections between Western forms of capitalism and religion were also studied by Max Weber. In his opinion, the Protestant Reformation led by Luther and Calvin in the sixteenth century caused a revolution in thinking and ethical practices. The new Protestant ethic became the first link in a complex chain of transformations in the traditional way of life and as a result there arose that system of thought and way of perceiving reality that can be called the "spirit of capitalism." It required centuries for this new ethic of acquisitiveness, this "spirit of capitalism," to take shape. Weber regarded the sermons of Richard Baxter, the seventeenth-century English preacher, as an early point in this evolution. The eighteenth-century homilies of Benjamin Franklin were a mature expression of this new outlook, and the high point, in Weber's view, was reached in the twentieth century with the American school of "scientific management" linked with the names of Taylor and Ford. (See A.I. Kravchenko, *Sotsiologiia Maksa Vebera* [Sociology of Max Weber], Moscow, 1997, pp. 110–121.) This kind of evolution in social mores and popular consciousness did not occur in Russia. The ethics of traditional Russian Orthodoxy, as well as the socialist currents of thought prevailing in nineteenth-century Russia, were far removed from the values of Western rationalism and the Western acquisitive spirit.

Of course the Protestant ethic is not the only basis for capitalist development. This was shown by the experience of Japan, which had its own traditions and religion. Yet the Japanese form of capitalism proved to be more efficient in many ways than the European one. An organization recently established in Russia, the National Democratic Vanguard Foundation, has as one of its aims to find a Russian road to capitalism, based on purely Russian values, which it hopes will prove even more efficient than the Japanese variety. But the foundation's statement to the public (in *Izvestia*, March 13, 1996) admitted that no Russian model has yet been found. If no one has yet discovered a Russian model of capitalism, wouldn't it be simpler to reform the model of socialism that already exists? Who would destroy their own home, where it is still possible to live, however uncomfortably, when there isn't even a blueprint for a new dwelling place?

5. Growing Resistance by the Population

The radical reformers' disregard for national values and traditions, the history of Russia, and the particular psychological features and ethical standards of the population has given rise not just to mass discontent but to growing opposition and resistance. Following the example of the coal miners, those who have engaged in various protest actions include workers in the energy industries, textile workers, metal workers, workers in the machine industry, teachers, doctors, scientists, pensioners, subway construction workers, workers in the defense industries, farmers, and students.

In 1991 Zbigniew Brzezinski wrote:

> Most Russians long for "normalcy," which they equate with political and economic Westernization. . . . Russians tend to fall into extreme boastfulness at one moment and extreme self-deprecation at another. Today they are experiencing an epidemic of self-denunciation. They see their fate as having been one of terrible historical failure, and they are looking abroad in desperate search for ideals. They would like to be like the United States or, even better, like Sweden, which pleases them with its ability to combine democracy and prosperity with social justice.
>
> (*Stolitsa*, 1992, no. 27, pp. 8–9.)

The author's arrogance and limited perception prevented him from making a sober evaluation of the superficial character and the motivation behind the upsurge of Russian Westernism.

Ulyukaev also failed to understand this when, in retrospect, he described the moods of 1991: "In a very short time the masses were won to the idea of democracy and the idea of capitalism. The ideological consensus that took shape on the basis of the blending of these two ideas . . . became the driving force of the political revolution" (*Segodnya*, September 20, 1996).

Ulyukaev's assertions are erroneous. The Westernism among Russians in 1990–91 did not go very deep; it was a passing mood; people had broken with Communist ideology but hadn't found a new, unifying national idea. As for wanting to "be like Sweden," there weren't many Russians who knew much about life in Sweden or the Swedish economy. In regard to the United States, most ordinary Russians had only a distorted notion of that country—based on movies, television, and books, especially detective novels. A poll taken in 1990 showed that 32 percent of Russian respondents considered the U.S. a model to be emulated; another 32 percent cited Japan; 17 percent, Germany; 11 percent, Sweden; and 4 percent, China.

However, the first few months of Gaidar's reforms altered such moods and opinions among Russians. A second poll, in 1992, based on the same questionnaire, gave a radically different picture. Only 13 percent now cited the U.S.; Japan, 12, and Germany, 7. The total number of pro-Western respondents fell from 90 to 40 percent. In late 1995 only 25 percent still considered Western models suitable for Russia. (*Izvestia*, October 13, 1995.) Although I haven't seen more recent polls, it seems to me likely that by 1997–98 the number of "Westernizers" would probably have fallen as low as 10 or 12 percent.

The "Westernizer" ideology in nineteenth-century Russia rested on much more substantial social strata and more stable moods. The philosopher Vadim Mezhuyev has commented on this:

> The old Westernizers, despite their critical attitudes, did not renounce Russia in favor of the West. For them Russia was more beloved than any country in the world, although it was backward in many respects. That backwardness, to them, was not a sign of limitation or decline, or of some sort of inherent freakishness in Russia. It was simply a sign of youthfulness, of a country for which everything still lay ahead. Recognition of backwardness did not give rise to a feeling of inferiority or hatred toward everything Russian. The Westernizers believed in a great future for Russia, whereas the Slavophiles focused on what they believed was Russia's great past. The Westernizers of today are different. . . . They have declared the state to be the main enemy of private property. Nihilism toward the Russian state is perhaps their most characteristic feature. I don't know of any Westernizing democrat in the past who would have wanted to achieve political and economic freedom at the expense of territorial loss and geopolitical defeat, the weakening and disintegration of his own state. . . . Today's Westernizers are indifferent toward national consciousness. For them patriotism is a dirty word.
>
> (*Nezavisimaya Gazeta*, February 13, 1997)

Yeltsin's victory in the 1996 election cannot be considered a victory for pro-Western or pro-capitalist ideology. He won, not by speaking with the Russian people in the language of Milton Friedman; he used the language of social democracy. He also spoke as a patriot and advocate of a strong state. After the 1996 election the promises of social democratic and patriotic measures were not kept. And resistance to capitalist reforms is growing, although it is still mainly passive. The patience of the population amazes even the reformers. But it is not unlimited. (See chapter 9, "War on the Rails.")

6. Market Complexities

The term capitalism is an abstraction. There are many forms of capitalism, depending on the history and traditions, nature and size of a country. There is American capitalism and European; Japanese and Turkish; Latin American and African; Indian and Pakistani. The Swedish model differs from the British; the model in Taiwan, from that in Thailand. Gaidar and his cothinkers wanted to follow the Anglo-Saxon model, although it is the farthest removed from conditions in Russia.

The problem is not just that Russia lacks the "Protestant ethic." Western capitalism today enjoys a highly advanced economy and high level of productivity, but it also rests on an enormous amount of capital accumulated over the course of centuries. Russia does not have this. The accumulation of capital in the West came not only from domestic sources; it was derived also from a far-flung system of colonies and semicolonies. Although the colonial system collapsed in the mid-twentieth century, the dependence of Third World countries on the metropolitan centers has persisted.

Advanced capitalism is a system of highly complex relations, which also took centuries to develop and cannot be reproduced by methods of "shock therapy." Oleg Pchelintsev, an economist with the Gorbachev Foundation, has rightly noted:

> Among us the market is often depicted as a simple mechanism (along the lines of such formulas as "demand creates supply," "goods produce money, which produces goods," etc.). Actually, the market is simple only in the imaginations of the ideologues of neoliberalism. In fact, it (or they, for there are a great many markets) is fantastically complex. Many volumes have been written about all the deviations from the model of "pure competition," and disregard for this knowledge, which has been arrived at through great effort by generations of economists, is probably the main defect of the neophytes on Gaidar's team.
>
> (Pchelintsev, *Rossiya na novom rubezhe* [Russia at a New Frontier], Moscow, 1995, p. 179)

Many well-informed people, as early as 1991, wrote about the unrealistic and utopian nature of the plans for a speedy introduction of market relations into Russia, but their arguments were rejected. In the fall of 1991, for example, an American political scientist with the Russian name of Igor Yefimov addressed his former countrymen:

> The market! The market economy is our only salvation. Place everything in private hands, allow producers to compete freely, let prices find their own levels, don't plan, or command, or regulate, and the country will revive. And there will be neither hunger revolts nor political strikes in Russia. But why wouldn't there be? What kind of fairy-tale country is Russia when through the ages in all countries of the world people have killed each other by the millions over property issues, but in Russia— after seventy years of the most ruthless political and economic oppression—some kind of fantastically kind-hearted population has supposedly grown up, so that people will stand in line peacefully and take what they like: one will take a mill, another an airport, another a high-voltage power line, another a nuclear reactor, or a railroad, or the Ostankino TV tower. And everyone will peacefully and harmoniously begin working and trading—to the envy of the rest of the world, which until now for some reason has been shaken by revolts, strikes, expropriations, gangsterism, confiscations, crisis, inflation, hunger, and destruction.
>
> To be sure, the market form of economic regulation has shown that it is the most efficient. But history has also shown just as clearly that the free market is a luxury that not every nation can allow itself, and certainly not at all times in its history. Solid and tested social structures are needed that will prevent the market from turning into a source of chaos and ruin. . . .
>
> Dear readers and fellow countrymen, look at the world around you with open eyes. You can see that socialism has not ruined Sweden, while capitalism has not saved Brazil. This is because there is something in the world more important than economics. . . . The name of this most important element in social existence is—cultural maturity. When we speak of culture we are not talking about the number of books read or poems memorized. By culture we mean the way in which a human community is constructed. Culture in this sense is slow to mature. If a country tries to move at too great a speed, one that is beyond its capabilities, it explodes from within, just as the

prosperous country of Lebanon exploded, and Iran, which was in such a great hurry to industrialize.

(*Nezavisimaya Gazeta*, October 17, 1991.)

These warnings went unheeded in 1991, but it is not too late to repeat them now. The mass of the people learn, not from slogans, as was said by Lenin, but from their own experience of life.

7. Lack of Resources

Even if it were true that the population of Russia, in its great majority, supported the idea of transforming "state socialism" into capitalism, still the accomplishment of this objective would require enormous material and financial resources, which neither the government nor the population have.

Western analysts consider the "systemic transformation" of the German Democratic Republic (GDR), the former East Germany, an example of a relatively successful transformation from socialism to capitalism. The GDR was numbered among the industrially developed countries of Europe. The general opinion was that the economy of the GDR functioned better than that of the Soviet Union or those of Poland, Hungary, and Romania. In labor productivity and living standards the GDR was ahead of all other countries of Comecon (the Council of Mutual Economic Assistance), the economic bloc of countries formerly allied with the Soviet Union. The crop yield in East Germany was less than in Hungary, but far more than in the USSR. The transition to a market economy began for the GDR in 1990 when it was merged with the Federal Republic of Germany, the former West Germany—the mightiest industrial country in Europe. The estimates of German economists were that it would take no less than four or five years, at a cost to West Germany of $250 billion, for the main part of this transition to be accomplished. Yet East Germany's territory was only 108,000 square kilometers, with a population of only 16.7 million. The German economists' estimates turned out to be greatly understated.

In March 1997, at the invitation of the German Party of Democratic Socialists, I visited Berlin and Thuringia, parts of the former East Germany. In the opinion of the residents I met there, the situation is still far from having reached the prosperity that was expected. Unemployment there is between 20 and 25 percent. Many factories that were fully viable under the standards of Comecon, but did not meet the technical requirements of the European community, have been closed. Also shut down were the eight nuclear power plants built on Soviet designs. All the state and collective farms of East Germany continue to exist, because no one has yet been able to finance a transition to private family farming. The actual expenditures on capitalist reforms in the former GDR have exceeded $400 billion, greatly increasing the national debt and the budget deficit for Germany as a whole. As a result of this overly hasty attempt at "transformation" the Germany economy has gone into a slump in recent years. In March 1997, mass demonstrations by German miners and construction workers, protesting unemployment, dominated the news in Germany. Yet the former GDR was about the size of only one province of Russia (not much bigger than Moscow province).

A plan for radical market reforms in Russia worked out by economists Grigory Yavlinsky and Stanislav Shatalin in 1991 said the main work could be done in—500 days! Gaidar promised to accomplish the job in two years. Galina Starovoitova predicted that if radical market reforms were carried out, Russia would be the economic leader of the world by 2000! What was all this—self-deception or deliberate deception of the people of Russia?

Many reformers, of course, hoped for Western aid. Valentin Pavlov asked American financial authorities to support a "structural perestroika" of the Soviet Union to the tune of "only" $24 billion. Gaidar hoped to obtain between $20 and $40 billion from the West for his reform program. Yavlinsky's "500 days" program envisaged Western investment in the Russian economy amounting to $500 billion over five years. Many other proposals were drawn up for a new variant of the Marshall Plan, the program by which the United States, from 1948 through 1951, provided large amounts of aid to restore the economies of Western Europe ravaged by World War II. All the proposals for a Marshall Plan for Russia were completely naive and utopian. The most advanced forms of capitalism in today's world are not noted for their philanthropic tendencies.

Many Western politicians and businessmen were of course happy to see the downfall of the CPSU, the dissolution of the USSR, and the adoption of a program of market reforms by the new government of the Russian Federation. But their comments became very guarded when the question of real material aid to the new Russia was raised. In 1991, George Kennan, a former U.S. ambassador to the Soviet Union, wrote about the changes in Russia (in *Foreign Affairs*, vol. 69, no. 5, Winter 1990/1991, p. 184):

"What is now emerging on the territory traditionally known as Russia will not be—cannot be—the Russia of the tsars. Nor can it be the Russia of the communists. It can only be something essentially new, the contours of which are still, for us and for the Russians themselves, obscure."

On the question of American aid to the new Russia, Kennan wrote: "The greatest help we can give will be of two kinds: understanding and example." By "understanding" Kennan meant simply a recognition that the Russian people were passing through a difficult and in many ways humiliating time. He saw "no reason why an understanding American attitude towards Russia at this juncture in its history should not include a reasonable measure of compassion."

So there you have it: understanding, compassion, setting an example. As for material aid, Kennan felt it should be "of minor importance." In his opinion, America had too many of its own problems that required the attention and resources of its taxpayers. Those problems included crime and drugs, urban decay, a decline in education, deterioration of the economic infrastructure and of the environment. We have the same problems in Russia, and in recent years they have reached dangerous proportions. But we cannot count on money from American taxpayers to solve our problems for us.

When they didn't receive the aid they had hoped for from the West, the Russian reformers began reaching more and more often into the shrunken wallets of their own countrymen, drastically reducing real income for most of the population. They did not hesitate to destroy a system of social welfare and social protections that had been built up in Russia over a period of decades. It proved impossible to begin the "systemic transformation" and at the same time preserve the social safety net.

8. Competition from the West

Western capitalism remains an egoistic society in spite of globalization and the increased international division of labor. Competition between countries, between multinational corporations, and between trading blocs persists. None of these entities wishes to see a strong new competitor emerge in Europe and Asia. Two Polish economists presenting a paper entitled "The Transition of an Economy from Socialism to Capitalism," at the Academy of Finance in Russia, drew on the experience of Poland in recent years to give their listeners a bit of good advice.

"Experience shows," they said,

> that the transition from a socialist economy to a capitalist one is possible, although the process is not easy. The more characteristic the socialist features of an economy were and the more it depended on trade with other socialist countries, the more significant were the difficulties of transition. However, trade with the West can also prove to be destructive. Because of Western protectionism a country with a transitional economy feels the temptation to abandon the policy of capitalist reforms, because trade barriers can simply choke off development possibilities for a country with a transitional economy.
>
> (*Belorusskaya Delovaya Gazeta* [Byelorussian Business Gazette], November 21, 1994)

Russian reformers were unable to persuade the West even to drop the harsh trade barriers erected in the late 1970s, supposedly because of human rights violations by the Soviet government. On its own side, Russia removed virtually all the barriers that had previously prevented the influx of Western goods. As a result Western companies have solidly established themselves in Russia and have undersold many of Russia's domestic industries. Russia is also entangled from head to foot in foreign debt. We have lost our economic independence and become an appendage to the Western economies as a supplier of raw materials.

Aleksandr Panikin, a leading Russian entrepreneur who successfully competes with the best Western firms on the knitted goods market, has given the following testimony:

> The attempt to enter the world economy has ended in the almost complete degradation of our domestic industry. Soviet industry was inefficient, sluggish, resource-intensive, and ecologically dangerous and could not operate successfully under normal conditions. . . .

Today there is beginning to take shape on our planet an economic system in which transnational corporations (TNCs) play the leading role. Can we expect mutually beneficial interaction with the TNCs? Is Russia of interest to them? . . . In the short term the interests of the TNCs are linked with the delivery and sale of food products to Russia (as long as we have something to pay with). As for mineral resources, the increasing costs of extraction and transportation dictate for the TNCs the strategy of penetrating and establishing their presence in the Russian raw materials market, not so much in order to quickly start up production, but to have a strong presence in Russia in case of changes on the world market.

The TNCs are obviously not interested in helping the development of advanced production of complex machinery by Russia's heavy engineering industries. They have no intention of strengthening our military-industrial complex, and in fact oppose any such thing with all the means at their disposal, including connections in Russian domestic politics. In relation to Russia, then, the TNCs of the developed countries are interested in only a few areas. First, transferring ecologically dangerous types of production to Russia. Second, draining off intellectual resources and the technical elite, including any ready-made inventions or high-tech ideas. Third, the recreational possibilities of Siberia.

We can enter the world market today only by gathering together all our resources and capabilities and exerting our will power to the utmost. Otherwise, we will not be able to control even our own territory and Russia will disintegrate into dozens of small feudal principalities.

(*Nezavisimaya Gazeta*, September 27, 1996)

No such harnessing of potential or exertion of will power is yet observable. In 1997, President Yeltsin did make an appeal to the citizenry to buy only Russian-made products. He also signed a decree that government officials had to use Volga automobiles, rather than foreign-made cars. But this is only a tiny part of what needs to be done to protect and restore the Russian economy. According to Panikin, the only solution is to create Russian transnational corporations—something that is easier said than done. Neither the government nor the private sector has the resources to accomplish that aim. The nomen-klatura-dominated type of capitalism in Russia, as Panikin himself admits, has not created a real market, and it stifles truly productive economic activity. Rather than opposing, it is helping the West to sub-jugate Russia.

Latvia, Lithuania, and Estonia have become part of an economic bloc of countries on the Baltic, but only as junior partners. Hungary, the Czech Republic, Slovenia, and Croatia have also apparently resigned themselves to the status of growing dependence on the pow-erful economy of Germany. But Russia is not a country that will resign itself to being a mere economic appendage to the wealthy countries of the West.

9. Lack of a National Idea or Radical Reform Ideology

No revolution can be successful unless the mass of the people are inspired by ideas that are strong and appealing, with a set of slogans that simply and concisely express the ideology of the leaders of the revolution and the revolutionary party.

But today's leaders in Russia have no new ideology, and the mass of the people have no strong new national idea. The slogans of democ-racy, freedom, and the fight against privilege which inspired a signifi-cant number of people in the years 1989–1991 have now been dis-credited by the democrats themselves, since their leaders have brought Russia only poverty and economic decline. No new slogans or ideas have come to replace those of 1989–91, to catch the imagination of the people and thereby become a material force. Why should the peo-ple of Russia suffer ever new difficulties and deprivations, with the prospect of more losses to come? Is there a believable purpose or ulti-mate aim in all this?

The absence of a unifying national idea is acknowledged by today's Russian leaders themselves. In 1996, President Yeltsin called on his supporters, and on all politicians and academic experts, to help find or create a national idea that could consolidate the population into a unified whole. The government newspaper, *Rossiyskaya Gazeta*, announced a contest entitled "An Idea for Russia," the winner to be awarded $2,000. Since then this newspaper has published several hun-dred suggestions, but no idea acceptable to the country as a whole has been found.

Russia lacks even an ideology justifying the radical reforms that have taken place. It has been said that a new liberal ideology should take the place of Communism. But where has this ideology been presented, and by whom? Who is the most authoritative advocate or theoretician of Russian liberalism? Is it Yeltsin? Or Chubais? Or Chernomyrdin? None of them aspire to that role, nor do they engage in theoretical study of the history and traditions of liberalism. As for the leader of the so-called Liberal Democratic Party of Russia—Zhirinovsky—he can hardly be considered a liberal.

Yegor Gaidar is most frequently cited as the chief ideologist of Russian liberalism. In 1997, Aleksandr Tsipko wrote that Gaidar's "anti-statist" ideology had won the support of the masses at the turn of the year from 1991 to 1992 and that the "new Westernizers" at that time had won a complete victory over the neo-Slavophile "statists." The ideology of Gaidar and his team, said Tsipko, has continued to be the ideology of the Russian reform movement and the new ruling party. Tsipko's assertions are mistaken in regard to both 1991–92 and 1997–98.

Before 1991 Gaidar, in his numerous articles and speeches, declared himself a supporter of democratic socialism, not liberalism. He did propose that market relations be encouraged, but only within the framework of a socialist economy. One of his articles in *Moscow News* (1989, no. 41) states, for example:

> A reform program that does not provide for the reinforcement of such values as equality, an equal start in life for all people without regard to wealth or property, social control over differences of income, and active participation by working people in economic management—a program without those is simply not viable. A policy course aimed at the renewal of socialism, including the democratization of social existence and the creation of a flexible, dynamic, multi-sectoral economy with a system of social guarantees, is not just a matter of paying tribute to the ideological orientations of the past. It is simply the result of a sound analysis of the actual, current disposition of social forces.

All the leaders of the democratic opposition from 1989 up through the first several months of 1991 adhered to the slogans of democratic socialism and called for socialist renewal. This was true of all the most prominent democrats, including Yuri Afanasyev, Gavriil Popov, Yuri

Chernichenko, Yuri Karyakin, Vladimir Lysenko, Vladimir Shumeiko, Vyacheslav Shostakovsky, and Ruslan Khasbulatov. When they called for an end to the political monopoly of the Communist Party, the democrats raised the demand "All power to the Soviets." Some members of the Inter-Regional Group of Deputies (IRGD) called themselves radical democrats, but none advocated "liberalism." In early 1990, in an appeal to voters during the election campaign for seats in the Supreme Soviet of the RSFSR, a group of radical democrats belonging to the IRGD—including Galina Starovoitova, Ilya Zaslavsky, Sergei Stankevich, and Telman Gdlyan—accused the leadership of the CPSU of having betrayed the legacy of the Bolsheviks. These radical democrats declared their adherence to the ideals of October 1917. The main slogans of the IRGD ideologists were: "Power to the people," "Factories to the work collectives," "Land to the peasants," and "Property to each and every one." The historian Vladimir Sogrin has justifiably described these slogans as "a modernized version of the program of the October revolution" (see *Otechestvennaya Istoriya* [Native History], 1997, no. 1, p. 109).

On July 6, 1990, Boris Yeltsin, in his capacity as chairman of the Supreme Soviet of the RSFSR, spoke at the seventh session of the Twenty-Eighth (and last) Congress of the CPSU. He criticized the conservative forces in the CPSU and the bureaucratic character of the party. Speaking in the name of "Communist democrats," Yeltsin declared:

> All of us, who have given dozens of years of our lives to the party, considered it our duty to come here and try to say that there is still a way forward for the CPSU. The party's name must be changed. It should be the Party [or League] of Democratic Socialism. . . . Members should pay minimum dues to the new party or league. Any group or faction having a socialist orientation but belonging to another party could join this league of the democratic forces of Russia. The people would recognize this league and follow it if it proposed an economic program for getting out of the present crisis, but not one based on deceiving the people or piling further burdens on their shoulders.
>
> ("Biulleten' No. 6. Dlia delegatov s"ezda" [Bulletin No. 6 for Congress Delegates], in *XXVIII s"ezd KPCC* [Twenty-Eighth Congress of the CPSU], Moscow, 1990, pp. 43–44)

No one at that time talked about Gaidar. He came to Russia's attention only in December 1991, and then as an economist, not as an ideologist or political leader. At that time the mass of the people, and much of the intellectual elite, supported Yeltsin, not Gaidar. And Yeltsin called himself sometimes a left radical, sometimes a radical democrat, sometimes a social democrat, but never a liberal. Even in the years 1992–94 Gaidar resolutely refused to distinctly formulate his credo. He wrote: "Free capitalism or the social state? . . . This is a topic for academic discussion only. Neither von Hajek nor Lord Keynes constructed his theory to be applied to an 'Asiatic' bureaucratic state that finds itself under powerful criminal influence. Let us change the system and lay the groundwork at least for a Western-type society, and then such questions will become relevant" (Gaidar, *Gosudarstvo i evoliutsiia* [The State and Evolution], Moscow, 1995, p. 198).

The chief ideologist in Yeltsin's circle in 1991–92 was of course Gennady Burbulis, rather than Gaidar. But Burbulis, too, was unable to elaborate a new liberal ideology for Russia. He spoke a great deal about "the freedom of the individual" and the need to defend the institution of private property, urging reformers to "renounce the hypocritical and false task of regulating relations among citizens on the basis of social justice" (*Izvestia*, August 31, 1992). Yet equality and justice are central concepts, along with freedom, in most twentieth-century varieties of liberalism.

As a social and political movement and as a theory, liberalism is a highly complex phenomenon and not at all homogeneous. Nineteenth-century liberal theories differ substantially from those of the twentieth century, and European liberalism is quite distinct from the American variety. The Western press has printed many articles on the crisis of classical liberalism and the attempts to create some sort of "neoliberalism." Yet the names of the ideologists of this new liberalism are not known in Russia—e.g., Dahrendorf, Vorlander, Sorman.

A group of Russian ideologists of liberalism who were prominent at the turn of the century—Peter Struve, Boris Chicherin, Pavel Novgorodtsev, and Konstantin Kavelin—have also, for the most part, been forgotten. Hardly any of present-day Russia's ideologists, political leaders, or social activists have even a superficial knowledge of the ideas and doctrines of the founders of liberalism—such as Adam Smith, John Locke, Jeremy Bentham, John Stuart Mill, Thomas

Jefferson, Wilhelm Humboldt, or Count Camillo Cavour. A first attempt at a discussion of liberalism and neo-liberalism was carried by the magazine *Novoye Vremya* in 1997, but as the editors of the magazine themselves admitted, the result was "only a monstrous piling up of questions" with no clarification of "what is really going on in the Russian economy, what the theoretical basis is for the current awful mess, and whether there is any reason to expect something qualitatively better" (*Novoye Vremya*, 1997, no. 17–18, p. 19). Only in recent years have books on the history of Western or Russian liberalism begun to appear in Moscow. The number of copies printed is small, and there is no great demand for these books.

It is also a mistake to say, as Tsipko does, that "the liberal ideology of Gaidar" was the ideology of the ruling party. In the 1995 Duma elections, Gaidar and his party suffered a crushing defeat. None of the parties of the democrats became "ruling parties." As for Our Home Is Russia, the center-right party created by Yeltsin and Chernomyrdin, it differentiated itself emphatically from the liberal democrats of 1991–92. The party of power as constituted after the 1996 elections did not wish to be seen as an heir to the Gaidar type of reformer of 1991–92. It refused to join the coalition of liberal parties set up by Gaidar and others in 1996. Gennady Shepilov, a leader and theoretician of Our Home Is Russia, dismissed the liberal parties as marginal and unpopular. An alliance with them, he said, would "destroy the image of our party as a solidly centrist movement" (see the supplement to the government newspaper *Rossiyskaya Gazeta*, October 19–25, 1996).

This "solidly centrist movement," the ruling party of Russia, also refrained from any clear formulation of its main slogans and ideology. It, too, lacked any inspiring new idea capable of winning wide support within the population.

10. Weak and Diffuse Character of the Forces Moving Toward Capitalism

Evaluation of the nature and prospects of any revolution requires a clear conception of its driving forces, which are not always homogeneous in social and political respects. Moreover, the role and conduct of various classes and groups within the population can change fundamentally at different stages of the revolutionary process, advancing one or another leader from their midst or, alternatively, casting them aside. In the historical and political writing, no precise or well-grounded analysis has been made so far in regard to the driving forces behind the new Russian revolution at its various stages. The political and social shifts of the last five or six years have been so complex and contradictory, and subject to varying interpretations, that it is no easy task to make an adequate assessment.

The struggle for personal power by individual leaders, the struggles between parties, social classes, and ethnic groups, spontaneous movements and conscious actions—all this has blended into a single mass of events whose overall outcome is difficult to evaluate or predict. It is still unclear which classes or social strata in the former Soviet Union and in the Russian Federation have had a particularly vital interest in the new dispensation.

The historian Andrei Ryabov has written that what occurred after August 1991 was "an anti-Communist political revolution that overthrew the party nomenklatura [or bureaucracy] that had dominated for more than seventy years. The driving force in this revolution was the Soviet middle class—a social entity to which too little attention has yet been paid by science and scholarship in our homeland" (*Kentavr* [Centaur], 1993, no. 1, p. 3).

Aleksandr Buzgalin, a Moscow University economist, proposes a more complex schematic diagram of the driving forces behind the historical shifts and changes of the 1990s which he does not think can properly be called a "revolution." As he sees it,

> In the depths of the decaying Brezhnev system, social forces took shape that had an objective interest in the establishment of a "nomenklatura-and-speculator-dominated type of capitalism." These social forces included a new, cynical generation of the upper and middle party-state bureaucracy and the "elite" strata of the intelligentsia: the children of those who had enjoyed the privileged life of the party and government "aristocracy," though on a secondary level. . . . These "sons" had an interest, objectively and subjectively, in a new dispensation, a change in the forms of power. No less interested in the development of a speculation-oriented capitalism were the wheelers and dealers of the shadow economy and the legalized entrepreneurs, mostly in cooperative businesses, who made their appearance in the late 1980s.

There is some truth in Buzgalin's account, but as I observed the development of the various people's fronts, democratic movements, and political clubs in the late 1980s, I did not see many from the "elite" among the leaders and activists. Those movements were made up mostly of people whose careers (in the party or the military or in business or academic life) had not been particularly successful and who saw a chance for social advancement through activism in protest movements. As for Yeltsin, in 1987–88 he was seeking rehabilitation in the ruling party, not advocating some form of "speculator capitalism."

Sergei Kurginyan, who is associated with a foundation called the Experimental Creative Center, gives a more complex account of the driving forces behind the capitalist revolution of the 1990s. In his opinion, five groups of "the Soviet and non-Soviet nomenklatura" entered the struggle for power. He describes these, in his own peculiar terminology, as "the Orthodox," "the cosmopolitans," "the Russian party," and the "super-nomenklaturas of New York and Moscow." Allied with "the cosmopolitans," in his view, were elements of the "Third Estate"—the intelligentsia and those active in the cooperatives and in the shadow economy. The struggle among these nomenklaturas and super-nomenklaturas, as he calls them, has passed through five phases during the 1990s and is still going on.

Kurginyan's constructs seem to me to be highly synthetic, abstract, and unconvincing. It isn't possible to discuss only the "elite" and various groupings in the nomenklatura without taking note of the political movements that involved substantial numbers of the urban population in the years 1988–91, including blue collar and white collar workers and the lower ranks of the intelligentsia. These citizens of Russia wanted to improve their material and social conditions but they were not "yearning for capitalism."

The Serbian philosopher Svetozar Stojanovic has written:

> History knows of no mass popular movements dedicated to private market-based commerce or oriented toward making bigger profits. On the contrary, mass social movements have always had as their goal the fight for justice, equality, freedom, civil rights, national rights, human rights, and have protested against hunger, unemployment, and exploitation. The rise of mass movements in support of capitalism is not to be expected, including in the post-Communist era.

Freedom and social justice—not market reform—were the slogans that attracted rank-and-file participation in the "democratic" movements in Russia. Most of these participants withdrew their support for Yeltsin in early 1992, when they felt the results of "shock therapy" on their own backs. To hold onto power, Yeltsin was obliged to disperse by force the very same Congress of People's Deputies that had elected him head of the Russian government in 1990 and had supported his campaign for the presidency of Russia in 1991, then voted to grant him special powers later that same year. As it turned out, the main social support of the Yeltsin regime in the years 1994–96 continued to be the Russian government officialdom, whose privileges and corruption far exceeded those of the Soviet party and government bureaucracy of the 1970s. The new entrepreneurs also support Yeltsin, of course, but in the last few years the Russian nationalist and "patriotic" opposition has also found increasing support among entrepreneurs. (We look more closely at this group in chapter 5.)

In early 1995 one of the sociological institutes of the Russian Academy of Sciences conducted a poll among various parts of the population on ideas that might serve as the basis for policies to revive Russia. The following ideas were chosen by the following percentages: justice, 44 percent; human rights, 37; order, 36; peace, 33; freedom, 20; private property, 14; spirituality, 13; equality, 10; loyalty to a strong state (*derzhavnost*), 10; Orthodoxy, 8; internationalism, 7; brotherhood, 6; the nation, 4; nationality, 4; religion, 3; capitalism, 3. (These results were published in Moscow by the Realists Club [Klub "Realisty"] in their *Informatsionno-analiticheskii biulleten* [Informational-Analytical Bulletin], no. 19, 1996, pp. 54–55.)

Jeffrey Sachs, when asked about the reasons for the failure of liberal reforms in Russia, replied: "When we undertook the reforms we felt ourselves to be doctors who had been called to someone's sickbed. But when we placed the patient on the operating table and opened him up, we found that his anatomical structure and internal organs were completely different, of a kind we never encountered in medical school" (*Novoye Vremya*, 1995, no. 28). Sachs simply left Russia, but Yeltsin has brought his young "democrat" associates back into the government—including Anatoly Chubais and his friends, as well as Boris Nemtsov—in order to "deepen the reforms."

Aleksei Ulyukaev, one of the most outspoken ideological defenders of the "reforms," justifies in advance the imposition of capitalism in its cruelest forms:

> When people perform a vitally necessary operation (in the absence of antibiotics, sterile instruments, bandages and dressings, or even electricity)—what they do is painful, and rarely does anyone express gratitude or have anything good to say about them. On the contrary, harsh, sometimes furious, criticism is their lot . . . But what does that matter? Let our common monument be the capitalism we have built through struggle. Amen.
>
> (*Segodnya*, September 20, 1996)

Such statements are not worth commenting on. It is quite obvious that with reformers such as these the only monument most Russians will have is a common grave.

3

Privatization, Government Crisis, and Elections (1993)

After the liberalization of prices the most important element of the market reforms was privatization, several variants of which had been discussed as early as 1990–91. The most active phase of privatization began in the fall of 1992 and continued through the whole of 1993.

Many different forms and methods of privatization and "de-statization" had been worked out and tested, both in the West (especially in the Reagan-Thatcher era of the 1980s) and in 1990–91 in Eastern Europe. In the West, among the most common reasons for carrying out privatization, or the offering of shares in government-owned property to private buyers, were: to attract resources for modernization purposes, to increase the efficiency of operations, to reduce spending from the government budget, or to increase budgetary income.

FIRST STAGE OF PSEUDO PRIVATIZATION

Privatization in Russia has been different. In its goals, its scale, and its time frame it has no precedent in world history. It was proposed that over a period of two or three years the greater part of the publicly owned enterprises and property that had been accumulated in Russia, not just in the Soviet era but ever since industrialization began in Russia in the 1870s—all this was to be sold or auctioned off or somehow distributed among the citizens of our country. It was expected that a new class of entrepreneurs and property owners would make its appearance and complete the transition from socialism to a capitalist market economy.

General supervision of the enormous changes envisaged in this program was entrusted to the State Committee for the Management of State Property, which was established as part of the government of the Russian Federation in mid-1991, around the time of Yeltsin's election as president. (We will refer to it as the State Property Committee, for short.) All the best-known economists and people with practical experience in the economy were kept away from this committee and its operations.

In November 1991, on Gaidar's recommendation, a new chairman of the State Property Committee was appointed—Anatoly Chubais. Relatively unknown at the time, he went on to become one of the most prominent figures in the Yeltsin government.

Chubais and Gaidar together drew up a privatization program, whose basic features were confirmed and given legal authority by a presidential decree that Yeltsin signed on December 29, 1991. This marked the beginning of what has been called "the biggest transformation of property relations in world history" (*Argumenty i Fakty*, 1997, no. 48, p. 5).

In view of his later prominence, a few words about Chubais are in order here. A 35-year-old engineer with a candidate's degree in economics when he was placed in charge of privatization, Chubais had worked in 1990–91 as chief economic adviser to the mayor of St. Petersburg, Anatoly Sobchak. He had not otherwise distinguished himself in either science and scholarship or politics.

Born in the Byelorussian Soviet Republic, Chubais had graduated in 1977 from the Leningrad Engineering and Economics Institute. His dream had been to become a factory manager, but reality kept him at his alma mater, as a junior member of the teaching staff and later a senior lecturer. Like anyone seeking a career in the Soviet Union, he joined the CPSU. After gaining his candidate's degree, he began to think about a doctoral dissertation.

In the late 1980s, St. Petersburg (then Leningrad) became a center for the "informal" groups that later evolved into the democratic movement. As a Komsomol activist in 1989, Chubais could be seen at a number of different unofficial clubs and "communes," where he sometimes spoke on economic questions. He also served as a consultant to several candidates for the Congress of People's Deputies. His older brother, the philosopher Igor Chubais, was a far more visible and authoritative figure in the "informal" movement, however. People who knew Anatoly at that time thought of him merely as a moderately ambitious social movement activist. Chubais was always extremely loyal to his superiors, a person who was easily guided. In later years he often repeated the remark, "I never sweated and strained to be Number One." Under Sobchak he headed the mayoral committee for economic reform in St. Petersburg. Sobchak and Chubais had many ideas but in fact accomplished little.

We probably never would have heard of Chubais if Gaidar had not tapped him. They first met in 1986 at an economics seminar outside Leningrad. Chubais later spoke of this meeting as "historic." The young economists discussed almost every question, from the possibility of their coming to power to the probable length of their future prison terms (if the old-line Communist officialdom reasserted itself). Gaidar didn't forget his new Leningrad friend, and when he was given carte-blanche by Yeltsin and Burbulis to form a government, Gaidar summoned Chubais to fill an important post.

Chubais displayed an ability to work long and hard hours as a government minister. Lack of experience and knowledge were combined with great energy, organizational ability, and extreme radicalism. "The aim of privatization," Chubais said later, "was to build capitalism in Russia, and to do so in a few years of frontal assault, thus accomplishing production norms that had taken the rest of the world centuries." (He made these remarks on the television show "Podrobnosti" ["Details"] on June 29, 1994.)

There were many vacancies at the State Property Committee in late 1991-early 1992, and Chubais invited numerous friends and acquaintances, mostly from St. Petersburg, to come work with him. These included Alfred Kokh, Pyotr Mostovoi, Sergei Belyaev, Sergei and Dmitry Vasilyev, Sergei Ignatyev, Maksim Boiko, Aleksandr Kazakov, Andrei Illarionov, and Pyotr Filippov, among others. After Yeltin's "Sverdlovsk mafia" (which included Burbulis, Lobov, Ilyushin, Yuri

Petrov, and others) this group of "homeboys" from St. Petersburg was the largest such regional grouping in the new Moscow government.

Since there were no Russian officials with experience or knowledge of privatization, several dozen foreign specialists were brought in to work with the State Property Committee, and their number grew steadily both in the committee and in the Russian government apparatus.

Disputes over the goals, methods, and principles of privatization continued in every part of the Russian Federation during the entire time that it was being carried out. By no means did it always go according to Chubais's plans. Moscow mayor, Yuri Luzhkov, compared privatization to "a drunkard in the street selling his belongings for a pittance."

The first stage of preparation involved a plan to transfer most state property in equal shares to all citizens of Russia without exception. Each citizen was to have a privatization account in his or her own name into which a certain sum would be deposited—its size to determined by the Government Privatization Program. Another law defined the sources of funds for obtaining privatized property. In effect, the government guaranteed each citizen a cash payment to be used only for purposes of privatization. On the other hand, a decree by Yeltsin specified that all large or medium-sized enterprises (other than military or extractive) must be reorganized as "joint stock companies," that plans must be drafted for privatization through the sale of shares, and that each such plan must be approved by a meeting of the work collective, then submitted to the government for approval.

Each citizen was to receive ten thousand rubles. Why that exact figure? The plan for a "people's privatization" took as its starting point the idea that the total productive capacity of the country was the property of the people as a whole and therefore each citizen should receive equal initial opportunity to own some of it. This took the form of each citizen receiving an "equal share." Every enterprise—whether a power plant, airport, or factory—had a certain "base value" (*balansovaya stoimost*), reflecting the original cost of building it and putting it into operation. The "base value" was usually not revised or reevaluated after construction of the enterprise, but was simply added together with the "base values" of other enterprises in the same branch of industry. The resulting totals from all branches of industry were added up to arrive at an estimate of the national wealth in money terms. In

1991 the "base value" of the Russian Federation's productive capacity was set at 1,260,500,000,000,000 rubles—that is, one trillion, 260.5 billion. This sum was divided by the population of Russia (148.7 million in 1991), giving the sum of 8,467 rubles, which was rounded off to ten thousand.

In 1991, ten thousand rubles seemed a fairly large amount. It was proposed, in addition, that the shares citizens would buy in privatized enterprises would increase in value—in other words, each citizen's ten thousand rubles would grow. Chubais declared that in effect each citizen would be receiving an amount equal to the value of one Volga automobile, perhaps even two Volgas.

That was the plan. The reality turned out to be quite different.

First of all, the government decided against establishing a cash account in each citizen's name. Instead, anonymous privatization certificates called "vouchers" were issued. These were nondescript pieces of paper, not backed by any government guarantee. All citizens were to receive their vouchers by December 31, 1992. The anonymity of the vouchers removed the question of how one or another person happened to possess them. Obviously they could be bought or sold, used as collateral for loans, etc. On the other hand, a privatized enterprise did not have to accept vouchers as payment for shares. Moreover, not all of the enterprises with the most favorable prospects were included in the voucher form of privatization. The inflation that followed liberalization of prices dealt the final blow to the voucher system. As the mass distribution of vouchers began, prices increased by as much of 15-20 times and continued to rise, but no revaluation of the vouchers occurred. By the fall of 1992, ten thousand rubles would buy no more than a man's suit of average quality.

Not knowing what to do with their vouchers, people began selling them. Buyers or brokerage firms at first offered 7–8 thousand rubles per voucher, but their value fell as the number of vouchers increased. At a time when other prices were soaring, the vouchers were the only commodity on the market whose value kept going down, both relatively and absolutely. By May 1993 a voucher would bring only 3–4 thousand rubles. In 1991 prices, that was the equivalent of only 30–40 rubles. Many citizens never did receive their vouchers, and many who received them did not use them to buy shares. Even those who did exchange vouchers for shares did not actually acquire ownership or income. No dividends have been paid by the new joint stock companies, neither in 1993 nor since. In the public mind the term voucher has become a synonym for gigantic swindle. For most ordinary Russians, "Chubais" and "voucher" are dirty words.

"People's privatization" was not the only form of denationalization in 1993. There was also the sale of "municipal" property. Stores, barber shops, laundries, restaurants, cafes, and so on were auctioned off to the highest bidder. In a number of cases the work collectives were offered the chance to buy the business from the municipal authorities — for example, drivers at a taxi depot could buy their cabs, or hairdressers could become owners of their salons. In these cases the "base price" was just the starting price. The auction process would determine the current "real market value." In the end a piece of property might sell for 50–200 times more than the starting price, a reflection of the hyperinflation in 1993.

This form of privatization proceeded at a brisk pace, involving a large number of enterprises in the service industry. Some of the new owners in the service sector gained from this, and services did improve, especially in retail commerce. But in many cases, instead of improving, services deteriorated

After taxi drivers had purchased their vehicles, for example, they found they could not afford to repair them or replace them when they wore out. Taxi service almost completely disappeared. Many services confronted a dilemma: whether to cater to a large number of customers at relatively low prices or to serve a small number at higher rates. The second path was usually preferred. Thus, in almost every case where a cafe, restaurant, or the like passed into private hands it reoriented toward a wealthy clientele, particularly those with foreign currency. Even the youngsters washing cars understood that it was better to wash two foreign cars and make twenty dollars than to wash ten Russian cars.

Waiting lines disappeared, but this was mainly because people went less often for a haircut or to the store or laundromat. They didn't take taxis any more and went less often to the movies or theater. For some the number of conveniences increased, but for the great majority everyday life became harder

The Russian government's decree on the formation of joint stock companies provided for a number of variants. Under the first variant, the employees of an enterprise (the "work collective") were given 25 percent of all shares free of charge, and could buy another 10 percent at reduced cost. This variant was not very popular. Although workers could obtain shares at low prices, they would have little opportunity to affect the fate of their company. Their consent was not required for any reorganization of the business, including layoffs. This variant, although it opened the greatest possibilities for modernization and reconstruction, had no success with work collectives at enterprises. Only 2 percent of the total number of enterprises were privatized according to this first variant. The third variant was the most "market-oriented" of them all. It provided for the free sale, on the stock exchange, of all shares in a company, and at market prices—no matter what those prices might be.

The work collectives at most enterprises chose the *second* variant, viewing it as the most conservative. Under this variant the work collective received a controlling block of shares—51 percent—and became the real owner of the enterprise. It could therefore influence the appointment of the management and decisions about what to do with profits. It was obvious that workers would not be interested in allocating profits to pay dividends to incidental shareholders instead of increasing their own wages. On the other hand, this variant of privatization made it difficult to carry out reorganization and modernization, especially if laying off workers was involved. In other words, productivity of labor would be raised very slowly. Few people were interested in buying shares in such enterprises. Not surprisingly the formation of such joint stock companies did not result in greater efficiency of production and in many cases made the operation of plants and factories more difficult.

A certain number of very large factories became joint stock companies under the first or third variants. There were hardly any individuals or organizations that could pay the large sums of money needed to buy stock in these enterprises. Vouchers had to be accepted. On the other hand, some businessmen and recently formed "voucher funds" had bought up vouchers from the rest of the population at very low prices and were seeking ways to invest them profitably. No auctions were held in these cases, and the properties were sold for their "base value." Thus, some very large enterprises passed into private hands at ridiculously low prices.

For example, a celebrated shipyard in St. Petersburg, the Baltic Works, was put up for sale for 150 million rubles, payable in vouchers. At the same time the price for a children's store, Malysh, on

Nevsky Prospekt, the main shopping street in St. Petersburg, was 701 million rubles. The Minsk Hotel in Moscow, a medium-sized structure, was sold for vouchers with a nominal "worth" of 200,000 rubles. In contrast, the gigantic ZIL auto plant, which occupies more than a thousand hectares in Moscow, was privatized (under the first variant) for about 800,000 rubles worth of vouchers that had been collected from all parts of Russia. A number of sports complexes, port facilities, and factories were sold at very low prices for vouchers. The Urals Machinery Manufacturing Plant, better known by its Russian acronym Uralmash, which had been the largest plant in the USSR and was still the largest in Russia and which employed more than 100,000 workers, was privatized for vouchers in June 1993. Its value was set at 1.8 billion rubles, or $2 million at the exchange rate of that time. What would $2 million buy in the heart of New York City by comparison? Nothing more than a luxury apartment.

The controlling block of shares in Uralmash was bought by the Moscow businessman Kakha Bendukidze (whom we discuss further in the chapter "Russia's New Class"). He had established a biotechnology company called Bioprotsess.

A giant plant like Uralmash did not benefit by passing into private hands. For meaningful investment that would modernize the plant what was needed was not vouchers but real dollars, in the millions, if not tens of millions, but the new owners did not have that kind of money. The new owners of these giant plants also did not benefit much from their acquisitions, because in the general conditions of industrial decline the plants were not making profits; in fact, they were barely able to stay afloat. The expectation was that in the future these plants would become sources of enrichment. Bendukidze explained to the *Financial Times* (July 15, 1995): "For us privatization was manna from heaven. It meant that we could move forward and buy from the government on favorable terms whatever we wanted. . . . We have taken a hefty bite out of Russia's industrial capacity, although we weren't able to buy a single square meter of real estate in Moscow. It turned out to be easier to grab Uralmash than to get even one warehouse in Moscow. . . . We bought that plant for one thousandth of its real worth. The most profitable way to invest capital in today's Russia is to buy up factories at a reduced price. Of course, if someone offered us a billion dollars for Uralmash we would say, Yes. . . . In my past life I was a biologist and a Communist. Now I am a businessman and a liberal."

Although privatization was "manna from heaven" for businessmen like Bendukidze, ordinary people could find no advantage in it. After losing their savings, after being hoodwinked and robbed by various pyramid schemes, and seeing prices going up wildly all around them, most people were in no hurry to obtain or sell their vouchers. The government proposed to complete "voucher privatization" in 1993, but in fact by the fall of that year only 36 million out of a total 148 million vouchers had been used. The management of an enterprise did not obtain any real capital as the result of privatization, but it found itself more dependent on "workers control" (new decision-making powers in the hands of the work force) or on the whims of new owners like Bendukidze. The government, for its part, gained no economic benefits from privatization.

In view of this poor showing, both the Yeltsin-Gaidar government and the Supreme Soviet began drafting plans to change the way privatization was being carried out; in particular, the concept of distributing state property free of charge to the population as a whole was to be abandoned. The government's new plan was drafted by Vice Premier Oleg Lobov, who on August 30, 1993, submitted to Yeltsin a memorandum on the need to revaluate the basic productive capacity of the country, since by July 1993 its real market value was no longer 1.5 trillion rubles, but more than 300 trillion. It was necessary to make a corresponding revaluation of privatization vouchers and joint stock company shares.

That would have meant a fiasco for the reformers on Gaidar's team. According to reports in the September 14 issue of *Rossiyskie Vesti*, a newspaper close to the government, Yeltsin at first agreed with Lobov, then changed his mind when he realized what a blow to the authority of his government it would be to alter the course of privatization at that point. Lobov was reassigned. He was removed from the cabinet and given the post of secretary of the Security Council under Yeltsin. Gaidar was given Lobov's former vice premier's position.

Even after Gaidar's return, privatization proceeded very slowly, because its internal resources had been practically exhausted. The government felt obliged to look to the West, to give Western capital equal opportunity in the matter of buying up state-owned property in Russia. In the next chapter we will examine how that process unfolded in 1994–95.

As we have said, the main aim of privatization was to form a class or stratum of property owners who could become a reliable base of support for the new social system being created. There was no precedent in economic history for this kind of privatization.

The commentator Anatoly Strelyany, a supporter of the radical democrats, gave a rather candid explanation of the philosophy of privatization in Russia: "Gaidar and Chubais proposed to achieve something small, which they hoped would develop into something great. Property would be distributed to anyone at all, even to a gangster, as long as it was taken out of government hands. If a gangster proved to be a capable manager of his capital, he would thereby cease to be a gangster, and if not, he would lose his wealth" (*Literaturnaya Gazeta*, June 25, 1997).

The economist M. Gelvanovsky wrote in 1993: "In the West there have been no precedents, no instances in which all the property in a country was transformed in an extremely compressed time frame from publicly-owned, or state-owned, to privately-owned. . . . Russia is facing an event of truly epochal proportions: privatization, if it is carried out according to its authors' conception, will mean a lightning-fast redistribution of property on a gigantic scale, comparable only to the Bolshevik revolution of 1917, but going in the opposite direction. But this 'return' of property to private hands will for the most part lack any historical legitimacy, and therefore the consequences in store for the economy and for social and political stability would appear to be rather dismal" (*Voprosy ekonomiki*, no. 10, pp. 64–65).

Chubais, in the "Introduction" to his book *Istoriya rossiyskoi privatizatsii* [History of Russian Privatization], which achieved a rather scandalous notoriety, admitted that his hastily conducted privatization program had lowered the economic efficiency of production and had not in fact created a broad and substantial stratum of property owners: "We constantly had to decide questions of the relations between ends and means. But I held, and still hold, that the creation of private property in Russia was an absolute value [to strive for]. In order to achieve this goal, it was necessary at times to sacrifice certain schematic notions of economic efficiency. These are categories that are measured by different yardsticks. Economic efficiency exists on a scale of one or two or ten years; private property operates on a scale of a hundred or a thousand years, and so on" (*Novoye Vremya*, 1997, no. 48, p. 10).

Most Russians have a very low opinion of Chubais and his privatization program. And even in the West, he is not universally praised. Writing in the *Washington Post* of August 24, 1997, the Russian expert Peter Reddaway observed that Chubais's dubious integrity as a politician and his authoritarian administrative methods raised a question whether the U.S. government should continue its friendly relations with Russia. Reddaway held that the U.S. should stop aiding a corrupt government and stop supporting people who did not work in the interests of their own nation. Similarly, in the fall of 1997 the *Chicago Tribune* wrote that Chubais's privatization program had been thoroughly corrupt from the start and that it had not produced a viable private sector that could help restore the ruined Russian economy.

SHARPENING POLITICAL CONFLICT, SPRING 1993

The change of prime ministers in December 1992 did not lead to any noticeable change in foreign or domestic policy. The underlying causes of the sharp conflict between legislative and executive branches that had been revealed at the Seventh Congress of People's Deputies persisted. Opinion polls showed a loss of confidence in Yeltsin. His popularity ratings in February 1993 had fallen to 20–25 percent. But confidence in the legislative branch had fallen even lower. Khasbulatov's ratings that same month were around 10–12 percent.

The economic situation in the Russian Federation continued to worsen, and public dissatisfaction kept growing. Under these conditions a renewal of the conflict between the two branches of government seemed inevitable. The first move in the new round was made by Yeltsin.

On Saturday evening, March 20, 1993, regular broadcasting on Russian television was interrupted, and it was reported that President Yeltsin would make an address to the people of Russia. We all waited apprehensively to hear what he would say. The president was brief. He announced that he had just signed a decree placing Russia under "special administrative rule," a condition in which the Supreme Soviet and Congress of People's Deputies would be subordinated to the president and would not have the right to cancel his decrees or to pass laws contradicting them.

Yeltsin's action was in violation of specific clauses of the constitution. It was a new attempt to carry out a coup d'etat from above and to change by decree the relations between the two branches of government. Before Yeltsin was off the air the Presiding Committee of the Supreme Soviet had gathered at the parliament building, the so-called Russian White House. It condemned Yeltsin's words and action. This was reported by Russian television, which also announced that at midnight it would broadcast statements by top government figures. Almost everyone in the country tuned in. The first to speak was Yuri Voronin, deputy chairman of the Supreme Soviet. (Khasbulatov was visiting Kazakstan at the time.) Aleksandr Rutskoi spoke next, criticizing and condemning Yeltsin. Valery Zorkin, chairman of the Constitutional Court, was the third to speak. After them Attorney General Valentin Stepankov, a man Yeltsin had been able to rely un until then, also condemned the president's action. This was a strong blow to Yeltsin's intentions.

Later it became known that Yeltsin had videotaped his speech the morning of March 20, and copies of the videotape had been delivered to foreign diplomats so that they could inform their governments. Yeltsin had acted in haste, even before his staff had completed the wording of the decree. Prime Minister Chernomyrdin supported the president, but Yuri Skokov, secretary of the Security Council, refused to endorse the new decree and tried to persuade his boss not to take this risky step. Vice President Rutskoi also refused to endorse the decree.

On Sunday afternoon, March 21, a full session of the Supreme Soviet was held. It condemned the president's action and passed a resolution calling for an emergency session of the Congress of People's Deputies to be held immediately. The heads of the "power ministries," army head Pavel Grachev, internal affairs minister Viktor Yerin, and state security chief Viktor Barannikov, were summoned to appear before the Supreme Soviet. They all felt obliged to support the Soviet. The evening of that same day the Constitutional Court convened and held an all-night session. On Monday morning, March 22, it declared Yeltsin's decree unconstitutional. Yeltsin realized he had misplayed his hand and retreated. His decree, published on March 24, no longer spoke of "special administrative rule," and several other points discussed in his speech of March 20 were omitted.

On March 26, the Ninth Congress of People's Deputies of the Russian Federation convened in the Kremlin. Unlike the Eighth

Congress, it promised to be of great significance: I followed its proceedings very closely. On the first day Valery Zorkin presented a report. Yeltsin took the floor several times, seeking to justify himself and take the offensive. Deputies spoke, one after another, very sharply. At the same time, behind the scenes, a search for a compromise was under way. Outside the Kremlin mass rallies were going on continuously. On one side several thousand Yeltsin supporters demanded that he not give in to the Congress. On the other side supporters of the opposition loudly chanted anti-Yeltsin slogans.

Tensions at the Congress kept rising. One version of an agreement with the president was proposed, but most deputies objected to it, and many of them demanded the removal of Khasbulatov from his post as chairman of the Supreme Soviet. A break in the proceedings was announced, so that deputies could consult with one another. I listened in on the discussions of one group. Its leader was trying to convince his fellow deputies: "It's too early for us to try to remove Khasbulatov." A simple majority was all that was needed to remove the chairman, and it was with some anxiety that Khasbulatov awaited the results of the secret balloting. Those who voted to remove him numbered 339; those opposed, 558.

During the first several days no one raised the question of removing Yeltsin from power. Khasbulatov tried to persuade the deputies to pass a resolution calling for elections ahead of schedule, both for deputies to the Congress and for president. Yeltsin very much feared such a resolution. He was not at all sure that the population would reelect him. The deputies, too, had reason to fear this proposal. They did not wish to risk losing their seats. They voted against consideration of the proposal, although a peaceful resolution of the conflict might have resulted if new elections for both branches of government had been held.

On the evening of March 27, there was a change in the relatively smooth proceedings of the Congress. Yeltsin, who was displeased with a number of the Congress's resolutions, asked for the floor. He spoke slowly and uncertainly, proposing that the Congress pass a resolution criticizing both branches of government and then disperse. Puffy in the face, hair uncombed, Yeltsin made a strange impression. He did not seem to be fully in command of his faculties. After his speech the session closed, but the deputies, guests, and reporters were in no hurry to leave. They stood around in the lobby discussing the events of the day. Suddenly a door at one end of the lobby opened and Yeltsin entered, propped up firmly by a bodyguard on either side. Video cameramen were quick to film the unsteady steps of the president and his rather incoherent answers to the questions that poured forth. Still surrounded and supported by his guards, Yeltsin went out of the building onto Red Square, and to the shouts of his supporters continued on down Tverskaya Street almost as far as the building of the Moscow Soviet. Several foreign correspondents I knew asked me: "Can we sleep calmly? What if Yeltsin, in the shape he's in, decided to push *the* button?"

On March 28 the morning session of the Congress opened in a very tense atmosphere. No less than a hundred thousand Yeltsin supporters had gathered on Red Square, and they were fired by passions that were not purely political. Yeltsin spoke to the rally. He declared that if the Congress passed a resolution calling for his dismissal from office, he would not submit to it but would submit only to the verdict of the people. The mood of those at the rally was at such a fever pitch that Yuri Luzhkov, the mayor of Moscow, asked deputies not to leave the Kremlin even during breaks. This smacked of blackmail, an attempt to pressure or intimidate the deputies.

A secret ballot on impeachment of the president was held the afternoon of March 28. Under the constitution, three-fourths of the total membership of the Congress were required—that is, 780 votes. Yeltsin was nervous awaiting the results, as he admits in his memoirs.

The evening session of the Congress began at 9 p.m., but it was not until 10 that the members of the government entered the room, and it was even later before the members of the Constitutional Court took their seats. Yeltsin did not appear. The results of the secret ballot were announced at 10:30 p.m. For Yeltsin's dismissal there were 617 votes, or 66 percent of those voting. Against dismissal were 268, or slightly more than one quarter of the total number of deputies. Such a close vote was in fact a political defeat for Yeltsin, but speaking before a crowd of his supporters on Red Square, he proclaimed victory.

The fourth day of the congress went relatively smoothly. Against Khasbulatov's objections the Congress passed a resolution for a referendum to be held at the end of April in which the public could vote on whether they had confidence in Yeltsin and whether elections should be held ahead of schedule.

Preparations for the referendum developed into a regular political campaign. Vice President Rutskoi was especially active during this time. In addition to dealing with problems of agriculture and agrarian reform, he had been assigned by the president to head an interdepartmental government commission to combat organized crime. This gave him the opportunity to collect quite a lot of information about corruption and abuse of power in the upper echelons of government. It was during this time, on April 10, that I met with the vice president to discuss questions of collaboration between the Socialist Party of Working People, of which I was one of seven co-chairs, and the Free Russia People's Party, which was headed by Rutskoi.

Many newspapers and magazines at the time were waging a campaign to denounce and discredit the vice president. Some of these publications were lying on his desk, in particular the magazine *Stolitsa*, which had a major article with the insulting title, "The Hussar Born of a Sow." "These scum," said Rutskoi. "What they don't write." We agreed on a number of joint measures to be taken by our two parties, but it proved impossible to carry them out. On April 11, by order of President Yeltsin, Rutskoi's bodyguard was reduced and a different car was assigned to him. Two days later he was removed from his position in charge of agrarian matters. His assistants dealing with agricultural questions and the staff he had built up were dismissed.

On April 16, Rutskoi gave a major report on crime and corruption to a session of the Supreme Soviet. He cited numerous cases of connections between organized crime and highly placed government figures, including military officers, especially in the Western Group of the Russian army. Many newspapers published the full text of his report, and by decision of the Supreme Soviet it was broadcast in full on television. Some of the government ministers accused in the report disputed the facts and documentation presented by Rutskoi and threatened to take him to court for slander, but they never did. Yeltsin answered Rutskoi's report in his own way. He announced that from then on he himself would take charge of the interdepartmental commission to combat crime and corruption. Chernomyrdin was added to this commission, and Rutskoi was removed from it. The press of the "democrats" continued the campaign against Rutskoi, accusing him of all sorts of sins, including the absurd charge that he had misappropriated several million dollars, allegedly hiding this money in secret Swiss bank accounts.

At the end of April a referendum was held throughout the territory of Russia on four questions:

1. Do you have confidence in the President of the Russian Federation, Boris Yeltsin?
2. Do you approve the social and economic policies carried out by the President and the government of the Russian Federation since 1992?
3. Do you consider it necessary that elections for President of the Russian Federation be held ahead of schedule?
4. Do you consider it necessary that elections for People's Deputies of the Russian Federation be held ahead of schedule?

Yeltsin and his supporters called for a Yes vote on the first two questions, and a No vote on the third and fourth. The opposition called for a No vote on the first two and a Yes vote on the last two. The referendum results were disappointing for the opposition. On the rolls of the Electoral Commission, 107 million voters were listed. Of these, 64.5 percent took part in the referendum. On the first and second questions, the Yes vote was 58.5 and 52.9 percent, respectively. On the third and fourth questions, the Yes vote was 32.64 and 41.4 percent, respectively. Thus, the citizens of Russia expressed confidence in Yeltsin as president and rejected the proposal for early elections. The bitterest pill for the opposition was the voters' approval of the social and economic policies since January 1992.

Yeltsin of course was quite pleased with the referendum results and began preparations for the next phase of battle against the Supreme Soviet. The president's staff and a so-called Constitutional Conference began compiling drafts of a new constitution in which the powers of the president would be increased and the powers of the Supreme Soviet reduced proportionately. A May Day demonstration by Toiling Russia and a number of Communist organizations was ruthlessly dispersed by government forces. Many demonstrators were beaten and one was killed by a blow to the head. On May 6, Yeltsin appeared on television to present his program of action for the next few months. In this speech he made a surprise announcement: "The referendum was a defeat for Vice President Rutskoi. During the preparations for the referendum the vice president in fact became a leader of the opponents of reform. I have lost confidence in

Rutskoi and have relieved him of all assignments entrusted to him by the president."

As we have seen, a major political division had developed in Russia. A majority of the Russian Congress of People's Deputies and the Russian Supreme Soviet, which had been pro-Yeltsin in 1990–91, were opposed to him, and Rutskoi and Khasbulatov, both former Yeltsin supporters, were now leaders of the opposition.

During June and July 1993 the political tension in Russia continued to grow. By August it was plain to virtually all observers that the situation had become critical. Vitaly Tretyakov, chief editor of *Nezavisimaya Gazeta*, published a long article on August 11 with the heading "Death Agony of Regime Evident: Only new elections and a new government can save the country." An article of mine, published in several Western newspapers, discussed the danger of radicalism in Russia:

> The events of the last few months have revealed a harsh reality: a deep division is endangering Russian society. Rallies by supporters and opponents of Yeltsin are attracting approximately the same numbers, and the speakers at these rallies seem equally deaf to the arguments of the other side. An irreconcilable hostility separates these two sections of our society, which remain relatively small (at least for now), but with every day the gap between them grows wider and the confrontation intensifies. . . . The political struggle is taking cruder and cruder form; it is hard to call it civilized—or justifiable. The apparent success of the president's supporters is accompanied by a deepening of the political and economic crisis, a growing embitterment in the politically active part of society, and apathy in the majority of the population. . . .
>
> In what other country could the president start a campaign of denunciation against the vice president? Or a president walk unsteadily to the speaker's stand before the highest legislative body in the land, so that hardly anyone could doubt the instability of his physical condition? Or declare at a rally that he

would not abide by the constitution? Where else could a government remain in power, unchallenged, after its actions had led to a decline in production by nearly one-half, to a fall in living standards to many times below the previous level, and to destruction of the systems of health care, education, and culture? . . .

Before our eyes a new Russia has been born, but it is a very strange country. It does not have clearly defined borders, but it has an army. Yet that army does not always carry out the orders of its commanders. This country does not have a clear foreign policy or military doctrine, but it has thousands of nuclear warheads—aimed at who knows what?

We don't know what kind of economy this government is constructing. More than half of 1993 has gone by, but we don't have a budget; we don't know what the government's income and expenditures are. Things cannot, and will not, go on this way for long. One cannot fail to see that the inner logic of such a crisis narrows the choices and creates the possibility of a right-wing or left-wing dictatorship. Neither would make things any easier for Russia or the world. . . .

The experience of the twentieth century has shown that radicals of any orientation, left or right, should not have the power to decide the fate of nations or of humanity as a whole. Today's world is too fragile to be entrusted to people bent on destruction.

On August 21, 1993, the "left" forces organized a demonstration with tens of thousands outside the Russian White House (nickname of the building housing the Supreme Soviet) to mark the second anniversary of the failed coup of August 1991. The demonstrators carried signs saying "All Power to the Soviets." Yeltsin, for his part, declared that in September "decisive events" would occur in Russia and that the remaining days of August should be used for "artillery practice." It soon became clear that this choice of words was no accident.

CIVIL WAR IN MOSCOW

Like the events of August 18–22, 1991, the eruption of civil war in Moscow on October 3–4, 1993, and the preceding two-week standoff between the Yeltsin government and the Russian parliament have given rise to a voluminous literature with quite a few differing versions of the events based on extensive investigations, both official and unofficial. The greater number of publications have been produced by the opposition. Many opposition leaders, including Khasbulatov and Rutskoi, have published books; others have confined themselves to articles and interviews. Several books and hundreds of articles on the subject have come from the pens of both Russian and Western journalists. The magazine *Twentieth Century and the World*, headed by Gleb Pavlovsky, printed a large volume with a chronology and analysis, entitled *'93 - October - Moscow*. Yeltsin's memoirs devote only one chapter, "Difficult Autumn," to the events of September–October 1993. In 1995, another large volume, entitled *Moscow, Autumn 1993: Chronology of a Confrontation*, presented the views of those in charge on the government side, including Yeltsin, Gaidar, Chubais, Kulikov, Volkogonov, and Luzhkov.

There is nothing strange in the fact that various authors view the events of "Black October" in different ways. Sometimes they merely supplement one another's accounts. In many cases they present contradictory, mutually exclusive versions. Within the limits of the present work I cannot go into detail about the events or examine the different versions in depth. But a general account is necessary and at least a preliminary analysis of specific versions.

For a long time Yeltsin had been making preparations for abolishing the existing Russian parliament, but in early September 1993 he intensified his efforts. His first secretary, Viktor Ilyushin, assigned to draft a decree annulling the powers of the Russian Supreme Soviet and Congress of People's Deputies, learned of these plans earlier than others. (Ilyushin, one of Yeltsin's closest collaborators, had worked with Yeltsin in the CPSU's Sverdlovsk province committee and had been his assistant in the party's Central Committee and Moscow city committee.)

After a week Yury Baturin, Yeltsin's assistant on legal matters, was brought in to help on the project. Earlier Baturin had served Gorbachev as part of the staff of the president of the USSR. A few weeks later the heads of the three "power ministries" were made privy to Yeltsin's plans. They were Pavel Grachev, minister of defense, Viktor Yerin, head of the Ministry of Internal Affairs (Russian initials, MVD), and Nikolai Golushko, Russia's new minister of state security. Yeltsin had dismissed the previous security minister, Viktor Barannikov, in late July. The official reason cited was corruption, but the real reason was Barannikov's sympathy with the opposition to Yeltsin.

Initially it was proposed that MVD units occupy the Supreme Soviet building on Sunday, September 19, since no members of the Supreme Soviet or their staffs would be in the building on a Sunday. An announcement of the dissolution of the Supreme Soviet and the Congress of People's Deputies would be made in the evening that same day. Later, Yeltsin rescheduled operations to September 21, on the assumption that seizure of the White House would not be necessary. On September 15 a pay increase of 180 percent for employees of the "power ministries" and the presidential guard was announced. MVD and OMON units from all over Russia were assembled outside of Moscow and in the city itself. (The OMON was an organization of "volunteers" trained to assist the police, created in the Gorbachev era. The acronym OMON means "special purpose militia detachment"—or in Russian, *otdel militsii osobogo naznacheniya*. Its members were not ordinary volunteers, but transferees from the military to the police, selected on the basis of physical features—tall, strong men trained to deal with "special" situations, including ethnic conflicts.)

Yeltsin signed the decree annulling the powers of the Soviet and Congress on September 15, but did not inform anyone except his chief associates. At 5 p.m. on September 21 a speech by Yeltsin was videotaped by a special unit, which was then sent to the central television office after 7 p.m. Broadcasting of the president of Russia's appeal to the people began on all TV channels exactly at 8 p.m. The speech lasted about twenty minutes. Simultaneously copies of Yeltsin's decree, which was named Decree No. 1400, were sent by official messenger service to all the chief centers of power throughout Russia.

The chairman of the Supreme Soviet, Ruslan Khasbulatov, received a packet of papers from the Kremlin, containing the text of the decree, just five minutes before it was broadcast to the country. The title of the decree was rather obscure: "On Step-by-Step Constitutional Reform in the Russian Federation."

The essence of this "reform" was as follows:

1. The functions of the Russian Congress of People's Deputies and Supreme Soviet would cease and a new, dual-chambered

Federal Assembly of the Russian Federation would begin operation.

2. A draft constitution would be presented by a constitutional commission by December 12, 1993.

3. Temporarily, until a new constitution was adopted and new elections were held for a Federal Assembly, the country would be governed by the decrees of the president and resolutions issued by the government of the Russian Federation (that is, the cabinet appointed by Yeltsin).

4. The proposal for the election of representatives to a State Duma, drafted by the constitutional commission, would go into effect immediately. Elections for the State Duma would be held on December 11 and 12, 1993. The Federal Assembly would take up the question of presidential elections.

5. A Central Electoral Commission would be established to oversee the elections to the State Duma, the lower chamber of the two-chambered Federal Assembly of the Russian Federation. (The upper chamber would represent geographic units, especially the non-Russian republics, regions, and districts.)

6. No session of the Russian Congress of People's Deputies would be called. The powers of the people's deputies would cease to exist.

7. It was proposed that no session of the Constitutional Court of the Russian Federation be held before the Federal Assembly began operation.

At 6 p.m. on September 21, Yeltsin left the Kremlin for his residence outside of Moscow, from which he would watch the unfolding of events. He gave orders to cut off all phone service to the Russian White House, including the government's internal telephone system.

At 8:15 p.m. a session of the Presidium of the Supreme Soviet began. From all directions people converged on the White House—members of the Supreme Soviet, journalists, and certain members of the Russian government, including Vice President Aleksandr Rutskoi.

The constitution of the Russian Federation contained a significant provision, Article 121, Clause 6. This stated that in the event of an attempt by the president to disperse a legally elected representative body, his powers would immediately—that is to say, automatically—

cease to exist. This constitutional clause became the basis for all the resolutions passed by the Presidium of the Supreme Soviet on the evening of September 21. During the night, in the early hours of September 22, the Supreme Soviet as a whole adopted these same resolutions. By September 23 many people's deputies who were not members of the Supreme Soviet had gathered in the Russian White House, and the opening of the Tenth (Extraordinary) Congress of People's Deputies was announced. This body confirmed the resolutions passed by the Supreme Soviet, which were essentially as follows:

1. In accordance with Article 121, Clause 6, the powers vested in President Yeltsin ceased to exist as of 8 p.m., September 21, 1993.
2. In accordance with Article 121, Clause 11, the presidential powers were vested in the vice president of the Russian Federation, Aleksandr Rutskoi.
3. The actions of President Yeltsin were to be regarded as a coup d'etat.

Rutskoi began performing the duties of president of Russia, issuing his first decrees the night of September 21 and in the early hours of September 22.

The Constitutional Court also handed down a decision on the night of September 21. It ruled Yeltsin's Decree No. 1400 unconstitutional and stated that his actions provided sufficient grounds "for his removal from office and for other special mechanisms to go into effect."

The law and the constitution were on the side of the Supreme Soviet, but what practical effect could this have? All the power ministries were siding with Yeltsin. Only the head of the Attorney General's Office, V. Stepankov, came to the White House.

Ordinary Muscovites also began to gather at the White House, including leaders of the more radical opposition groups, but they added up to only about two thousand. Rutskoi was constantly on the phone to various military units, but none were in any hurry to follow his orders.

Yeltsin, too, encountered disappointments. Defense Minister Grachev, who sided with Yeltsin, was unable to convince the Collegium of the Defense Ministry to adopt a resolution supporting the president. The army did not wish to go to war against the civilian population or to disperse the Supreme Soviet. Moods within the army were complex and contradictory. Opinion polls of active-duty soldiers and retirees showed that sympathy for Yeltsin was not prevalent. During 1992 and 1993, before the dissolution of the Soviet Union, one out of two serviceman questioned by pollsters expressed support for Rutskoi. The same was true among retired military personnel and skilled workers in military industries. In August and September 1993 in these circles Yeltsin's ratings hovered around 25–30 percent, while Rutskoi's were 35–45 percent. These polling results were reported in *Itogi*, June 30, 1996, but they were known to the initiated in 1993, and it was no wonder that the Defense Ministry Collegium decided on neutrality.

Those in charge of the television system sided with Yeltsin almost from the start, a great advantage for him. The TV channels gave no details on the actions taken by the Supreme Soviet, the People's Congress, and Rutskoi. The newspapers, on the other hand, mostly took a neutral position or sided with the Supreme Soviet. On September 23, under the general heading "President Tramples Constitution" *Rossiyskaya Gazeta* published Decree No. 1400 alongside the resolutions of the Supreme Soviet and the decrees issued by Rutskoi.

Among the resolutions of the Supreme Soviet was one removing Grachev, Yerin, and Golushko from office. New "power ministers" were appointed: Colonel-General Vladislav Achalov as defense minister, Andrei Dunaev as head of the MVD, and Viktor Barannikov as head of state security. They all accepted their appointments and went to the White House. But no army units, MVD troops or police, or state security personnel responded to the orders they issued. Only some individual officers from the power ministries went to the White House. From the ranks of these scattered individuals the new "president," Rutskoi, with Achalov's assistance, organized a defense guard for the White House and a personal bodyguard.

From the provinces reports were contradictory. Almost all local administrative chiefs sided with the president, while the majority of representative bodies of local government sided with the Supreme Soviet. Some heads of provinces or autonomous units of the Russian Federation declared their neutrality or offered to act as intermediaries. Thus, during the first days of the confrontation neither side had the overwhelming advantage. The American politician Zbigniew Brzezinski was right when in answer to a question about the standoff in Moscow he predicted, "Whoever sheds blood first will lose."

Meanwhile, all leaders of the Western powers declared their support for Yeltsin. I directly experienced this pro-Yeltsin sympathy in the West during a visit to Germany on September 15–26, 1993. Lyudmila Vartazarova, chairperson of the Socialist Party of the Working People (Russian initials, SPT), and I were there on an invitation from the Democratic Socialist Party of Germany. I observed that German television and most of the German press were on Yeltsin's side. On the evening of September 23 we met with a large group of businessmen and Bundestag members. Vartazarova spoke on the economic situation in Russia, and I on the political situation. My sympathies were with the Russian White House, but most of my listeners obviously sympathized with the Kremlin. I asked the audience, "What would you say if here in Bonn the president or chancellor suddenly dissolved the Bundestag, declared the German constitution null and void, and called for the establishment of new government institutions?"

"Russia is not Germany," was the reply of one Bundestag member.

September 22–23

As the standoff continued on September 22–23, barricades were built around the White House, but its defenders were not numerous. The people of Moscow displayed an obvious indifference to the appeals coming from either side. The leaders of the parliament had counted on mass support. Not much earlier, on May 9, 1993, more than 100,000 Muscovites had turned out for an opposition demonstration. The unofficial street leaders had given their chiefs definite assurances, but as it turned out, they were unable to fulfill their promises.

The trade unions made no response to Yeltsin's dissolution of the Supreme Soviet. There were various limp statements of protest, but no calls for action. No political strikes were declared in Moscow or anywhere else in Russia—actions Rutskoi and Khasbulatov had counted on. Small groups came to the White House from St. Petersburg, from the Trans-Dniester region, from Abkhazia, and from other regions to show support for the Soviet, but they numbered in the dozens or at best hundreds, not tens of thousands.

This absence of large-scale street support for the legislative branch worked to the advantage of Yeltsin and company, who gradually stepped up the pressure on the Supreme Soviet and Congress of People's Deputies. It was announced that any deputy who would leave the White House would be assured an influential post in the executive branch. These promises had an effect. Khasbulatov's deputy, Nikolai Ryabov, was one of the first to quit the White House; he was immediately appointed chairman of the newly created Central Electoral Commission. Aleksandr Pochinok, a member of the Soviet's budget committee, left and was appointed deputy minister of finance in Yeltsin's government.

The White House and neighboring buildings were sealed off by reinforced police units, which did not, however, interfere in any of the proceedings. Sessions of the Supreme Soviet and of the Congress of People's Deputies were broadcast to the territory surrounding the White House. By the end of the day on September 23, 632 people's deputies were present in the building. This was not a sufficient number to pass constitutionally binding resolutions. Nevertheless, the Congress voted to abrogate the powers of people's deputies who had declared support for Yeltsin and who refused to attend sessions of the Supreme Soviet or Congress. The first resolution on this point contained 88 names.[*] A separate resolution stripped Ryabov and Pochinok of their mandates as deputies for "supporting a coup d'etat." Several similar resolutions were adopted later on.

September 24

On September 24 it was still relatively easy to enter and leave the White House. Delegations from various regions arrived one after another. Groups of deputies went to talk with representatives of the MVD and Defense Ministry and with the media. A group from the Union of Officers arrived at the White House in uniform and bearing arms. Armed groups of Cossacks and others from the Trans-Dniester region also arrived. No one responded to an ultimatum issued by Yeltsin and Moscow's Mayor Yuri Luzhkov demanding the surrender of all weapons and military supplies. A surprise attack by a group of armed men on the staff headquarters of the Unified Armed Forces of the Commonwealth of Independent States provoked a stormy reaction

---

[*] The author lists 20 of those who would be most famous to Russian readers, but we have omitted this list.—G.S.

in the mass media. The attack was beaten off and the attackers fled. One officer defending the headquarters was killed. The Defense Ministry blamed the Union of Officers and the Supreme Soviet for the attack. The White House, for its part, charged that it was a provocation organized by the government.

The number of people around the White House was smaller on this day. A poll of Muscovites showed that more than 75 percent sympathized with neither side. The overwhelming majority were not interested in demonstrations or strikes in support of Yeltsin or of the Supreme Soviet. This situation suited Yeltsin just fine, but for Khasbulatov it was a big disappointment. He proposed that the work of the Congress of People's Deputies be interrupted.

"Much has been accomplished," he declared, "but the main thing has not been done—the rule of law has not been restored in our country. This has happened as a result of the apathy of our fellow citizens and the behavior of officeholders who, from careerist considerations, do not wish to submit to the law."

The ring of MVD and OMON forces around the White House was strengthened, giving rise to rumors that the building was about to be stormed. But Yeltsin and Grachev both announced that there would be no storming of the White House. Nevertheless, the units protecting the building were reinforced. The Congress passed a resolution calling for elections ahead of schedule both for president and for the people's deputies "no later than March 1994." Such resolutions did not become widely known. Russian television ignored them, and *Rossiyskaya Gazeta*, which had remained loyal to the Supreme Soviet, was closed down. Khasbulatov's motion for the Congress to cease operations was not carried. Some deputies accused Khasbulatov of cowardice and called for the election of a new chairman. These motions were voted on and rejected.

Late in the evening the White House's electricity was turned off. The blockade of the building was reinforced, and now only members of parliament and staff were allowed through.

September 25

On September 25 more than 5,000 gathered for a rally outside the White House. The building of barricades continued. Rutskoi came out of the parliament building and walked the whole length of the police and OMON cordon surrounding the White House, appealing to these men to abide by the law. They listened in silence with no show of emotion. During that same day Khasbulatov held several press conferences and meetings with opposition party leaders. Yeltsin also gave several interviews. He claimed that one deputy after another was leaving the White House and soon only Rutskoi and Khasbulatov would remain. "But I don't understand what the two of them, alone, will be doing in that building," he joked.

At an evening rally outside the White House, according to press reports, there were about ten thousand people. Among defenders of the White House a regiment was formed which took a vow of loyalty to the constitution. Rutskoi and Achalov attended this ceremony.

Toward evening the cordon around the White House was tightened. Private citizens and the press were no longer admitted, but anyone could leave the White House without interference. Some of those rallying to support the Supreme Soviet gathered by the subway station that bore the name "Barrikadnaya" (of the barricades). New police units and some ambulances were brought up to the ring around the White House. The defenders of the White House were now joined by a group of neo-fascists from the ultra-nationalist organization Russian National Unity, headed by Aleksandr Barkashov. They were given several rooms in the building but no weapons were issued to them. Inside the building all the reins of leadership were held firmly by Khasbulatov.

September 26

On September 26 rumors began to circulate both inside and outside the White House that the building was going to be stormed late that night. Indeed, the cordon around it was reinforced with elite units from the Dzerzhinsky Division. Snipers took their places in many buildings around the White House perimeter. The encirclement of the building was strengthened by the placement of dozens of trucks and buses.

More than two thousand people were on constant duty guarding the White House. Food was regularly brought into the building by various means. On the other hand, Yeltsin continued his efforts to buy deputies off. He decreed that anyone leaving the White House would be awarded a million rubles, a permanent residence permit for Moscow, and deputies' quarters. The eminent cellist Mstislav Rostropovich arrived in Moscow and directed a big concert on Red Square at noon on September 26, with Yeltsin, Grachev, Yerin, and Luzhkov among those in attendance. At 2 p.m. a rally of Yeltsin supporters was held on Soviet Square, with about 30,000 in attendance. At the White House rumors spread that military units coming to rescue the Supreme Soviet were already in the suburbs of Moscow. A religious procession headed by several priests made its way around the White House building. Several times each day Rutskoi came out on a balcony and gave a speech to the defenders of parliament. A continuous rally went on at Free Russia Square. Rutskoi announced that the Urals and Volga military districts had come over to the side of the parliament. The Defense Ministry denied the report.

In the evening the pumps providing water to the upper stories of the building stopped working. Sessions were held by candlelight. Many foreign correspondents attended Khasbulatov's evening press conference. Although representatives of the press were supposedly not allowed through the cordon, their number in the White House increased. The strictness of controls at the cordon had been relaxed somewhat that evening, and the ring of police and OMON units was pulled back several hundred meters.

Prime Minister Chernomyrdin for the first time offered to negotiate. Yuri Voronin, a spokesman for the opposition side, replied that before any negotiations, the water and electricity would have to be turned back on.

September 27

On the morning of September 27, rumors of an imminent storming of the White House again began to circulate. Gas masks were issued to many of the building's defenders, who were joined by an armed unit from Moldavia, the "Dniester Detachment." Observers estimated the total number of people around the building at 5,000–6,000. The Congress of People's Deputies voted to send out various appeals: to particular regions of Russia, to the patriarch of the Russian Orthodox Church, to the United Nations. The police again stopped journalists from entering the White House, and even people who worked in the building. Crowds of people gathered around the outside of the police cordon, and here and there clashes broke out between them and the

OMON troopers, who made free use of their clubs. Among the defenders of the White House calls for marching on the television center at Ostankino were heard for the first time.

Negotiations went on all day long between some of Yeltsin's cabinet ministers and some leaders of the Supreme Soviet, with Valery Zorin presiding as intermediary. In the evening Rutskoi and Khasbulatov addressed the crowd at another rally.

September 28

An operation aimed at blocking off the White House completely began early on the morning of September 28. The encirclement of the building was reinforced with MVD units accompanied by trucks with water cannon, and OMON troopers occupied passageways and courtyards in streets adjacent to the parliament. Many of the OMON carried automatic weapons. Mounted police were among the many new units brought up around the White House. A public address system was set up near the building, and an ultimatum was announced to its defenders to put down their weapons and surrender to the authorities. That morning roughly one hundred people's deputies who were away from the parliament building for various reasons were not allowed to reenter. Patriarch Aleksiy II of the Russian Orthodox Church joined the negotiations, where attempts were being made to work out a compromise.

Telephones in the White House and neighboring buildings were cut off. One-third of the buildings in Moscow's Krasnaya Presnya district, where the White House is located, were left without telephone service. Among foreign correspondents, only Americans were allowed into the building. Barbed wire began to go up around the White House, and many fire trucks and bulldozers for breaking down barricades joined the encircling forces. The number of White House defenders grew smaller. It rained all night, and some people left their posts in order to dry off and rest. By then the ring enclosing the White House was sealed tight. People were allowed to leave but no one could enter any more. All the schools in central Moscow were asked to suspend classes.

Another session of the Congress of People's Deputies began in the White House. Khasbulatov reported that 514 deputies were present. A large number of people gathered outside the police encirclement, and again there were clashes between police and demonstrators, with injuries on both sides. Demonstrators closed off the Sadovoye Koltso, or Garden Ring, and construction of another barricade began there. A barricade also went up at the "Barricades" subway station blocking entrances and exits.

Toward evening more barbed wire began to go up around the White House. Tension and bitterness mounted on both sides. Even foreign observers assessed the situation as explosive.

September 29

On this day the cordon around the White House was expanded outward. At the same time, Khasbulatov's deputy Veniamin Sokolov began negotiations with representatives of Yeltsin and his cabinet. Later in the day Ramazan Abdulatipov, another spokesman for the Supreme Soviet, joined the talks. A break in the continuous sessions of the Congress was announced as the shortage of food and water in the White House began to make itself felt. In the Kremlin a session of the Security Council, with Yeltsin presiding, was under way. The MVD gave the mass media greatly exaggerated information on the arms in the possession of the White House defenders. One headline proclaimed, "Parliament Armed to the Teeth." Other newspaper reports indicated that most Muscovites, and most people in the provinces, continued to favor neither side and had no desire to get involved. Though numerous rallies were held in various parts of Moscow, the number of participants remained small.

I visited different areas in Moscow that day—including the area around the White House, the Arbat, and the Garden Ring. Except for the immediate vicinity of the confrontation, life in the city went on undisturbed. The events around the White House did not seem to be on the minds of Moscow's residents. In the crowds that did gather along the Krasnaya Presnya embankment, by the Hotel Ukraina, at the Barricades subway station, and on the outer side of the police cordon around the White House, people who were simply curious seemed to predominate. Some people, after standing around near the parliament building for two or three hours, would leave, and their places would be taken by new arrivals.

At a few locations near the police cordon indignation reigned. At another spot, however, some elderly people were treating OMON troopers to homemade pirozhki. Elsewhere the men of OMON were pushing the crowd back, waving their clubs in a threatening way, curses and insults were flying. Khasbulatov's claim that more than 300,000 had taken part in protest meetings in Moscow and that a wave of opposition was starting to roll across Moscow and all of Russia simply didn't correspond to reality.

In the evening the usual rally was held at the White House, and there were rallies on the other side of the police cordon. Here and there police used their clubs, and demonstrators threw stones and iron bars. An especially large rally went on at the Barricades subway station.

September 30

On this day armored personnel carriers made their first appearance in the cordon around the White House. Journalists counted six of them. The Congress resumed its sessions, passing various laws and issuing decrees.

In the building of the Constitutional Court there began a conference of representatives of all the components of the federation: 54 provinces and autonomous republics were represented. The aim was to establish a new government body, the Council of the Federation.

In the Kremlin, Yeltsin met with Patriarch Aleksiy II and agreed to his intercession. Negotiations were to be conducted at the Svyato-Danilovsky (St. Daniel's) Monastery. Sergei Filatov and Oleg Soskovets were to represent the president in these talks.

A headquarters for processing renegade deputies began operation at 17 Novy Arbat Street. This was where deputies abandoning the White House could receive their million rubles apiece, permits for Moscow residences, and posts in various government ministries. Several dozen deputies were milling around in the reception room. Many were arguing about the jobs being offered them, demanding more prestigious posts. Even the pro-Yeltsin paper *Komsomolskaya Pravda* wrote about these people contemptuously, calling them "turncoats tempted by a mess of pottage."

About 150 people's deputies who had not been allowed to return to the White House found a place to work at Moscow's Krasnaya Presnya District Soviet. That evening the police prohibited people from gathering in groups of more than ten in the area near the Barricades subway station. Violators of this ban were beaten with police clubs or arrested and taken away. Nevertheless there were constantly 500–600 people crowding the vestibule of the subway station. Small rallies were also held on Pushkin Square.

October 1

On this day the two sides began negotiations mediated by the church. Voronin and Abdulatipov represented the parliament; the president and his cabinet were represented by Luzhkov, Filatov, and Soskovets. Some telephone service was restored at the White House, and electricity was turned back on at 6 a.m. Abdulatipov and Voronin agreed to some preliminary conditions—all weapons in the possession of the White House defenders were to be placed in a pile, and monitoring groups from both sides would oversee these stores of weapons. However, the Supreme Soviet would not accept this condition and denounced the negotiated agreement. In the afternoon, negotiations continued. The Supreme Soviet demanded that all its functions and powers be restored, but this condition was unacceptable to Yeltsin. He announced that he saw no way out of the conflict other than a peaceful conclusion; still, he would continue negotiations only after White House defenders laid down their arms.

"We will not resort to force," Yeltsin assured journalists. "But we don't want irregulars from Trans-Dniester or OMON troopers from Riga spilling Russian blood."

Kirsan Ilyumzhinov, the president of Kalmykia, was able to make his way through to the Russian White House. He warned that the police cordon had been reinforced again, and that by then there were several dozen armored vehicles surrounding the building. Meanwhile, the award for deputies leaving the White House was increased to two million rubles. But deputies were told they had only until October 4 to take advantage of these benefits. The office on the Arbat was to be closed on October 5.

On the morning of October 1 about 100 journalists, native and foreign, were allowed into the Russian White House. Achalov reported that several dozen OMON troopers had come over to the Supreme Soviet. Hundreds of new police and OMON troopers had been added to the cordon, bringing the total above 10,000, according to the estimates of observers. Police units from neighboring provinces had arrived in Moscow. On this day rallies were dispersed (as had occurred at the Barricades subway station the day before), and several hundred people were arrested. All the police stations in the neighborhood of the White House were overflowing with arrested demonstrators. Rallies were held, nevertheless, at Insurrection Square and some other squares in Moscow. These were broken up mostly by police, but some military squads were also used.

In the evening the Congress went into session again. A new delegation to the peace talks included the people's deputies Vladimir Isakov and Valentin Agafonov, as well as the chairmen of both chambers of the Supreme Soviet. An amateur arts entertainment was presented at the evening session, with delegates singing songs and reciting verse. Rutskoi declared that he would never allow the White House to be surrendered and vowed he would take part in any new presidential elections. More armored vehicles were brought up around the White House, and high-powered lighting systems were set up. Journalists in the White House were warned that beginning Saturday, October 2, their permits would be canceled and admission to the building would be closed off completely.

A government spokesman, Mikhail Poltoranin, told newspapers that people should take an understanding attitude toward "the action that the president has decided to carry out on October 4."

October 2

On the morning of this day another session of the Congress began. Many deputies who had been outside the walls of the White House managed to return. Despite the previous day's announcement, journalists were admitted to the building. Early in the day conditions in the city were generally calm. Negotiations continued at the Svyato-Danilovsky Monastery, but only specialist advisers from each side were involved, rather than direct representatives.

Khasbulatov and Rutskoi held another press conference. They called on residents in all regions of Russia to support the Supreme Soviet more actively, including stopping railroad traffic, pipeline flows, and communications in general. No one responded to these suggestions. Khasbulatov reported that the number of armed personnel in the cordon around the White House had risen to 50,000. Rutskoi appealed to residents of Moscow and other cities to "come out into the streets and join the protest rallies." In particular, he asked officers and veterans to take part in protest actions. In the afternoon a big rally began on Smolensk Square. When attempts were made to disperse it demonstrators resisted. Stones and chunks of wood were thrown. Several police and demonstrators were seriously wounded. Trouble continued at Smolensk Square for several hours, with activists from the organizations Toiling Russia and National Salvation Front taking part. On the Garden Ring barricades went up again, and tires were burned. By 4 p.m. the number of protesters had reached about 5,000, some of them carrying iron bars and Molotov cocktails. Barricaded areas were blocked off by the police. The rally on Smolensk Square was led by Viktor Anpilov, who called on Muscovites to offer open resistance. Not until nightfall did the demonstrators disperse after passing a resolution to renew the protest the following day.

At the White House rationing of food and water began, in expectation of a long siege. At the Svyato-Danilovsky Monastery the two sides resumed negotiations aimed at reducing tensions around the Supreme Soviet building.

October 3

On Sunday a small room in the White House became a church where a number of the building's defenders were baptized. Khasbulatov and Rutskoi attended the service. At 10 a.m. a session of the Congress began, and resolutions were adopted appealing to local Soviets, military personnel, and police. Meanwhile Yeltsin and the top personnel of his government were meeting in the Kremlin.

At 2 p.m. on October Square there began a large rally organized by Toiling Russia and the National Salvation Front. The Moscow mayor's office had ruled this rally illegal, but the Salvation Front leader, Ilya Konstantinov, urged demonstrators not to disperse but to march toward Zubovskaya Square. The column of demonstrators turned and headed toward the Crimea Bridge in the direction of the White House. OMON units blocking the bridge were meant to stop this movement, but the demonstrators broke through the OMON lines. By 3 p.m. the column appeared on Smolensk Square, heading for the White House. Marching in the forefront were several hundred demonstrators wielding iron bars. Four armored vehicles and two

OMON squads were sent to confront them. Automatic weapons fire rang out, but the troopers were firing in the air.

At this point events took a strange turn. Although no fewer than 15,000 men of OMON and other units were surrounding the White House, the demonstrators were able to break through the cordon and reach the Supreme Soviet building. Several thousand people from the Krasnaya Presnya embankment also got through the cordon at the same time. The blockade of the White House was broken. A mass meeting began outside the walls of the building. Above the crowd waved banners with such slogans as "Hang Yeltsin," "Rutskoi Is President," and "Judas Yeltsin." Addressing the crowd, Rutskoi called several times for the seizure of the mayoralty building and the Ostankino television tower. This was more than an appeal. It was an order. Under the leadership of Rutskoi and Makashov the formation of combat detachments began. Personnel included both White House defenders and newly arrived demonstrators. The mission of these units was no longer just to defend the building, but to conduct offensive operations. The nature of events in central Moscow was swiftly changing.

Why Did the Police Withdraw?

To this day sharp debate continues over the events of October 3 and 4, which marked a turning point not only in the standoff between president and parliament but in the history of modern Russia as a whole.

One of the most important but least comprehensible aspects of the events has to do with the October 3 behavior of the police, OMON, and MVD units surrounding the White House. Why were they unable to prevent the demonstrators from breaking through to the Supreme Soviet building? Throughout the confrontation the MVD had maintained a headquarters in the building of the Moscow mayoralty. Why did the MVD suddenly wrap up its business and leave the building, making it easy prey for Makashov's detachments?

From midday on, military helicopters were flying low over the Supreme Soviet building. Dozens of trucks with MVD troops were brought up to the cordon surrounding the building. Suddenly, within 20–30 minutes, the police, OMON, and MVD troops all disappeared from the vicinity of the White House. The armored vehicles also withdrew. On the square in front of the Supreme Soviet building and next to the mayoralty building trucks were left standing, without drivers, but with full tanks and keys in the ignition.

The OMON and MVD troops did not return to their barracks. They gathered in side streets and courtyards a few blocks from the White House. What was this? A retreat? Had they fled in defeat? Or was this an ambush, a lure, an invitation for Supreme Soviet supporters to engage in offensive operations? Military and police units don't leave their positions unless ordered. Doesn't that mean that an order was issued?

Toward evening on October 3 it was not only the officers and troops of the cordon around the White House that disappeared. All police in central Moscow did likewise. Even traffic police were suddenly gone from the Garden Ring district. The illusion was created that all authority in the city had evaporated. This encouraged the defenders of parliament to make an insane show of force, when in fact their forces were pitifully inadequate to accomplish anything in a city as huge as Moscow.

Subsequently the police and MVD were frequently denounced in the press that reflects the views of the "democrats." The police were accused of cowardice and vacillation, of abandoning Moscow, leaving it to be sacked and pillaged by the raging bands of Makashov and Anpilov. Viktor Yerin, head of the MVD, was singled out especially for denunciation, although a few weeks after the events of October 3–4 Yeltsin gave him a "Hero of Russia" award. Is this because Yerin carried out a deceptive maneuver with particular skill and verisimilitude?

October 2 and 3 saw the first shedding of blood in the confrontation. Several police and several demonstrators or defenders of parliament were killed. Each side blamed the other, and no investigation has been able to determine with any certainty who was the first to fire. It was very important for Yeltsin to portray himself as being on the defensive. Kremlin analysts had studied the opposition leaders, drawing up psychological profiles of how they might act under extreme circumstances. They were regarded as people inclined toward adventurous actions, people who did not think things through and consider their actions carefully. After twelve days of siege and isolation it was possible for Rutskoi, Khasbulatov, and Makashov—and even for Achalov and Barannikov—to believe that the other side had been defeated, that the police had panicked, that the people had come out on the side of the parliament. After all, hadn't thousands of demonstrators broken through to the White House from both sides? The opposition leaders fell into the carefully prepared trap. They played out their parts to perfection in a drama written by the other side.

As long as the supporters of the parliament were only defending the building, their position had many advantages from both the legal and the political point of view. They were defending themselves and upholding the existing constitution. Yeltsin had no valid justification for storming the Supreme Soviet building. To have a parliament that defended itself and perished under a hail of bullets was not to his advantage. On the other hand, an armed uprising, a putsch, a dangerous insurgency by the opposition forces benefitted him politically.

When Rutskoi and Makashov ordered the seizure of the mayoralty building and Ostankino, the putsch Yeltsin was looking for finally happened. The mayoralty building was quickly and easily taken. Makashov's detachments had it under their control by 5 p.m. There was great rejoicing among the defenders of the White House and the demonstrators gathered outside it. The order was given to march to Ostankino and seize the television tower. Some supporters of parliament reached Ostankino by taking trucks that had been left standing near the White House and mayor's building. Others marched through the city in a crowd. No one tried to prevent them. Armored personnel carriers with OMON troopers were encountered along the way, but the troopers shouted, "We're with you, fellows!" Rumors spread among the supporters of parliament that many police units had come over to their side.

General Makashov commanded the Ostankino operation. He was leading several thousand people, but only a few were armed. Viktor Anpilov also acted as a leader of the crowd. In the Ostankino building only some of its regular guards were on duty, but the MVD's special Vityaz brigade was stationed there. Between 12 and 15 armored vehicles were moving slowly back and forth at some distance from the besieged television tower. The thousands of angry demonstrators found the doors of the tower locked. Makashov ordered the doors broken down. Grenade launchers were used to fire at windows where lights were on, and as a result a member of the Vityaz brigade was killed. This served as a signal. A dump truck had been used to break down the doors, and a group of Makashov's men had gotten as far as the first floor.

Now a battle began. The troops of the Vityaz brigade, OMON troopers, and the armored vehicles began to fire directly into the crowd. Dozens of people fell dead and wounded. The wave of attackers swept back from the television building, people taking cover wherever they could. Renewed attempts to take the building were repelled with many more casualties. Nevertheless, all television broadcasting stopped except for the government news channel. Lines of print appeared on TV screens, stating that the station had been seized by an armed mob. But of course it had not.

The truth came out later that broadcasting had been stopped by the director of the television center, acting on orders from Chernomyrdin. Next to the Kremlin were parallel TV broadcasting centers belonging to the Defense Ministry, the Communications Ministry, and the Ministry for Emergency Situations. They immediately offered their services to the government, but were not taken up on their offer. For several hours the country had no television news. This worked to the advantage of the president's side. At 4 a.m. on October 4 Yeltsin signed a decree declaring a state of emergency in Moscow. At 6:30 p.m. he arrived in the Kremlin by helicopter and assumed personal leadership over the operation to crush the parliament by force. At 8 p,m. the state of emergency decree was announced over all radio stations. At the same time the government issued a statement to the citizens of Moscow and all of Russia that an insurrection had begun and that the government was obliged to use force to suppress it.

Monday, October 4: Bombardment of the White House

Neither Moscow nor the rest of the country knew as yet that Makashov's units had been defeated at Ostankino. News that the police had withdrawn and the mayor's offices had been seized caused a panic among many of the "democrats." Over the radio and on the still-operative Russian News television channel, Yegor Gaidar called on Muscovites to gather at the building of the Moscow City Soviet in defense of the government. Several thousand unarmed citizens turned out in response to this appeal. Many other prominent "democrats," both politicians and celebrities, called for the use of force to defend the government. Late on the night of Sunday, October 3, both Yeltsin and Chernomyrdin spoke along the same lines. A government-controlled television station at Shabolovka, which had begun broadcasting, carried their messages.

During the night army troops were brought up to the White House.

Units of the Ryazan paratroop division had been hastily deployed to Moscow. The 27th Motorized Infantry Division was relocated to the center of Moscow. Chernomyrdin appealed to the Collegium of the Defense Ministry, and the generals changed their minds, abandoning their former neutrality. They passed a resolution authorizing army participation in the suppression of armed rebellion. Paratroop units from Tula were also brought to Moscow. Tanks rolled out onto the embankment facing the White House. Dozens of armored vehicles took up positions on the other side of the building. A special anti-terrorist unit, the Alpha brigade, was given orders to arrest the leaders of parliament, Khasbulatov and Rutskoi first of all. Units of the Taman and Kantemir tank divisions were also brought into Moscow. As early as October 2 or 3, an American television news company had received permission to set up equipment at convenient locations around the White House. On the morning of October 4, CNN began broadcasting the bombardment and storming of the Supreme Soviet building for all the world to see.

Early on the morning of October 4 the armored vehicles around the White House opened up a heavy, concentrated fire on the positions held by the defenders of the building. There was hardly any return fire. Several dozen deputies managed to make their way through side entrances and backyards of neighboring buildings to safety. Some of them even showed up at the Novy Arbat office and claimed their 2 million rubles. Approximately 200 deputies remained. They and the staff of the Supreme Soviet building gathered in the large meeting room belonging to the Council of Nationalities, which was protected by walls all around. It was in the interior of the building and had no windows opening onto courtyards or streets. The parliament building was raked with fire from large-caliber machine guns. At 9 a.m., guns from armored units began bombarding the building, the upper stories first of all. The boom of artillery and the crash and rumble of shells hitting the building could be heard.

Rutskoi let it be known that the besieged defenders were ready to surrender. No one fired back at the armored units. The surrender signals and calls for help for the wounded were disregarded. It was necessary to terrify and punish. The building began to burn. The whole world witnessed the flames coming out the White House windows. It was no longer possible to get out of the building. It was enclosed by a solid ring of fire and a renewed police cordon. The police and OMON units which had disappeared the day before were back, forming a large second ring around the White House. They detained and checked the identification of everyone who did somehow get out of the building. Such people were beaten up, then taken off somewhere.

Soon the bombardment was directed at the lower stories, not just the upper ones. Elite units approached the building, preparing to take it by storm. Helicopters circled above. At 10 a.m. some of the defenders surrendered, since resistance was useless. They too were beaten up and taken off somewhere. Later there were reports that some of them were executed, but no one could verify these reports. At 10 a.m. the helicopters began firing at the White House roof. A huge crowd of Muscovites had gathered around the distant approaches to the building, beyond the cordon of military and police. But they were merely onlookers, not demonstrators. They came to watch the spectacle of the White House being bombarded. Stray bullets flew in their direction, too, and several people were wounded. Some were even killed. Nevertheless the crowd of rubberneckers kept growing.

Now and then people would run from the White House. Some were shot and killed, some taken as "prisoners of war," some allowed to reach the crowd of onlookers. The armored units kept maneuvering around the building and firing on it. The seventh floor was burning, black smoke pouring out the windows. Toward 11 a.m. firing intensified. Inside the White House there were many dead and wounded. Now people in civilian clothes, some of them wounded, were fleeing the building in groups of ten or more. Official reports claim there was firing from the White House, but it is hard to give any credence to that. After the events, it was reported that very few spent cartridge were found inside the building. Resistance was useless, and what would have been the point in firing with rifles at tanks?

At 11 a.m. the first attack units entered the building. Fire directed at the lower floors was redirected to the upper ones.

Wounded people were arriving at hospitals, and already about 20 of them had died. In the end more than 200 were hospitalized. It was not possible to make a count of the total number killed or wounded. Many who fled did not go to hospitals.

Who Was Firing from the Roofs?

During the bombardment of the White House snipers from nearby rooftops kept up a steady fire. This was another enigma of the "battle" in Moscow. According to the Yeltsin government, the snipers firing from the roofs were Rutskoi supporters who at an earlier time had ensconced themselves in those positions. There was no evidence to confirm this version. Some left-wing publications contended that the snipers belonged to certain secret units of the MVD or the FSB, successor to the KGB?

In the newspaper *Zavtra* some surviving participants in the battle wrote that the snipers were under the command of Aleksandr Korzhakov, chief of the presidential bodyguard (Russian initials, GUOP—Gosudarstvennoe Upravlenie Okhrany Prezidenta).

Several publications claimed that the snipers were shooting not only from the rooftop of the Hotel Ukraina but also from the top of the nearby U.S. Embassy. They charged that the snipers were foreigners, a special unit trained in Romania and Israel. None of the snipers was captured and questioned. It is known for certain that the snipers' fire was directed not only at the White House defenders but also at OMON troopers and the special attack forces. One officer of the Alpha brigade was killed by a sniper's bullet. There were snipers among the defenders of the building as well as among the attackers. But the snipers on the nearby rooftops clearly belonged to some separate, special unit. Several people in the crowd of onlookers were also killed by their fire.

The End Comes

Not until 12 noon of October 4 did Channel One, the main television channel, resume broadcasting from Ostankino. The very first reports by news announcers spoke of fighting around the Supreme Soviet building and placed the blame on Rutskoi and Khasbulatov for innocent blood being shed.

At 12:30 p.m. the defenders of the White House and some of the building's staff began coming out of the building in large numbers with their hands up. The heavy, concentrated fire stopped, but then it started up again just as intensely. General Konstantin Kobets was directly in charge of the storming of the building. His assistant was Colonel-General Dmitry Volkogonov, the well-known historian.

More people came out of the building; among them were journalists and the group accompanying Kirsan Ilyumzhinov, president of Kalmykia. Some people were detained, others allowed to go free. Firing stopped again, and people began coming out of the building in a steady stream. Around 4 p.m., firing at the building started again, including cannon fire from the tanks. The upper stories had been burning for quite a while, but still the tanks fired on them.

Around 5 p.m. firing stopped again, and approximately three hundred people came out of the building. A little later, several hundred more came out, including many deputies.

Soldiers of the Alpha brigade had entered the White House. It was they who brought the deputies out, along with Rutskoi, Khasbulatov, Achalov, and Barannikov, who had all surrendered to the Alpha unit. All the leaders were arrested and taken away to Lefortovo prison, Yeltsin being immediately informed of this. Some deputies were taken away in buses, others set free. Not until 7 p.m. did the MVD announce that fighting had ended, and not until 9 p.m. did firefighters begin putting out the fires in the Supreme Soviet building and at nearby barricades.

The Mass Beating of Deputies and White House Defenders

During the evening and night of October 4 a large number of people who had been in the White House were subjected to ferocious beatings. These beatings were mainly the work of the OMON and police who had formed the second, outer line of encirclement. The beatings occurred in the courtyards and entrances of buildings near the White House, in the Krasnaya Presnya stadium, and at local police stations. Two people's deputies, Ivan Sashviashvili and Oleg Rumyantsev, gave me first-hand accounts of these beatings. Rumyantsev was beaten in the entranceway of a building, Shashviashvili at the stadium. Several times the police pretended they were about to execute the deputies. They took their documents and some of their clothing, then left them. No deputies were killed on October 3 or 4, but dozens of them were made to suffer severely.

This was not a spontaneous outburst by drunken or irate police. It was a conscious act of intimidation. In carrying out these actions, the police were following orders from higher up.

According to reports by a number of deputies and the opposition press, many White House defenders who were caught bearing arms were executed. Those mainly singled out for execution were the fighters who had come from the Baltic, the Trans-Dniester, and other regions, as well as the neo-fascist followers of Barkashov. These reports remain unconfirmed.

127

A Battle Without Heroes

Salvador Allende, the president of Chile, died with an automatic weapon in hand, defending the presidential palace against a military coup. This made him a hero for many—not only in Chile. None of the leaders of the White House became heroes in the eyes of public opinion in Russia. They do bear their share of responsibility for the bloodshed on October 3 and 4. Even the anti-Yeltsin press subsequently acknowledged the bravery as well as the crudity and stupidity of General Albert Makashov, who led the takeover of the mayoralty building and the storming of Ostankino. Khasbulatov was pathetic and frightened during the decisive moments of the defense of the White House. On October 3 he was talking about marching on the Kremlin, but on October 4 he became almost hysterical and was barely able to talk, even with those closest to him. Rutskoi displayed great inconsistency. He *pleaded* with the enemy to stop the cannon fire from the tanks. But he ordered defenders to keep firing from the windows and doorways. He begged for help—from the soldiers of the Russian army and from foreign embassies. He really did not know what to do. He obviously feared reprisals against his person. When he surrendered his automatic weapon to an officer of the Alpha brigade he pointed out that the weapon had not been fired; the grease it was packed in was still clean. As though that were of any significance at the end of the day on October 4.

How Many Were Killed or Wounded?

The answer to this question was still not known three years after the events. According to official accounts, about twenty government soldiers and police were killed, while the death toll for supporters of Rutskoi and Khasbulatov was between 150 and 200. (There was disparity in the numbers provided by various official sources.) The number of wounded on both sides was roughly three to four times the number killed.

Kirsan Ilyumzhinov and the president of Ingushetia, Ruslan Aushev, stated that inside the Supreme Soviet building they had seen several hundred corpses and that the total number of White House defenders exceeded five hundred. According to the opposition press, about two hundred were killed outside the Ostankino television tower and no less than 1,500 died at the White House. Some MVD officers confirmed these estimates (*Nezavisimaya Gazeta*, October 30, 1993). There are reports that the bodies of those who died in the parliament building were secretly removed on October 5 and 6 through underground passageways leading to the Barricades subway station. From there they were shipped out of the city and burned. In this operation no attempt was made to identify the dead. There is no confirmation of these reports.

No journalists or independent observers were able to gain access to the White House immediately after it was stormed. Even physicians from the Moscow public health department were not admitted to the building until after "investigative activities" had been completed. No bodies were brought to Moscow morgues after October 3 and 4. An investigative report on this subject appeared in the pro-Yeltsin paper *Komsomolskaya Pravda* (October 15, 1993) under the heading "Did the White House Become a Mass Grave?" It should be noted, incidentally, that there has been no official publication of the names of all those killed or wounded at the White House and Ostankino.

Post-Confrontation Repression

In the heat of the confrontation between the executive and legislative branches of government, the executive side temporarily banned almost all pro-Communist newspapers and the more radical "national-patriotic" publications in Moscow. In St. Petersburg the newspaper *Narodnaya Pravda* was banned, and in Kemerovo, the newspaper *Kuzbas*.

Most of the Communist and trade union papers soon resumed operations, some of them appearing under different names. For example, *Den* became *Zavtra*. But some of these papers never reappeared.

When the state of emergency was declared in Moscow many parties and social organizations that had opposed Yeltsin were ordered to cease their activities. The Ministry of Justice ruling on this point named the National Salvation Front, the Toiling Russia movement, Russian National Unity, the United Front of Toilers, the Union of Officers, the Shield Union of Military Personnel, the Free Russia People's Party, the Communist Party of the Russian Federation, the Russian Communist Workers Party, and several other less well known organizations. After the Moscow state of emergency was lifted, however, almost all of these organizations resumed their activities.

129

For several days after the arrest of Rutskoi, Khasbulatov, and the other White House leaders, further arrests were made among former White House defenders and among active members of left-wing and "national-patriotic" organizations. Also imprisoned were Viktor Anpilov and Ilya Konstantinov, the organizers of the October 3 demonstrations. Many criminal cases involving charges of "civil rebellion" were instituted.

Pro-Yeltsin politicians and other prominent public figures justified his actions without qualification. Opposition supporters and many legal experts regarded his actions of September–October 1993 as criminal. Some legal experts calculated that from September 21 to October 5 the Russian president violated the laws and constitution of the Russian Federation more than fifty times. These violations were enumerated by the opposition and by a number of legal defense organizations, but not by the prosecutor's office. "Victors are not judged."

ELECTIONS TO THE STATE DUMA, DECEMBER 1993

Yeltsin's Decree No. 1400, aside from abolishing the Congress of People's Deputies and Supreme Soviet, setting the stage for the elimination of all remnants in Russia of the system of Soviets (originally, workers' councils), cited a new law regarding the election of deputies to a State Duma. This election law, drafted by the presidential staff, was published in almost all Russian newspapers on September 25, 1993. It established new "rules of the game" and scheduled elections for December 12, 1993. As early as late September, many Russian political leaders and organizations began to make preparations for these elections. In early October, even before all the bodies of those who died in and around the White House had been buried, the election campaign went into full swing. After all, only two months remained before the voting.

From the legal point of view, this election was highly questionable. Yeltsin had violated the constitution but he had not abrogated it. The constitution still in effect, to which Yeltsin had vowed loyalty when he was sworn in as president in July 1991, made no provision for a Federal Assembly or a State Duma. Those were provided for in the draft of a new constitution, which was not even going to be published until mid-November. People were supposed to vote on this new constitution in a referendum on December 12 at the same time they were electing a Duma. But what if the constitution wasn't approved? How could the Duma it provided for be valid?

Hardly anyone troubled themselves about these legal niceties, however. Yeltsin's opponents decided to take part in the Duma elections. After eliminating the previously existing legislative bodies, Yeltsin obviously could not remain in the legal framework of which they were a part. The new rules of the game, arbitrarily established, would be given legal validity after the fact, and the new constitution would have retroactive effect.

The new election law differed substantially from the laws and regulations that had governed the earlier elections of Supreme Soviets and Congresses of People's Deputies. Only half the deputies to the Duma, 225 out of 450, were to be elected under the winner-take-all (majoritarian) system, in which one candidate would be elected from each electoral district. The election of a candidate was considered valid if at least 25 percent of the registered voters in the given district had cast ballots. Only one round of voting was held, and the candidate with the largest number of votes was considered the winner (whether with a plurality or an outright majority).

The other half of the Duma was to be chosen on the basis of proportional representation, with people voting for party lists rather than individual candidates. Any competing party, electoral bloc, or other organization that received more than 5 percent of the vote was given a certain number of seats in the Duma, based on the proportion it won out of the total number of votes cast. Under the draft of the new constitution the Duma was to be elected for a four-year term. The first Duma would be an exception, however. It would serve only two years, from 1993 to 1995.

There was sharp and convincing criticism in the Russian press in regard to the new election law, as well as the draft of the new constitution (published on November 10), and the hasty scheduling of the Duma elections and the constitutional referendum. Even members of the intelligentsia sympathetic to Yeltsin asked, Why go galloping into an electoral contest of dubious outcome? Why the rush?

Yeltsin was in a hurry, however, because he knew, based on his experience in 1991, that a relatively short campaign favored the incumbent and created greater difficulties for the opposition. In addition, Yeltsin and his circle wished to distract public opinion from the bloody tragedy just played out in Moscow.

With doubts and hesitations the opposition parties decided to take part in the elections. Three parties could not participate; they were still banned, with their leaders in Lefortovo prison—these were Rutskoi's Free Russia party, Anpilov's Russian Communist Workers Party, and Konstantinov's National Salvation Front. Left-wing participants in the campaign included the Communist Party of the Russian Federation, the Agrarian Party, and the Socialist Party of the Working People (SPT). The Liberal Democratic Party of Russia (LDPR), headed by Vladimir Zhirinovsky, also stood in opposition to Yeltsin's government. It would be more accurate to call this a radical Russian nationalist party, rather than "liberal democratic."

In the center of the political spectrum were such groups as the Civic Alliance, the Russian Movement for Democratic Reforms, and Women of Russia. On the right, but still in opposition to the Yeltsin government was Yabloko, an electoral bloc headed by Grigory Yavlinsky.

In strong support of Yeltsin's government were two parties that had been formed in 1993: Russia's Choice, headed by the former prime minister, Yegor Gaidar; and the Party of Russian Unity and Concord (Russian initials, PRES), headed by Sergei Shakhrai. Gaidar's party—whose slogans included "Russia's Choice Is President Yeltsin"—was considered the front-runner. In November Gaidar said that his party counted on winning 40 percent of the seats and, together with its allies, would command a majority in the new Duma. Shakhrai and the center parties also made highly optimistic statements, backed up by polling agencies sympathetic to them.

The election results were a surprise to everyone. In the contest among party lists Gaidar's party made a showing of only 12 percent, a significant defeat. The bloc headed by Shakhrai barely won 7 percent. Success came to Zhirinovksy's LDPR, whose political pretensions had been viewed with scorn by most Russian leaders. Yet the LDPR won more than 22 percent of the vote. The Communist Party of the Russian Federation (CPRF), headed by Gennady Zuganov, gained about 14 percent, which was regarded as a big success. The Agrarian Party, headed by Mikhail Lapshin, also made a good showing, with about 9 percent, but the main center parties suffered a complete defeat: their leaders, such as Gavriil Popov, Anatoly Sobchak, and Arkady Volsky, did not even win seats in the Duma.

What were the reasons for the defeat of the pro-Yeltsin parties and the victory of the opposition, especially the radical Russian nationalists? There were many, but the main reason was the population's sharp reaction against the "shock therapy" that had been going on for two years, with no end in sight. As the poet Yevgeny Yevtushenko wrote, "Through cracks in the voting booth walls, Poverty's icy breath blew in."

All the promises of President Yeltsin and his cabinet, including those made before the April 1993 referendum, remained unfulfilled. Prices for basic consumer goods were five times higher in December 1993 than they had been in April, while wages and pensions were only 2.5–3 times higher.

I would cite another important reason: the difficult, sometimes humiliating position the Russian population found itself in after the dissolution of the Soviet Union. Russians had grown used to thinking of themselves as one of the largest and most influential nations in the world. But now, even in tiny Estonia, Russians were abused and denied citizenship. The Russian population was being driven out of Tuva and Chechnya; thousands of Russian families had fled from Central Asia and Transcaucasia. In Ukraine Russians were scorned as "Moskali" (an insulting term meaning "Muscovite"); in Moldava and the Dniester region they were beaten up. All this was a painful blow to the Russian nation's self-esteem. It is not surprising that these conditions gave rise to many radical Russian nationalist organizations, the main ones being the National Salvation Front, the Russian National Assembly (Sobor), and Russian Unity.

Another factor explains the large vote for Zhirinovsky. After the Russian Supreme Soviet was crushed by force of arms, most of the radical Russian nationalist organizations were banned, as we have said. Zhirinovsky's LDPR was the only such group to remain on the ballot. Those who might have voted for other Russian nationalist groups gave their support to Zhirinovsky. The LDPR also enjoyed overwhelming support among military personnel and substantial support among those working in military industries. Most of the sailors and officers of the Pacific and Black Sea fleets voted for Zhirinovsky, as did a large number of servicemen in the elite Taman Division, whose tanks had bombarded the White House.

There were other reasons for the poor showing of pro-Yeltsin parties. The "democrats" were divided and bogged down in petty feuds and squabbling. Their campaigning had been uninspired; they really had nothing to say to the electorate. Half the voters—young people mainly—boycotted the election.

Each of the participating electoral blocs made fairly extensive use of television. Zhirinovsky used it more effectively than his rivals. His broadcasts had the most specific content and were the most interesting. To be sure, he indulged in populist demagogy and made a lot of promises that he couldn't keep. But Yeltsin and the democrats came to power in 1990–91 on a wave of populist demagogy, scattering false promises right and left. Zhirinovsky simply used the democrats' own weapon against them. Some of Zhirinovsky's speeches were quite dangerous and inflammatory, as is typical of radical nationalists. He spoke insultingly about other nations, including former Soviet republics. But his speeches touched on some truths. As one newspaper observed, a great many problems existed in Russia that the democrats had been avoiding for two years. Only Zhirinovsky and extremists like him cried out about the lonely old people dying of hunger as food prices soared, about the collapse of the social safety net, about Russians being driven out of former Soviet republics just because they were Russians, about Russia being a great power whose distinct geopolitical interests were being disregarded by other world powers.

The defeat of the president and his cabinet was so obvious that the pro-Yeltsin press didn't even try to put a good face on it. *Rossiyskaya Gazeta* wrote that the new Duma would be "more conservative, more leftist, and more evil than the parliament that was dispersed in September–October . . . The thunder of victory is heard on the extreme left wing. All that remains for the democrats is to lick their wounds and shake themselves thoroughly out of their torpor."

"What Have You Chosen, Russia?" exclaimed *Izvestia*. "The world is troubled and aghast over the outcome of our elections . . . You can almost hear people sighing for the 'good old days' of recent vintage when the chief villain was Aleksandr Rutskoi, and Vladimir Zhirinovsky was considered not so much a danger as an entertainment."

The most radical "democrats" were not only upset; they were panicked. Writing in *Komsomolskaya Pravda*, the leader of the Democratic Union, Valeria Novodvorskaya, called on Yeltsin to immediately ban the parties of Zhirinovsky and Zyuganov. Otherwise, she warned, what awaits us are dungeons, gas chambers, crematoria. I would urge Boris Nikolayevich [Yeltsin] to forget the word "democracy." Russia has shown its incapacity for democracy. Those who voted for the Communists and Zhirinovsky are not the people, but the mob, dark and ignorant. What the mob likes is fascism. Therefore within the next few weeks a National Guard must be formed. We must all join it. Equipped with the latest weaponry and air power, we will then have something to defend ourselves with.

Leaders of "democrats" like this had just gotten through applauding the bombardment of the legally elected Russian parliament and reveling in their imagined victory.

The December 1993 Duma elections were of course a disappointment for Yeltsin, but they did not result in a weakening of his power and influence. On the contrary, his power grew. All those who feared the left rallied around him. Among these were the intellectual "elite" and many businessmen. His main support, however, came from the *bureaucracy*, whose numbers and influence, far from declining in the now "democratic" Russia, increased rapidly.

Hardly any of the more than two million Soviet bureaucrats and party apparatchiks were left without jobs in the new Russia. In fact, the government apparatus of Russia expanded by 20 percent, compared to that of the former Soviet Union. This apparatus became the mainstay of the "democratic" Yeltsin regime.

4

The End of Market Romanticism

The social and political conflicts of 1993 took place against a background of continuing economic decline and social degradation. The establishment of new political structures and the relative consolidation of a "democratic authoritarianism" also required fundamental corrections in economic policy. In the aftermath of the December 1993 Duma elections, Prime Minister Chernomyrdin declared: "The period of market romanticism has ended for us today." The winter of 1993–94 was long and severe. Heating fuel had to be supplied to the cities. A budget for the first quarter of 1994 had to be drawn up. It was also necessary to pay back wages owed to millions and millions of people in all sectors of the economy, but especially those in the North who were owed for November and December 1993.

"The era of market romanticism has ended not only for Gaidar's economic reforms," wrote Vladimir Orlov in *Moskovskiye Novosti* ([Moscow News], 1994, no. 4, January 23–30). "For the president, too, it has exhausted itself." Orlov wrote that Chernomyrdin had support and confidence in many quarters, particularly in the "power ministries" and among government officials tired of constant reorganization and unpredictability and longing for stability.

Changes in the makeup of the cabinet accompanied the shift toward pragmatism. Disheartened by his poor showing in the Duma elections, Vice Premier Gaidar submitted his resignation. The number two figure in the cabinet had been Finance Minister Boris Fyodorov. Chernomyrdin insisted on his departure as well. On becoming an ex-minister, Fyodorov sent Yeltsin a letter predicting terrible disasters for Russia now that he and Gaidar were no longer in the cabinet. But Yeltsin ignored the "warning" and appointed Sergei Dubinin as minister of finance. Mikhail Poltoranin also left the government. Earlier he had been very close to Yeltsin and had been called "unsinkable." Vladimir Shumeiko, the first deputy vice premier, to whom Chernomyrdin was obviously unsympathetic, also withdrew.

Ella Pamfilova, the minister for social protection, also sent Yeltsin a letter of resignation, charging that the government's social policy was a complete fiasco. In the Supreme Soviet of the USSR Pamfilova had headed a committee to investigate official privilege, and I remember well her speeches describing the fancy villas of various Soviet marshals and generals. She knew quite well how the top officials of the Brezhnev and Gorbachev eras had lived. But now she wrote: "Compared to the current abuses of power, those of the past seem like child's play. . . . There is a growing epidemic of suicides. People are drinking themselves to death and becoming brutalized in other ways. More and more children with birth defects are being born, and the ranks of orphans, homeless people, and beggars are constantly growing. Against this background of increasing impoverishment the same old corrupt bureaucracy, bound by ties of mutual loyalty and mutual protection, continues to grow fat and to run the show" (see *Argumenty i Fakty*, 1994, no. 5, p. 3).

Only one person remained in the cabinet from the former Gaidar team—Anatoly Chubais. On March 4, 1994, a session of the cabinet was held in the hastily repaired White House, which had now become the seat of Yeltsin's government. At this session the president and the prime minister supported one another on all aspects of economic policy. Chernomyrdin made no promises of a better life in 1994. In order to keep the situation under control, to reduce inflation and stop the decline in production and in living standards, and to avoid a massive rise in unemployment, the government, according to Chernomyrdin, would have to act not only firmly and decisively, but also with extreme caution, "for we are walking on the razor's edge."

Credits and subsidies would be forthcoming, Chernomyrdin said, but only if the recipient enterprises guaranteed results and only on the basis of strict and rigorous repayment. All areas of production that showed good prospects would be supported. Russia would not become a raw-materials appendage to the West.

Chernomyrdin spoke critically of the ministers and vice premiers who had engaged in irresponsible experimentation and then left office when their experiments and theories failed. "Russia is not a racing car," said Chernomyrdin, concluding his report, "that you can drive for a while and then get out—leaving the entire country shaking." This part of his speech was shown on all television channels, with the camera switching back and forth between Chernomyrdin and Gaidar.

On the other hand, Chernomyrdin did not propose a change of course, but called for increasing "the cruising speed" of market reforms. Corrections were to be made only in some areas, for example, conversion from military to civilian production, tax policy, imported alcohol, and monitoring of the financial activity of banks and enterprises.

The overall goal set for the government by the president and the premier was to stop the decline of production in 1994 and, in 1995, to complete "structural reforms" for the most part, so that in the period 1996–99 economic growth would be assured and Russia would return to the ranks of advanced industrial countries. It was necessary to avoid a prolonged depression, which would throw Russia into Third World status as a helpless supplier of raw materials to more efficient economies. Unfortunately, the goal they set was not achieved. You can't reach a destination if the road you're on doesn't go that way.

END OF THE "THIRTEENTH FIVE-YEAR PLAN"

For many decades (since 1928–29) we had planned our country's economic development and assessed its progress on the basis of five-year plans. The most successful five-year plan, to judge by the economic indicators, seems to have been the eighth, from 1966 through 1970— and the least successful, the twelfth, 1986–1990. But when it came to the "thirteenth five-year plan," that is, the 1991–1995 period, to call it merely "unsuccessful" would be a mockery. Appraising the results of those years, the authors of sober economic studies, not given to hyperbole, used words like "crash" or "catastrophe." However, even a crash requires analysis, probably more, in fact, than success or victory.

The economic measures taken by the Yeltsin, Gaidar, and Chernomyrdin governments did have some positive results. One undeniable achievement was the elimination of shortages. The market was saturated, and sometimes oversaturated, with consumer goods, and in real terms, prices have stopped rising to such an extreme degree. The service sector has grown quickly and occupies a larger share in the gross domestic product. Millions of people lost their jobs in production but found a way to apply themselves in trade, including such rather uncivilized forms as the "shuttle trade" and the enormous markets, bazaars, and swap meets that have grown up. Supply now exceeds demand in almost all areas, and according to the market economists, that is the primary basis for a healthy economy.

In 1994–95 the average real income of the population declined more slowly than in 1992–93. Opportunities to display initiative and earn additional income expanded. Inflation was substantially reduced, and the authority of the ruble rose. It almost became convertible. Banks in Poland, Finland, Austria, even Germany began trading in rubles. A system of financial institutions and other basic elements of a market infrastructure had essentially taken shape: there were commercial banks, commodity exchanges, markets for securities and government bonds, foreign currency markets, insurance companies, pension funds, and a body of arbitrators, notaries, and attorneys dealing with civil cases. Many economists saw this as indicating a healing process in the economy. The majority of the population did not see it that way, however, since their living standards continued to decline.

A relatively stable correlation between the dollar and domestic Russian prices expressed in rubles gradually developed. For holders of foreign currency, life in Russia ceased to be incredibly cheap. The plundering of the country through the export of all sorts of cheaply purchased Russian goods and materials also came to an end. The reliability of savings banks was partially restored and confidence in them began to revive. Many healthy forms of private enterprise developed. For about 10 percent of the population life obviously became better,

139

and for approximately 200–500,000 it began to seem simply splendid. (See chapter 5.)

In November 1994, Chernomydin commented that the citizens of our country had "already experienced all the negative aspects of the breakdown of the old economy, but had little experience of the positive aspects inherent in the new economy." He promised that in 1994–95 the government would be more responsible in turning toward a "new, normal life under market conditions" (*Rossiyskaya Gazeta*, November 29, 1994).

This promise, unfortunately, was not fulfilled. In the first half of 1994 the decline of production was 26 percent of that in 1993 and almost 50 percent of the decline in 1991. The falling off in investment activity was even greater. The state of affairs in material production continued to worsen.

In the second half of 1994, in an effort to check the continuing downturn, a program was adopted to restore financial balance, ensure the bringing in of the harvest, and increase the capacity of native industry to compete on the world market. The proposal was made to establish a real estate market and to expand opportunities for foreign investors. Most of this program, however, went no farther than the paper it was written on.

The government did not have the necessary resources to make investments or even repair worn-out equipment. Private capital had no desire to invest in industrial and agricultural production that promised only low returns. Owners of capital preferred trade, services, and semi-criminal operations where return on investment was high.

Chernomyrdin complained about discrimination against Russia on the world market. "We have things to trade. We have competitive products. Not just raw materials! We have metal products, machine tools, items produced for the space program, products related to atomic energy and the nuclear industry, areas where we can compete. But we are kept in the waiting room of the world market like poor relations. We are in fact being discriminated against" (*Rossiyskaya Gazeta*, May 6, 1994).

Chernomyrdin criticized Gaidar for relying too much on aid from abroad. The promised $40 billion—or even $26 billion—never materialized. Yet Chernomyrdin's government was incapable of mobilizing internal sources of investment capital and itself began to look hopefully toward the West, seeking to create a favorable climate for foreign investment. The statistics, however, were unrelenting. Only about 0.1 percent of all foreign investment in the world was going to Russia. In this respect, such countries as Poland, the Czech Republic, Hungary, and even Estonia were doing better.

Overall results for 1994 were not at all consoling, with basic economic indicators making an even worse showing than in 1993. The press spoke of a year of "lost opportunities" (*Delovoi Mir*, March 4, 1995). The budget deficit increased noticeably in 1994. Expenditures for the maintenance of government bodies and administrative agencies increased more than twofold relative to gross domestic product. Production continued to decline, and GDP was only 85 percent of what it had been in 1993. Agricultural production shrank by almost 10 percent. The inflation rate remained high, and the debt for unpaid wages was enormous. An unexpected financial crisis hit in the fall of 1994 (so-called Black Tuesday), and only with difficulty did the government overcome the consequences of that disaster. According to official statistics, approximately half the population was below the poverty line, and some 30 percent were living in such extreme poverty that malnutrition, even starvation, threatened.

The situation did not change substantially in 1995. The war in Chechnya, which began in December 1994, proved to be bloody and prolonged, and contributed to a worsening of the economic situation. But there were hopeful signs. There was a slowing of inflation and production declined more slowly. The State Statistical Committee even noted increased production in metallurgy and in the oil and chemical industries. The functioning of the transportation system improved. But there was no increase of capital investments, not even in these improving sectors. Equipment was hardly even being repaired, let alone renewed, with the result that serious accidents were on the rise.

From April to June 1995 the decline of the economy continued, but at a slower pace—3 percent in the second quarter, as opposed to 4.5 percent in the first. The biggest downturn was in the garment industry and in consumer durables. Investment in production was also contracting slowly. There was a substantial increase in housing construction for wealthy customers in suburban areas. Thousands of beautiful homes, sometimes small palaces, made their appearance in picturesque areas outside of Moscow. Most of this work was done by construction crews brought in from Ukraine, Belarus, and Yugoslavia. Naturally demand for building supplies, tools, and equipment increased. Major urban construction projects were also being carried out, especially in Moscow. Foreign trade continued to expand, both imports and exports, with a favorable trade balance of $15 billion, which helped to service Russia's foreign debt. The decline of production in electric power, ferrous metallurgy, and even heavy engineering came to a stop. The exchange rate of the ruble improved. At the beginning of the year it had been 5,400 rubles to the dollar, but from June to December it remained steady at 4,600 to the dollar. Of course, with prices generally continuing to rise, people's savings lost value; as a result people used any surplus income they had to buy foreign currency, rather than trust in Russia's savings banks.

During the third quarter of 1995 the decline of industrial production practically stopped. It remained at about the same level as the second quarter (98–102 percent of the level in April). The grain harvest, however, was substantially below average, and the number of livestock declined. Inflation continued, so that by September prices had risen by 100 percent for the year. The number of people living in poverty continued to grow, as did unemployment. The birth rate declined and the death rate rose.

There had been hopes that 1995 would mark a turning point, but that did not happen. In the press, economists appraised the results not only for the year, but for the whole five-year period. It was generally agreed that an economic collapse of such proportions had not been seen since the civil war of 1918–21. Gross domestic product in 1995 was about 40 percent of what it had been in 1990; industrial production was 42 percent of 1990; agricultural, 65 percent. Capital investments had fallen to only 28 percent of those in 1990. These figures (published by *Ekonomicheskaya Gazeta*, 1996, no. 2) were disputed by some economists, who presented statistics indicating that the downturn was even greater. Production was down substantially in some branches of extractive industry but also in the processing of raw materials intended for export to the West. Yet earnings from these exports paid for the consumer goods being imported. Oil production, for example, was 307 million tons in 1995, or 58 percent of the 1990 level.

High technology production in many areas was on the verge of extinction. Some very important centers for fundamental and applied research had been destroyed, and the brain drain continued at a threatening pace.

Over the five-year period the system by which the country had provided its own food supply was brought to the verge of destruction. In industry, iron and steel production had been reduced by 40 percent in five years. The production of trucks in 1995 was 39 percent of the 1990 level; of tractors, 10 percent; of combines, only 6 percent! Production of synthetic fiber was only 33 percent of the 1990 level; of refrigerators, 47 percent; washing machines, 25 percent; color television sets, 15 percent; tape recorders, 10 percent. The production of textiles was 21 percent of 1990, and of shoes, only 14 percent. Figures like these, testifying to a general breakdown rather than "successful reform," could fill many pages (as they do in a special section of *Pravda-5*, 1996, nos. 3 and 4, entitled "The Orphan Economy" [*Besprizornaya Ekonomika*]).

Disregarding the special features of Russia's economy, ignoring Russia's history and the difficulties of its geographical position, the "reformers" succeeded over a five-year period in creating a situation of virtually unparalleled difficulty.

In some regions the "reforms" produced genuine disaster areas. This was especially true of the coal-mining regions of Vorkuta and the Kuznetsk Basin (Kuzbas). Another disaster area was the Ivanovo-Voznesensk textile-manufacturing region. It was affected by reduced levels of production and delivery of cotton from Uzbekistan, while at the same time Russia was flooded with cheap textiles from China, Turkey, Korea, and Vietnam. Among the newly impoverished areas were almost all the former top-secret centers of scientific research, which had previously been closed to foreign visitors, including certain "atomic cities" and many research centers near Moscow and Novosibirsk.

The rural regions also found themselves in an extremely difficult situation. In the past, state farms and collective farms had suffered from forcible government requisitioning as well as from planning quotas that were impossible to meet. Now there was often a simple refusal to purchase the products of Russian agriculture. For example, 70 percent of Moscow's food requirements were being met by imports from Europe, North Africa, and the Near East. In other major cities the share of imports in the food supply varied between 30 and 50 percent.

The weaknesses and inadequacies of the Soviet economy were no secret to many economists. No less than half of Russia's industrial capacity needed radical modernization or conversion. Our "science cities" did not always function efficiently. The condition of roads and communications systems, and the quality of services in the Soviet Union, hardly bear mention. Problems like these needed to be dealt with, and a reform program was necessary. But such problems could not be solved in one year or even several years. The Russian economy at the end of 1995 could be likened to a sick person in whom the doctors have discovered ulcers, tumors, and other diseased conditions that could not be eliminated easily, a situation in which it was not at all clear what course of treatment to pursue. The doctors from Yeltsin's government kept fussing over the patient, trying to keep him alive with various injections, but still not knowing what to do to get him back on his feet.

In seeking to explain the failures of what I call the "capitalist thirteenth five-year plan," Gaidar has repeatedly insisted that the legacy of socialism was too heavy, that the "bankruptcy of the socialist system" was the reason for these terribly painful social costs. According to Gaidar, the reforms were begun in the ruins of an economy where the Communists had stolen or sold off everything that could be stolen or sold off. That was why the reformers were unable to stabilize and correct the situation to save Russia and its people from hunger and destruction (see *Nezavisimaya Gazeta*, January 5, 1996).

The economist Galina Rakitskaya gives another explanation for the failure of the reforms:

> The president and his administration quite successfully—quickly and competently—carried out the program of the International Monetary Fund, which envisaged the destruction, to a significant extent, of the Russian economy, the transformation of Russia into a country of the colonial type, with a standard of living for most of the population much lower than before, with mass unemployment, and with an industry incapable of competing on the world market, the transformation of Russia into a source exclusively of cheap labor and cheap raw materials for the First World.
>
> (*Voprosy Ekonomiki*, 1995, no. 6, p. 58)

Rakitskaya's explanation for the painful results of the reforms put through by Yeltsin, Gaidar, and Chernomyrdin is the same one that some of Gorbachev's opponents used to explain the failure of perestroika—it places all blame on Western financial circles and on Russia's political (or geopolitical) opponents in general.

In my opinion, the reasons for the failures of the past decade are to be found in a combination of incompetence and voluntarism, or willfulness, on the part of those in power, their inability to foresee the results of their actions or to forestall negative consequences, their haste and impatience, and their infatuation with grandiose, but unrealistic projects. Lenin's attempt at a "cavalry charge against capitalism" in 1918 was of the same order, as were Stalin's "all-out collectivization" and many of Khrushchev's misguided reforms. Besides this, however, there was another element present in some of the reforms of recent years—a desire to destroy all the previous existing structures, or as Chubais, Gaidar, and Shokhin put it, to bring the Russian economy to a "point of no return." This element comes to mind above all when we review the course and results of the privatization campaign, whose absurd and destructive character seems to defy all rational explanation.

NEW STAGE OF PRIVATIZATION

Privatization had begun early: the process had started during the premierships of Nikolai Ryzhkov and Valentin Pavlov in 1990 and 1991. Continuing and intensifying under Gaidar and Chernomyrdin in 1992–93, privatization led to a substantial redistribution of property in Russia. A large proportion of urban housing passed into private hands. Buildings or structures not used for housing were reequipped and turned into stores, warehouses, offices, cafes, workshops, and so forth, whereas previously they had hardly been used at all for purposes useful to society. A substantial part of the commercial trade, including public catering and other services, also passed into private hands. Despite all the costs of this process its overall results may be regarded as positive. The swift expansion of all kinds of trade and services created millions of new jobs, easing the negative social consequences of incipient unemployment.

In rural areas tens of millions of household plots, summer gardens, and lands allotted for use as orchards or vegetable gardens became the private property of the citizens who worked that land. Both urban and rural inhabitants acquired ownership of about 40 million hectares, which undeniably resulted in improved economic utilization of this portion of Russia's arable lands.

Less useful, and less comprehensible to the population, was the voucher form of privatization. Essentially it provided nothing for the ordinary citizen except annoyance over the great but empty fuss and the unrealized hopes and promises. The government budget, as we have said, did not benefit. Some benefits did accrue to certain broker-ages that bought up vouchers and to some individual businessmen, but this is an area less suitable for economic analysis than for investi-gation by prosecutors. We have already seen that 51 percent of the stock in Uralmash was purchased by a single businessman, but at least he was a Russian citizen.

Certain more questionable purchases were made under the voucher form of privatization. For example, the American aircraft companies Boeing and Sikorsky made use of certain local firms, the MMM Company and Sadko-Arkada, as agents to buy up cheaply one-third of the stock in the celebrated M. L. Mil Helicopter Works. The aim of this purchase was to gain access to technology and designs and also to remove from the world market a dangerous competitor in aviation technology.

In 1994 a new stage of privatization began. Thousands of enter-prises in Russia's basic industries were put up for sale. Formally this was supposed to be done through auctions—but for real money, not vouchers. By this time the Chubais team had set up an apparatus to oversee privatization. Chubais himself never stopped praising his staff for its professionalism and competence. This narrow group of indi-viduals was given practically uncontrolled authority to dispose of some of the largest industrial plant in the world. This was industrial property that had been built up over a period of seventy years, a uni-fied economic complex embracing all levels of social production, dis-tribution, and exchange (as described in Article 16 of the USSR Constitution).

I will not argue that the party-state bureaucracy and economic management staff of the Soviet Union disposed of the property entrusted to it in the best way. Much has been said, and still can be said, about lack of efficiency, excessive privilege, and abuse of power by the ruling circles of the USSR. However, in comparison to the new "democratic" nomenklatura the ruling circles of the Soviet Union now appear as highly diligent and conscientious managers who took care to see that state property steadily expanded if only because their own well-being depended on the effective functioning of the productive apparatus under their control.

In 1992 the situation changed. With Yeltsin's blessing the management of Russia's state-owned property and its privatization was turned over to Anatoly Chubais, to the directors of the State Property Committee, to the Federal Property Fund, and to various subordinate units of the executive branch of government connected with the Committee and Fund. Chubais's team has been zealously protected from public opinion, the press, the work collectives, and also from business circles, from so-called national capital, and from directors of various branches of the economy. This protection has been provided both by President Yeltsin's administrative apparatus and by the cabinet ministers, as well as by the Federal Assembly of 1994–95. Only Moscow was able to preserve its autonomy against Chubais's destructive monopoly, whose activity has been described by the well-informed newspaper *Delovoi Mir* (February 3, 1996) as "secretive and inexplicable."

It is generally understood that the market economy is based on the sacred right of private property. Article 8 of the Constitution of the Russian Federation states that "private, state, municipal, and other forms of property are recognized equally and equally protected." Acquaintance with just a few examples of the activity of Chubais and his State Property Committee will show that this article of the constitution was continually violated during the course of privatization. State property was treated as though it were a burden, like escheated property, property that had been used up and worn out, as useless goods to be gotten rid of as quickly as possible. The process of getting rid of state property proceeded very quickly. As early as 1994 Chubais's staff proudly announced that more than 50 percent of all productive capacity in Russia had passed into private hands. By the end of 1995 the state had sold or delivered into private hands about 80 percent of all formerly state-owned enterprises. The next question on the order of the day was the sale of urban real estate belonging to the government and of economically valuable land: forests, farmland, and land of other types. Several groups of economists have drafted programs for selling the resources beneath the land surface of Russia. Apparently the question of selling Russia's territorial waters, including its rivers and lakes, has not yet arisen.

The motives for this vast selling-off of government property, which has no parallel in world economic history, are incomprehensible. Here and there references are made to the needs of the budget, but the budget received very little from privatization, because the government's property was sold at extremely low, almost symbolic prices. For example, a controlling block of shares in the Northwest Steamship Line, consisting of more than a hundred oceangoing vessels, worth more than $450 million, and an enormous amount of property on dry land, worth more than $400 million, was pawned off for only $6 million, a value equivalent to just one ship. The Hercules plant, located near Moscow, which marketed breakfast cereals familiar to all Muscovites, was sold to the Menatep Bank for only $20,000. (See *Delovoi Vtornik* [the Tuesday business supplement of *Komsomolskaya Pravda*], January 30, 1996.) This was less than two or three months wages for a Western diplomat or correspondent working in Moscow.

The Russian press was brimful of examples of this kind. The sale of very large and important state enterprises went through even when the seller, that is, Chubais's office, knew very well that the buyer was insolvent. For example, the Vnukovo Airlines, which had annual receipts of $400 million, became the property of a company named VIL, which no one had ever heard of and which had assets of only $1 million. Acting as a guarantor in this deal was the Ratobank, which had a total capital, its own and borrowed, of only $30 million. (*Delovoi Mir*, February 3, 1996.)

In a market economy it is a customary practice to sell at low, or almost symbolic prices, if a property is antiquated or a business is debt-ridden and nearly bankrupt. In such cases the new owner modernizes the property, introduces new management techniques, and finds new markets or new incentives to raise the productivity of labor. In Western Europe and the United States almost all employee-owned businesses came into existence through such processes. China purchased dozens of obsolete plants and factories at low prices in industrially developed countries and shipped them home on special vessels. Given the condition of cheap labor in China these properties could produce effectively for the domestic market, and even for foreign markets, for another ten or twenty years. Nothing like that happened in Russia during the years of privatization.

In 1994–95 it was not just antiquated or money-losing operations, whose maintenance was a burden on the state, that were put up for sale;

148

highly profitable enterprises were also sold off. For example, in November 1994 a group of Western investors bought 55 percent of the stock in a famous Moscow candy factory—Krasny Oktyabr (Red October). This was the first case in which Western capital was able to buy a controlling share in a successful and prospering Russian business. After this first instance came many more. A previous case involved the purchase by an American company of 49 percent of the stock in the Moscow textile factory Bolshevichka, Russia's largest maker of men's clothing. This purchase cost the Americans $5.5 million.

Some specialists expressed the opinion that Chubais's office did not know how to correctly gauge the real value of stocks or to take advantage of rivalry among potential buyers. There were other explanations as well. *Komsomolskaya Pravda* recounted in detail how the multinational Philip Morris Corporation was able to buy for $100 million a number of large tobacco factories in the Kuban region of Russia, when other tobacco companies were ready to pay $140–150 million for the same properties. The deal was put through under the direction of Vladimir Shumeiko, who was still an influential politician at the time. Since then many people in the Kuban refer to him, not as Vladimir Filippovich (his middle name), but as Vladimir Filipp-Morrisovich.

Many furniture and woodworking enterprises that were doing quite well were sold cheaply for dollars or marks. Even the largest oil and gas companies in Russia were put up for auction in 1995. In the colorful expression used by several commentators, these "geese that could still lay golden eggs" were being hustled off to market. In this case the buyers had to pay tens or hundreds of millions of dollars, but the companies being privatized had a market value of hundreds of *billions* of dollars. The behavior of Chubais's office in these cases caused bewilderment, anger, and protests within the branch of industry affected. At the end of 1995 the Association of Oil and Gas Industrialists sent a message to Yeltsin and Chernomyrdin noting that market value had been reduced by 50–70 times for enterprises being sold in their branch of industry. The hasty and disorderly sale of shares in oil and gas companies, in the Association's opinion, could result in serious losses for the state and reduced investments in this vital sector of the economy. The Yukos oil company was worth probably more than $2 billion, yet 78 percent of the stock in this company was sold for $350 million.

Bewilderment was the reaction to the sale not only of profitable enterprises but also of obsolete or money-losing operations. These were neither taken out of the country (as China had done) nor modernized. Privatization created no incentive to reconstruct these plants or pay their debts. Most often the buyers themselves did not have the means to carry out modernization. Reconstruction of Uralmash or of the Moscow ZIL auto plant would have required a hundred times the capital used to buy them. If the new owners were small, but greedy private firms, why would they spend huge sums to modernize these plants? In these cases privatization was simply a gift from the state to a private individual at the expense of the taxpayers.

Former Minister of the Economy Aleksandr Shokhin explained to the uninitiated the aims of this phase of privatization. "When we entered the monetary phase of privatization [as opposed to the voucher stage] an obvious clash of choices revealed itself: would it be privatization for purposes of investment or privatization for the budget? The ideal scheme would have been one in which income from monetary privatization could go toward real investment in the economy. This was a road leading directly toward revival of the economy. But the financial and budgetary situation in 1995 forced us to think about the necessity of selling as much property as possible to cover the noninflationary budget deficit" (*Rabochaya Tribuna*, July 15, 1995). Shokhin's arguments cannot stand up to the slightest criticism. After parting with an enormous amount of state property in 1995, Russia made only about $1 billion, or 5 trillion rubles, which accounted for approximately 1.5 percent of budgetary income. This was of little help in eliminating the budget deficit or combating inflation. On the other hand, the government had reduced the possibility of earning income from its own property and had blocked investment in many large and important enterprises.

In an attempt to somehow justify privatization at such low prices, the officials of Chubais's commission stated that no one in Russia had sufficient capital to acquire the biggest "chunks" of publicly owned property. Yet it was necessary, they argued, to create as quickly as possible a stratum of private owners who could manage their newly acquired property more efficiently than the state. This was an illusion. The new owners had neither the ability nor the incentive to manage these cheaply bought enterprises efficiently. The Russian press is full of examples in which the production performance of enterprises was worse after privatization. Nowhere have I encountered convincing examples in which new owners introduced more efficient management. Undoubtedly such cases exist, but there cannot be many of them.

A more troubling aspect of this phase of privatization is that in many cases foreign companies were known to be using Russian firms as agents or false fronts in order to buy up important Russian enterprises. Here are some examples given by one of the directors of the State Property Committee, who became frightened upon discovering the enormous scale on which Russian industry was being sold to Western firms:

> The British company Madrima acquired 19 percent of the shares in the famous St. Petersburg plant Elektrosila. Another 20 percent of the shares in this plant were acquired by a major German firm. Their aim was not to help the plant but to force Elektrosila out of the traditional markets in which it sold its products. . . .
>
> [One] corporation from the United States, through local individuals acting as its agents, bought 30 percent of the shares in the Moscow enterprise Aviazapchast [an acronym meaning Aircraft Spare Parts] . . . .
>
> Through a local dummy firm, Bransvill, the American company Baldwin Enterprises bought more than 10 percent of the shares in a defense plant by the name of Komponent, most of whose production goes to fill military orders for the General Staff of the Armed Forces and the Counter-Intelligence Service of Russia. . . .
>
> Two former citizens of the USSR, M. and L. Cherny, having established themselves abroad, were able to buy, through local dummy firms, 28 percent of the shares in the Krasnoyarsk Aluminum Plant and 48 percent of the shares in the Bratsk Aluminum Plant.

This information was published by the newspaper *Argumenty i Fakty* (1995, no. 22) under a rather expressive headline "The Homeland Has Been Sold Out" (*Rodina prodana*).

Numerous protests appeared in the Russian press when the top-secret government enterprise NIIgrafit [which means Scientific Research Institute on Graphite] was sold along with the Moscow Electrode Works, which was used as the institute's proving ground. This enterprise produces uranium-graphite elements for nuclear submarines and power plants, as well as tips for nuclear warheads and technology for stealth airplanes and the space program. In the opinion of specialists, NIIgrafit was one of the key enterprises at the heart of Russia's military industrial complex. This deal was carried through by a Russian company called Graniks, whose capital had been supplied by a U.S. citizen named Jonathan Hay, a person completely unknown to the business world. Journalists were able to locate this not very wealthy American rather quickly. It turned out that since 1991 he had worked in Chubais's office, heading a department providing expert advice and technical assistance to the State Property Committee. Four other U.S. citizens worked in that department. But who supplied Mr. Hay with the hundreds of millions of dollars used in this purchase?

According to information provided by the Duma Committee on Property and Privatization, by the end of 1993 approximately 500 major Russian enterprises in the fields of metallurgy and machine manufacture, and in the oil, gas, and chemical industries, having a real market value of $200 billion, had been sold for a total of only $7.2 billion and had ended up in the hands of foreign companies, purchased through local dummy firms (see *Rossiyskaya Gazeta*, January 24, 1995). We do not know how much of the $7.2 billion mentioned by Burkov actually went into the government treasury and how much remained abroad in the bank accounts of various intermediaries and sharp operators. The process of selling Russian enterprises to foreign firms at low prices continued in 1995. If we take only the case of one American company, Credit Suisse-First Boston, a transnational at the heart of the Mellon empire, we find that it was able to buy up substantial blocks of shares in more than *eighty* major Russian enterprises, including Norilsk Nickel, the Novo-Lipetsk Metallurgical Complex, the telephone systems of Moscow, St. Petersburg, and Novosibirsk, and even the Leningrad Optical Mechanical Works (Russian initials, LOMO), which produced optical instruments for Soviet spy satellites and launching systems for nuclear missiles.

The intermediary in these very favorable deals turned out to be the Russian Privatization Center, an organization subordinate to the government of the Russian Federation, but headed—according to the newspaper *Moskovsky Komsomolets*—by an American citizen, one Bruce Gardner, and a fellow countryman of his, whose name is given by *Moskovsky Komsomolets* as Boris Bostonets (which means "Boris of Boston"). A third person in this group was a Russian emigre by the name of Leonid Rozhetskin, who was in charge of drafting most of

Russia's laws having to do with privatization. The scandal that began to unfold during the Duma investigation of all these deals and the revelations about them in the press was one of the main reasons for Chubais's resignation (see *Moskovsky Komsomolets*, February 7, 1996). Boris Shilov, writing in the newspaper *Delovoi Mir* (February 12, 1996) summed up Chubais's work:

> It is understood that the work Chubais carried out was done by government order. But it was done crudely, without the necessary qualifications, and with an inclination toward laxness. He does not deny the very serious charges against him, even after his resignation, but instead conducts himself with great self-assurance, sometimes even arrogance. Why? Because he knows too much and feels that he is protected—that is the only possible answer. But here, too, he is going astray. Under any new government—a government of the left or of the right or a coalition government—under any, he will have to answer for his actions. It is to be hoped that the Attorney General's Office of Russia, having undertaken an investigation of the privatization process, will not limit itself to exposing isolated infringements of the law or put the blame on "the little man." This would only be a way of covering up for the main actors in the drama.

A question arises about what was behind Chubais's activity. It is the same question Shilov raises in the title of his article: "Economic Illiteracy or Malice Aforethought?"

The scandal involving the Mellon firm, incidentally, did not put a stop to the sale of military enterprises. According to the League for Assistance to Defense Plants, at the very end of 1995 preparations began for the sale of a famous planning and design office, the Sukhoy, and of certain production installations connected with it, where aircraft are produced for the Russian Air Force, Navy, and Civil Defense. On top of that, Anatoly Chubais was brought back into the government and given an even higher post than his previous one.

THE NEW RUSSIA AND THE WEST

Hope of receiving economic aid, with no strings attached, from the developed capitalist countries proved illusory. Western governments and financial institutions, even when providing credits at high interest rates, set increasingly strict, sometimes humiliating terms. The U.S. Congress, for example, to this day refuses to give Russia "most favored nation" status, although such status has long been granted to China and the Eastern European countries. Russia has not been allowed to join GATT (the General Agreement on Tariffs and Trade), which embraces nearly 120 countries. This kind of discrimination is especially inappropriate because Russia itself has given its Western partners every conceivable and even inconceivable kind of advantage, and not only in trade.

Western business organizations were unable to resist temptation in the years 1992–95 when Russian properties were being sold for a song. If the port facilities at Novorossiysk were being offered for sale for only $22.5 million, if the famous Krasnoye Sormovo shipyard in Nizhny Novgorod was valued at only $21 million, what were Western buyers to do? Be offended at the low price and demand that it be raised ten times, or fifty times, higher?

It is difficult to estimate the overall size of Western acquisitions in Russia's economy, because many deals were made by "Russian" firms fronting for Western ones. What has become known, however, is mind-boggling and arouses feelings stronger than mere concern or anxiety. In some cases the aim of the Western buyers was clearly to gain control of potential competitors. In others, their aim was to acquire high technology and trained personnel.

Not surprisingly, Western governments were interested above all in technology developed by the Soviet defense industry, which had previously been top secret. Yevgeny Primakov, who was head of Russia's foreign intelligence service in the period 1992–95, reported to his government at the end of 1994: "On the whole, the West has acquired new technology from Russia on such a large scale that NATO has established a special program to process it all. . . . As part of this program there is an organized effort to invite Russian specialists to help classify this newly obtained technology to conform with European standards" (see *Pravda-5*, January 19–26, 1996). Often the aim of Western businessmen and politicians has been to increase the delivery of Russian raw materials to the West.

Together with the process of privatization, the delivery and sale to the West of oil, gas, and metals (aluminum and others) increased markedly. The export of timber and all other types of raw materials also increased. Certainly the export of raw materials had existed before that. Without exports it would have been hard for Russia to plan on restructuring its economy. But in some cases from 1992 on Russia began to export resources it might better have held back for later sale at a better price or sold in smaller quantities. This applies to timber, unprocessed diamonds, and at least some of the oil and gas that was exported. Our own diamond and woodworking industries might have been expanded to make use of these raw materials.

No small part of the exported raw materials was sold to various middlemen at prices considerably below those prevailing on the world market. Besides that, much of the foreign currency earned from these exports went into private accounts in Western banks. As a result, it was not Russia that grew richer, but various enterprise directors, commercial middlemen, and officials in the Ministry of Foreign Trade and other parts of the government. Some of the earnings from exports went to pay for imported food and consumer goods rather than Western technology or know-how. Many of these imports were not particularly needed and a goodly number were of poor quality, including perishables whose expiration dates had passed. The very large scale of alcohol imports had the effect of undermining the government budget (since the sale of domestic alcohol had traditionally been a government monopoly and a major source of revenue). The sale of an enormous quantity of imported food products undermined domestic agriculture, including private farmers. Sometimes competition from imports stimulated our native producers to do better, but more often the Russian competitor lost market share and was forced out of business.

The Gaidar team deliberately introduced this kind of competition, although they did not publicize the fact. Among themselves they were more candid. They would say, confidentially, that if Russian agriculture and industry were unable to compete with the West, so much the better. They would rather let such inefficient production be ruined than try to reorganize it or provide government aid. Russia could be supplied with food and consumer goods, they felt, in exchange for the natural resources it was exporting. This was the policy of the Yeltsin-Gaidar government, and it was undeniably harmful to the long-term interests of the Russian economy.

Under the privatization program many Western companies were able to gain control of some quite efficient and productive Russian enterprises. Having gained such control, they were naturally concerned above all with their own interests, not those of the Russian economy. We can take as an example the operations on the Russian market of one of the largest transnational corporations, United Technologies, which established itself quite confidently in some previously top-secret parts of the military and space industries. Through subsidiary firms in Russia, United Technologies took control, for example, of Energiya, an industrial and scientific conglomerate in Moscow which produced rocket engines for the space program but which had fallen on hard times. A joint venture was established by an agreement signed in the United States, for the purpose of development, production, and sale of RD-120M, formerly a top-secret engine that now has been exported to the U.S. A director of United Technologies' space program stated not without satisfaction: "The first Russian serial-production rocket engine in history has been delivered to the United States" (*Pravda-5*, January 19–26, 1996).

Joint ventures like this did not always choose the best model for research, development, and production. Pratt and Whitney, a subdivision of United Technologies, gained control of the Ilyushin Aircraft Complex and also "came to the rescue" of two impoverished Russian firms, Perm Motors (formerly known as the Sverdlov Works) and a company called Aviadvigatel (meaning "Aircraft Engine"; formerly the Perm aircraft engine manufacturing enterprise KB). As a result, production of the PS-90, the best aircraft engine in Russia, was shelved. This engine had been developed jointly by the skilled personnel of the aircraft industry in Perm and the Central Institute for Aircraft Engine Production (which had been declared bankrupt even though the Russian government owed it more than 19 billion rubles). In place of the PS-90, the American company's design went into production—even though the American engine cost $12 million, while the Russian one cost only $1.5 million and matched its rival in terms of reliability, noise level, fuel consumption, and other qualities (see *Pravda-5*, January 19–26, 1996). A great many examples of this kind are recorded in the Russian press.

According to data provided by Russian economists, 55 percent of the consumer market in Russia had been taken over by foreign companies or their Russian subsidiaries by the end of 1995. This figure had been expected to rise to 70 percent in 1996. Russian producers of food products and other consumer goods were being driven out of the market, and so were such giants of the heavy engineering industry as Uralmash, Izhorsk, and Kramatorsk. "Don't let ourselves be turned into a raw-materials appendage to the West!" warned Ivan Silaev, the former Russian premier and current president of the Machine-Building Association of the CIS (in *Delovoi Mir*, December 5–11, 1994).

Quite a few painful blows have already been dealt to the Russian economy under the guise of Western "aid." In 1992–93, Russia was virtually forced out of the world arms market, although Russian weapons systems were often better and cheaper than Western ones. In 1994–96, with great difficulty, Russia reestablished itself as an exporter of arms. Without such exports it would be difficult, if not impossible, to carry through a conversion of military industry to civilian uses. Russia has not been able to use the advantages it has in the market for space technology or the peaceful uses of atomic energy. Only with difficulty was Russia's Ministry of Atomic Industry able to defend its contract with Iran to build a nuclear power plant in that country against objections by the U.S. government.

The West also waged a surreptitious campaign to discredit Russia's financial structures: "In Russian business circles the opinion is growing stronger that the demonstrative Western friendliness toward Russia is hypocritical. They like us as long as we make no attempts to stand on our own feet. Our slightest move toward lifting ourselves off our knees results in a blow to the head. . . . They don't hit someone that's lying down. They hit them trying to get up" (*Komsomolskaya Pravda*, December 20, 1994). No large sums of foreign currency were earned by selling shares in Russian industries to Western firms. Often the money brought in was enough only to pay some debts of the Russian company and to meet its payroll, but not for very long. This was no substitute for direct investments. In recent years there has been a slowdown in the economies of the advanced capitalist countries. Bankers have encountered difficulties in placing capital investments and have been forced to lower interest rates. They have very large reserves of investment capital, but hardly any of it has flowed into Russia. Russia's unstable economic and political conditions are only partial explanations for the caution displayed here. Direct Western investment in the Russian economy was $1.4 billion in 1993, $1.05 billion in 1994, and $1.85 billion in 1995 (see *Delovye Lyudi*, January–February 1996, p. 52). Under normal market-economy conditions, no country would refuse foreign capital investments. Western investments in China in recent years are valued at tens of billions of dollars. But Russia has been slow to establish a system of laws covering foreign investments, and this is just as important to potential investors as political stability.

Among Russian economists, the country's increasing indebtedness is also a cause for concern. Criticizing the administration of Nikolai Ryzhkov, who was Soviet premier under Gorbachev from 1985 to 1990, Yegor Gaidar has often complained that he began his reform program with a government treasury that was empty and with a huge debt to Western creditors. But Gaidar fails to mention that since 1991 Russia's indebtedness has not been reduced, but in fact has doubled.

In 1985 the Soviet Union's foreign debt was not large. The USSR's role in the world economy was primarily that of a creditor nation. Soviet leaders gave generous credits to their allies of the Comecon countries and to such Third World countries as Iraq, Ethiopia, Angola, Nicaragua, and Southern Yemen. During "perestroika" (1985–1991) the Soviet foreign debt grew quickly. Some economists considered this quite normal and even urged Gorbachev to borrow more from Western creditors, because it would be possible, they argued, to simply pay interest for decades, rather than immediately repay the loans in full. Gorbachev was dubious about such advice. Nevertheless, in the difficult situation facing the Soviet economy he turned more and more often to Western creditors for assistance.

By the beginning of 1991, the total Soviet debt was $71 billion. This was not an excessively large amount in proportion to the number of inhabitants of the USSR and the size of its gross domestic product. The IMF determines a country's creditworthiness in terms of the size of its foreign trade and its overall trade balance. Before 1986 the Soviet Union exported more than it imported, but a sharp drop in world oil prices in the spring of 1986 (from $30 per barrel to $10) changed the picture. Prices fell proportionately for natural gas, which was the USSR's second most important source of foreign currency. Imports should have been reduced, but the government could not bring itself to take such measures, because that would have affected people's living standards. For all its difficulties, the Soviet government had no serious problem in paying its debts, although to do so, it had to borrow further from Western banks and deplete some of its gold and hard currency reserves.

When the Soviet Union dissolved, Russia assumed most of its foreign debt. At the beginning of 1992, Russia's foreign debt was $69 billion. (Data concerning foreign debt comes from materials provided by Zhores Medvedev and from the newspaper *Delovoi Mir*, November 27–December 3, 1995.) The new government team headed by Yegor Gaidar apparently nourished the illusion that Russia's debts might be written off in exchange for political and economic reforms that were favorable to Western interests.

Past precedents did exist in which debts had been written off when positive political changes took place, particularly in Greece, Turkey, Portugal, and Spain, during those countries' transitions from dictatorship to democracy. Likewise, in the case of Poland, some debts had been canceled. But in all these cases, the debts had been incurred by intergovernmental agreement and serviced through the so-called Paris Club of creditor nations. Debts to commercial banks are serviced though another creditors' institution, the London Club, and they as a rule are influenced less by political considerations. The situation had been more favorable in regard to the Polish debt—although it amounted to more than $40 billion—because 74 percent of that debt was to Western governments and only 26 percent to commercial banks. The structure of Russia's debt was much less favorable: only 22 percent of it was paid through the Paris Club, while 78 percent derived from the London Club (with involvement by more than 600 private commercial banks). There were no strong financial grounds for writing off the Russian debt. Russia's "credit rating" was quite high and kept going higher as its favorable trade balance increased, reaching $18 billion in 1993.

Gradually the illusions about a possible writing-off of Russia's debt dissipated. In order to increase its foreign currency reserves, Russia began selling oil and gas to other former Soviet countries at world market prices and in exchange for dollars only. This drastically reduced deliveries of these energy sources to Ukraine, Belarus, and other countries of the "near abroad" because they did not have dollars. Oil exports to the "far abroad" were stepped up, raising the level of profits from export. Also, the number of Russian companies licensed to export oil, gas, and the like was sharply reduced. This measure was intended to restrict the flight of Russian capital, which was ending up in foreign bank accounts. Foreign currency trading inside Russia was forbidden, and all the stores that had appeared in Moscow, St. Petersburg, and other major Russian cities to sell imported goods for foreign currency (mostly joint ventures) were told they could sell only for rubles. Import tariffs were raised, and strict measures were imposed for collecting taxes on foreign currency transactions. Certain favorable terms for foreign investments were introduced, and some foreign banks, including Chase Manhattan, were given the opportunity to open branches in Moscow.

Western investors preferred not to carry out financial transactions through Russian commercial banks, whose number had risen above two thousand. Thus, the presence in Russia of foreign banks with reliable reputations was expected to help increase the influx of investment capital. These measures did have some effect, and the hard currency reserves of Russia's Central Bank and other financial institutions began to increase.

In 1993 Russia's foreign debt was $82 billion. In 1994, this grew quickly to $120 billion—an increase of 46.3 percent. By the end of 1995 the debt had reached $130 billion, and at the end of 1996 it was $150 billion. This is the biggest debt owed by any country lacking a convertible currency. By 1997 Russia's debt to the West had reached $900 per capita and continued to grow.

In early October 1994, at a regular session of the IMF in Madrid, the Russian delegation was waiting for a decision on the release of credits that had been promised earlier, in 1993, and on the rescheduling of current debt payments. Russia hoped these payments could be extended over a ten-year period, with a five-year moratorium on repayment, effective immediately. These hopes were dashed. Neither credits nor rescheduling of payments was forthcoming. The IMF experts had concluded that no real structural transformation had yet taken place in the Russian economy. In their opinion, the unemployment rate was still "too low" and no "inefficient" enterprises had been allowed to go bankrupt. The average consumption level in Russia had even risen, they complained. (This was because of imported consumer goods.) "Capital flight" remained high, and the self-indulgent life of "new Russians" abroad had already become legendary.

Commenting on the IMF meeting, the London *Financial Times* (October 4, 1994) wrote: "The message from Madrid is that the world cares less about Russia and is less well disposed toward it than many in its government had thought." Western financial officials were annoyed by the Russian willingness to live at others' expense. The prevailing attitude was to let the Russians solve their own problems.

From a creditor nation Russia had been transformed, by Gorbachev's perestroika and Yeltsin's "reforms," into a country living on borrowed money. Even under the most favorable of circumstances the people of Russia are doomed to financial dependence on the West for the next 15–20 years. And how can we count on favorable circumstances?

In order to change this situation, ruinous financial and economic policies must be altered. In particular, a policy of government regulation and intervention in the economy must be adopted. The market, as the experience of the last several years has shown, is not able to allocate resources rationally. The Yeltsin government, however, is in no hurry to change its policies. Instead, it continues to lead the country toward financial and economic disaster.

A DISASTER FOR THE HEALTH OF RUSSIA (AND A DEMOGRAPHIC DISASTER)

[This section is based on materials provided by Zhores Medvedev.—R.M.]

The economic decline in Russia, accompanied by reduced living standards for most of the population and a drastic reduction in all forms of social protection, has had serious consequences for the health of the Russian people.

In 1988 the population of the Russian Federation was 147.4 million. According to data from the World Health Organization (WHO), there were 1,569,112 deaths in Russia that year: 732,710 men and 836,402 women. (The disparity in these unhappy statistics reflected the simple fact that there were 9.4 million more women than men.) By 1992 the population of the Russian Federation had increased by only 300,000, but there were 1,807,444 deaths that year. Moreover, this was the first time since the period of World War II (1939–45) that more men than women had died. In 1993 the trend continued, although the death rate for women also rose sharply. In 1993, deaths from all causes reached 2,129,339, of which 1,112,689 were men and 1,016,650 were women.

There had been times in the past when an increase in the death rate had been observed—most recently the decade 1972–82. But in 1985 the death rate moderated, especially for men and children, and average longevity increased. In 1990 this trend began to reverse, and by

161

1992–93 the Russian nation was experiencing a demographic disaster, for the death rate began to significantly exceed the birth rate. The only reason the population as a whole did not grow smaller was because Russian refugees from Central Asia, Transcaucasia, and the Baltic region made up the difference. If the influx of refugees had not camouflaged the picture, the population of Russia by 1995 would have declined by 2 million.

Only in the famine years of 1932–33 and the Stalin terror of 1937–38 did the Russian people suffer such losses during peacetime. The artificial nature of this demographic catastrophe is indicated by the fact that the sharpest increase in the death rate was not among children and the elderly, as usually happens when a country suffers a sharp decline in living standards because of economic difficulties. It was among men of working age.

The death rate for children from 1988 to 1993 did not change in relative terms, but it did change absolutely—it declined because of a lower birth rate. In Russia in 1993, 25,946 children died. At the same time among men aged 35–54 the death rate nearly *doubled*. In 1988, 287,223 men of that age died, and 90,191 women. During this period the average life expectancy for men dropped from 64.8 to 58.9, with the sharpest drop occurring in 1992–93. In 1994, according to data from the World Health Organization, life expectancy for men fell to 57.7, and it barely started to rise again in 1995–96. In average life expectancy for men Russia not only lost its place among the economically developed countries, where it had already been in last place. It exceeded the parameters for practically every country whose death rate for men had until then been close to Russia's.

In the case of comparable death rates in Africa, the occurrence of death is mainly among male children or elderly males. The only countries where men of working age die at the Russian rate is in African countries with prolonged civil wars (Angola, Sudan, Somalia).

The high death rate in Russia cannot be explained by economic factors alone. After the dissolution of the USSR, the economic situation in Kazakstan, Ukraine, and Belarus, for example, was worse than in Russia. But life expectancy for men did not drop so drastically in those republics. In Kazakstan, from 1988 to 1993 life expectancy for men fell from 64.7 years of age to 61.3, and in Belarus the corresponding figures were 67.0 and 63.8. In Ukraine the decline in life expectancy was less, from 66.6 to 65.0. In Eastern and Central Europe life expectancy fell for both men and women, but the difference was a matter of months, not years.

A question naturally arises. Why is it that Ukraine "paid" for the transitional period of economic reforms with one year off the life expectancy of its men, and Belarus about three years, while Russia "paid" *seven years*? Making things worse, of all the countries undergoing "reforms," Russia also suffered from the most severe decline in birth rate.

There is no direct connection between the economic conditions in a country and the health of its population, although of course on the average people live longer in wealthy countries than in poor ones. Such factors as climate and national peculiarities of diet and lifestyle affect the health of a population no less than income level. In Europe, the poorest country—Greece—leads the pack in average life expectancy for men, 75.5 years of age. The wealthiest European countries, Sweden and Switzerland, whose per capita GNP is three or four times larger than that of Greece, have the same life expectancy for newborns but lag behind Greece in life expectancy for older males. In Spain, men live longer than in Germany, Denmark, or Britain, although Spain is twice as poor as any of those countries. Gerontologists explain these differences by the more favorable climate of the Mediterranean and the Greek and Spanish habit of using olive oil rather than butterfat. They also credit the southern Europeans for their healthy custom of the siesta, a two-hour rest or sleep in the afternoon. In recent years another positive factor has been noted: it seems that wine, when taken in moderation, helps lower the instance of arteriosclerosis.

France holds the record in Europe for longevity among women, with a life expectancy of 82.3 years of age—over ten years more than Russia's in 1993. In the Western Hemisphere, Canada is ahead of the United States in health statistics, although the United States not only has a larger per capita GNP but also spends three times more of its GNP on health care and medicine.

On our planet the region of greatest demographic catastrophe is unquestionably Africa. The average annual per capita income in most African countries ranges between U.S. $110 and $500, that is, it borders on the most extreme poverty. The largest African country, Nigeria, with a population of nearly 100 million, had a life expectancy for men of only 53.5 in 1993 (for women, the figure was 55.9). The worst health statistics for a country not suffering from civil war were in Tanzania. Owing to a crisis of indebtedness and an unsuccessful attempt to make a transition from "African socialism" to a market economy, the country was bankrupted and the annual per capita income fell to $110. Average life expectancy for men also fell from 50.0 years of age in 1987 to 41.5 in 1994.

Among the larger countries of Asia, the worst situation was in Bangladesh and the best in Japan, where in 1980 life expectancy for men was 76.5 years, for women, 83.1. But the standard of living in Japan is lower than in the United States or Western Europe despite the comparable per capital GNP, because a greater part of income goes to savings and investment. In Japan, pensions are small, there is a six-day workweek, and workers receive only two weeks paid vacation (in contrast to Germany, where they get six weeks). The Japanese spend three times less per person on health care than the United States. In Japan, there is one doctor for every 570 persons; in the United States, one for every 390; in Russia, one for every 225. Nevertheless, men in Japan, on average, live 4.3 years longer than men in the United States. And many years longer than men in Russia. Japan's advantages apparently stem from several factors: the absence of unemployment, a homogeneous ethnic composition, and the predominance of fish rather than meat in the diet. Japanese also drink less alcohol.

Why, then, have Russian men been dying so much earlier? The Russian press almost unanimously blames the excessive use of distilled alcoholic drinks, especially vodka. Similar explanations were presented in a survey of Western experts (published in the *British Medical Journal*, no 310, 1995, pp. 646–648). Indeed, Russia holds first place in the world for annual per capita consumption of pure alcohol—14.5 liters in 1994. In the 1970s the consumption of alcohol was higher in France and Italy (17.6 and 16 liters, respectively)—though, to be sure, this was in the form of wine. These countries are now paying for those excesses with Europe's highest death rate from cirrhosis of the liver.

According to international statistics, there is not a direct link between the level of alcohol consumption and the average length of life. In fact, an increase in the consumption of alcoholic beverages usually reflects a rising standard of living. Alcoholic drinks are of course not among the prime necessities of life. Thus, spending on alcohol is higher in countries where people have more money left over after the basic necessities. In the 1970s the number of people recorded in medical institutions as suffering from alcoholism was highest in the richest country, the United States, and reached as high as 5.4 million (with an annual per capita alcohol consumption of 11 liters). In France, the annual per capita consumption of alcohol reached a peak of 22.6 liters in 1968, and the figure for those suffering from alcoholism was correspondingly high (1.5 million). In Russia at various times between 1980 and 1991 the number of people on record as being under treatment with a diagnosis of alcoholism was between 2.5 and 2.9 million, relatively less than in France or the United States.

In Western countries the recognition that alcoholism endangered public health resulted in a systematic increase in taxes on the sale of alcoholic beverages and tariffs on wine and vodka imported from other countries. Thus prices for alcoholic beverages rose continually and invariably exceeded the rate of inflation.

In the USSR from 1970 to 1982 the increased consumption of alcohol was also related to the generally rising income of the population. But in 1985 Gorbachev, instead of using the tested method of raising prices, decided to drastically restrict the production and sale of vodka, wine, and even beer. This led to a completely predictable increase in the illegal production of alcohol, and by 1987 the production of "samogon" (homemade vodka) exceeded the production of vodka at government-owned distilleries. The incidence of alcoholic poisoning also rose accordingly.

The era of drastic economic reform in Russia in 1992–93 differed markedly from generally accepted practices until then, both internationally and in the Soviet Union. During those two years, (and to a lesser degree in 1994–95 as well) the consumption of alcohol increased greatly under conditions of precipitous decline in the monetary income of the population and a decline in the standard of living by a factor of two or three for most of the population. For nearly half the families in Russia income fell below the "survival minimum." Yet at the same time, consumption of alcohol increased rapidly, and the same thing occurred with cigarettes and other tobacco products.

The press tends to maintain the absurd theory that there is an inclination among the Russian people as a whole to abuse alcohol. Any nation is capable of drinking too much—especially if it is government policy to promote such behavior. The sharp rise of alcoholism in recent years can be directly linked with government policy. In early 1992, President Yeltsin issued two decrees. The first abolished the government monopoly on vodka production and introduced complete freedom, an unprecedented absence of restrictions, on all forms of sale of alcoholic beverages. No other country in the world has every had such free and unrestricted sale of alcohol. In no time there suddenly appeared dozens of new kinds of vodka of unknown origin, and they were sold everywhere, out of boxes, and from booths set up on the streets and along the highways. At the same time the unrestricted import of alcohol, free of any tariffs, was permitted, Also many organizations that previously had nothing to do with the sale of liquor were given special permission to import alcoholic beverages (this included sports organizations, veterans organizations, and associations of invalids).

An enormous flood of inexpensive foreign liquor poured into Russia. Vodka became incredibly cheap. The purchasing power of the average wage fell by nearly half in 1992–93, but relative to vodka it *increased* three times over. This was a quite conscious attempt by the government to encourage the use of alcohol by making it accessible to even the poorest strata of the population. (In 1994 the same was done in regard to imported tobacco products, whose prices, instead of increasing, fell.) The result of all this "opium for the people" was something that greatly surprised Western observers—there were hardly any serious social disturbances in Russia as government-owned property was redistributed in haste and passed into private hands. In Kazakstan, Ukraine, and Belarus these changes took place at a much slower pace, but it was also true that in those three former Soviet republics the incidence of homicide, suicide, death by poisoning, and death from cardiovascular or other diseases was much lower than in Russia. In 1993, Russia took first place in the world in the number of fatal poisonings (48,342 men and 14,555 women). In the number of homicides Russia outpaced the United States not only relatively (per 100,000 persons) but absolutely. In 1993, there were 45,060 murders in Russia, but in the United States, only 26,254. In this regard Russia pulled even with Brazil, although it still lagged behind Colombia, which leads the world in crime statistics.

The shortening of the average life span in Russia cannot be attributed solely to alcohol. In the years 1992–94, death from infectious diseases increased sharply in Russia. Nearly 20,000 people a year die from tuberculosis now in Russia. This is the result of increased poverty and the collapse of the former system of epidemiological and clinical services.

The sharp increase in the number of suicides, especially among men—from 26,796 in 1988 to 46,016 in 1993—can only partly be attributed to alcohol. Latvia, Estonia, and Lithuania hold first place among former Soviet republics in the number of suicides relative to total population. They also hold first place in Europe (displacing Hungary). This is an indication of the extreme social tension in those countries, where economic reforms have been accompanied by mass violations of civil rights, especially in regard to the Russian-speaking part of the population.

The generally poor nutrition or malnutrition being observed in Russia today of course has a major negative effect on the health of the population. According to figures compiled by experts, the average per capita daily calorie intake is 2,100 calories, less than the minimum recommended by the WHO. In the Soviet Union from 1980 to 1985 the average daily intake was 3,400 calories, which exceeded WHO recommendations. In the United States in 1993, the average per capita annual intake was 3,732 calories.

Of course, even the wealthy countries have discouraging problems when it comes to death rates and causes of death. In the years 1992–1994 the United States was the only developed country in which AIDS figured as one of the ten chief causes of death (with 13.7 persons per 100,000 of the population dying of AIDS). Kidney disease and homicide preceded AIDS as primary causes of death. In Japan diseases of the nervous system were among the main causes of death, a reflection of the stressful character of work in that super-disciplined country.

In 1995, after the most trying phase of economic reform and redistribution of property, the Russian government tried to bring order into the anarchy surrounding the production, import, and sale of alcohol. Tariffs on imported alcohol were introduced, and began to rise rapidly. Stricter rules for quality control and regulation of the sale of alcohol were also established. Vodka had played its social role in reducing combativity during the harshest period of the economic reforms, and it was now necessary to restore alcohol's previous function as a source of funds for the budget. This process is likely to proceed rather slowly, and it is to be hoped that the health of the population will improve accordingly—but of course other problems besides that of alcohol will need to be resolved.

5

Russia's New Class

One aim of the market reforms carried out in the last few years was to assist in the rapid formation of a new class of property owners and businessmen who could become a solid base of support for the post-Soviet system in Russia. Although there has been some progress, this goal has not been reached.. It would be premature to refer to Russian businessmen—or the "new Russians," as they are called in the West—as a fully formed social class. We are observing only the first stages in the formation of such a class, the beginning of its consolidation and arrival at self-consciousness.

Nevertheless, it is important to understand how it is that capitalist entrepreneurs are making their appearance in a society in which the heritage of state socialism persists. By what means have large private fortunes been created in Russia? What will the rise of a new class bring to Russia and its economy? These and many other questions related to the emergence of a new social structure in Russian society are at the center of attention for many economists, sociologists, historians, and political scientists. Russia is once again the scene of a social experiment unparalleled in history and on a huge scale. It is not that a capitalist bourgeoisie, taking shape over the course of centuries in the interstices of a feudal society, is creating a layer of government bureaucrats and officials obedient to capitalist class interests while encouraging ideologues promoting laissez-faire liberalism. On the contrary, it is ideologists and government bureaucrats, trained in the depths of a "developed socialist society," who are helping a capitalist bourgeoisie take shape—and hoping to accomplish this in a very short time.

"BUSINESS PEOPLE" IN THE GORBACHEV ERA

While in Hungary and the Baltic countries many previous property owners or their children have returned to make a claim, the "new Russians" have no links with the bourgeois classes of old Russia. The same can't be said, however, about the complex world of illegal business, the black market or "shadow economy," which existed for decades in the USSR and gained great scope during the years of "stagnation," the Brezhnev era. Those active in the shadow economy lived not just by the laws of the market but by those of the criminal world. The legalization of private enterprise opened up major possibilities for them. Nearly everyone who had been sentenced to prison for economic offenses was amnestied. Their years in prison or labor camp now became a source of pride, just as hard labor under the tsars had been for revolutionaries in the past. Few of the kingpins of the shadow economy, however, were able to adapt to legal businesses conditions. The swift growth of organized crime offered them far greater opportunities. That is why any continuity between those active in the shadow economy of the 1970s and the "new Russians" of the 1990s is rather the exception than the rule.

In 1987–88 legal businesses and large private fortunes first began to appear in the USSR. A law "On Individual Labor Activity" (adopted in November 1986 by the Supreme Soviet) permitted the establishment of tens of thousands of small workshops. In Marxist terms, this was only a "petty bourgeoisie," however. There were few opportunities for big business or enrichment on a large scale in that situation. The law "On Cooperatives" was a different matter. Its hidden potential was not apparent even to those who drafted the law. Tens of thousands of cooperatives were soon formed—by private individuals as well as government enterprises and organizations. Commercial and "middleman" cooperatives predominated, but quite a few associations were formed to engage in production or construction. Through the cooperatives it was possible to transform billions of rubles worth of non-liquid assets into cash. The liberalization of foreign trade—that is, the relaxation of the previous government monopoly on such trade—also made it possible to swing commercial deals on a large scale through the cooperatives.

The orders authorizing formation of some cooperatives were signed by top-ranking ministers, even by the prime minister, Nikolai Ryzhkov. Many people who are now part of the Russian business elite made their first millions at that time. They even say it was easier for them to work under Gorbachev than under Yeltsin. According to many present-day millionaires, the years 1988 and 1989 were the most favorable for their businesses. Ivan Kivilidi, who has since been killed, recalled how easily he was able to make money in those years by selling aluminum abroad for dollars, after purchasing it inside the USSR for rubles, then using the dollars to import computers and fax machines. In three or four months $500 would grow into $50,000—or a million rubles would become a hundred million. Brokers could make money even faster. Our first rich people were aided by more than their entrepreneurial talent. They had no serious competition, and they had those all-important "right connections."

By the late 1980s, "shuttle" trade had already made its appearance in the USSR. Tens of thousands of Soviet citizens went streaming into "socialist" Poland, Hungary, or China. (It was still hard to get visas to capitalist countries.) They brought home not only computers and faxes, but also clothing and cosmetics. But to do as the Kivilidis did, to ship to the West flatbed rail cars full of aluminum or raw petroleum—which of them had that kind of opportunity? They had to be content with exporting, in the trunks of their cars, Russian matryoshka dolls, needlework, or mushrooms from the forests of Russia or Byelorussia.

The Komsomol (Young Communist League), the only permitted youth organization for teenagers and young adults in the USSR, with as many as 15 million members in the late 1980s, had been the starting point for anyone wishing a successful career in the one-party state dominated by the CPSU. It began to engage in business ventures quite extensively, of course with encouragement from the ruling party. It was a disciplined organization, and now it was being steered toward profit-making. "My assignment was to become a millionaire," several young people have testified. A new term arose: "the Komsomol economy." (See the discussion of this in the Komsomol magazine *Molodoi Kommunist* [Young Communist], 1990, no. 2, p. 39.)

Government assets could be transformed into ready money through the Komsomol organizational structure, and through this same structure the first commercial banks and stock exchanges were set up, as well as cooperatives for the construction of housing, especially for young people. Impulse, a young people's "creative production association," produced a variety of consumer goods, primarily aimed at the youth market; it also built a children's hospital in Moscow province, in the town of Kaliningrad. The Siberian youth center "Magistral" provided equipment for computer classes and video viewing centers and organized cooperatives for making garments of fur and for processing timber. There were also Komsomol brickyards in Ryazan province, and in Dnepropetrovsk, a Komsomol operation for producing artificial marble and fiberboard panels.

The main source of profit for the youthful entrepreneurs lay elsewhere, however. Komsomol businessmen dominated the show business and video markets, as well as tourism and the gambling business. A substantial part of the super profits from international trade also passed through their hands. The dissolution of the Komsomol, in 1990, a surprise to many, did not damage "the Komsomol economy." By then it was able to get along without the organization's tutelage. Besides, it became possible to put some of the property formerly belonging to the Komsomol into profitable circulation.

Within the government apparatus and in the official structures of the state-owned economy, there was significant activity along similar lines, although it was kept hidden. Many managers and directors were allowed a previously unheard-of degree of independence, and their enterprises were placed partly on a self-financing basis, instead of depending on government subsidies. In place of several ministries, large trusts or conglomerates were formed, Gazprom being a prime example. Government supply centers and exchange centers were reorganized as privately owned trading centers, stock or commodity exchanges, or joint ventures (with foreign firms). Regional banks or banks serving particular branches of the economy were transformed into commercial banks. All this was regarded at the time as part of the economic aspect of perestroika, which was moving toward a market economy. In this connection, however, the leadership of the CPSU did not have a clear conception or program, and it had difficulty in keeping the anarchic tendencies of the market economy under control.

It has been said that the young, aggressive, predatory businessmen who emerged in 1988–89 were among those who dealt the final blow to perestroika, because its ideal of social justice interfered with their aims. (See the article by the historian Vladimir Iordansky in *Svobodnaya Mysl*, 1996, no. 11, p. 3.) The ideals of social justice, however, do not necessarily exclude individual initiative, private enterprise, and private ownership, especially when those are based on the natural, material needs and interests of the population. Restrictions were necessary only in regard to anti-social forms and methods of enrichment: businesses engaged in plundering the wealth of the country and its citizens should not have been permitted. But under perestroika, the necessary limits were not set. The leaders of perestroika went to an extreme in allowing highly parasitic forms of business to flourish.

Among the Russian businessmen of 1988–89 there were really not that many who were purely aggressive and predatory, concerned only with maximizing profits regardless of the cost to society. I met a young Moscow businessman in Rome in 1990 who, after obtaining the necessary credit, had purchased old military transport planes destined for the scrap heap, transferred them to Latin America, and set up a successful air transport company moving cargo between Peru, Brazil, and Venezuela. His pilots were also from Russia, flying at their own risk for no more than $2,000 per month. My acquaintance was on his way to Moscow to buy another dozen planes that had been written off by the Soviet military. He was not troubled by any moral aspects of the business. But he was less of a money grubber than the customs official who relieved him of his massive gold watch, providing no official record of the transaction.

Many small businessmen of the late 1980s were driven by poverty and need, but many were drawn by the possibility of taking initiative, engaging in a form of self-expression. These were people whose talents went unutilized by the bureaucratic-administrative system. People's motives and interests varied widely at that time. We can see this in two typical, but quite different, examples of Russian businessmen of the period 1989–91. There was Vadim Tumanov, who built bridges and roads in Karelia and Moscow that were cheaper and better than those of the state-owned construction organizations; he paid his workers well and made a good profit for himself and his company. Then there was Sergei Mavrodi, who deliberately tricked and defrauded millions of his fellow citizens by organizing an elaborate pyramid scheme (the MMM Company).

THE "NEW RUSSIANS" OF 1992–93

Some use the term "shock therapy" for the changes that occurred in Russia after the downfall of the CPSU and dissolution of the USSR; others call it a "structural transformation"; still others speak of the triumph of a capitalist revolution. However one views it, there is no question that for the business elite, conditions changed fundamentally in 1992–93. The coming to power of the "democrats," the liberalization of prices, and the swift upward spiral of inflation created opportunities for some to get rich quick. A number of foreigners as well as native Russians wasted no time seizing these opportunities. With the demand for dollars rising rapidly, the purchasing power of foreign currency in Russia greatly exceeded its purchasing power in the West. Thus the purchase of almost any commodity at the domestic Russian price, followed by its resale at world market prices, resulted in a quick and substantial profit. Western dealers did not have to operate on an especially large scale, as long as they had dollars or marks, and they came to dominate in the massive buying-up of everyday consumer goods, as well as objets d'art and folk handicrafts, pottery and china, antiques, and musical instruments. Vietnamese citizens who were working in the USSR in the 1980s also engaged in these activities.

When it came to selling major types of raw materials in Western markets—oil, petroleum products, metals, especially ferrous and rare earth metals, lumber and other forest products, chemical fertilizers, and furs—it was Russian citizens, not foreigners, who predominated. They did so because of their positions and connections, enabling them to obtain the necessary licenses and authorizations.

Export privileges made it possible for a number of high-ranking Russian officials as well as businessmen to make huge fortunes along these lines in a short time. Thus, Kirsan Ilyumzhinov, the youthful president of Kalmykia and a millionaire, makes no bones about the fact that he made his millions by selling oil and petroleum products. Konstantin Zatulin, who in 1988 held the modest position of an assistant secretary on the Komsomol Central Committee and who was responsible for promoting the "youth economy," had by 1992 become the chairman of the board of a company called Brokers of Russia, a member of the board of the company Russian Gold, vice president of the Council of Entrepreneurs of the Moscow city government, one of the directors of the Moscow commodities exchange, and an adviser to President Yeltsin on foreign policy and defense.

In export matters, actual business ability played a secondary role. Inside information, connections, and bribes were decisive. In 1992–93, according to the businessmen themselves, no important deal involving timber exports went through without the intermediary services of the *son* of a top official of the former Ministry of the Forest Industry, who did not himself own any company or put his name on any contract. The volume of exports by the gas, oil, and metals industries far outpaced those of the forest industry, but even so, timber exports in 1993 were valued at $1.4 billion. Also highly profitable in 1992–93 was the purchase of real estate. A two-room apartment in Moscow in fairly good condition would sell for $2–3,000, and for $8–9,000 in cash you could buy a good three-or four-room unit.

The legalization of dealings in foreign currency and credit became a major source of enrichment. The government granted credits to agriculture and other vitally important industries at annual interest rates of from 10 to 25 percent. But in most cases the money did not reach its destination very quickly. With inflation soaring at a yearly rate of 2,500–3,000 percent, other uses were found for these credits. If a banker "sat on" the money for a while, using it for foreign currency dealings, he could make huge profits. In the same way money earmarked for the payment of wages to miners, teachers, and military personnel, if it was held up for two or three months, could bring in enormous profits. Even in the military there were financial officers who couldn't resist this temptation. Commercial banks set up foreign currency exchange locations almost everywhere. It wasn't only the wealth of the already existing banks and bankers that grew. The number of banks increased rapidly, and Russia soon emerged as the number one country in the world for the number of banks per capita. Thousands of banks collapsed later on, bringing ruin to many customers, but not to the bankers. They had covered themselves by making big deposits in Western financial institutions or buying real estate—also as far from Russia as possible.

Many bankers or exporters established dual citizenship, not only in Israel but also in every country that facilitates such procedures for well-to-do people who own real estate or have business interests in the given country. Some big businessmen left Russia altogether—for example, Artyom Tarasov, who took up permanent residence in England. Tarasov was one of the first Soviet millionaires. He made huge sums of money as early as 1990–91 through his involvement in the scandal-ridden "Harvest 1990" campaign. Thousands of collective farms at that time delivered to the Russian government quantities of grain above the quota set by the plan in exchange for special government certificates with which they could obtain certain goods that were in short supply and hard to get. Most of these certificates were not honored, but instead large sums ended up in Tarasov's pockets. He went on to work as a middleman, was involved in gambling operations, financed television shows and the lottery called Russkoye Lotto. When he heard that a criminal case was being prepared against him, he fled the country, feeling endangered by the excessive attention being paid to his person by the minions of the law.

The Western press, as early as the 1950s, wrote a lot about "the managerial revolution." In the big corporations top officers were not only receiving huge salaries—as much as a million dollars a year—but they also had the opportunity to acquire company stock on favorable terms. Still, these men did not become owners of the corporation and could be removed from their posts by those who owned controlling blocks of shares or at meetings of shareholders. Similar, but not identical, processes have been under way in Russia. The hasty privatization of state-owned enterprises at very low prices created opportunities for the directors of those firms and others in leading positions in economic management to acquire large "chunks" of formerly state-owned property. It would have been difficult, if not impossible, to carry out privatization against the will and interests of the actual managers of the enterprises. The factory managers as a group did not wish merely to be paid higher salaries. A substantial portion of the shares in the newly privatized firms were distributed among the managers on the basis of a secret subscription list. The former directors did not obtain controlling blocks of shares, but when combined with their influential positions even a block of several percent was enough to make them the actual new owners of the enterprises.

Even in the Gorbachev phase of perestroika, these former directors had been able to successfully adapt to the new conditions. The term "nomenklatura privatization" refers to this reality—ownership of newly privatized firms by managers who had been part of the top-level party-state bureaucracy, the "nomenklatura."

Failure awaited attempts by newcomers or outsiders to obtain ownership of major state-owned enterprises. Take the case of Aleksandr Yepifanov, owner of the private company Mikrodin, who was able to purchase, for a million dollars, 25 percent of the shares in a newly privatized auto plant in Moscow, the ZIL plant. After privatization the functioning of the plant deteriorated drastically; instead of profits there were mounting debts and losses. In this state of affairs, the Moscow mayor's office could not look on with indifference, since the livelihoods of hundreds of thousands of Moscow residents depended on the ZIL plant. In the end, Moscow Mayor Yuri Luzhkov felt obliged to buy up the shares of the plant, which now became municipal property.

A similar situation involved a famous heavy machinery plant in the Urals, Uralmash. The Moscow businessman Kakha Bendukidze, owner of the private firm Bioprotsess, purchased a controlling share of Uralmash stock for only $2 million. He of course was not about to start managing the giant Uralmash plant himself, even when the privatized plant's functioning deteriorated. In fact, Bendukidze soon expressed willingness to sell his shares—although he was asking $1 billion.

Even when 51 percent of the shares in a state-owned enterprise were distributed among its blue-collar and white-collar workers, the directors became the de facto owners. It was virtually impossible to impose new owners from the outside. It made considerable political sense for the post-Soviet regime to allow this merger of power and property in the hands of the corps of former "Red directors": this reduced the strength and intensity of opposition. To have left influential and powerful managerial personnel, who also had experience as party leaders, without property or positions would have strengthened the opposition many times over.

"Property passed into the hands of those most ready to take it. At the same time revolutionary pressure from the masses in favor of alternatives pointing in a socialist direction—such as placing control over the means of production in the hands of the work collectives—proved to be very weak. What can one say? Perhaps it was all for the best," writes Yuri Aleksandrov (in *Novoye Vremya*, 1995, no. 43, p. 19).

Let us note well: *Property passed into the hands of those most ready to take it.* Not to those who had a greater right to it, not even to those most able to use it efficiently in the broader social interest. Nor to those who could pay real market value for it. (Neither the directors nor the "work collectives" had that kind of money.) This unusual mode of formation of a new class of property owners has probably never been seen during the period of formation of capitalist society in any other country in the world.

Different authors take different attitudes toward this unique mode of class formation and toward the activities of Russia's "new class." The economist Aleksei Ulyukaev, a former assistant of Gaidar, writes glowingly about the appearance in Russia of a large number of the rich and super-rich.

"For a long time," he writes, "America was the land of opportunity. People there could make something of themselves, rising from 'pauper to prince.' The fastest careers happened there, the biggest fortunes were piled up, the highest degree of individual freedom was found there, the broadest opportunity for the individual to pursue his happiness and prosper.

"Today Russia is this kind of Eldorado. The fastest careers happen here, and the biggest fortunes are made. Real men of affairs, all those oriented toward success, toward free and unencumbered creativity in their personal lives, are drawn here. For that reason the ideology of practical liberalism, the concept that 'God loves those who work hard and enrich themselves,' not the poor, the downtrodden, the humble, the miserable—these ideas are taking root in Russia and will soon have pride of place here" (*Svobodnaya Mysl*, 1995, no. 3, pl. 53). Ulyukaev seems to forget the God of the New Testament who said it is easier for a camel to pass through the eye of a needle than for a rich man to enter the kingdom of heaven.

Some calmer observations on this subject are made by Olga Kryshtanovskaya, who heads a unit at the Sociology Institute of the Russian Academy of Sciences engaged in research on "the elite."

Kryshtanovkskaya writes:

At the core of Russian's economy is a class of "authorized personnel," owners of major properties to whom the state has entrusted the task of developing a market. The economy operates in the absence of equal "money-making" opportunity for all. . . . The state capitalism of today has *itself* nurtured these businessmen, giving birth from its own inner recesses to this *class of authorized property owners.* This was a positive, productive move. First, these government-authorized owners had a personal interest in making a profit (as did the state, personified in its top officials); second, government-authorized business was guaranteed against bankruptcy and all sorts of disorder and consequently brought an element of stability into the chaos of the market; third, this new economic elite was a natural obstacle in the path of any "plutocracy" that might be formed by the nouveaux riches of Russia, for whom the laws had *not* been written.

(*Izvestia*, January 10, 1996)

Kryshtanovskaya exaggerates the productive qualities of this "authorized class," a class that was not so much nurtured by the government as appointed from within its own ranks. Certainly these operators are different from the nouveaux riches and plutocrats whose praises Ulyukaev sings, those who rose "from pauper to prince." But the "authorized" millionaires, like their counterparts among government officials, have quickly learned how to put substantial sums in their own pockets—whether their businesses are doing well or not. There have been many cases in which operations at a mine, mill, or factory were going from bad to worse, with workers receiving no pay for months on end, while the directors found the money to build themselves luxurious villas or go on vacations to the Canary Islands.

The historian Vladimir Iordansky is more critical:

The tense relations within the "new class" were predetermined by the conditions under which it originated. It is misbegotten and internally disharmonious because its development was unnatural. Upon it lies the ineradicable mark of the post-perestroika government's artificial efforts to promote its existence.

179

. . . Given these circumstances, the predominant characteristic of the "new class" is parasitism.

(*Svobodnaya Mysl*, 1995, no. 11, p.8)

Vadim Kortunov, director of the Humanities Center at the State Academy of Management, has an equally low opinion of Russia's new class.

The new generation of Russian "businessmen" has been formed, for the most part, on the basis of leftovers. Above all these are people incapable of marketing their own intellectual property, incapable of constructive, creative activity. Consequently they are people who have been left on the sidelines by society, in the margins of cultural and spiritual life. . . . They are either former members of the nomenklatura who were in the right place at the right time when their enterprises were privatized, people who found it easy to exchange their "Communist convictions" for the psychology of monetarism. Or else they are openly criminal elements who shrewdly grasped that under conditions of social, political, and legal instability it was more efficient and safer for them to operate by hanging up a commercial sign. Or else they were youthful newcomers who hadn't absorbed what they were taught in school but, to make up for it, were not burdened with any symptoms of the thinking process. . . . This generation of "new Russians" is united by such characteristics as moral nihilism, a total inability to engage in spiritual or intellectual activity, a monetarist psychology, and consequently a parasitic mode of existence displaying the flag of "free enterprise." It is therefore quite logical that the growing prosperity of today's Russian businessmen takes place against a backdrop of overall decline in production, impoverishment of the population, inflation, and the ruination of our country's economy as a whole.

(*Nezavisimaya Gazeta*, December 5, 1996)

These assertions are justified in regard to a great many contemporary Russian businessmen, but by no means all. Recently I became acquainted with the operations of a joint stock company called Izmailovo, which runs a group of tourist hotels in the Moscow suburb of that name. Despite the fierce competition that now prevails in the tourist and hotel business, the very large units at Izmailovo would have been doomed to bankruptcy if the owners of the controlling shares in this complex had been free of any "symptoms of the thinking process." Valery Ryazantsev, the new general director of the Izmailovo complex, has been able to provide excellent services for his foreign and Russian guests and has also transformed the complex into a kind of cultural center for the region. The Izmailovo hotel corporation sponsors interesting exhibits and has shown a generosity toward artists and sculptors that is rare in these times. It is not by chance that many of Russia's parties and social movements, ranging across the political spectrum, have in recent years held their conferences and congresses at the Izmailovo complex. The company's good reputation has helped it succeed in business.

The harshest appraisal of the ways in which Russia's new class has been created belongs to none other than Boris Fyodorov, the prominent politician and leader of the "Forward, Russia" movement.

"It's as though we were present at the biggest robbery of the century," he writes, "perhaps even the biggest in human history. But no protests are heard. Heads are bowed and people are intoning, 'Oh, please, just don't let things get worse.' As if everything was as it should be. Very kind, forgiving, and generous people we are" (*Izvestia*, March 21, 1995).

There is justification of course for the charge "biggest robbery of the century"—although it is strange that Boris Fyodorov became aware of it only after he lost his post as finance minister and vice premier of the Russian government. At the height of "shock therapy" Fyodorov was not only an adviser to Yeltsin on financial questions but also a director at the World Bank representing the Russian Federation. He had many opportunities, particularly in 1992–93, to influence the ways in which Russia's new class took shape, being part of that class himself. Even Gaidar in recent times has more than once referred to Russia's new capitalists as incompetent and thieving—although he relates these negative qualities to the "Soviet upbringing" of these new property owners, not to the haste, incompetence, and lack of system in the program of "systemic transformation" drafted by his own governmental team. The Russian language is rich in proverbs and sayings along the lines of "Haste makes waste." One of them is: "Haste gives birth to the blind." (*Toropit—slepykh rodit.*)

Wealth that is not earned by the sweat of one's brow, whose source one feels must be kept secret, has produced a kind of inferiority complex and fearfulness in many "new Russians," often combined with arrogance and snobbery. It is not surprising that in 1992–93, ruined and impoverished Russia became an exporter of capital to the West to the tune of $20–30 billion, a process that continues to this day. The "new Russians" are afraid to invest their money in the Russian economy, and they don't want it held in Russian bank accounts. Better to buy or build a villa in Cyprus, Nice, or Spain or squander a year's worth of their company's payroll money on a pleasure trip to Italy

"What is this?" asks the political commentator Kirill Kholodkovsky (in *Izvestia*, April 10, 1996). "The inevitable overhead costs of a transitional period, after which everything will gradually settle down and return to normal? Or the outlines of a new kind of system in the making, in which society will have to feed a new type of parasite, shoving Russia's wealth into his bottomless pockets, lining a purse that is usually sequestered somewhere outside our country?"

The answers to these questions depend on the kind of government and economic policy Russia is to have in the coming decade.

THE BUSINESS ELITE, 1994–96

Among the democrats of the first or second wave—those who paved Yeltsin's way to power and helped ensure the swift growth of Russia's new class—hardly any kept their posts in the Russian government after 1993 or their status as part of the business elite. The government and the elite are now closely linked with the "nomenklatura"—the highly placed bureaucrats who dominated the party, government, and economy in the 1980s. Studies by the Sociology Institute of the Russian Academy of Sciences showed that at the end of 1995 as much as 75 percent of Yeltsin's administration and immediate entourage consisted of members of the former Soviet elite—that is, had been prominent in the Communist Party of the Soviet Union, the Soviet government, the Young Communist League (Komsomol), and Soviet economic administration. Also originating in the Soviet nomenklatura were 82 percent of the regional "post-Soviet" elite and 74 percent of the government of the Russian Federation. As for the business elite, 61 percent of it was recruited from the same source, mainly from the Young Communist League or from Soviet economic administration (*Izvestia*, January 10, 1996).

By 1996–97 a fairly stable leading group of Russian entrepreneurs had emerged. In all the listings of the members of this group the experts generally give Rem Vyakhirev, head of Gazprom, first place in terms of economic power and political influence. Of the fifty most influential entrepreneurs in Russia, five came from the gas, oil, and energy sector in 1996, seven in 1997. Dominating the listings were the bankers—twenty-seven of them in 1996, twenty-six in 1997. In the listings we also find three heads of auto companies in 1996 (four in 1997); two from the diamond and gold mining sector; and two from the sphere of commerce and export. Advertising, publishing, show business, the airlines, and ferrous metals were represented by one big businessman each in the top listings. Three heads of diversified companies made the top fifty in 1996; four in 1997. Also on the list, and not in the lowest spot, was Svyatoslav Fyodorov, the world-famous eye surgeon who heads a company called Microsurgery of the Eye. (He is no relation to Boris Fyodorov.]

These listings, based on assessments by experts, are published quarterly by the newspaper *Nezavisimaya Gazeta*. (See, for example, the February 20, 1997, issue of that publication.) Other listings, published by *Delovoi Mir* (Business World), do not differ significantly from these.

Other statistics have taken note of the average age of our home-grown businessmen (36 years), their marital status (few women are numbered among the business elite, only 6 percent of the total), the number of former Communist Party members (85 percent), and their educational level (70 percent have had higher education; 7.5 percent are holders of candidate's or doctor's degrees). (See *Argumenty i Fakty*, 1996, no. 4, p. 6.)

It is much harder to estimate the personal fortunes of the richest people in Russia or their annual incomes, because they try to keep much of this information hidden from the tax collectors. The experts guess that no more than a thousand people in Russia measure their annual profits in millions of dollars. Approximately ten thousand make profits of between $100,000 and $500,000 annually—not that many by American, German, or Japanese standards. To the businessmen themselves, the "rich" are those who make no less than twenty to thirty thousand dollars a month. To the average resident of Moscow, anyone who makes even *one* thousand dollars a month is pretty well off. I speak of Moscow because most of Russia's rich live in that capital city. In the provinces, even five hundred dollars a month is a good income.

The Russian press more often than not writes in a critical vein about the business elite—although the magazines *Delovye Lyudi* (Business People) and *Dengi* (Money) and the newspapers *Kapital* and *Kommersant* (Merchant) are exceptions. The Christian Democrat Viktor Aksyuchits places the blame for the defects of the new class once again on the Communists. His article "The Bright Future of Nomenklatura Capitalism" states in part:

> Capitalists with a Communist Party apparatchik mentality— where has that ever been seen before? All the big fortunes in Russia can be traced to the most varied sources, except for their economic origins. There was always party or Komsomol money or credit on favorable terms from the State Bank or Western credits distributed to the right people, or licenses to export raw materials, or government orders, or delivery of goods on favorable terms, or subsidies, or permission to privatize desirable state-owned properties at throwaway prices—something like this can invariably be dug up as the source of the primary accumulation of capital for all our homegrown nouveaux riches. The question of who would be richer was not decided by objective economic laws, but by a very specific, bureaucratic "subjective factor"— government officials and the personal ties which the future rich had with them. In addition to that, favorable conditions were created for the legalization of businesses run by organized crime. Therefore, when measured by other yardsticks, this form of capitalism could be called bureaucratic-Mafia capitalism.
>
> (*Nezavisimaya Gazeta*, February 16, 1996)

In contrast Western newspapers and magazines have written with unconcealed admiration about the wealthiest figures among the new Russian businessmen. *Forbes* magazine, for example, had an article about Mikhail Khodorkovsky, who it described as "one of Russia's richest men":

> As he sips coffee in his office, the skin of an Ussuri tiger glistens on the floor. . . . Khodorkovsky is all of 31. His first financial backing came from one of the communist-controlled district councils of Moscow. Later, apparently Khodorkovsky bought out the district council. Now this swarthy young man runs a vast conglomerate. It includes the Menatep Bank, a dozen other

banks, Moscow real estate, a steel mill, one of Russia's largest producers of titanium, as well as food processing and chemical companies.

"We don't invest in companies that do less than $50 million in sales," Khodorkovsky smirks. He is a Russian equivalent of the misnamed robber barons who came to dominate American capitalism in its early days—capable, energetic men with vision, but ruthless: Cornelius Vanderbilt, John D. Rockefeller, Andrew Carnegie, James J. Hill, Jay Gould, and J. P. Morgan. These men gained control of vast assets not through theft, as the popularizers thought, but through organizational skills and financial leverage. . . . The Russian robber barons, like their American predecessors, are not creators or builders but consolidators—capitalists in short, rather than industrialists. They are restructuring existing companies into capitalist units.

[Translator's Note: The quoted passage about Khodorkovsky originally appeared in *Forbes* magazine, November 21, 1994, pp. 74ff. The author cites the translation published in *Za Rubezhom* (a Russian-language review of the foreign press), 1944, no. 46]

Two years later the German magazine *Wirtschaftswoche* wrote more candidly about Khodorkovsky. We quote from the Russian translation, published in *Za Rubezhom*, 1996, no. 48, p. 4.

Drops of sweat stood out on the brow of Mikhail Radayev, director of the oil refinery in Samara. But not from the heat. For about an hour he had been showing his guest—an unassuming-looking intellectual type wearing glasses and a tweed jacket—around the refinery. . . . The huge pipes and giant holding tanks made no big impression on the guest from Moscow. To every suggestion by the director about improvements he replied with the same words: "What would that give us? How much profit would that bring?" The director shrugged his shoulders: in Soviet times it had not been axiomatic for a plant manager to know how to produce a profit.

This inspection tour of his empire by the 33-year-old Mikhail Khodorkovsky showed that "the clash of two worlds" is not just a theoretical concept. In only a few years this banker has bought up about fifty enterprises with a work force numbering more than 300,000 (blue collar and white collar employees) and an annual turnover equivalent to more than 12 billion marks. His methods are not always elegant. His prize possession is Yukos, the second largest oil firm in Russia, of which the Samara oil refinery is a part. He bought it from the Russian government, paying much less than it was worth. Ever since the time in 1987 when this Yeltsin supporter, with a university education in chemistry, began selling computers from the basement of a building, he has had good relations with the powers that be. To begin with, he persuaded the rector of his institute to let him open a cafe. Then as a Komsomol activist he persuaded the Soviet government to give him a license to start a bank, thus founding Menatep, one of the first commercial banks in the country.

During the years of hyperinflation up to 1995 the bankers, more craftily than others, with the help of foreign currency deals and credit speculation, when interest rates on loans reached a height of tens of percentage points per day, contrived to make fortunes literally overnight. Here, too, Khodorkovsky went one step further. For a long time he had been helping with complex government financial deals. At one point he was responsible for reorganizing the entire Russian oil industry. In 1992, when privatization of the Russian economy began, he acquired at laughable prices the "tastiest morsels" in the chemical industry, raw materials, and light industry—that is, in those sectors which, in the event of an economic upturn, would be the first to bring in a profit.

In 1992, and even in 1994, it was possible to buy up quite a few businesses at "laughable prices"—if one was in the right position, with the right contacts and resources. But getting them to work efficiently was another question. Khodorkovsky promises to accomplish this over the course of "no more than . . . a few generations." It so happens that I own several shares in Khodorkovsky's company called Moscow Real Estate, but it has not earned even twenty kopecks worth of dividends for my family and myself. Consequently I have a different opinion about how decent and competent these new financial magnates are. What is this company doing for its shareholders? I don't know how accurate it is to use the term "robber baron" for the founders of America's biggest financial and industrial dynasties, but it can be said with certainty that neither Morgan nor Rockefeller, neither Carnegie nor Vanderbilt were assisted in the early stages of their business careers by any district committees of the Young Communist League or municipal district Soviets. (The term "Soviet," which of course originally meant "workers' council" and was a representative body consisting of delegates from various factories and other workplaces in a city, was still used for local government bodies, such as city councils and municipal district councils in the Soviet Union, but after the early 1920s they were dominated by the single ruling party, the CPSU.)

LIFESTYLES OF THE RUSSIAN RICH

Hardly any of the magnates listed as the richest and most powerful will display their wealth openly in impoverished Russia. They are more concerned with guards and security. Most of the denizens of the night clubs and casinos, expensive restaurants and deluxe saunas are not part of the top one thousand wealthiest Russians.

For all who have risen above a certain line a Mercedes 500 or 600 has become de rigeur: in the years 1992–1996 in the Moscow region alone, more of these models were purchased than in all of Europe over a ten-year period. Every month in Moscow three or four thousand apartments in exclusive buildings are bought by "new Russians." In recent years thousands of red-brick fortress homes have been built for "new Russians" in the suburban areas near Moscow, and similar construction has been under way on a smaller scale in other regions. Much larger sums have gone for the purchase of real estate outside of Russia. The most popular countries are Spain, the United States, Cyprus, Portugal, Greece, and France, but the "new Russians" have not overlooked Switzerland, England, Italy, Canada, Germany, and Austria. Besides houses and lots, they are also buying securities. Russian businessmen have invested billions of dollars in American and German banks.

The "new Russians" also love to travel. In 1994 their spending on tourism in countries outside the former USSR amounted to about $7 billion—that is, more than the IMF loaned Russia in 1995. Experts estimate the total amount spent on personal consumption by the Russian rich at $45 billion—several times more than Russia's annual spending on military and defense needs. (These figures come from the Sociology

Institute of the Russian Academy of Sciences and were published in *Izvestia*, March 13, 1996, and *Argumenty i Fakty*, 1996, no. 44.)

Most of Russia's rich do not appreciate attention from their own mass media. Some of them have been willing to open their palace doors to Western correspondents, but were unhappy to see reports from the Western press reprinted in Russian publications. Vladimir Bryntsalov, for example, was at first glad to see the dozens of photographs in the French magazine *Paris-Match* and the German *Bunte* showing the luxury he lived in. The French magazine reported:

> Vladimir Bryntsalov is one of the richest men in Russia. His personal fortune is estimated at $1.5–1.8 billion. Bryntsalov lives, eats, and dresses like a tsar. He is protected by 20–30 bodyguards armed to the teeth. His villa is located not far from Moscow. It is a palace of gold, every corner of which glistens with wealth. He seems to have everything: antiques, icons, table service of gold, crystal, paintings by old masters—no fewer treasures than in the vaults of the Kremlin.
>
> He has ordered furniture from Versace, luxurious chandeliers from Baccard, and Russia's best icon painters have decorated the ceilings of his palace rooms with images of the saints. The inlay work on his walls comes from his own workshops, the porcelain for his feasts is of his own manufacture, and the silk cloths are from his own textile mills. Thus he lives with his tsarina, Natalya. She is his second wife and has blessed him with a son and heir, Prince Alyosha, and an heiress, Princess Alena. Three governesses—two English and one French—keep his heirs busy learning to speak foreign tongues fluently. He also has a daughter by his first marriage, for whom he is building a palace of carrara marble near the Kremlin.
>
> How is it possible to become so wealthy so fast without being a criminal? After putting together his first million, Bryntsalov began buying up pharmaceutical firms one after another. He says, "I concentrated on pharmaceuticals, because medicine is something everyone needs." Today he owns a holding company that produces 30 percent of all medications in Russia.

(The passages above are translated from the Russian version of the *Paris-Match* article, which appeared in *Za Rubezhom*, 1996, no. 10, p. 10.)

Bryntsalov was quite unhappy when, in early 1996, the *Paris-Match* article appeared in Russian—in many regional papers, as well as *Za Rubezhom*. At that time he had just entered the presidential race after announcing formation of the Russian Socialist Party under his own leadership. The aim of the party, he declared, was prosperity for the Russian people and for Russian capitalists. The program of his party states, "A socialist government would serve two masters, His Majesty the Russian people, and Russian capital." It also says that birth certificates should state the bearer's nationality. In other words, in a Bryntsalovan Russia the government, not the family, would decide what a child's nationality is. The voters did not show much support for this billionaire "socialist." He received less than 0.5 percent of the vote.

THE MOST IMPORTANT BUSINESS FOR RUSSIA— CONSUMER GOODS PRODUCTION

According to Russian businessmen themselves, their biggest profits in 1995–96 came from trade, especially trade in raw materials, foreign currency, electronic goods, and real estate. Second-highest earnings were in banking. The third-ranking position went to government service. Certainly government salaries, even for top officials, are not that big. But the businessmen know what they're talking about. According to privately circulated surveys that businessmen have responded to anonymously, 91 percent claim that in any dealings with the authorities they are obliged to pay bribes. Fourth place in the list of top sources of income was held by the brokerage business, which earlier, in the years 1992–93, was the quickest way to get rich. Fifth place was assigned to theft. Strange as it may seem, this category is broken down into several subdivisions, not only by Russians but also by Western businessmen. Hardly anyone among the really substantial men of commerce would buy a stolen fur coat or car, although it has been known to happen. There are other stolen goods that are easier to deal in: for example, museum pieces, icons, paintings by Russian or Western masters, rare books. And no one feels a pang of conscience about buying carloads of nonferrous metals or tanker cars of oil that have been diverted from the (usually state-owned) enterprises producing them. Sixth place in the list of most profitable businesses goes to real estate; seventh to consulting. Not until eighth place do we come to a type of business that is fundamental for any healthy economy—consumer goods production.

Hardly any of the "super-rich" can be found among those who have established successful consumer-goods or construction companies and maintain them at a high level. People in these fields aren't even in the second or third rank as far as wealth and political influence go, though this is where the major part of what is customarily called "national capital" is concentrated. Productive business people of this kind find it harder than others to evade taxes or register their corporations outside of Russia—in Cyprus, for example. Many of them are able to stay afloat only because they themselves advertise and sell the goods they produce. The term "new Russians" is rarely applied to these people.

Take for example the firm Agrodorspetsstroi (an acronym meaning "Rural Roads Special Construction") headed by Pavel Golyshev. The work it does is very difficult, but very much needed. Like Vadim Tumanov, mentioned earlier, Golyshev builds roads. By early 1994 his company had built more than a thousand kilometers of road. But it did not bring in very large profits, and Golyshev was forced to diversify. His company began cutting timber and mining gold in remote parts of Siberia. Its productivity, and the wages it paid, were three or four times higher than those of state-owned enterprises in this area. Nevertheless, his business was given no special treatment by the banks or the government.

"Yes, we are prospering and moving ahead," Golyshev has written. "But how much effort it has cost us! We've been oppressed by senseless tax policies, nonpayment of bills, and the unbridled behavior (*bespredel*) of the banks. We would have been able to develop much further and bring in much more if it hadn't been for these harsh economic conditions. It's nearly impossible now to work productively and profitably, and soon we'll make it completely impossible" (*Delovoi Mir*, April 23, 1994).

The Doka Pizza Company, which began operations in 1991 with a capital of forty thousand rubles, within three years owned dozens of pizzerias and restaurants in Russia and other former Soviet countries and was producing and selling dozens of lines of potato chips. This firm, with its headquarters in Togliatti, in Samara province, is headed by Vladimir Dovgan. It has produced and delivered to all parts of the country hundreds of miniature ovens for baking various kinds of breads. They were no worse than imported ovens, but were six to seven times cheaper. The company has also issued stocks and securities, which have done well and brought in earnings for the shareholders.

"Feeding people is the most reliable and stable business," says Dovgan. "Judge for yourself. There are 160 million people in Russia, who spend a large part of their income on food. Besides, with a minimum of investment there is a big volume of business and maximum return on investment" (*Argumenty i Fakty*, 1994, no. 16, p. 15).

Anis Mukhametshin, founder of a company called Anis, draws the same conclusion. His first endeavors were in show business, and he is still a leader in that field, but he branched out and made a fairly substantial investment in ice cream. Taking just one of his plants as an example, it produces as much as 180 tons a day of ice cream that is of excellent quality but sells for half the price of imported Western ice cream. Anis has also built a cigarette factory outside Moscow, plus a distillery for liqueurs and cognacs and a pharmaceutical plant. Here too his products are several times cheaper than their imported Western equivalents. He recently completed construction of an ice cream plant in a suburb of Moscow, while in Tatarstan there is a big soft drink plant that produces "Anis Cola." He does not, however, operate on the "robber baron" model of either Andrew Carnegie or Mikhail Khodorkovsky, much to the regret, no doubt, of *Forbes* magazine. Here is what the magazine *Delovye Lyudi* (June 1995, pp. 25, 29) wrote about Mukhametshin:

In his youth this 42-year-old Tatar passed through "the Uzbek school" of life in the former Soviet Union, one of the harshest forms of schooling one can imagine. He was hardened by the continuous round of pitiless and exhausting battles in that "school," and in this respect he differs fundamentally from most Russian entrepreneurs, who tend to fall into nervous paralysis at the slightest unpleasantness. Many of the habits of the lone wolf remain with Anis to this day. He does not trust hangers-on or consultants, nor cooks, drivers, and bodyguards. He is always alone, both at his business and behind the wheel of his armored Mercedes, and there is no cavalcade of guards' cars rushing along behind him. His home is always full of guests, and rather than burden anyone else, Anis himself cooks pilaf and shurpa [a

Tatar dish] for them. . . . Many of his old friends have been in Europe or America or South Africa for a long time—they prefer to cultivate their businesses on less stony soil, under a kinder sun. Anis builds his factories and houses here, as well as his mosques and churches and theaters, and a school for deaf children, the only one of its kind, not in order to leave the country some day. He does this in order to stay.

Almost all types of textile products are the output of the Russian company Paninter, with which I personally became acquainted in March 1996. The firm is headed by Aleksandr Panikin, a mathematician by education, who in the recent past worked as an administrator in the theatre world. He started out in business in 1988 with some garment-making machinery and 25,000 rubles. By 1994 the Paninter textile plant was producing more than a million items per year with a work force of 700. Efficient organization of labor, high productivity, but above all high quality standards—these have ensured quick sale of the company's products. Here, too, the prices have helped. They are two or three times lower than comparable imported Western goods. The best Russian clothes designers are working for Paninter, and all its products are marketed through its own network of stores. Goods received are sold within two or three days. All this is at a time of seemingly insoluble crisis for Russia's textile industry, whose warehouses are bursting with unsalable goods. Paninter outlet stores have been opened in St. Petersburg and Krasnoyarsk, in the Urals, and in other regions. Production is expanding quickly, and not only stitching and weaving. In the distant suburbs of Moscow, the company has established a commercial farm, from which dairy products are already being delivered to Russia's capital.

Additionally, Paninter runs the Center for Practical Free Enterprise, which has already graduated several classes of students hailing from many different parts of Russia. The company also gives large sums to charity. Two hundred retirees living near the Paninter plant receive regular pension payments, and the company has created green spaces and other improvements in the neighborhood, including aid to the schools and to a children's sculpture center. Paninter also sponsors round-table discussions and other public events. A newspaper called *Paninter* carries major articles by leading political figures from many different points of view, as well as material about the firm itself.

Aleksandr Panikin is actively engaged is seeking ways to bring Russia out of its present crisis. His proposals are debatable—especial ly the one about helping successful Russian companies become transnational corporations. He is convinced that such a venture would succeed, given government support. But there are certain stages of growth that a market economy must pass through, and they cannot simply be skipped over.

There is another firm, the Hobbit Company, whose successful operations I have observed for the past several years. It was founded in Moscow by several young science researchers who were friends of mine and former parliamentary assistants. The company began with furniture making, but switched over to mass production of all types of "mini-garages" (basically, plastic shells). It produces and installs as many as 2,000 mini-garages per month—without any prepayment or additional fees required. In 1995–96 Hobbit established ties with a successful German firm and organized the production of plastic windows and doors that provide good sound and heat insulation. The Hobbit Company is also expanding into advertising, providing services in this field to many companies in Moscow, St. Petersburg, and even Berlin. In the first two years Hobbit increased its work force from thirty to three hundred, and in the next two years the number grew to one thousand.

In discussing the productive entrepreneurs of Russia, we should say something more about Vladimir Bryntsalov. It is true that his lifestyle and many of his public statements, which are deliberately intended to shock, have damaged him as a public figure. But the way he built his business operations was not through currency speculation or special access to cheap credit. The medications he produces are the result of a total revamping of the Karpov chemical and pharmaceutical plant, which had fallen into decline. It is true that a state-owned enterprise Mosmedpreparaty (acronym for Moscow Medical Preparations) did transfer a unit to Bryntsalov, or sold it to him for practically nothing—the Antigen plant, which is located on a large plot of land (80 hectares). In this instance I do not condemn Bryntsalov. Hundreds of enterprises privatized from 1993 through 1995 have ended up being less economically productive than before. That is not true of Bryntsalov's businesses, which are part of a conglomerate called FAO Verein.

There are many other companies working successfully and productively in Russia. They include industrial plants, advertising agencies, publishing and information companies, and self-supporting (i.e., nonsubsidized) hospitals and clinics. These successful Russian enterprises, in almost all cases, have connections with Western companies in one form or another. Paninter, for example, uses high-productivity Western equipment in its plants. Golyshev's company has purchased Swedish enrichment processes and equipment and Italian road-building technology. Doka Pizza uses organizational methods pioneered by McDonald's and Coca Cola. The Anis Company places orders for equipment and even labels with Western firms. The Hobbit Company cooperates with the German firm UEKA. It uses German technology, and also sells that technology in many parts of Russia. We should make a distinction between businesses like these and the purely parasitical operations of the comprador type, which are committed only to making profits for their Western corporate masters and which are the worst type of Russian business today. The examples above show that intelligent and mutually beneficial economic integration is possible.

SMALL BUSINESS

An enormous field of free-enterprise activity in Russia today, and in many cases the most important, is constituted by medium-sized and, especially, small business. But this sector enjoys hardly any support from the Russian government, the big banks, or the "free-market" reformers.

As one author, A. Neshchadin, has noted:

> After small business emerged as a significant factor, the promises of the Gaidar government to support this sphere took the form of outright suppression of virtually any free-enterprise activity. If the legislation on free enterprise in the Gaidar era is compared with that under Ryzhkov it is easy to see that current legislation blocks virtually any possibility for small business to develop. This applies to the systems of registration and taxation as well as the system for monitoring the conduct of operations.

(*Izvestia*, September 21, 1994)

The predictions of Marxists in the late nineteenth and early twentieth centuries that small and medium-sized businesses would inevitably be squeezed out by giant monopolies have not come true. Even today in the developed countries small- and medium-sized businesses are the main component of each nation's business activity and the chief hope for the healthy development of business in general. In Western Europe from 50 to 80 percent of the gross national product comes from small- and medium-sized businesses.

There is little hope that true entrepreneurs will develop among people who do not start their businesses themselves, relying on their own material and financial bases and drawing on their own abilities and initiative. The school of business, like all others, has its own lessons that must be learned and stages that must be passed through. If a class of entrepreneurs is to take shape in Russia, its core will consist of people who started their businesses at their own risk, using their own financial means or the credit they were able to obtain. Thus far in the upper strata of the Russian business class, such people are few and far between. They are to be found predominantly in small- and medium-sized enterprises. But it is precisely in this sector that many feel obliged to go out of business after two or three years of hard work and trying experiences, because they did not receive the support that small and medium-sized businesses most frequently need in order to last through the first phases of their development. It seems that in this area, too, the post-Soviet Russian government is experimenting according to the principle "sink or swim."

The number of enterprises that can be counted as small businesses are defined in different ways by different authors, using different criteria. The Russian Economics Academy estimates that by the end of 1995 there were about 900,000 small businesses in Russia, employing about 9 million people (*Voprosy Ekonomiki*, 1996, no. 7, p. 39). The biggest growth in the number of small businesses was seen in 1992, but in the years since then the rate of growth has declined considerably, a decline connected with the very high rates of taxation, from 60 to 90 percent of all profits. The largest number of small businesses were in the fields of commerce, science, and the servicing of scientific institutions, public education, and several other areas where it was easier to avoid tax pressures. In consumer goods production, agriculture, and other sectors of greater importance to society, small businesses found the going much tougher.

195

In 1995 and 1996 the number of small businesses in commerce, science-related fields, and public catering also began to dwindle. Even the most radical parties from the Communist part of the spectrum are now trying to exploit the disastrous situation for small business, calling on the "proletarians of the business world" to support them.

For example, in the Communist publication *Glasnost* (October 11, 1996) we find:

> The proletarians of the business world cannot be forgotten, those 20 or 30 million small property owners, traders, people doing "shuttle" commerce, owners of trucks, small booths, shops, or studios, people who sell doughnuts or hawk things from trays around their necks, people who, following their own desires or (more often) forced by the will of harsh circumstance, have plunged into the abyss that is normally called "business" in hope of surviving, making it, feeding their families, and maybe acquiring some wealth . . .

> It has already been forgotten for some reason that the formation of cooperatives was encouraged by the Communist Party in the 1980s, that that was the best era for those who dreamed of having their own business but didn't have the capital for it: it was easier then to obtain credit or to rent space, and the arbitrariness of government officials was kept under strict control. The small property owners no longer understand that, were Communists to hold the reins of power, things would be simpler and better for them. . . .

> The existence of small- and medium-sized businesses (and the prospering of the same) is an unstoppable process, like the growth of bamboo. A fairly large number of theoretical precepts and practical examples confirm that the world of small business is perfectly compatible with Communist ideology and the socialist cause.

I do not know about "Communist ideology" but as far as the programs of most socialist parties are concerned, they do favor the development of small business and its coexistence with socialism. However, people in this field still remember only too well the foolish campaign against "unearned income" conducted by the ruling Soviet Communist Party in 1986, as well as the anti-alcohol campaign of 1985–90 and all the persecution of small business from the 1930s through the 1970s. That is why people in the small business sector did not support the Communist Party of the Russian Federation in the 1996 elections.

The many difficulties and few achievements of small business were topics of discussion at the First All-Russia Congress of Representatives of Small Business, held in February 1996. The participants heard quite a few promises from government spokesmen, but the fates of most small businesses continue to be governed by the "sink or swim" principle. Yet all serious economic analysts are warning the government that support and development of small business should be a top policy priority. It is not just that small businesses are playing an increasingly vital role in the national economy, that they can become and in some cases already are the fastest growing sector. The most important aspect of small business is that, more than any other branch of the economy, it can ensure stability in society, both politically and economically.

Only small business can ensure the quickest possible return on investment and the most efficient use of resources. Yet even those small businesses that have the greatest possibilities for rapid growth and major innovation have not received the necessary government support.

Today we are all surrounded by or drawn into some form of business activity. One of my friends, after losing his job with a district committee of the Communist Party, began using his own sedan, a Zhiguli, to deliver flour and sunflowers produced by relatives in the Kuban region to members of his wife's extended family in the colder, more northern region of Vyatka. Today he is the owner of a Kamaz truck and a Mercedes van. He has a store in Stavropol where he sells goods from the north of Russia and one in Kirov, where he sells products from the south. As many as twenty people work for his small company, whose operations make life better for hundreds of customers.

Another acquaintance of mine, a former CPSU employee, organized a warehouse for the storage of paper products and runs a retail business dealing in office supplies. Several young people I know, unable to maintain their families on their miserable salaries as engineers or researchers, took up the "shuttle" trade, organizing their own stores, located in their homes, as part of the process.

Many of the people I know personally are engaged in small business. One of my acquaintances, a journalist, organized a successful

197

advertising agency. I know physicians with private practices, publishers, owners of book shops, brokers, and jewelers. An acquaintance of mine is a private farmer, who has an apartment in Moscow and does a successful truck gardening business on two hectares of land with the help of a mini-tractor and a number of contrivances that he invented himself. Six months out of the year I myself work in my thousand-square-meter garden and orchard, providing my family with a year-round supply of vegetables and berries. I prepare my own books for publication without benefit of editor or censor, paying for each small print run myself and selling them through intermediaries. I also see to the syndication of my own articles in Russia and those of my twin brother, Zhores Medvedev.

This is a reality that is in some ways better, some ways worse, than the previously existing one. None of my friends and acquaintances consider themselves "new Russians." Necessity, as a rule, was the mother of their business ventures, but these have helped fortify them in the present day and prepare them for whatever reality tomorrow may bring.

A BALANCE SHEET

Healthy entrepreneurship is just taking its first steps in Russia. The experiment begun in 1991 of producing an entrepreneurial class by hothouse methods has not been especially successful. No such class has yet taken shape. In fact, the process of formation is just beginning, and it is proceeding in a way that is very painful for our society and country. The Russian bourgeoisie, large, small, and medium, remains a class "in itself," to use Marx's terminology, rather than one "for itself." That is, it is not united by an enlightened self-awareness, but is divided into various groups and strata, not only by social position, income, and mode of operation but also by competing interests. The tone is set by the most egoistic and parasitic groups, which have fattened on the ailments of society and continue to do so. Rather than contribute to overcoming society's difficulties, they aggravate the ailments of our economy.

The super profits of its business elite do nothing to enlarge Russia's economic possibilities. Rather, they have the effect of constricting its domestic market. Research by the Institute of Systems Analysis of the

Russian Academy of Sciences has shown that even today the main income of the elite neither seeks nor finds application within Russia, but "goes West" at the rate of $2–3 billion per year. (This was reported in the newspaper *Finansovye Izvestia* [Financial News], November 12, 1996.)]

Russia is unable to break out of a vicious circle: while its own economy is declining, it continues to serve as a donor to the economies of the West, resulting in greater domestic and foreign indebtedness. The Russian government, by increasing the tax burden, makes Russian goods less competitive, thereby shrinking the tax base for its own budget. As a result there is a persistent danger of generalized bankruptcy. Against this background the elation expressed by Chubais at the end of 1996—over the fact that more than half the property in Russia was in private, rather than government, hands—seems rather strange. It is all too reminiscent of the glowing reports in the early 1930s of success in the campaign for "total collectivization."

A round table discussion, sponsored by the magazine *Rossiysky Obozrevatel* (Russian Observer, 1995, no. 1), took up the theme "The 'New Russians'—What's Russian About Them, and What's New?" Some participants in the discussion likened the present situation to the sinking of the *Titanic*. Once the ship's officers knew that all was lost, all the best delicacies in the restaurant were given out free, champagne flowed like water, and the orchestra played till it could play no more.

"Everything the 'new Russians' do indicates lack of confidence in the future," said one of the participants, Anatoly Utkin. "Their social irresponsibility will be their undoing . . . They don't represent any positive idea Getting rich as an end in itself cannot serve as a social ideal." The Russian *Titanic* is already sinking, as Utkin sees it. Some of the 1500 passengers have made it into the far too few lifeboats and are heading for foreign shores; others are perishing in the icy seas. But the "new Russians" are unaware of the danger. They are playing banking games, selling fuel, or popping into other people's cabins to grab things left behind. Perhaps it is true that they are displaying a lot of energy and initiative, but in their greed they are the most irrational passengers on the doomed liner. "Their energy," says Utkin, "might have been used for constructive purposes, but they are standing on the captain's bridge trying to direct the orchestra instead of trying to stop leaks or provide lifeboats for the weakest and most defenseless."

Another dark side of Russia's new class, in addition to the egoism and social irresponsibility typical of many of them, is their connection with the criminal world. In 1994 the Institute of Applied Policy did a study on the question "The New Millionaires." In the course of research and investigation approximately 40 percent of those surveyed admitted they had previously been involved in illegal business dealings; 22.5 percent admitted they had been taken to court because of this; and 25 percent at the time of the survey still had connections with organized crime. And we are only talking about those who *admitted* illegal connections. Unfortunately, the criminalization of Russian society has proceeded much more quickly in the last seven or eight years than the development of legitimate private business.

PART 2

THE ELECTIONS OF 1995–96

AND THEIR AFTERMATH

6

Duma Elections, December 1995

During much of 1995 and 1996 public attention in Russia centered on two sets of elections: for the parliament, or State Duma, in December 1995; and for president, in June and July 1996. These elections did not lead to any change in regime or in the character of the government. They did, however, reveal much about the disposition of political forces in Russia, the nature and influence of the main political parties and groups and of the individual leaders.

Russia's "Third Republic," born in the bloody events of October 1993, lacked legitimacy. The first Duma elections, in December 1993, were conducted in extreme haste, before the new constitution had been adopted. Society had not yet recovered from the shock of the bombardment of the building that housed the Supreme Soviet. Some political parties and groups had been banned during the 1993 elections, while many prominent political figures had been in prison. The regime needed new elections to gain greater legitimacy, but it also feared the possible outcome of elections.

Yeltsin had been elected in 1991 to a five-year term as president of the Russian Federation, but the constitution he had sworn to defend had been annulled by his government.

DUMA ELECTIONS

In outlining a series of social, economic, and political measures for 1994–95, Yeltsin and his entourage, together with the Chernomyrdin administration, were sure they could change direction and improve the social and economic conditions in Russia. They proposed to stop the decline in production and stabilize finances, and expected market mechanisms to start working full force. This would strengthen the regime's political base.

But it did not happen. The economic situation kept growing worse, and financial stabilization remained as elusive as ever. Discontent mounted, while the political groups that had consistently supported Yeltsin and his government grew weaker and began to fall apart. The unpopular war against Chechnya (begun in the winter of 1994–95) with its heavy casualties and severe setbacks aroused opposition even among "democrats" who had always supported Yeltsin.

All this caused concern in the president's inner circle, and proposals were made to postpone or cancel the elections. But such a step would have required political and ideological resources that the Yeltsin regime no longer had. To many in his circle, the risk entailed in any use of force or threat of dictatorship was greater than the risk of democratic elections.

On top of that, Yeltsin's health kept getting worse. Nevertheless, and with some doubt and hesitation, Yeltsin announced that the elections would be held as stipulated by the new Russian constitution: Duma elections in December 1995; and presidential elections in June 1996. Thus, the Duma elections became a test of strength and a dress rehearsal for the more significant presidential elections. From the spring of 1995 on, all the political events in Russia and all realignments of political forces were viewed and analyzed by political observers from the point of view of the upcoming election campaigns. In particular, the pollsters began to assess the standings of the various parties and candidates.

Two years earlier, in the Duma elections of December 1993, the parties and groups supporting Yeltsin's government had suffered a palpable defeat: they had failed to win control of the Duma. The parties of the left had not won control either. At best they could swing about 30 percent of the vote. Small groups in the center of the political spectrum had taken different tacks at different times, while Zhirinovsky's Liberal Democratic Party of Russia (LDPR), one of the largest groups in the Duma, had supported the government rather than the Communist opposition on all the most important questions.

A special factor was the role of Ivan Rybkin. As a leader of the Agrarian Party he had been elected Duma chairman, but he soon went over to the Yeltsin camp. In 1991, Rybkin had led the "Communists of Russia" group in the Russian Supreme Soviet. In 1992, when the Socialist Party of Working People was founded, he became one of its co-chairs. In 1993, he switched parties and became a deputy chair of the CPRF and a leader of the Agrarian Party. Making one more switch, in 1994 he became one of Yeltsin's closest cohorts. Both Communists and Agrarians denounced him as a turncoat, but attempts to remove him as Duma chairman were in vain. The right-wing bloc, the center, and the LDPR supported him. Most groups in the Duma found him amenable, especially because he managed to obtain unheard-of benefits for all Duma members, supplying their offices with all sorts of hi-tech equipment for communications and other purposes.

The adherence of Rybkin meant a lot to Yeltsin and Chernomyrdin, but it could not compensate for the general disarray on the right. The Russia's Choice Party soon lost whatever authority it had, and the smaller groups of "democrats" broke up into warring factions. Yeltsin needed some sort of new organization, and so the government, rather than being formed by a party, set out to create a party to fill the void beneath it. President Charles DeGaulle of France had acted in a similar way in the 1960s, creating his own Gaullist party to support his regime.

The government officials in the Kremlin and on Old Square were much taken with the idea of creating a "party of power." Many felt inspired, convinced that at last they had the key to all the government's problems. A political scientist, using the pen name "N.B.," analyzed the Yeltsin's camp's strategy:

The idea of a "party of power" is the ingenious product of Yeltsin's entourage. If brought into being, such a party could keep

205

the intransigent opposition from gaining access to any real power. Meanwhile, the present ruling stratum, by ridding itself of the ballast of the "democrats," could avoid a crushing political defeat.

Political life in Russia is not very highly structured. Its most structured component is the state apparatus, the government administration. There, all structure is quite clear and reliable. In view of the ordinary Russian citizen's inclination, fostered by decades of Communist rule, to support the existing regime, it can be assumed with considerable certainty that a substantial portion of the electorate will indeed vote for the "party of power." Only accident could prevent such a party from winning in the presidential elections.

In the Duma elections, the chances are also high that such a party could win leading positions in the lower house of parliament. In the center of power, this party would control the main television channels and radio stations, as well as several daily newspapers. It would have no great problem obtaining the financial means for its election campaigns. Its main constituency would be in the government administration and in the "power ministries" [defense, security police, interior ministry troops and police], among those working in the "budget sphere" [services or occupations supported by the government budget] and in state-owned enterprises, a section of the entrepreneurial class, and most ordinary "loyal citizens." Consequently, such a party could win no less than 30–35 percent of the seats in the Duma.

(*Levaya gazeta*, 1995, no. 31, pp. 4–5)

Of course, there were doubts and hesitations about this strategy. The government and its actions had become increasingly unpopular. Who could guarantee that a "party of power" would succeed with the voters? Nevertheless, in the spring of 1995 Yeltsin warmly supported the idea and announced it publicly. At one of his press conferences he stated, as if in passing: "We have decided to establish two big political parties of the center. One will be a party of the right center; the other, a party of the left center. The first might be headed, for example, by Chernomyrdin. The other by Ivan Rybkin." Together, these two parties, as Yeltsin saw it, might be able to garner more than half the votes in the Duma elections.

Yeltsin's wish for a "party of power" was Chernomyrdin's command: he immediately began taking practical steps to bring such a party into being. As for the "party of the left center," a kind of loyal opposition, that was a different matter. There were already several parties opposing the government from various points of view. The creation of one more, and a *tame* opposition at that, simply wasn't feasible. Anyone who took up Yeltsin's assignment was bound to lose face, and it was only with reluctance and after much delay that Ivan Rybkin began the effort. Though provided with ample resources, he was unable to produce anything by the fall except a diverse and not very numerous conglomeration of several dozen small, uninfluential groups. They couldn't even agree on a name, and in the end the party registered as "the Rybkin Bloc."

Chernomyrdin did better, though his results were not brilliant either. The founding conference of the new "party of power," which was given the name Our Home Is Russia (Nash Dom Rossiya, or NDR), was held in May 1995. Chernomyrdin of course became the party's leader. Its executive body was made up of top government officials, as was its membership both centrally and locally, but there were also factory managers, directors of banks and insurance companies, chief administrators of libraries, top physicians at hospitals, rectors of universities, and the like. Three main goals were singled out in the NDR program: "a strong state," "liberal foundations for the economic life of Russia," and "appreciable social measures."

Virtually every politician and political party in Russia entered the Duma election campaign. The number of political groups vying for the electorate's attention reached as high as five hundred.

Gaidar's Failure

On the right wing appeared a Bloc of United Democrats: Yegor Gaidar's party, Russia's Choice; Yuri Chernichenko's Peasant Party; Aleksandr Yakovlev's Party of Social Democracy; and the Congress of National Organizations of Russia. This was the core group of "democrats," to which most ministers of the first Yeltsin government had belonged. This bloc paid the price for the failures of that government, for the *bespredel* (lack of restraint; lawlessness) that accompanied market reforms, for the "shock therapy," for the fleecing of investors, for all the unfulfilled promises.

In spite of all that, the Russia's Choice representatives were able to form a fairly solid bloc in the 1993 Duma. By 1995 their bloc had weakened. Several prominent figures had left, among them Boris Fyodorov, Mikhail Poltoranin, Ella Pamfilova, Gennady Burbulis, and Andrei Kozyrev. They had founded their own groups with such names as Forward Russia, Common Cause, and Transformation of the Fatherland.

The pollsters guessed that only Gaidar's main group would pass the 5 percent barrier and make it into the Duma. That did not happen. In the 1995 elections, Gaidar suffered a humiliating defeat. His bloc won only 3.9 percent of the vote, and none of its leaders won a seat, neither on the basis of party lists nor in districts where votes went to individual candidates. None of the other groups of right-wing "democrats" made it into the Duma, although together they accounted for about 10 percent of the vote.

Yavlinsky's Showing

Grigory Yavlinsky ran a more successful campaign with the Yabloko electoral bloc that he put together with five other small political groups. Although he was usually numbered among the right-wing "democrats," he had been critical of the Yeltsin-Gaidar policies since as early as 1991 and bore no responsibility for the sorry results of the "structural reforms." He had rejected all offers from Gaidar to unite their blocs, correctly assuming that any alliance with Gaidar would only worsen Yabloko's prospects. In late November and early December 1995 the pollsters' predictions gave Yavlinsky's bloc 9–10 percent of the vote, but the Yabloko group won only 7 percent. This did nevertheless allow Yavlinsky to form his own independent faction in the Duma.

Setback for Yeltsin's "Center" Formation

The Our Home Is Russia group defined itself politically as "right-center." In the early summer it counted on winning as much as 24–30 percent of the vote, and its aim was to establish a large and influential voting bloc in the Duma. In the fall, predictions were more modest. The pollsters guessed that the "party of power" would gain no more than 12 percent of the vote. Although the bloc had an impressive list of candidates, including Chernomyrdin himself, the popular film director Nikita Mikhalkov, and General Lev Rokhlin, who had won fame in the Chechnya war, it was able to win only 9.9 percent. Yet this bloc had conducted the most lavish and energetic election campaign. Tens of millions of dollars had gone to promote Our Home Is Russia. The most highly placed administrators and many regional politicians had participated in the campaign. The "party of power" bought 7.5 hours of television advertising time. But the results achieved were less than modest. The "party of power" did succeed in placing quite a few deputies in the Duma, but it was unable to obtain a controlling bloc of votes. Such a situation is understandably seen as a defeat for a party representing the government in power.

Of course Chernomyrdin was not about to resign, but it was obvious he had to substantially alter the policies and composition of the government. As premier, Chernomyrdin did make some changes as early as January 1996, postponing until the presidential elections any more fundamental reshufflings of the cabinet.

Some of the smaller political groups that declared themselves allies of Our Home Is Russia were not even noticed by the voters, bringing in between zero (!) and 0.3 percent of the vote. Sergei Shakhrai, who ran as a center-right candidate together with his Party of Unity and Concord, also suffered a crushing defeat. His party gained only 0.36 percent. Yet two years earlier his party had won about 7 percent and had a solid bloc of votes in the first Duma. The Women of Russia movement also ran as an ally of Chernomyrdin's. It, too, had been quite successful in the 1993 election. The pollsters did not predict a repeat performance, but were confident that the women's group would have seats in the Duma. To the surprise of many observers, however, Women of Russia won only 4.6 percent of the vote. Only some individual members of this grouping entered the Duma, elected in districts where the voting was by individual candidate rather than party list.

The Defeat of Rybkin's Bloc

As early as August 1995 it might have seemed that Ivan Rybkin had succeeded in carrying out Yeltsin's assignment of forming a "loyal opposition" party of the center-left. At any rate he faced no financial obstacles: Rybkin's bloc held a leading position when it came to campaign spending; it was second only to the "party of power." During

September, however, many members of his bloc began to abandon Rybkin, fearing they would be compromised by associating with him. The group Trade Unions for the Elections left him, as did the United Industrial Party. Another group, My Fatherland, went off on its own. Rybkin continued to make optimistic pronouncements and frequent television appearances. Only Our Home Is Russia bought more television time than Rybkin. But the millions of dollars he got from the Yeltsin administration did not help him.

Rybkin's bloc won only 1.1 percent of the vote. All together, the blocs and groupings taking a center-left position won more than 15 percent, but the votes were divided among ten different "left of center" party lists, with the result that none of them won representation in the Duma. Among those roundly defeated was the Bloc of Social Democrats, headed by Gavriil Popov and Vasily Lipitsky. They won only 90,000 votes, or 0.13 percent. The election also revealed that the official trade unions enjoyed very little authority: they, too, won only about 1 percent of the vote. The so-called Party of Workers Self-Management, founded by the ophthalmologist Stanislav Fyodorov, was more successful, with 4 percent. This was an undeniable achievement for a left-wing party that had just recently been founded.

Setback for Zhirinovsky

Zhirinovsky's Liberal Democratic Party of Russia (LDPR) waged a fairly ambitious campaign. In the opinion of many specialists, it was Zhirinovsky who made the most effective use of television time. But to repeat the success of 1993, when the LDPR obtained 23 percent of the vote, proved impossible. In 1995, Zhirinovsky's party won 11.1 percent, which still enabled him to form a fairly solid voting bloc in the Duma. One newspaper commented that the LDPR differed from the other opposition parties "in being too obviously 'easy to buy' and too accommodating toward the executive branch, as well as in its leader's lack of concern with principles. . . ."

Failure of the Congress of Russian Communities

The Congress of Russian Communities (Russian initials, KRO) had been founded in 1992 to defend the interests of Russian communities in the "near abroad," the former Soviet republics bordering Russia. A young politician by the name of Dmitry Rogozin had emerged as its first leader. This organization did not stand out, however, among the welter of Russian nationalist and "patriotic" groups and movements. In 1993 it was unable to obtain the support of even 100,000 voters, the minimum necessary to participate in those elections. In early 1995 General Aleksandr Lebed and Yury Skokov, head of the Commodity Producers Federation, joined the KRO leadership, which immediately attracted attention to this formation. Skokov, who had left Yeltsin's entourage, was still considered an influential politician, with links to the "shadow economy" and extensive connections in the business world of Russia. Lebed, at that time, was still commander of the Fourteenth Russian Army, deployed in the Trans-Dniester region. He was well known and popular throughout the country and among the troops. Several other prominent figures, well known in Russia, belonged to the KRO's National Council: S. Glazyev, K. Zatulin, S. Burkov, and V. Rastorguyev. Local KRO organizations were set up in all the provinces and republics of the Russian Federation. The program and aims of the KRO were expanded to include not only problems of Russian-speaking populations outside Russia but all ethnic problems as well.

The KRO distinguished itself from the extreme Russian nationalist organizations. As early as the summer of 1995 it came to be regarded as one of the favorites in the election campaign: the polls gave it no less than 10 percent of the votes. A bloc of about a dozen parties and groups formed around the KRO, including the Socialist Party of Working People, of which I was a leader. During September and October the prognosis for the KRO remained favorable. But with the onset of televised debates the KRO's popularity began to decline. Although General Lebed was the most popular KRO leader in every respect, he occupied second place on the party's list of candidates and hardly ever appeared on television. All we saw and heard on our TV screens was Skokov, who was a poor speaker, lacking in interest. With every TV appearance by Skokov the KRO, instead of gaining, lost support. Rumors of behind-the-scenes negotiations between Skokov and Yeltsin, widely circulated by the media, also hurt the KRO among opposition-minded voters.

Although the KRO leaders were confident of success, disillusion awaited us all. The KRO received only 4.3 percent of the vote and failed to win representation in the Duma. To be sure, Aleksandr Lebed and his brother, Aleksei, were elected as individuals, but the party slate did not make it.

The Agrarians and the Radical Communists

Nearly twenty members of the Agrarian Party were elected as individuals, but the party slate was unable to pass the 5 percent barrier. As a party the Agrarians won only 3.8 percent. Even the party's leader, Mikhail Lapshin, failed to win reelection. This was a big setback and disappointment for the Agrarians.

As for the radical Communists, they had not run in the 1993 elections; they were not allowed to. Many of their organizations were banned in 1993, and some of their leaders, Viktor Anpilov among them, were in prison at the time.

In 1995, the radical Communists decided to take part in the elections—by supporting the Toiling Russia (Trudovaya Rossiya) group. Their debut was relatively successful. Toiling Russia received more than 3 million votes, giving it 4.5 percent of the total. Although none of them won seats in the Duma, the radical Communists could view the results as an undeniable gain.

Success for the CPRF

The Communist Party of the Russian Federation (CPRF) turned out to be the favorite in the elections of December 1995. It was able to win the support of a large percentage of opposition-minded voters. As early as the summer, voting forecasts gave the CPRF 12–13 percent. During the fall this figure kept growing, even though the CPRF hardly ever appeared on television. Of course the Central Electoral Commission did allocate some TV time to the CPRF, as it did to all the competing parties, but the CPRF purchased hardly any separate advertising time—six minutes all together. In contrast, the Rybkin bloc bought 7 hours of TV time, and the KRO, 2.5 hours.

The main CPRF candidates, Zyuganov and Kuptsov, won 22.3 percent of the vote, more than any other group or bloc. By comparison with the 1993 voting results, this was an undeniable success, but it did not indicate a fundamental change of mood among the majority of Russian voters. Subsequent analysis showed that many who in 1993 had voted for the Agrarians or Zhirinovsky, in 1995 gave their votes to the CPRF. Very few voters who had previously held center or left-center positions switched their votes to the CPRF.

In the 1995 Duma elections the votes of all the groups that supported Yeltsin and his government, taken together, added up to about 25 percent, while the votes of those in the "Communist" part of the electorate added up to 32 percent. About 4 percent of the vote went to groups with no clear political coloration. And the remaining 39 percent were divided among a variety of groups—Russian nationalists, "social reformers," and others.

No single group had a controlling vote in the Duma, although the preponderance of the CPRF was obvious—out of 450 seats in the Duma, the Communists and their allies held 186. A member of the CPRF leadership, Gennady Seleznyov, was elected chairman of the Duma, and many Duma committees came to be headed by Communists.

The Duma went into session in late January 1996, but the country's attention was not on Duma activities; it was on the presidential election campaign that was just beginning. By early February more than twenty candidates had declared their intention to run for the office of president of the Russian Federation.

THE 1996 PRESIDENTIAL ELECTIONS IN RUSSIA: LESSONS AND PARADOXES

These elections constituted what was till then the most important political event in post-Soviet Russian history. They proved to be a central experience for all political parties and movements in Russia, for the individual politicians, and for the people as a whole. Few distinguished themselves in this campaign and far from everyone stood up to this difficult test. Some parties and politicians disappeared from the scene completely; quite a few who had seemed to loom large shrank instead to minor proportions, and some entirely new people appeared on the political scene.

(After reviewing the course and outcome of the election campaign, we will take a closer look at the candidate who emerged as Yeltsin's chief opponent—Gennady Zyuganov—and what he and his party represent.)

The stakes in the elections were high. The 1993 constitution established a strong presidency in Russia. The office of president stood above all other branches of government. Although the president was not part of the cabinet responsible for current administration of the country, it was appointed by him. Only the prime minister required approval by the Duma; all other members of the cabinet were appointed by the president—and could be replaced by him. He also had legislative powers, unlike the presidents of France or the United States. On matters not covered by existing laws—and their number is still quite large in Russia—the president may issue decrees.

The president is the commander in chief, and all the "power ministries" are under his control, as are the Foreign Ministry and the Security Council. The administrative bodies under the president have no less authority than the government bodies under the prime minister and other members of the cabinet. Housed in the offices of the former Central Committee of the CPSU, these administrative bodies carry out essentially the same functions that the party's Central Committee apparatus did previously—serving as the country's "guiding and directing force." The president's influence on the government bodies of the non-Russian parts of the Federation is also enormous.

The results of the 1996 presidential elections are well known. Yeltsin remained as president of Russia. But the conditions under which he was to rule Russia from 1996 to 2000 had changed. The hopes, needs, and expectations of the population had changed, and it was dangerous to ignore that.

The most important fact about the elections was that they were held. On the whole, all political forces in the country accepted "the rules of the game." This shows that our new democracy, for all its inadequacies, is not just an illusion or a screen for despotism. Only extreme radicals of various stripes have questioned the results of these elections—the first time in the history of Russia when nationwide popular elections for the head of state have been held.

Of course there was pressure from those in power and pressure from the West to influence the election outcome. Leaders of other former Soviet countries and international financial institutions sought to intervene in our internal affairs. And there were violations of election law. But these were not decisive in the final outcome. Thus, the best thing Gennady Zyuganov did after the elections was to state that he would respect the choice made by the people and to send Yeltsin a telegram congratulating him on his victory.

On July 3, 1996, it was up to the voters of the Russian Federation not simply to select a leader but to decide the general sociopolitical course their country would take in the next few years and what its governmental and economic structure would be. Anyone who believed that Yeltsin's election signified approval of his social and economic policies of 1991–95 would be profoundly mistaken. To be sure, the people of Russia once again confirmed their rejection of the ideas and practices of totalitarianism or a primitive "levelers' " type of communism. But they also rejected the ideas and practices of a chaotic, unregulated market economy, "savage capitalism," a piratical kind of primitive capitalist accumulation, and primitive liberalism.

When Yeltsin began his campaign his ratings stood near zero. He had presided over five years of "shock therapy," unfulfilled promises, constantly rising prices, the hoodwinking of small investors, a declining standard of living, overnight enrichment for tens of thousands accompanied by impoverishment for tens of millions, destruction of the educational system, health care, and science and culture in general, rampant crime of all kinds, a falling birth rate and a rising death rate, the war in Chechnya, the degradation of the army, the decline of industry and agriculture, the weakening of all forms of social protection, unemployment, homeless children, refugees, strikes, and ecological disasters. The list could go on and on.

With Yeltsin loaded down by such baggage, it seemed inconceivable that he would win. In December 1995, opinion polls gave him an approval rating of no higher than 5 percent. The following month his ratings on all questions were significantly lower than those of Gennady Zyuganov, the man expected to be his chief rival. A survey conducted in January 1996 by Moscow's Bureau of Applied Sociological Research gave the following percentages for Yeltsin and Zyuganov in reply to specific questions. (The percentages are of the total number of people surveyed. These results were published in the newspaper *Segodnya*, July 17, 1996.)

In your opinion, which politician, after becoming president, could most quickly stop inflation?

Yeltsin   8.4
Zyuganov 24.8

Which politician, after becoming president, could straighten out the economic situation most quickly?

Yeltsin   7.9
Zyuganov 21.8

Which politician could stop the war in Chechnya more quickly?

Yeltsin   6.1
Zyuganov 15.4

Which politician could solve the crime problem more quickly?

Yeltsin   6.0
Zyuganov 16.0

Which politician could improve health care more quickly?

Yeltsin   8.1
Zyuganov 30.6

Only 15 percent replied that they were living better than before perestroika, while 68 percent said they were living worse or much worse, and 14 percent said there was no significant change in their standard of living. When asked, "Do you now approve the social and economic policies followed by the president and the government since 1992?" an overwhelming 66 *percent* replied in the negative.

It is not surprising that a number of people in Yeltsin's circle repeatedly urged that the elections be postponed or canceled, even if that meant resorting to the use of force. Others feverishly searched for someone to stand in Yeltsin's place: Chernomyrdin? Nemtsov? Luzhkov? A bloc between Gaidar and Yavlinsky?

In mid-February, when Zyuganov and Yeltsin began collecting signatures for their candidacies, Zyuganov's ratings were as high as 20–22 percent, twice as high as Yeltsin's. When asked what chance Yeltsin had of regaining the presidency, Zyuganov confidently replied: "No chance." The highly experienced Anatoly Lukyanov answered more cautiously: "Yeltsin is a serious opponent."

Yeltsin displayed energy, activity, resourcefulness, even zeal that no one expected of him. He looked hale and hearty. One morning he would preside at a parade in Moscow, and on the same afternoon he would climb a hill to visit the war memorial outside Volgograd, and then the same evening sail down the Volga River to Astrakhan. He "went to the people," visiting 24 different regions and cities, more than during his entire presidency. But it was not the handshaking on the streets with residents of Yekaterinburg or Krasnodar or the dancing with young people at a stadium in Rostov on the Don, or the concerts with stars of stage and screen that changed the attitudes of millions toward Yeltsin; it was the new social orientation reflected in his decisions, decrees, and promises. It was his campaign to have arrears in wages and pensions paid up, to have scholarships for students and pensions for retired people increased, and to have the first compensation payments made for savings wiped out by inflation.

Prices virtually stopped rising as inflation dropped to about 2 percent per month. Hundreds of billions of additional rubles were spent on science, education, hospitals, and theaters. Decisions were made to give government support for the needs of northern Russia, to expand the Baltic merchant marine and the Novosibirsk subway system, to support suburban truck gardening and the domestic manufacture of airplanes, and on and on.

Yeltsin spoke not just about the market and private ownership, but about a "socially oriented market economy" as he shifted more and more toward the political center. One of Yeltsin's supporters, the economist Pavel Bunich, a member of the Russian Academy of Sciences, declared several times that Yeltsin had begun to carry out "a genuinely social democratic program." After Kozyrev's resignation foreign policy priorities also began to change. After Chubais's resignation his ruinous privatization program was stopped. Yeltsin issued a decree recognizing the red banner as one of the symbols of the Russian state, and on Victory Day [May 9—the equivalent of VE day] for the first time in many years the Russian head of state stood on Lenin's tomb to review the armed forces. Important agreements during a state visit to China and new treaties concerning economic integration with Kazakstan, Kirgizia, and especially Belarus—all these were new initiatives taken by Yeltsin, who also included in his election platform, and trumpeted widely, the notion of Russia as a great power that was being humiliated.

Even *Pravda*, on July 9, 1996, admitted that Yeltsin had "succeeded in creating the image of a strict but concerned father of his nation and impressing on an enormous number of people the idea that he represented progress, democracy, and freedom, in contrast to the undemocratic character of the previous Soviet social order."

A CPRF spokesperson, I. Bratishchev, protested: "The party of power has shamelessly appropriated our own economic demands." Zyuganov urged people, "Look at Yeltsin's decrees. Why, he is carrying out 80 percent of our program." But there was nothing in the electoral laws forbidding this. And it makes more sense to ask why so many people trusted Yeltsin rather than Zyuganov on questions of social protection and the needs of the Russian state. Yeltsin went so far as to meet in the Kremlin with leaders of the Chechen separatists and sign a cease-fire agreement with them; later he made a surprise visit to Chechnya and gave a speech to one of the Russian military units there. At that point he had serious grounds to hope for a victory in the first round of the elections.

He did not of course win the first round, or even gain a decisive advantage over his main opponent. By early May, Yeltsin had fully mobilized his own electoral following and won over many wavering "centrists" and doubtful "democrats." But the hopes Yeltsin and his staff had of winning a section of Zyuganov's ideologically consolidated following proved vain. Although Yeltsin did take up many of the Communists' demands, he succeeded only partially in distancing himself from the disastrous consequences of "shock therapy." For most citizens he continued to embody the painful economic course begun in 1992. He remained in this sense a symbolic figure.

Yeltsin's showing in the first round represented an unquestioned gain over the low ratings of January and February. But on the whole, the first round represented a serious defeat for him. On June 16 the overwhelming majority of voters condemned the policies of the previous 4–5 years. Only 35 percent of those voting cast their ballots for Yeltsin, while 65 percent voted against him. About 30 percent voted for Lebed, Yavlinsky, Fyodorov, or Gorbachev, all of whom considered themselves "democrats" but stood as opponents of Yeltsin in the elections.

The first round was not a victory for Zyuganov either. He, too, had campaigned with great energy, traveling to many parts of the country and drawing large audiences. He could not issue any decrees, of course, but his criticisms of the Yeltsin regime were persuasive and his promises attractive. He tried to avoid orthodox Communist slogans and promised to renounce revolutionary measures or even any sharp turns in the economic field. Still, he was only partially able to distance himself from the disastrous results of Communist policy in the USSR from 1917 to 1991. In the eyes of millions of Russian citizens he embodied both the significant achievements and the many crimes of Communist rule. He too remained a symbolic figure.

One poster seen on the walls of buildings proclaimed, "The Communist Party has not dropped its name: it will not abandon its methods." Zyuganov did not wish to take his distance even from the worst crimes of Stalinism. He frequently referred to Stalin and quoted him. This was attractive to extremists like the Anpilov group, but it repelled the best elements among the intelligentsia. One Moscow University professor said to me: "How could I vote for Zyuganov? I was at one of his demonstrations. Thousands of people were marching along Tverskaya Street, carrying portraits of Zyuganov and Stalin."

Zyuganov got a large vote in the countryside, but he didn't win the sympathy of most workers. Even striking miners in the north and unemployed textile workers in Ivanovo-Voznesensk voted mostly for Yeltsin. Zyuganov's program and demands were good in many respects. But the Communists had been in power not long before, and voters preferred to judge this party by its deeds, not its words. How many attractive Communist programs had been heard since 1917! But which promises had been kept and at what cost? It's no wonder that all of Zyuganov's attempts to portray the CPRF as a completely new Communist Party failed. He won 32 percent of the vote in the first round. That means that 68 percent quite definitely voted against him, and for the CPRF leader this was a serious defeat.

For Grigory Yavlinksy the first round of voting also represented a major setback. His name was well known, but almost nothing was known of him as a real player on the political stage. "Intelligent, handsome, knowledgeable, self-assured"—these are not political definitions. It was unclear whether he stood on the left or the right, or in the center. Refusal to compromise is a good quality in a scientist but not in a politician. It was not only Chernomyrdin who asked, "What has he done for the country? What can he do?" His movement, with its exotic name Yabloko (Apple), never acquired clear outlines or a clear program. That seems to be why the vote for Yavlinsky has steadily declined from election to election, from 1993 to 1995 to 1996.

The 1996 elections brought defeat to Zhirinovsky as well. The time for political clowning and tightrope walking had passed. Chauvinism had little resonance either. Had Zhirinovsky accomplished anything useful for Russia while in the opposition? Few seemed to think so. He lost three-quarters of the votes he won in 1993.

The Russian press had little comment on the crushing rejection of Gorbachev. Not even one percent voted for him. He was able to attract some attention of course, but not sympathy. It is obvious that the voters charged the disastrous situation in Russia to Gorbachev's account even more than to Yeltsin's.

In regard to General Aleksandr Lebed, much has been said and written, both during the election campaign and especially afterward. In the first round nearly 15 percent voted for him—a big victory for a man who had just started a political career, one who, besides, had been relieved of his military command only a year earlier, in June 1995. None of the pollsters had predicted anything like this. Even his campaign staff was surprised. They later admitted that the most they expected was 8 percent.

People on Zyuganov's campaign staff, and also Gorbachev in an article in *La Stampa* (Rome), charged that Lebed's "15 percent blitzkrieg" had been organized and funded by Yeltsin's campaign. Material published in the newspaper *Kapital* shows that Lebed received funds from the Electoral Commission and from several thousand supporters. Among these were several financial and commercial entities. There was no money from Yeltsin's campaign staff. On the other hand, no one placed any obstacles in the way of Lebed's frequent appearances on television.

Of course the Yeltsin campaign tried to calculate what the possible voting results might be and what might be gained by making a bloc with one or another "third force" candidate. In May, Yeltsin met with Yavlinsky and Fyodorov, and twice with Lebed. And this was only natural. I do not exclude the possibility that Yeltsin's campaign might have given some money to promote Lebed in June. If so, it would have been strange for Lebed and his staff to refuse. But Lebed's success was not primarily due to financing. In December 1995, enormous sums were of no help to Rybkin or Gaidar. And in June 1996 the billionaire Bryntsalov's wealth was no advantage. As for fame, that hurt Gorbachev more than it helped. The weak candidate Shakkum could have appeared five times more often on television; he still would not have reached the one percent mark.

Lebed's image and his slogan "Justice and order" simply coincided with, and corresponded closely to, the needs and aspirations of many voters.

Thus, Yeltsin and Zyuganov faced each other in the second round of voting. Their chances were about even. Each of them had exhausted his opportunities as a single candidate, and everything now depended on some kind of coalition based on compromise. There were other factors at work as well. The example of St. Petersburg was indicative. There, in gubernatorial elections, Anatoly Sobchak had received the largest number of votes in the first round, but he lost in the second round.

An alliance with Zhirinovsky was not desirable. Zyuganov or Yeltsin could lose more among his own supporters than he would gain by such a move. Yavlinsky's conditions for an alliance Yeltsin considered excessive. They weren't in keeping with the modest extent of Yavlinsky's electoral support.

Zyuganov proposed a very broad coalition. He was willing to include not only Tuleyev in the next government of Russia, but also Lebed, Fyodorov, Glazyev (a former minister of foreign trade), Luzhkov (the mayor of Moscow), Yegor Stroyeva (governor of Saratov province), Rakhimov (the head of Bashkiria), Yavlinsky, and others. This proposal was not very realistic, and it was made public rather late in the game, on June 25. Not until then, apparently, did Zyuganov realize that an alliance with extremist "orthodox Communists" such as Anpilov, Makashov, and Terekhov repelled more voters than it attracted.

Yeltsin was more decisive and acted more quickly. He reached an agreement with Lebed on June 17 and announced it on June 18. Lebed was appointed secretary of Russia's Security Council and assistant to the president for national security affairs: he was promised considerable power and authority in the government. Defense Minister Pavel Grachev, the most unpopular man in Yeltsin's entourage, was retired to "the reserves." Three others in Yeltsin's inner circle were dismissed: General Barsukov, the chief of the security police (FSB), Aleksandr Korzhakov, head of the presidential guard, and vice premier Oleg Soskovets. Seven more generals linked with Grachev were soon dismissed as well. Lebed expressed his satisfaction. A program drawn up by the group around Lebed, entitled "Main Directions of Activity for the Security Council of the Russian Federation in the Present Period," was made public before the July 3 second round. Of all the programs known to me it was at once the most radical and the most realistic for bringing Russia out of its present crisis. "He laughs best who shoots first," said Lebed at a press conference on July 2.

Yeltsin's political alliance with Lebed was greeted with unconcealed anger both by the CPRF and by the radical "democrats." Voices in the Communist Duma group could be heard defending the dismissed generals. Zyuganov predicted that Lebed would experience the same fate as Rutskoi, who also began an anti-crime campaign but ended behind bars himself.

The Yeltsin-Lebed alliance was a conjunctural agreement and, though advantageous to both sides for the moment, was not stable. During Lebed's first days as secretary of the Security Council it became clear he would not be just another official in Yeltsin's administration. He was given a significant amount of autonomy and power. At his first press conference he declared: "Eleven million voters believed that I could restore order and guarantee security. I am an officer and must carry out these orders. Having finished third, I am assuming these difficult duties. I think that no less than 80 percent of the voters will understand me and follow my lead" (*Krasnaya Zvezda*, June 19, 1996).

The commentator Mikhail Leontyev wrote later, in the newspaper *Segodnya* (July 10, 1996): "The position and powers of the Security Council are determined by the presence of the 'first nationally elected secretary of the Security Council' and by the personality of this secretary. . . . He will not be able to exist in the structures of power at a position lower than No. 2 man in the government. . . . It is another question to what extent an adequate embodiment of this situation will be found."

Some Communist newspapers wrote at the end of June that voters would be repelled by the Yeltsin-Lebed alliance and the departure of "patriotic" generals from the Kremlin and that those who had supported Lebed in the first round would not vote for him in the second.

"Against this background," wrote *Sovetskaya Rossiya* on June 22,

the actions of Zyuganov rise to new heights. Despite all the mud-slinging accompanying the election campaign, Zyuganov remains an unbesmirched politician, who has conducted the struggle with the use of methods that are exceptionally clean, honest, and legitimate. At the finish of the presidential race, when passions it seems are at their height, Zyuganov demonstrates a high level of political culture, coolness, and restraint, and the voters cannot help but see this and appreciate it.

> After the unseemly events of June 19–20 [the ouster of Korzhakov, Barsukov, and Soskovets], there can no longer be any doubt of Zyuganov's victory.

This was obviously an expression of the Communists' wishful thinking, not the reality.

After June 23, Yeltsin's health failed him. He pulled back from his intense participation in the election campaign, canceled his scheduled trips and meetings, and made only some brief television appearances. In contrast, Zyuganov continued a very energetic campaign, holding a press conference every day. But he was not able to spruce up his image or show new faces on his team. He no longer had much hope of winning, but he expressed confidence that, whoever the victor, the margin of victory would be small. Yeltsin's campaign staff feared that would be so.

The results were a surprise to both sides: 67.3 percent of the electorate took part, with 53.7 percent voting for Yeltsin and 40.4 percent for Zyuganov. Only 5 percent voted for "none of the above." Most of the Russian press greeted the results with enthusiasm. However, Yeltsin's was not a triumphal victory; it was won at great cost, both literally and figuratively. Opinion polls showed that many had voted not so much for one candidate as against the other. Many who voted for Yeltsin did not like him, but they disliked the Communists more. Many who opposed Yeltsin voted for Zyuganov, although they didn't particularly like him either. Both groups were voting for the lesser evil. Yeltsin's staff understood this. One of his campaign slogans was: "I'm no Communist. Communism's worse than me." Of Lebed's supporters, 75 percent voted for Yeltsin; of Yavlinsky's, 80 percent. About 70 percent of Zhirinovsky's supporters voted for Zyuganov. All these facts placed a limit on Yeltsin's freedom of maneuver, as did the 40 percent vote for Zyuganov. Yeltsin had to take these forces into account, and he could not ignore the simple fact that in the first round only 46 out of 89 administrative units of the Russian Federation gave him more votes than Zyuganov.

Analysts in the CPRF camp, it seems to me, were unable to evaluate correctly the reasons for their defeat. They pointed to many factors that, in my opinion, were secondary. The 1996 presidential elections showed how strongly most citizens of Russia oppose any return to power by the Communists, who were unable to draw a clear line between their past and the present and future.

223

Yegor Ligachev (the former Politburo member) wrote that the election results were a success. "The CPRF has existed just a little more than three years. It was founded after the CPSU was banned and has been working under conditions of moral terror. The CPRF and its candidate, Zyuganov, were in fact denied access to central television and radio, and they did not possess one tenth of the financial resources spent on Yeltsin's campaign" (*Pravda*, July 30, 1996).

This view is too superficial. Of course Yeltsin had many advantages, but his position also had many weaknesses. Some other opposition party might have taken advantage of those, but it was difficult for the CPRF to do so. Only in a formal sense had it existed "little more than three years." Those who voted for the Communists or withheld their votes from them undoubtedly thought about not just the last three years but the many decades of Communist rule. Even in the elections of 1989–91 the Communist regime had not given its opponents as many opportunities as the CPRF was given in 1996.

Yeltsin remained president, but the situation in Russia did not improve. Numerous promises were waiting to be kept. Talk about "completing the reforms that have been started" covered up the real need for fundamental corrections. Russia actually needed a new reform program, but Yeltsin did not have the strength or energy to start anew or make a fairly sharp about-face.

As I have written elsewhere, Yeltsin is a politician whose main objective is to stay in power. He is willing to change his image, his policies, and his advisers to achieve that end. In the Sverdlovsk province committee of the CPSU he was a despotic boss. As secretary of the CPSU's Moscow city committee, and after breaking with Gorbachev in 1989, he took the stance of a tough fighter against party privilege and corruption. From 1989 to 1992 he was a pro-Western democrat and liberal. Riding to power on the wave of an amorphous "democratic movement," he soon pushed the "first wave" of democrats out of government, figures like Yuri Afanasyev, Gavriil Popov, and Galina Starovoitova. In 1992–93 he began to get rid of a second line of "democrats"—figures like Burbulis, Gaidar, and Shakhrai. Later, in 1994 and after, Chubais, Kozyrev, and others had to go. In their place came professionals from the party and state apparatus of the 1980s, men like Chernomyrdin, Primakov, Kadannikov, and Yegorov.

Meanwhile there was little change in economic policy, and the country continued its downward spiral. By the end of 1995 the Yeltsin regime's social support consisted only of the following: commercial and financial capital, backed by Western capital, the comprador bourgeoisie (business people working for foreign capital), corrupt bureaucrats, a section of the officer corps, a section of the regional elite, and a section of the intelligentsia in the capital, plus criminal and semi-criminal elements. Things were heading toward a social explosion. To hold onto power and extricate Russia from its crisis, Yeltsin needed to find mass support in the ranks of the working class and wider strata of the intelligentsia, within the army, and among the masses of the rural population; also among students and retired people, among the new national bourgeoisie, and among the owners of small and medium-sized businesses.

The political shifts Yeltsin made from January to June 1996 were only the first necessary steps in the right direction, but they were not continued after the election. Many of the social programs announced in the spring and summer were discontinued in the fall of 1996. Of all the campaign promises Yeltsin made, he kept only one: the war in Chechnya was finally ended. But this was mainly the work of Lebed, with little obvious help from Yeltsin or Chernomyrdin. After the election, the return of privatization mastermind Chubais to a high post in Yeltsin's administration canceled many of the hopes held by those who voted for the Russian president.

Explaining the reasons for his bloc with Yeltsin, General Lebed contrasted "the old idea," which no longer inspired anyone, to "the new idea," which was being put into practice poorly, but which he preferred. The Russian people did reject the idea of totalitarianism and the primitive "leveling" type of orthodox Communism, but it also rejected the even older idea of an unregulated market economy, "savage capitalism," criminal-dominated "primitive capitalist accumulation," and crude laissez-faire liberalism. Neither Communist fundamentalism nor Western liberalism is foremost in the thinking of most Russians today. Instead, uppermost in their minds are some ideas that for Russia are truly new—political liberty and social justice, democracy and order, individual initiative and government regulation, protection of citizens' social rights and their equality before the law. This spectrum of ideas is customarily linked with the social democratic movement. It is no accident that in addition to the Socialist Party of Working People, which in 1996 observed its fifth anniversary, a goodly dozen social democratic parties and groups have made their appearance in Russia in recent years.

Ideas relating to a strong Russian state (*derzhavnost*) and defense of Russia's national interests have also taken on much greater urgency.

New shifts in public opinion have not found adequate expression in the policies of those in power nor among those in opposition. Many CPRF leaders understand the importance of pluralism and a mixed economy, a combination of public and private ownership. But when the CPRF was founded in 1990, and when it was reestablished in 1993, it was by no means based on the most progressive sections of the CPSU. From the party of the retrograde Ivan Polozkov, Zyuganov has inherited not only a conservative ideology but also a large part of the active party membership. Thus, after the party's failure in the 1996 elections it is no accident that attempts to reorganize a National-Patriotic Assembly along less radical lines have been combined with increased adulation of—Stalin. At his first press conference after the elections Zyuganov admitted that he had not known how to adequately oppose the concentrated pressure of the "party of power," exerted through all the mass media. "However," he commented, "if in the face of such pressure on the voters and such use of the media, Generalissimo Stalin had been running in the election, he would have won" (*Pravda*, July 6, 1996).

The attitude of the West toward the Russian presidential elections is a separate subject, too big to go into here. The general attitude was summed up by one English newspaper, which asserted that Yeltsin's victory made Westerners happy, but that his health was cause for concern. Official circles in the West were also troubled by Lebed's rapid rise. Some were inclined to regard his program for strengthening Russia's national security as a "throwback to the Cold War." There was no shortage of caustic comments in the Western press to the effect that a "tank division had been brought in to hold a single department store," and there were frequent references to Lebed as a "loose cannon." An influential American newspaper advised Yeltsin "to cast Lebed aside after a decent interval" and place his reliance on Chernomyrdin, who had proven himself to be a "most loyal servant to the head of state." Yeltsin followed this advice almost to the letter, but that was hardly to his advantage.

7

Gennady Zyuganov as Politician and Ideologist

The reestablishment of the CPRF and its success in the Duma elections of 1995 focused universal attention on its leader, Gennady Zyuganov. The 1996 presidential campaign transformed him into a political figure of national importance. In all opinion polls the previous year he was invariably listed as one of the four or five most influential politicians in Russia. His position and importance in the Russian Communist movement was the result of his role as an ideologist, one aspiring to map out new ideological terrain not only on social questions but in the sphere of nation-building and state structure as well.

I first became acquainted with Zyuganov in late 1990 at one of several meetings of leaders of the Russian Communist Party with people's deputies of the RSFSR and party activists. I was drawn to these conferences by a historian's curiosity as well as my great concern for the fate of our country in my capacity as a people's deputy, a position to which I had just been elected. It was at that time, in the winter of 1990–91, that destructive processes in the party and the country were starting to build up quickly. Top leaders of the Russian Communist Party, who had lost any illusions about perestroika, progressive reform, and the new thinking much earlier than those in the Central Committee of the CPSU, still were uncertain how to proceed. Almost all the leaders of the RSFSR Communist Party were already in opposition to Gorbachev, but they were even more opposed to Yeltsin and the "democrats" around him, who were in power in the Russian Federation. What to do? How to conduct oneself in this two-sided oppositional position? No one had the answers to these questions.

The second time I met Zyuganov was on a day quite memorable for all of us, August 19, 1991 (the first day of the attempted coup against Gorbachev). We met in a mountain park at Kislovodsk. It turned out that we were vacationing in neighboring sanatoria. Our conversations of course turned on the events in Moscow, which were a complete surprise for both of us. During the next few days, up to August 23, we continued to encounter one another in Kislovodsk. On the morning of August 24 I flew to Moscow for a session of the Supreme Soviet (in which I was a people's deputy).

The impression I had of Zyuganov was of a strong, energetic, and well-educated man. He was at ease in conversation and tended to listen rather than try to impose his point of view. In his way of talking and addressing others, there was none of the self-importance one so often encountered among party officials. He was often harsh in his articles or speeches of that time, but not in conversation. Even later, when Zyuganov attended the first congresses of our Socialist Party or when we met at congresses of people's deputies of the Russian Federation, he was calm, even cheerful; I never saw him angry or rude. Somehow or other he easily withstood criticism from his rivals or his colleagues—something especially notable at the sessions of the Constitutional Court.

Zyuganov's biography is not rich and eventful. He was born at the end of 1944 in the village of Mymrino, in the Khotynets district of Oryol province. "I come from a family of three generations of teachers," he has written. "Some were party members, some were not, but there were two special things: everyone in my family worked from morning till night; and practically everyone took part in the defense of the Fatherland. Many of them didn't come back; my father lost his leg at Sevastopol; and none of them were ever investigated or put on trial" (*Sovetskaya Rossiya*, February 11, 1993).

In one of his interviews a third feature of the Zyuganov family was noted: They were pure Russian, "pure as spring water."

"In our village the cock's crow reached three provinces—Oryol, Bryansk, and Kaluga. It was the edge of the mixed zone of forest and steppeland. Beyond us stretched the forests of Bryansk. It's the area between the Oka and Volga rivers, the area from which the Russian people came" (Zyuganov, *Drama vlasti*, Moscow, 1993, p. 3).

In his family's tradition the Great Patriotic War was the main event. The fighting hit the Oryol region hard, both when it went from west to east (during the German invasion) and when it went from east to west (as the invaders were driven out). After completing school, Zyuganov taught for a year, then took up studies at the physics and mathematics department of the Oryol Teachers Institute. After his second year he was drafted into the army, and served in an intelligence unit dealing with radiological, chemical, and bacteriological warfare. In 1966, while in the army, he joined the CPSU. After graduating from the Oryol Teachers Institute, Zyuganov briefly taught mathematics there, but party work occupied much of his time and soon became his profession.

His party career went in a perfectly straight line: he was first secretary of a district committee of the Komsomol (Young Communist League) in Oryol, then first secretary of the Komsomol city committee, then first secretary of the Komsomol for all of Oryol province; subsequently he became second secretary of the CPSU's city committee in Oryol, after which for nearly a decade (1974–1983) he was head of the propaganda and agitation department of the party's Oryol province committee. During that time he graduated from the Academy of Social Sciences under the CPSU Central Committee, defending his dissertation in philosophy. The purpose of that academy was to train cadre for the Central Committee apparatus, and in 1983 Zyuganov began work in Moscow as an instructor in the Central Committee's Ideological Department. He was a diligent worker and soon became head of one of the sectors in the Ideological Department.

In 1989, four years into the Gorbachev era, he was appointed to a high post in the Central Committee apparatus: deputy head of the Ideological Department. The head of the department was Aleksandr Yavovlev, a secretary of the Central Committee and at that time a close ally of Gorbachev. By then Zyuganov had traveled widely within the USSR. He drafted memoranda for the Central Committee analyzing the situation in Central Asia, in the Baltic region, and in the

229

Caucasus. These were the years of perestroika, which the Central Committee apparatus accepted without any enthusiasm.

> I saw everything from the inside, wrote memoranda to the higher-ups in which I asserted that because of what Gorbachev had initiated perestroika was turning into 'perestrelka' (a shooting match). For which I was reprimanded, including by the Politburo. Specifically I wrote that there was going to be war in Tadzhikistan and in the Caucasus, that there would be serious upheavals in other regions, that prices would rise to ten times their former level . . . as a result of the last-named item Gorbachev became highly allergic to me. Of course, our country was ripe for reform. Even Kosygin, back in 1965, had begun some. . . . But for reform to succeed there needed to be a capable team in charge, a clear program, a refined methodology, and powerful levers of information that would make it possible for the people to participate in the reforms. In addition, the social gains of our society needed to be preserved, everything that our citizens had suffered to achieve. Gorbachev had none of that and did none of that. His talents had not shone brilliantly in his less responsible posts; as the highest leader of the state he simply fell on his face.

(*Delovoi mir*, April 8, 1995)

As a rule the people who worked in the Central Committee's Ideology Department and International Department were quite well trained and well informed. But discipline in the CC was stricter perhaps than in the army. Initiative and independence were not encouraged. Thus, for many Central Committee apparatchiks the establishment of a separate Communist Party of the Russian Federation in 1990 was doubly important; it opened up possibilities for independent political work.

Zyuganov was elected a member of the Politburo of the Russian Communist Party and Central Committee secretary in charge of ideology. The apparatus of this new party was small, as were its possibilities. It was at this time that Zyuganov began developing his new conception of Russia's path to socialism, in which the issue of a national-patriotic orientation played an important part. In late 1990, as we have said, the crisis in the USSR intensified rapidly—an economic crisis interwoven with a crisis of power and ideology. Gorbachev's authority plummeted. There was a mounting wave of criticism of the "center," including from regional party leaders. Several publications by Aleksandr Yakovlev sought to reply to these criticisms. In one interview Yakovlev commented on "the danger from the leadership and apparatus of the Russian Communist Party for the implementation of perestroika along the indicated course." On May 7, 1991, the newspaper *Sovetskaya Rossiya* published an "Open Letter" from Zyuganov to Yakovlev "in regard to his recent statements and not only those." Zyuganov's letter, to which the newspaper added the flashy headline "Architect Beside the Ruins," attracted quite a bit of interest and was widely discussed in all party organizations and government structures.

Although Zyuganov's letter referred only to Yakovlev, who was then a senior adviser to President Gorbachev, everyone understood that the president was its real target. Neither Gorbachev nor Yakovlev undertook to answer Zyuganov publicly. Several newspapers did try to answer him, but they were not very convincing, for none of them spoke of perestroika's "successes." The main argument in one newspaper was that Yakovlev, "one of our best and brightest minds," was being attacked by "a petty functionary no one has ever heard of, who by some incredible chance has risen to the top in the scandalously established hierarchy of leaders of the Russian Communist Party."

The political scientist Aleksei Kiva agreed: "Yes, we are standing in the ruins, but they are the ruins of a totalitarian, inhuman, antidemocratic system."

"The architect faces the task of reconstructing a prison as a temple. How can this be done without destroying the prison walls and ceilings? Marxism-Leninism itself teaches that in order to construct a new social order, it is necessary first to destroy the old one" (*Komsomolskaya Pravda*, May 22, 1991). This was a peculiar logic. A prison could be reconstructed to serve as a temple without destroying its walls and ceilings, just as under Stalin many churches were turned into storehouses for grain—or into prisons.

At that time, however, Zyuganov kept the pressure on, intensifying his criticism. This was when he drafted a public protest against perestroika, which was published in July 1991 under the title "A Word to the People." It was cosigned by a number of conservative, pro-Stalin, and "patriotic" Communists. Even today Zyuganov considers the

"Word to the People" a work of great importance. He included the full text of it in his book *The Drama of Power* (*Drama vlasti*).

Its concluding section states in part: "We are appealing to representatives of all professions and social classes, all ideologies and faiths, all parties and movements. . . . Let's wake up, come to our senses, and stand up, young and old, for our country. . . . We are starting a movement of all the people, calling on all who recognize the terrible disaster that has befallen our country: join our ranks."

Few responded to this call. All sorts of appeals to the people were being made in June and July 1991 by dozens of politicians and political groups. Yeltsin, who on July 10 had been triumphantly proclaimed president of the RSFSR, issued many appeals to the people for support. Gorbachev appealed to CPSU members and to all Soviet citizens to support the party's new program (adopted in the summer of 1991) and the new union treaty. A month later the number of appeals increased manyfold. August 1991 had come.

The "Word to the People" was greeted with a flood of invective. Its authors were accused of provocation. For the most part they had no authority. Like Zyuganov, most were known only among relatively small circles. The text consists mostly of fiery accusations and emotional statements, rather than logical arguments or specific proposals. People held many different views on Russia's past history. It was no easy task for any one group to unite them under its leadership.

Later on, some political writers in the camp of the "democrats" made a connection between the "Word to the People" and the August coup attempt by the so-called State Committee for the State of Emergency. In August 1994 several CPRF newspapers published the "Word to the People" together with and alongside of Decree No. 1 of the State Committee. "Read the State Committee's action program calmly," wrote *Pravda Moskvy* (no. 3, 1994), "and tell us what there was in it that did not correspond to our country's best interests." This is a strange request. There were of course many tempting promises and reasonable recommendations in the State Committee's Decree No. 1. But who believed in promises by then? Hardly anyone was willing to follow Gennady Yanaev, Boris Pugo, and Valentin Pavlov as leaders. The State Committee took measures not only against the elected leadership of the Russian Federation (Yeltsin and his supporters) but also against the Russian Communist Party, toward whom all the top leaders of the CPSU, not just Yakovlev, had been hostile. The

Russian Federation's declaration of sovereignty was far more divisive for the Soviet Union than similar actions by Estonia, Georgia, or Armenia, but most of the Communist representatives in the Supreme Soviet of the RSFSR supported that declaration.

Zyuganov returned to Moscow from Kislovodsk in late August or early September. The Communist parties of the Soviet Union and the RSFSR had by then been outlawed and their offices ransacked, including of course Zyuganov's. He did not participate in any of the attempts begun then to establish new Communist parties, although he followed these efforts closely. In December 1991 the Union of Soviet Socialist Republics was dissolved, bringing with it the danger of a partial breakup of the Russian Federation. This prompted a number of politicians and public figures to form the Council of People's Patriotic Forces (Russian initials, SNPS, for Sovet Narodno-Patrioticheskikh Sil). People of many different views joined the Council—from Communists to some recently formed "councils of the nobility." Zyuganov was elected chairman of the SNPS. It had a variety of aims—to help patriots in prison, to intervene in various ways in defense of the national interests of the Russian state, and to defend socially weak groups in the population, especially the intelligentsia.

In the winter of 1991–92 Zyuganov could be found in attendance almost everywhere—at congresses of people's deputies of the RSFSR, at congresses of commodity producers, or entrepreneurs, at congresses of Russian writers. He also attended the first congress of the Socialist Party of Working People (of which I was a leader) and many conferences of the "Communists of Russia" group in the Russian Supreme Soviet (which met in the Russian White House).

To earn his living in this period, according to his own account, he compiled various reports, prognoses, and analytical memoranda. Many of these were sold to clients under various pen names. I have no doubt that such memoranda were professionally produced. People working for the CPSU Central Committee were taught how to do such things well. Confusion reigned at that time among many of the Russian Communists. They were accustomed to being in the ruling party and didn't know how to function as oppositionists. The new ruling groups and government organizations energetically recruited among former Communist cadre. At the beginning of 1991 no fewer than 300 people's deputies of the RSFSR considered themselves members of the Communist parliamentary group. At the end of that year only 60 remained, and even they did not function as any sort of real opposition to the Yeltsin government. Many of them voted to grant Yeltsin emergency powers and to ratify the treaty dissolving the Soviet Union. The mood among people's deputies began to change during the spring of 1992, and by summer more than half the deputies were backing one or another opposition group.

At that time Zyuganov did a lot of work at the Russian Supreme Soviet and the Constitutional Court, but his main arena of activity in 1992 was with the large national-patriotic groups and associations that arose then. He took part in the First Congress of the Russian National Assembly (Russky Naordny Sobor), headed at that time by KGB General Aleksandr Sterligov. Three co-chairmen of the organization were elected: Gennady Zyuganov, the Siberian author Valentin Rasputin, and Pyotr Romanov, director of a major chemical complex in Krasnoyarsk. The documents of this organization included a call for the restoration of the Russian state with its 1914 borders and the elimination of autonomous non-Russian territorial units. Non-Russian nationalities should be assured of cultural autonomy only. Socialism was rejected. "Instead of the twin evils of 'savage capitalism' and utopian socialism, the Assembly (Sobor) chooses a 'third way,' the path of rationally combined administration, state regulation of the economy and market mechanisms, and the gradual transformation of property relations and all social institutions on the basis of national interests and priorities" (*Pravda*, June 16, 1992).

The Sobor addressed itself above all to the Russian population and could hardly expect that non-Russian nationalities of the RSFSR or the former USSR would support its program of creating a unitary state "on the foundation of Russian Orthodox values." The appeals of this Russian nationalist organization found little response even within the Russian population. No mass movement emerged to follow this group of would-be leaders.

In October 1992 Zyuganov helped found the National Salvation Front, which was more of a mass organization than the Sobor, with more radical methods of struggle. People's deputy Ilya Konstantinov was elected coordinator of the Front, and among its co-chairmen were Zyuganov, Mikhail Astafyev, Albert Makashov, Vladimir Isakov, and Sergei Baburin. Zyuganov also became a member of the editorial board of the newspaper *Den*, which in 1994 changed its name to

Zavtra. Also toward the end of 1992 Zyuganov joined the Organizing Committee for the Reestablishment of the Russian Communist Party.

In the preparations for the "Refoundation Congress" of the CPRF there was no discussion of who its future leader might be. Some members of the Organizing Committee thought the party head should be Valentin Kuptsov, who had been elected first secretary of the Central Committee of the CP RSFSR to replace Ivan Polozkov, when the latter resigned and in fact abandoned political activity. Kuptsov, however, proposed a collective leadership. The delegates didn't go along with his proposal. They were in a very radical mood, and on a motion by Albert Makashov they elected Zyuganov chairman of the CPRF. During the evening before the vote a number of Zyuganov supporters were busy urging the delegates to vote this way. But there was no contest. Zyuganov was elected almost unanimously, and Kuptsov became first deputy chairman. Since then Zyuganov's energies have been mainly devoted to the CPRF, which quickly became the strongest and most widely ramified political organization in Russia.

The October days in Moscow in 1993 were a serious test for the CPRF. Zyuganov and his party of course supported Khasbulatov and Rutskoi from the very beginning of the confrontation. But this support was not unqualified. Zyuganov insisted that the use of force by either side should be emphatically ruled out. He visited the White House many times. When "peace talks" began Zyuganov supported this initiative. None of the CPRF leaders took part in the demonstrations of October 2 and 3. On the contrary, on October 3 Zyuganov met with Khasbulatov in an attempt to persuade him to renounce any military move against the Kremlin, the Ostankino television tower, or any other strategic objective. Several times on October 3 Zyuganov spoke before audiences of many thousands, arguing that any foray from the White House would be used by the authorities as an excuse to bombard the building, disperse its defenders, and eradicate the surviving institutions of Soviet power in Russia. Zyuganov later said he had reliable information on this matter.

Anpilov's supporters and some of Zyuganov's allies in the National Salvation Front were too radically minded and would not listen to Zyuganov. General Albert Makashov also refused to heed Zyuganov's advice. Late in the evening of October 3, when bloody clashes had already begun at Ostankino and the Moscow mayor's office had been captured, Zyuganov asked for and received permission to appear on

235

television. He appealed to all participants in the confrontation to abstain from any further use of force. But "revolutionary ardor" carried the day, and the tragic results are well known. When martial law was introduced in Moscow the CPRF was temporarily banned and Zyuganov went into hiding for several days. But the authorities had no grounds for banning the CPRF permanently.

Not only did the CPRF avoid destruction in October 1993 but in the Duma elections in December that year it achieved a substantial success. A strong and influential CPRF group was formed in the Duma, with Zyuganov and Kuptsov at its head, and the party found it had significant new opportunities for legal activity.

The work of the CPRF and Zyuganov in the Duma was quite successful. Zyuganov has often said that the Duma was really a screen for one-man rule by a president intent on destroying Russia. But he has also noted that the Duma can function constructively as both a legislative and a representative body. At any rate the Communists were very assiduous about attending all Duma sessions. Both as a Duma delegate and as leader of the CPRF Zyuganov traveled around the country a great deal and spoke before the most varied audiences. During the course of a year he visited forty or fifty different regions of Russia. This was of great importance in helping to establish local party organizations.

As a result of the very intense activity of the CPRF and of Zyuganov in particular, and because of the continued worsening of the economic situation in Russia, increased crime, and general instability in society, not to mention the war in Chechnya, the political influence of the CPRF rose dramatically. In the Duma elections of 1995, as we have seen, the CPRF emerged confidently as the main winner.

It was evident to all political observers that if the presidential elections were held, the CPRF and its allies would be the chief opponents of the Yeltsin regime. In 1994–95 Zyuganov himself replied in the negative when asked if he would run for president. But on February 15, 1996, an all-Russia conference of the CPRF officially nominated him as the party's candidate, and he immediately emerged as the favorite in all the polls.

Zyuganov's energetic participation in the election campaign, his numerous appearances before the most varied audiences, his replies to questions, and his effective polemics all made it possible for observers to assess his capacities as a politician and his potential as a leader. His speeches held the attention and won the approval of sympathetic audiences, but he did not arouse his listeners. His answers to questions rarely drew applause. I never observed the kind of enthusiasm that was frequently seen during Yeltsin's speeches in 1989–90, or in 1996 when Lebed spoke.

Zyuganov himself says, "I am not a charismatic person." One might add that he is also not demagogic—in either the positive or the negative sense of the word. Andrei Fyodorov, of the Political Research Foundation, who knows Zyuganov well, wrote at the beginning of the 1996 campaign:

> Zyuganov today bears little resemblance to the man he was two or three years ago. Today he is above all a self-confident politician who thinks out his steps with care and precision. He no longer needs to prove his legitimacy or the legitimacy of the Communist Party—society's change of mood in that respect is evident.
>
> But one thing has remained unchanged—Zyuganov still has no charisma in the traditional sense of the term. Some other politician might turn himself inside out trying to achieve charisma. But not Zyuganov.
>
> Zyuganov has the backing of the most numerous and best organized political party in Russia. Therefore he doesn't have to be overly concerned with charisma. The press seizes upon his every word, and his frequent appearances . . . to judge from opinion polls, have had a palpable effect.
>
> (*Nezavisimaya Gazeta*, March 20, 1996)

Miroslav Buzhkevich, a political commentator, appraised Zyuganov's personal qualities this way:

> Zyuganov is not hasty about making decisions; he is undeniably thoughtful and reflective. He is not a poseur, although he knows how to present himself and his party in a favorable light. He is harsh but not noisy and obstreperous like Zhirinovsky. About such people it is said: they make their bed softly but sleep hard. A real fighter in debate, he is never at a loss for words, but he cannot be called a fanatic. His views and convictions are fully formed. He does not retreat from them, although he knows how to tack and veer. He is far sighted. The CPRF already has a shad-

ow cabinet, a Zyuganov team, which would go with him to the Kremlin if he won the election. . . .

Objectively the CPRF leader is in a better position than his main opponent. For now he is not under the gun because of promises he failed to keep. And he has an ace up his sleeve—the only party in Russia with a real mass membership and a reliable organizational structure.

(*Delovoi Mir* [Business World], March 2, 1996)

ZYUGANOV'S IDEOLOGY: GENERAL FEATURES

For the mass audience in Russia, the general impression a politician makes is very important. The ordinary voter does not study party programs or election campaign literature or read the books written by the leading candidates, like those by Yeltsin, Zyuganov, and Lebed in the last few years.

However, for political observers and commentators, for party activists, for journalists and scholars who help shape public opinion, the ideologies of the leading politicians are also quite important. What do they think about Ukraine, Transcaucasia, Kazakstan, and Central Asia? What about Russia's relations with the West? What are their priorities in domestic and foreign policy? What are their views on such questions as private property and religion, the army, the mass media, democracy, problems of ethnic relations?

It is not easy to evaluate or study Yeltsin's ideology, which is subordinated to the pragmatic consideration of holding onto power. To remain in power, Yeltsin is willing to alter many, if not all, his ideological priorities. Zyuganov, however, as the leader of a Communist Party, cannot allow himself that kind of latitude. His statements on prime questions of political theory are fairly consistent. In the 1996 election campaign he continued to expound many of the same views on social and national questions that he had in 1991–92. This consistency does not, however, mean he has a unitary conception. His views are eclectic. He borrows something from Lenin, something from the Russian religious philosopher Ivan Ilyin, something from Marx and something from the Russian nationalist writer Aleksandr Prokhanov, something from Stalin and something from the German geopolitical theorist Karl Haushofer.

Zyuganov enthusiastically accepts some of the ideas of the nine-teenth-century writer Constantine Leontiev, advocate of a strong monarchical state, a fixed hierarchy of social castes, and strict reli-giosity as well as some of the ideas of Lev Gumilyov, a contemporary Russian thinker and ethnographer who has studied the fates of many past civilizations on the territory of today's Russia. Zyuganov mixes certain ideas taken from Marxist doctrine or the works of Lenin with concepts of official patriotism and Russian nationalism that are alien to classical Marxism. In Zyuganov's writings, some very modern ideas on humanity's need for "sustainable development," as proposed by Valentin Koptyug, vice president of the Russian Academy of Sciences, alternate with the conception of Moscow as "the third Rome," as pre-sented by the abbot Filofei in the late fifteenth and early sixteenth cen-turies.

Zyuganov makes no attempt to tie all these heterogeneous ideas into a single internally consistent system—an impossible task anyway. Nor does he try to go very deeply into any particular aspect of this hodgepodge ideology, for that might lead him into a blind alley or cause his none-too-stable ideological construction to fly apart.

In replying to critics of his theoretical "system," he usually resorts to superficial historical analogies. In 1992 he wrote: "Certain objec-tions are made against our views, not without malice. 'Excuse us,' they say, 'but you are proposing to unite that which cannot be united—democracy, socialism, and the Russian idea.' History gives quite a few examples of things that, it seemed, could not be united, but that *were* united when the need for self-preservation arose. Who would have thought in 1933 that the anti-Hitler coalition could have been creat-ed, when the U.S., England, and France, on the one hand, and the USSR, on the other, were separated by a chasm of irreconcilable inter-ests?" (see Zyuganov, *Drama vlasti* [The Drama of Power], Moscow, 1993, p. 63).

This analogy is wrong. There have been many coalitions of various kinds in history among governments with differing regimes and ide-ologies. The most unusual pairings of political partners are possible. One example is the "right-left" coalition at the heart of the opposition to Yeltsin in 1992–93. In forming coalitions, the various parties do not renounce their own ideologies or political platforms. On the other hand, it is impossible, for example, to unite Christianity, Judaism, and

Islam into a single whole, even though certain general historical and epistemological roots can be found in common for all three religions.

Nevertheless, Zyuganov does try to unite things that really cannot be united, and his books, pamphlets, articles, and interviews contain many completely contradictory assertions.

In all fairness we must admit that Zyuganov does not try to impose his ideology on others; it is not obligatory even for members of the CPRF. He seems to regard his ideas for the most part as provisional constructs. He doesn't exaggerate the theoretical merits or achievements of himself or his party. Noting how important it is that a new philosophical and historical theory be fashioned, Zyuganov has commented that "the CPRF has already accomplished something in this regard . . . , but an integrated, scientifically grounded theory of how the future of Russia will be shaped, one that breaks with the obsolete past but at the same time preserves traditionalism and acknowledges Russia's exceptional uniqueness, has not yet been created" (see Zyuganov, *Rossiya—Rodina moya* [Russia—My Motherland], Moscow: Informpechat, 1996, pp. 285–86).

Nevertheless the current ideology of the CPRF and its leader needs to be analyzed. Without pretending to do this thoroughly or entering into an exhaustive debate with Zyuganov, I outline below some of his more important ideas, many of which have found expression in the CPRF program.

Russia as Exceptional and Unique

Central to all of Zyuganov's ideological constructs is the idea that Russia is a society that has taken shape in historically unique and exceptional ways, as a "special civilization that has taken various governmental or state forms at various times, with varying borders and with varying sociopolitical structures, but always remaining ineradicably unique (*samobytny*—being unto itself, one of a kind) and internally, spiritually self-sufficient" (*Nezavisimaya Gazeta*, October 17, 1996).

"Russia is an autonomous economic organism, distinct from the Western free-market model" (Zyuganov, *Rossiya i sovremennyi mir*, Moscow: RAU Corporation, 1996, p. 20).

This definition lacks concreteness and does not answer the question, Which Russia should one seek to restore and defend? It is well known that Zhirinovsky thinks in terms of a Russia with the borders it had in 1913—plus Alaska, plus new territory extending southward to the warm waters of the Indian Ocean, a Russia divided into provinces that would be called *gubernia*s, as under the tsars, and without any autonomous non-Russian national republics, provinces, or districts. For Solzhenitsyn, on the other hand, Russia ought to be a single Slavic state uniting Russians, Ukrainians, and Byelorussians, but not the Baltic region, Central Asia, or Transcaucasia. For Boris Mironov, leader of the Russian Patriotic Party, Russia is above all a national state, created by and for the Russian nation.

What does Zyuganov think about all this? He does not want to restore the borders of 1913. For him, Finland, Poland, and Manchuria are not part of Russia, although they came under the domination of the Russian empire. On the other hand, the entire Caucasus region in his view is part of Russia. As for Central Asia, he holds his tongue, but he sharply criticizes the constitution of Tatarstan, which declares that Tatarstan is "a sovereign state, an entity under international law, associated with the Russian Federation." To recognize constitutions with such wording in Tatarstan, Chechnya, or Tuva is, in Zyuganov's view, for Russia to fall apart. But is it true, as he says, that Armenia, Georgia, and Chechnya are the "heirs and continuators of the thousand-year traditions of Kievan Rus and the Muscovite state"?

Aside from that, how are the traditions of the Muscovite state to be reconciled with those of the Union of Soviet Socialist Republics? How is the Islamic land of the Uzbeks to be included as part of the "unique organism" of Russia?

Zyuganov often repeats Ilyin's formulation regarding "the younger brothers of the Russian nation who as a result of mutual spiritual understanding have created a cultural and linguistic unity."

For Zyuganov, the fact that Russian civilization is "the result of the activity of the Russian nation should not be offensive to the Jew or the Yakut or the Cherkessian because the basis for the well-being of all the peoples who have linked their fates with Russia is the vital force of 'the Russian idea' " (*Nezavisimaya Gazeta*, October 17, 1996).

I will not go into the losses suffered in the realm of language and culture by the Jews, Yakuts, and Cherkessians, losses that could have been avoided while maintaining the integrity of Russia. Instead I will ask how two ancient civilizations, those of Armenia and Georgia (which existed thousands of years before the rise of the Kievan state or the Muscovite grand duchy) can be included in a single "Russian civilization" or "Russian idea"? As for Tatars and Kazakhs, whom Zyuganov includes among "the younger brothers of the Russian nation"—won't they regard his version of "Russian civilization" as insulting and unacceptable? Why should Chechens or Lezghians consider themselves "younger brethren" relative to Russians?

We could go on with such questions, but Zyuganov avoids answering them, preferring vague generalizations about Russia's "self-sufficiency."

The Soviet Union was broken up and destroyed first of all because of a clumsy and mistaken policy toward non-Russian nationalities and because of nationalist movements that consequently arose. Similar processes and movements are continuing within the Russian Federation. The unity of the Russian Federation can and should be strengthened and many ties with former Soviet republics can and should be restored, but this can't be done with slogans about "Holy Russia." Ideas and solutions of quite a different kind are needed.

Official Patriotism

This concept is an extension of Zyuganov's notion of Russia's uniqueness and is virtually the central component of his world outlook. He writes:

> "The state cannot live without an ideology. And if it is impossible to restore that by which society was guided in the last several decades, then it is necessary to create something new on the basis of traditional spiritual and cultural values. The Russian idea, supplemented by the current realities of life and the social conquests of socialism, achieved during the seventy years of Soviet rule— those are the components of the new state ideology that can be called the ideology of official government patriotism."

(*Pravda Rossii* [Russia's Truth], April 6, 1995)

Zyuganov often repeats: "For me the most important party is Russia." According to him, the Soviet state was the logical continuation of the Russian empire, which had taken shape over the course of centuries. It is therefore necessary, in his opinion, to reexamine all previous dogmatic interpretations of the history and nature of the Russian state, rejecting the negative appraisal of such terms and concepts as "autocracy" and "empire."

It is a commonly understood fact, however, that negative attitudes toward the Russian autocracy and empire became firmly lodged in the consciousness of many generations of Russian revolutionaries in the nineteenth and twentieth centuries. Such attitudes were dominant in the outlook of Russia's great writers, from Pushkin and Lermontov to Tolstoy and Nekrasov. For Zyuganov this doesn't matter. They were all terribly wrong, he claims.

> They tell us that *empire* and *government power (derzhava)* mean an all-powerful bureaucracy, suffocating censorship, and an absence of elementary liberties. That they represent the violation of national sensibilities, contempt for the individual, and a trampling underfoot of the natural standards of human coexistence. Lies! Empire is the historically and geopolitically predetermined form of the development of the Russian state. It is . . . the framework of a great power encompassing a multitude of variegated tribes and peoples, bound by the unifying force of a common, advanced culture, by a consciousness of the equality of all before the law and the supreme power of the state . . . Russia from ancient times was aware of itself as the heir and preserver of the imperial heritage. "Moscow is the third Rome." With this extremely precise formulation the abbot Filofei as long ago as the late fifteenth and early sixteenth century expressed the centuries-old continuity of the Russian state idea.
>
> (Zyuganov, *Derzhava* [The Mighty State], p. 15)

Zyuganov is enthralled not only with the formula "Moscow, the third Rome." He often cites another celebrated formula: "Autocracy, Orthodoxy, Nationality." Zyuganov writes:

> In the thinking of the latest interpreters of the formulation "Moscow, the third Rome," the historical movement from Rome through Byzantium to Moscow represented a consistent coming-into-being (*stanovlenie*) of the three fundamental principles of the imperial state system: the unity under law and under the power of the state that characterized Rome was enriched by the moral-spiritual, Christian unity of Byzantium, and finally achieved perfection in the national-popular unity of Muscovite

243

Rus, Russia. This was expressed in the formula Autocracy, Orthodoxy, Nationality, which was put forward a century and a half ago by Minister of Education S. S. Uvarov.

(Zyuganov, *Rossiya—Rodina moya*, pp. 224–225)

This line of argument is not very convincing. What national-popular unity or equality of all before the law can you speak of in regard to Muscovy or the tsarist empire? Zyuganov himself admits that the formulas he cites were controversial and that their critics in the Russian revolutionary-democratic press were justified. In the tradition of the Russian democratic movement of the nineteenth century, Count Sergei Uvarov (1785–1855) was customarily regarded as one of the most reactionary ideologues of the tsarist regime. Does it make sense to try now to revive his "theory of official nationality," which he presented in a memorandum to Tsar Nicholas I in 1832 and which, after receiving the tsar's approval, he sought to make the basis of a rigidly reactionary educational system for Russian youth?

Zyuganov thinks this is a good thing to do, and he defends Uvarov's "theory" with hardly any change of emphasis from that of its originator. Zyuganov even describes Uvarov's formula as "ingenious." "Autocracy," Zyuganov writes,

is the principle of state structure which assumes full sovereignty and political independence in concert with the conscious aims of a great power. The grand dukes of Muscovy began to refer to themselves as "autocrats" precisely at the time when Russia had finally become a country freed from foreign influences. For many long centuries, autocracy became the only possible principle for gathering together a country characterized by exceptional variety.

(Zyuganov, *Derzhava*, p. 17)

As was to be expected, Zyuganov's concept of official state patriotism was most sharply criticized by other Communists of many different tendencies. One of them, Mikhail Antonov, writing in *Pravda* (April 26, 1994), expressed the view that the CPRF, if it followed Zyuganov's proposals, would inevitably cease to be the vanguard of Russian working people, their leader and defender, and would become a national-patriotic party, a nationalist party loyal to the government, one that many of the wealthy "new Russians" would be willing to support. Others among Zyuganov's opponents have asked,

If patriotism is love for one's country, then what is official state patriotism? Love of the state? What state? How can one love a *state*, anyhow?

Zyuganov has not entered into this theoretical discussion. He contends that if the CPRF is not to become a party of "pensioners and supporters of the nomenklatura," a mere leftover of "the heritage of the past," it must be made a party of "Communist supporters of the state" (*kommunisty-derzhavniki*). "The new Communists," he writes,

> are different from their arrogant and stagnant predecessors of the nomenklatura. With the aim of restoring the collective (*soborny*) unity of society, they have rejected the extremist thesis of class struggle, which threatens to tear apart the body of the nation with internal conflicts and divisions. Thus, a decisive step has been taken toward ideological healing. . . . The chief advantage of the new ideological and political platform of the Communists . . . which allows them to look to the future with confidence, is their firm adherence to the ideals of social justice and social equality, which is in profound harmony with the traditional values of the structure of our national life, the life of the people.

(*Derzhava*, p. 127)

The logic of this sudden shift from the ideals of Count Uvarov to those of equality and justice is not at all clear. It is to be achieved, according to Zyuganov, by means of "dialectical unity, mutual tolerance, and constructive compromise." Along this path of "the unity of opposites" we encounter the concept of people's power (*narodovlastiye*) which would seem to stand in obvious contradiction to the ideal of autocratic power.

"People's Power"

Stalin's version of socialism and Brezhnev's "actually existing socialism" discredited the very concept of socialism in the minds of many. By the same token the "democratic" reforms of the last few years have discredited the very concept of democracy for many. Zyuganov rarely uses the term "democracy' but he writes at length about the establishment of "people's power" in Russia: "The decisive condition for preserving and strengthening the Russian state system," he writes, "is the

245

restoration of people's power—rule by the overwhelming majority of the working population" (*Derzhava*, p. 65).

What we have in power in Russia today, Zyuganov says, is a criminal comprador bourgeoisie and a bureaucracy interconnected with it. But these circles lack any justifying principle for their rule. They have produced nothing but declining living standards, social divisions, war, and civil war. They must be removed from power.

As for those in the section of the entrepreneurial class who think in terms of state interests, according to Zyuganov, they face a choice: "either to agree to the leading role of the toiling classes in the effort to save the country, or to end up in the camp of traitors to the fatherland." "People's power" is not just rule by the people. "We must now speak as loudly as possible," Zyuganov writes, "although at one time people were ashamed to speak of it—about the role of the Russian people in the great family of Soviet peoples, their role in the formation and preservation of the state system. In their collective (*sobornoi*) completeness the Russian people are the state preservers of the Russian state principle, its primary vehicle and main defender" (*Derzhava*, p. 69).

The "Russian Idea" and the Russian Nation

Zyuganov's concepts of "the Russian idea" and the Russian nation are closely linked with his notions of official state patriotism and of Russia as a "unique civilization." Ever since the many-years-long debate between Slavophiles and Westernizers in the nineteenth century, arguments over "the Russian idea" or "the question of Russia" have persisted. So many different notions have been advanced in this regard that simply listing them would require too much space and time. Zyuganov's conception is of course a compilation from various, disparate sources. Unlike Vladimir Solovyov, whom Zyuganov so admires, he interprets "the Russian idea" in its much narrower aspect—the particular features and fates of Russians as a nation.

Zyuganov cannot find words enough to describe the lofty qualities, the uniqueness of the Russian people and their self-concept (*samosoznanie*). The Russian nation arose, as he sees it, not only on the basis of an ethnic community of ancient Slavic tribes but also as a community on a loftier, more spiritual plane. For example:

Hence, in many respects our "universal humanness," our national quality of patience, the absence of ethnocratic tendencies in our state structure, the celebrated qualities of "the Russian soul" which remain incomprehensible to the West even today: mercy, compassion, and patience combined with amazing sturdiness, courage, and capacity for self-sacrifice. . . . Over the course of many centuries, the Russian has striven to embody in all aspects of his being the ideals of holiness and purity of heart . . . the universal maxims of morality.

(*Derzhava*, p. 34)

Another example:

The adoption of Christianity, which united the freedom-loving Polyane, Drevlyane, Krivichi, Vyatichi, Radimichi [Slavic tribes that came under the rule of Christianized Kievan Rus] . . . laid the basis for the formation of that unique ethno-political and spiritual-ideological community that is known to the world by the name of the Russian people. . . . We are an idealist people, a dreamer people, a people performing heroic feats and exploits, often guided in our practical activity not by considerations of reason, advantage, or sober calculation, but by bursts of passion of incredible force. Sometimes these have brought Russia to the heights, to pinnacles of nearly unimaginable self-denial, self-sacrifice, heroism, and holiness.

(*Veryu v Rossiyu* [I Believe in Russia], Voronezh, 1995, pp. 43–44)

Far be it from me to dispute these lofty sentiments. But I have no desire to counterpose the Russian people to the other nationalities of Russia or of the former USSR or of other countries. In speaking of the uniqueness of the Russian nation, are we implying that other nations don't really measure up as ethnic groups? When we say that the Russian people are not deformed by the lust for consumerism, have not been spoiled by "a well-fed Paradise," doesn't this imply that other populations have been spoiled, are living without ideals, and regard nothing as sacred? Zyuganov of course is not trying to insult the French or the Germans. He speaks of "Westerners" in the abstract, people who lack Russian spirituality, concerned only with satisfying their sensual desires and therefore incapable of self-limitation based on moral criteria.

247

What does the "holiness" of the Russian people refer to? For Aleksandr Prokhanov, one of Zyuganov's friends and colleagues, it is a synonym for being chosen by God. "Divine Providence," Prokhanov writes, "chose Russia as the land and the people for whom Love and Truth would become the main reason for existence. . . . We are united in the National Patriotic Assembly of Russia [Russian initials, NPSR], where to the howling of demons, among traitors and executioners, we continue the work entrusted to us of saving and restoring Russian civilization" (*Zavtra*, 1996, No. 31). For the Communist Zyuganov this kind of explanation for the NPSR, which was founded on his initiative, is unacceptable. But he himself far too often speaks of the "holy" Russian people and the "foreign devils" of the West.

For many radical nationalists, to be Russian means to have purely Russian blood, several generations of purely Russian descent. For Russia, with its long and complicated history of the intermixing of nations, this kind of approach is dangerous. Zyuganov, as a shrewd politician, rejects it. "Being Russian today," he writes,

> means feeling with one's heart an affinity (*prichastnost*) with the profound culture of our Fatherland, the inexhaustible thirst for justice and righteousness (*pravednost*), the willingness for voluntary sacrifice, qualities that over the course of many centuries helped Russia to survive, amazing the world with its heroism, majesty, and long suffering. This road is open to all, regardless of what 'nationality' may be recorded in their passport. At its heart lie not common ties of blood, but mighty brotherhood of the spirit.
>
> (*Rossiya—Rodina moya*, p. 231).

Nevertheless, many of Zyuganov's statements indicate that those who are Russian by heredity, "by blood," are more Russian than the others. His pamphlet *Beseda na Puti k Svyatyne* [Conversation on the Road to a Holy Place], published by the Electoral Foundation of Candidate for President of the Russian Federation, G. Zyuganov (Moscow, 1996), carries the heading "I Am Russian by Blood and by Spirit."

National feelings are powerful forces that can be constructive or destructive. The Russian Federation remains a multinational state and cannot therefore be based on "the Russian idea," although it cannot ignore Russian national sensibilities either. Arguments to the effect that Russians constitute 83 percent of the population mean little. More than half the territory of the Russian Federation is occupied by nationalities who do not consider themselves Russian and who identify themselves with their native territories (Tatarstan and Yakutia for example). It is impossible to rally the populations of former Soviet republics around "the Russian idea," although the CPRF considers that one of its chief aims. The tragic lesson of the war against Chechnya, whose population constitutes less than one percent of the Russian Federation, should be taken under advisement by all who wish to construct a Russian Federation on a basis of peace and harmony.

Zyuganov tries to blend "the Russian idea" with the idea of socialism. He has often said that "the Russian idea is a profoundly socialist idea." In the nineteenth century the Narodniks made the same contention, using different terminology and citing native traditions of communal ownership of land in the Russian countryside. On the other hand, Zyuganov emphatically rejects internationalism, which in his opinion masks "indifference to the fate of Russia itself and willingness to sacrifice the age-old special qualities of the Russian people and their national interests to the Moloch of world revolution" (*Derzhava*, p. 127).

Various distortions and perversions of the idea of internationalism have certainly occurred in our history. But must the very idea of internationalism therefore be rejected? To be sure, the present humiliated position of the Russian people, the Russian nation, and its growing dependence on Western countries and the International Monetary Fund give rise to feelings of protest that are national as well as social in character. But every form of nationalism conceals substantial dangers within itself. How can the energies of national protest be accumulated without their taking the bloody course followed in Yugoslavia? That problem has not been resolved by Zyuganov or the other ideologues of the CPRF.

The Special Role of the Orthodox Church

Many Communists are divided over the question of the role of the church. One of Zyuganov's ardent supporters, Natalya Morozova, wrote in her "Urgent Appeal to the Future Communist President."

Gennady Andreyevich, we believe in you. Only, please don't repeat the mistakes of the past. I personally am sure that you will succeed in maintaining loyalty to basic Communist principles. . . . What I find sickening, though, is your playing around with the church. How can you shut your eyes to the sinister role of the church in the downfall of our country? Why, it is a kind of vampire, sucking away material resources from our impoverished country—and the last vestiges of reason from our people. The classical Marxists were a hundred times correct: "Religion is the opium of the people!" . . . Is it really the business of Communists to support the pernicious influence of the church? Is it not the outright duty of the Communists to expose and denounce the role of the church as an accomplice of the criminal regime?

(*Vernost*, 1996, no. 14.)

Zyuganov decidedly disagrees with such views. Even Yegor Ligachev declared that the Communists and the church should not only coexist but cooperate. Zyuganov goes further. Socialist ideas and values, he says, are very close to Christian values. For example, the idea of social justice is an earthly, secular manifestation of the "heavenly" truth that all are equal in the eyes of the Lord. "It is time that we recognized," Zyuganov writes, "that precisely the Russian Orthodox Church has been the historical support and expression of 'the Russian idea' in a form polished to perfection by ten centuries of our Russian state system."

The counterposing of science to religion, accompanied by the use of force, has done no one any good. It is time for even the most militant atheists to understand that there are various forms of cognition, of knowledge of the world. Each of them has its own irreplaceable qualities and characteristics. To cut off any one of them artificially impoverishes the spiritual condition of the nation as a whole.

(*Derzhava*, p. 32)

"Without the extremely high level of morality of the Orthodox Church," Zyuganov wrote elsewhere, "it would have been impossible for our people to survive the numerous burdens that have fallen to their lot."

It would be appropriate to point out to some of my opponents who still insist on characterizing religion as 'opium,' as deception of the people, and who consider it inexpedient to cooperate with the church, that one cannot help admitting the obvious: despite the energetic struggle against religion during the Soviet era, there was no success in the attempt to 'sweep the minds' of the people clean of it. Many people were baptized or married or observed other religious rituals and celebrated church holidays. Why reject or fight against something that the people hold onto so dearly? Isn't it better to take an attitude of respect and understanding toward the people's faith? Wherever I have had occasion to meet with officials of the Russian Orthodox Church, I have met sympathy and support.

(*Rossiya—Rodina moya*, p. 277)

This is an understandable position, although in a number of cases it has led Zyuganov to idealize Russian history and the role of the church in our history. He writes, for example, that the vast expanses of Russian civilization "were not appropriated the way it was done in the New World. We went forward not with the sword, but with the cross" (Ibid., p. 279). Any historian could easily show that we "went forward" with both the cross and the sword. To the east, to the south, and to the west. Or with the Red Star and the sword.

The Oneness of "Reds" and "Whites"

The Russian civil war, as Zyuganov sees it, was a tragedy that disrupted the unity of the people and the continuity of Russian history. The time has come, he believes, to heal that division. There is no need to inquire who was right or wrong. "Having united the 'Red' ideal of social justice and the 'White' ideal of a nationally conscious state system, perceived as a form of existence of the centuries-old sacred values of the people, Russia will find at last the longed-for social harmony between classes and social groups, as well as the mighty power of the state bequeathed to us by dozens of generations of our forefathers" (*Derzhava*, p. 27).

This solution is required by the current threat to the very existence of the Russian people, who have become superfluous on their own territory, who have been separated by absurd, even criminal borders, who have been deprived of a healthy state system, and who are being deafened by the propaganda of the officially controlled media. What is happening to the Russian people, says Zyuganov, is genocide. All patriots must therefore unite, as during the Great Patriotic War against Hitler's Germany when Stalin appealed to the lessons and values of Russian history and received the support of the Orthodox Church and a section of White emigres. "We made a huge mistake," Zyuganov writes, "when we acted as though before 1917 there was 'no history,' nothing but evil . . . They are trying to drive us into the same blind alley today, only with the signs reversed—as though *after* 1917 there was 'no history,' nothing but a great black hole. This too is an unparalleled lie! . . . It can be countered effectively only by recognizing the historical unity of Russian life in all its tragic and heroic many-sidedness" (*Derzhava*, p. 41).

Slavic Unity

Zyuganov condemns the destruction and disintegration of the Soviet Union, which had been a powerful state, the successor to the Russian empire. Within Russia, as within the Soviet Union, as many as 130 nations and nationalities had been united. But the core of the state had been the unity of the Slavic populations, through which lies the road to the revival of a Great Russia. "What do we mean when we speak of 'Great Russia'?" Zyuganov asks.

> By this I mean the Russian state, which undeniably includes within its borders all the territories on which there lives a compact Russian or Russian-speaking population; a state founded on the inseparable fraternal unity of the Great Russians, the Little Russians, and the Byelorussians, as well as all the tribes and nationalities that voluntarily wish to adhere to such a union. I do not think its borders will differ essentially from those of the USSR.
>
> (*Derzhava*, p. 43)

"Two Parties" Inside the Soviet Communist Party

Zyuganov urges his supporters not to delve into the ancient history of the party and the country, since differing interpretations could divide patriots and hinder the struggle against the current "regime of occupation." But Zyuganov himself is quite free in giving his appraisals of past events and periods in our history. He has nothing to say about its dark sides; that is not a subject of discussion for today, in his view. But he cannot ignore the massive criticism of the mistakes and crimes of the Soviet era that has poured forth in the last ten years and that for the most part is based on undeniable factual documentation.

In his address to the Constitutional Court Zyuganov sought to evade this criticism with the concept that there really were "two parties" inside the Soviet Communist Party. He has often returned to this theme—for example, in an interview that appeared in *Pravda* September 10, 1993:

> In the USSR there was not one, but two parties, and a stubborn struggle went on between them, never dying down for an instant. The fact that they were formally united within a single organization does not change the essence of the matter, because they had different ideologies, different goals, and different political and national priorities.
>
> To the first party belonged Sholokhov and Korolyov, Zhukov and Gagarin, Kurchatov and Stakhanov. Also belonging to it were the greater part of the ordinary or run-of-the-mill administrators and apparatchiks of the party, who unfailingly gave their all in our country's most difficult days. Most importantly, it was this party that the fighters on the front of the Great Patriotic War joined by the thousands, and it was to this party that there belonged millions of hard-working patriotic people whose heroic labors turned this country from an ash heap into the greatest power in the world. For all of them the USSR, as the historical heir of Russia, was the Fatherland, beloved and dear to their hearts. . . . This is the party of which we consider ourselves the heir.
>
> There was another party in the Soviet Union. Numerically it could not compare with the first, but in its political weight and influence at the highest echelons of power it was disproportionately large and often decisive. To it belonged those for whom "this country" and "these people" were just an arena for realizing their own inordinate ambitions and power-hungry drives, a testing ground for adventuristic social experiments. This was the party of Trotsky and Kaganovich, of Beria and Mekhlis, of

Gorbachev and Yeltsin, of Yakovlev and Shevardnadze. We do not wish to have anything to do with this party.

It is generally recognized that within the Bolshevik party even before the 1917 revolution there was an organization of professional revolutionaries that stood over and above the mass of rank-and-file party members. After the Bolsheviks came to power this division persisted in the form of an apparatus of professional party leaders (the nomenklatura), on the one hand, and the mass of the rank and file, on the other. But Zyuganov is not talking about this division between the leadership and the rank and file. Most of the present CPRF leaders came directly from the former apparatus of the CPSU; they themselves belonged to the nomenklatura.

The division Zyuganov has in mind is of a different kind: the honest and good Communists were one party; the bad ones were another. He does not care to specify which "party" Lenin belonged to, or Stalin, and he barely mentions Khrushchev or Brezhnev.

From this point of view the CPRF is not just the successor of the CPSU, but in essence a new party in which only the "good" element from the former CPSU may be found. The "bad" element joined Yeltsin's circle or found posts in the new non-Communist government.

The "two parties" conception also finds reflection in the CPRF program, which states that a final line of demarcation has been drawn between the two component parts of the former Communist Party and that only "healthy elements" have entered the CPRF. This concept may be convenient for avoiding responsibility in regard to the mistakes and crimes of the former leadership of the USSR and CPSU, but it is too primitive and unconvincing.

Zyuganov's Attitude Toward Stalinism

Zyuganov is quite consistent in pursuing the line that to avoid conflicts within the CPRF or between that party and its allies, it is necessary to abstain from judgments about the past. While hardly ever mentioning Brezhnev or Khrushchev, he does quote Lenin—infrequently—and sometimes even Marx. But he makes no assessment of Lenin or Leninism, thereby frequently provoking criticism from party veterans. He very rarely expresses himself on the question of Stalinism either, explaining that he had no personal experience of the Stalin era. "I grew up after the war," he often says, "and in my time there was no repression." Of course there was repression under Stalin after World War II—except, as Zyuganov would have it, in the villages of Oryol province where he grew up.

Zyuganov knows about the crimes of the 1920s and 1930s and takes a negative view of them. Here are some quotations from scattered articles or interviews:

"As early as the 1950s our party condemned the repression."

"We have known everything. Businessmen were suppressed, churches and the estates of the gentry were destroyed, the intelligentsia were persecuted, the relics of saints were dug up, entire nationalities were declared enemies. Today we rehabilitate people and we repent, but at the same time we create new enemies. Pick up the newspapers of the 1930s—isn't there the same tone, the same kind of arguments, the same intolerance and incitement to violence?"

"The situation today is reminiscent of the eve of 1937, when the entire people was drawn into the rivalry among Bonapartist groups, and the blood of the best and most talented sons of Russia flowed in rivers."

"During the twentieth century we have passed through the crucible of civil war and repression, suffocating ideological dogmas and spiritual genocide."

Zyuganov draws a sharp distinction between the Stalin of the 1920s and 1930s and the Stalin of World War II and after, when he began to act and speak like a patriot and a man loyal to the state (*derzhavnik*), when he made peace with the church and acknowledged the greatness of the Russian people, "first among equals."

In Zyuganov's view, if Stalin had lived five to seven years longer, he would have made his "ideological perestroika" irreversible and would have restored the Russian spiritual and governmental tradition.

A close look at the main policies Stalin followed from 1945 to 1953 is enough to refute these assertions. Moreover, Zyuganov makes no objection to an increasingly insistent tendency expressed in *Zavtra*, where he is on the editorial board, in *Pravda Rossii*, whose editorial board he heads, in other CPRF papers, and in such allied papers as *Sovetskaya Rossiya*—a tendency to rehabilitate Stalin and Stalinism and to flagrantly falsify history. He has repeatedly stated his willingness to compromise for the sake of unity against today's *bespredel*, the prevailing criminal disorder and rampant lawlessness. But even compromise has its limits. I am sure that

255

the eulogies to Stalin in the Communist press repel far more people than they attract.

Socialism

Zyuganov never misses a chance to mention his commitment to socialism: "I favor clearly stated conceptions. At the core of our national goals will be the ideas of brotherhood, justice, humanism, Russian spirituality and loyalty to the state (*derzhavnost*). This fully corresponds to the ideals of socialism" (*Komsomolskaya Pravda*, September 20, 1994).

In speaking of socialism, Zyuganov rarely refers to Marx or Lenin. He does not try to analyze the evolution of socialist ideas, merely commenting occasionally in passing on the need to renounce concepts that are "a century old" or "two centuries old," to abandon "that uncompromising Communist orthodoxy by which an outlived dogmatism managed to preserve itself, blocking the development of constructive possibilities and the potential for a scientific socialism" (*Sovetskaya Rossiya*, April 26, 1994).

"Without the socialist idea," he argues, "without the 'socialization of life,' that is, establishment of the primacy of social interests, there is no way out of the difficulties confronting the world today. Without that, both Russia and our planet as a whole are doomed" (*Sovetskaya Rossiya*, February 11, 1993). At the same time, Zyuganov stresses that he is far from being an apologist for the model of socialism that arose in the USSR. There is a need, he says, for a new conception of socialism to be created, for a new contribution to be made to the theory of socialism, to outline a new economic and social profile— a twenty-first century socialism based on postindustrial information technology and new models of production and consumption (*Sovetskaya Rossiya*, March 17, 1994).

Zyuganov summed up his outlook in a very concise formula: "Not back to socialism, but forward to socialism." In explaining his concept of socialism, he does not analyze class conflicts in Russian or Western society. He does not of course deny the existence of classes or of class struggle, but he obviously rejects the Marxist notion that all social problems must be viewed from the standpoint of class interests and class struggle. For Zyuganov, national interests take primacy. He does not accept Marx's dictum that the workers "have no fatherland."

Rather than enter into debate over such questions with the "orthodox" Marxists, Zyuganov simply waves them aside. "To defend
Russia, to save the people from genocide," he says, "is much more
important than to maintain one's ideological purity" (*Sovetskaya
Rossiya*, February 11, 1993).

Zyuganov's Renunciation of Revolutionary Violence

Zyuganov advocates fundamental changes in economic and social life,
a changed constitution, and the restoration of Soviet power. But since
1992 he has stated more than once that "Russia has exhausted its
capacity for revolutions." In a *Pravda* interview (August 10, 1994) he
said: "The number one thing that we reject . . . is the revolutionary
way of solving problems. The situation in our country, the existing
systems of technology, the abundance of especially dangerous types of
production and explosive materials—all these make it impossible for
any party to use such methods to assert its dominance. That would be
an adventure that would end in disaster."

Such statements have provoked criticism by some party theoreti-
cians. Sergei Kara-Murza sought to instruct Zyuganov, in the pages of
Pravda (October 12, 1994), on the concepts of revolution and the revolutionary method by giving examples of peaceful revolution.
Without engaging in polemics, Zyuganov altered his terminology. In
his articles and interviews in 1995–96 he said "Russia has exhausted
its capacity for civil wars" and declared that in our programs and in
our practical activity, we should renounce "revolutionary violence."
Logically he also rejects the call for a dictatorship of the proletariat,
which is still found in the documents of more radical Communist
groups. When he is reminded that this is one of the most important
elements in the teachings of Marx and Lenin he simply asserts that
"any dictatorship—whether of the proletariat, the landed gentry, or
the bourgeoisie—bodes no good" (*Delovoi Mir*, April 8, 1996). Why
argue, he adds, with those who "remain stuck in the last century and
will never make the leap into the present."

Social Democratic Ideas

It has often been said of Zyuganov that when speaking to Western
audiences he sounds like a social democrat, but when speaking in the

cities of Russia he sounds like a nationalist and supporter of a strong Russian state. These charges are not really fair, because some social democratic conceptions do find a place in Zyuganov's ideology (although not a big one, thus far). His renunciation of revolutionary violence and the dictatorship of the proletariat are examples of social democratic views that he shares. He and the program of his party also accept pluralism and a mixed economy. (See *Pravda*, August 10, 1994.)

He has hardly ever commented on questions concerning the international Communist or Social Democratic movements. He is completely absorbed with Russian problems,. Nevertheless in several interviews he has stated emphatically that he is not a Social Democrat and that "Social Democracy has no support and no future in Russia" (*Argumenty i Fakty*, 1996, no. 15, p. 9).

Sustainable Development

Of all contemporary social theories Zyuganov refers most often to that of sustainable development, which has become widespread in recent years. This theory does not ask the question, Socialism or capitalism? It was originated and promoted by a number of Western scientists and scholars. In Russia it has been popularized especially by Valentin Koptyug, vice president of the Russian Academy of Sciences and head of its Siberian Division (in Novosibirsk). His field of specialization is chemistry, and he is also a member of the Central Committee of the CPRF.

The theory advocates changing the very concept of "progress" and renouncing unrestrained consumerism. Nature's resources and potential are limited, and the human race is starting to destroy the natural basis of its own existence. The character of development must be changed and the utilization of natural resources worldwide must be brought under control. Such relatively new disciplines as demography, ecology, and futurology find expression in this theory. A major world conference on problems of sustainable development was held in Rio de Janeiro in 1992, attended by several thousand scientists, government officials, and social activists.

Many scientists with leftist views, like Koptyug, seek to employ the concept of sustainable development as an argument in favor of socialism, for only a worldwide socialist planned economy would be capable of rationally combining the interests of particular countries, humanity as a whole, and individual needs.

Many of the radical nationalists—Prokhanov's group, for example—strenuously object to Russia's accepting the concept of "sustainable development." They criticize the "globalists" of Novosibirsk. Worldwide environmentalist projects, as they see it, would only strengthen world regulatory bodies and other agencies of control and ultimately lead to a world government that would be dominated by the wealthier Western countries. "Sustainable development is a trap for Russia," they argue. (See *Zavtra*, 1996, no. 10.) Zyuganov disagrees. Here is his view (as expressed in *Rossiya—Rodina moya*, pp. 160–161):

> It is impossible to solve an entire complex of problems facing humanity today if Western consumer society is to become the global model for development.
>
> The capitalist form of progress has reached the limits of its possibilities. The model for production and consumption must be changed; the vector along which scientific and technical progress is to travel must be redefined. The overall body of ideas aiming toward this goal and the projects being undertaken in many countries come under the generally accepted heading of "sustainable development." Whatever the specific technical or organizational details connected with this theory, its social content and the world-historical mission of making it a reality are connected, in our opinion, with socialism and communism in their contemporary meaning, which naturally follows from the urgent objective needs of world development.

The West as Russia's Enemy

Zyuganov does not try to analyze situations in detail in the various countries of the capitalist West. They cannot be a model for Russia even if they have achieved significant success in economic, scientific, and technical development, in solving social problems, in education and health care, or in controlling the activities of monopolies. Of course, to the extent possible, anything valuable or useful that has been created by Western civilization should be borrowed. But it should not be forgotten, in Zyuganov's view, that the wealthy Western

259

countries are for the most part enemies of Russia, its geopolitical, ideological, and economic adversaries. The better Russia understands this, the better its cooperation will work out with Western countries in areas where that is possible and desirable. Cooperation with the West requires a clear and basic knowledge of the hidden springs and levers by which those countries are ruled. Western democracy is in many respects just a screen concealing the real sources of influence and power.

Zyuganov singles out one of these forces: "An ever more perceptible impact on the world outlook, culture, and ideology of the Western world," he has written,

> is beginning to be made by the Jewish diaspora, whose influence is constantly growing. . . . The Jewish diaspora, which has traditionally controlled the financial life of the continent, as its "own market" has grown, has become a kind of holder of the "controlling block" of shares in the whole economic system of Western civilization. The motifs of the "chosen people," of "a higher calling" to rule the world, and of their own exceptional status—which are typical of the religious beliefs of the Jews— these motifs are beginning to have a substantial effect on Western consciousness. . . . Under these circumstances . . . Slavic civilization acquires special significance.
>
> (Zyuganov, *Za gorizontom* [Beyond the Horizon], Moscow, 1995, p. 18)

During the Russian presidential campaign of 1996 these statements were widely publicized with a great deal of commentary by virtually all the democratic and independent newspapers. The strength and influence of Jewish capital in the West does not have to be proved. But it is far from being "the holder of the controlling block of shares" either in the U.S. economy or in those of Western Europe or Japan.

A Secret World Conspiracy

In discussing the reasons for the downfall of the Soviet Union and the CPSU, Zyuganov hardly ever talks about the deep internal contradictions of Soviet society, and the multinational Soviet state, which were never more than partially resolved and which in many respects have continued to deepen. Zyuganov's criticism is directed above all at the defective and harmful or even criminal methods employed by the leadership of the party and the country which came to prevail in the Gorbachev era and are continued in the work of the "conscienceless, unprincipled, and traitorous regime of politicos and hustlers which has been established on the ruins of the Soviet empire."

The destruction of Russia is not simply the result of ever growing internal contradictions that its leaders could not manage to overcome and that ultimately sundered the unity of the party and the country. The defeat of Russia was the result of a prolonged, well-planned, and ruthless struggle conducted by the anti-Communist and anti-Russian forces in the West, above all in the United States, which after World War II became not only the leader of the capitalist world but also the chief geopolitical opponent of the USSR. It was in the United States that the cold war strategy against the Soviet Union and other socialist countries was elaborated; it was there that military confrontation against the USSR was worked out and the arms race, so ruinous for the USSR, was planned, along with various forms of ideological and psychological warfare against Russia. Enormous forces and resources, both material and intellectual, were mobilized for this struggle. "After the basic conceptual postulates relating to the destruction of the USSR were formulated in America, they were assigned to hundreds of research institutions, and the corresponding programs were developed" (*Drama vlasti*, Moscow: Paleus, 1993, p. 76).

Such assertions are hardly original. The Western campaign against the USSR and CPSU is easily documented. At the very beginning of his presidency, for example, Ronald Reagan declared that the West would not simply contain Communism but overcome it; it would not simply nail Soviet Communism to the wall, but would get rid of it altogether. Khrushchev had made similar belligerent statements. During his visit to the United States, he made his famous prediction, "We will bury you." The conflict was two-sided, and the responsibility for the cold war, the arms race, and the tension in international relations lies with both the capitalist West and the socialist East. For decades this struggle was depicted for Soviet citizens as a battle by the forces of decaying imperialism against the forces of progress and socialism. Zyuganov adds some new elements to this picture. In the struggle against Soviet Russia, in his opinion, the United States never acted entirely on its own.

"Look closer," he says,

it is not really the government at all [that was doing this], but an immensely overgrown industrial-commercial corporation. It does not have its own national interests as such. It uses this term, the 'national interest,' to conceal the lust of the international financial oligarchy, in whose hands the political, military, and economic might of America serves merely as an instrument for achieving its own selfish goals and serving its own clan-connected interests. The cosmopolitan elite of international capital—that is the real behind-the-scenes director responsible for Russia's time of troubles!

(*Pravda*, July 3, 1993)

Zyuganov does not stop here. Both the United States and the "cosmopolitan elite of international capital" have existed for more than 200 years, but the struggle to remove Russia from the historical scene has gone on for more than a thousand. According to Zyuganov, Western governments and the transnational banking and finance corporations are ultimately only "obedient transmitters of an aggressive and relentless anti-Russian policy." The source and inspiration for this age-old policy is hidden somewhere behind the scenes. It is a secret world conspiracy (*Mirovaya Zakulisa*) that seems to have established its rule throughout the world and to have created supranational bodies of political, economic, and military power. "This maniacal idea," Zyuganov writes, "has an ancient history, closely linked with the development of secret political societies, religious sects, and mystical beliefs. Only at the end of the twentieth century has it attained the possibility of practical realization owing to the scientific and technological advances and objective processes of global economic integration.

"Only awareness of this alarming fact can give clarity and purpose to the patriotic movement for the revival of a nationally conscious Russian state system" (*Pravda*, July 3, 1993).

But what clarity and purpose can there be in fighting mystical beliefs and secret religious sects?

Zyuganov's theory of a secret world conspiracy is very important to him, for he returns to it constantly, explaining in detail the methods and techniques, the "algebra of politics," that the "director behind the scenes" employs with perfect mastery, a "director" for whom even the Communists "at the dawn of their existence were loyal allies."

(*Derzhava*, p. 53.) How can we cope with these all-powerful secret organizations if they have already brought all the Western countries, including the United States, under their control?

> The world conspiracy has taken decisive action in forming a harshly centralized system of coercive control over the development of human civilization. . . . This plan represents something more complex and multifaceted. In seeking to draw historical analogies, we cannot fail to recognize that in essence it is a worldwide Messianic eschatological religious project which, in its dimensions, the extent to which it has been thought out, and its thoroughness of preparation, goes far beyond the planetary utopias known to history—whether those of the Roman imperium of Tiberius and Diocletian, the Abassid caliphate, the Protestant fundamentalist movement in Europe, or the Trotskyist daydreams of World Revolution.
>
> The ideologists of one-worldism (mondialism) are themselves convinced that what is involved is the imminent arrival of a Messiah who will establish on earth the laws of a perfect religion and be the founder of a "golden age" for all humanity under the rule of a single Worldwide Supergovernment.

(*Pravda Rossii*, April 13, 1995)

Zyuganov's doctrine cannot be proven or refuted. One can either believe in it or not. For my part, I am unable to place any credence in this secret world conspiracy with its mystical director behind the scenes.

8

The Inevitability of Change

The balance sheet of 1996 did not justify the expectations of the optimists in the government camp nor of the pessimists in the opposition. Russians had been promised an economic upturn by the end of 1992, but even by the end of 1997 it still had not started. There was no increased output, not even the 1–2 percent that some of the more cautious economists had predicted. On the other hand, the economic or financial crash that many oppositional economists predicted did not happen either, nor did the social explosion that many had feared.

The government's only major achievement was to reduce inflation to 1–2 percent per month. This strengthened confidence in the ruble, and some citizens, cautiously, began using the services of the central savings bank again. The strengthening of the financial system, however, led neither to increased investment nor to a repatriation of funds the business elite had converted into foreign currency. The Gross Domestic Product declined by 5–7 percent. Only one-third of capacity was being utilized in processing industries. Unemployment grew, as did Russia's foreign and internal debt, while the gold and foreign currencies reserves of the central bank were reduced by one-third.

The scourge of the economy continued to be delayed payment of wages and benefits on a massive scale. Tens of millions of people were not paid on time; factories and the army delayed payment of their bills for fuel and electric power; in many sectors payment in kind replaced monetary exchange. The 1996 budget was not met, for either income or expenditures. Taxes were so high (100–200 percent of profits!), and there were so many of them (more than 200), that virtually every economic entity in one way or another avoided paying them. Only the "shadow economy" continued to grow. Economic indicators for commercial banks grew worse, and hundreds of credit institutions ended the year with losses. Several dozen banks failed, including some large ones, like the Tver Universal Bank.

After the elections, Yeltsin and the government canceled many decrees that had been put into effect during the first half of 1996. Of the 12 trillion rubles that were supposed to come into the government's budget as a result of privatization, only about one trillion were received by the end of 1996. Agricultural production in Russia declined during the year by 6–7 percent. Plans to ship necessary goods and resources to northern parts of the country were not fulfilled. The number of poor people increased during the year, and their poverty deepened. Even the wealthy did not increase their income significantly.

The government's budget and economic projections for 1997 aimed only at small or partial improvements, plugging the worst leaks and catching up on unpaid wages. The government had neither the resources nor the imagination for any major change of direction.

Outside government circles, many proposals were made for bringing the country out of its crisis, including a variety of "breakthrough strategies" elaborated by business groups. All these programs and proposals required a sharp turn in economic and social policy—new priorities and new directions. They had many features in common: for example, they advocated reestablishing many of the previously existing instruments of government regulation, and in many cases urged direct government management of a substantial part of the economy(monopoly-dominated areas), much of the military-industrial complex, and, especially, large enterprises and some transport systems. In other words, the affected areas were those where regulation by the market based on private ownership had proved unworkable or inefficient.

All the new programs advocated rational and effective conversion of part of Russia's military industry, the utilization for Russia's economic development of the advanced technology achieved in the military-industrial complex, the millions of highly skilled workers employed there, as well as its engineers, draftsmen, and scientists, and its social infrastructure. To this day significant opportunities for Russia's military-industrial complex exist in the markets of Third World countries, especially Arab and Islamic countries, but they are going to waste. There is also underutilized potential for rational collaboration and cooperation with China and India.

All the new programs advocated support for and intensification of economic integration within the framework of the Commonwealth of Independent States, and partly within the former Council of Mutual Economic Assistance (Comecon). The single economic space that had been destroyed needed to be rebuilt wherever it was possible and advantageous for all partners.

All the new programs provided for rational regulation of imports and exports, and an end to those that were proving harmful. There should be no large-scale importing of products that can be produced just as well, given some state subsidies, by native industry and agriculture.

All the new programs envisaged revision and correction of the most harmful and illegal instances of privatization. On the other hand, they favored support for rational and legal commercial agreements, including joint ventures, that were advantageous.

I will not list all the various proposals for extricating Russia from its present crisis. Some of them were even advocated by the Yeltsin government, but it had neither the motivation nor the means for putting them into effect. These proposals included government support for small- and medium-sized business, reducing taxes and straightening out the tax system, restoring the government monopoly on the sale of alcohol and tobacco, government support for science, culture, and education, and suppression of gangsterism, especially in its most dangerous forms.

One thing must be made clear: any serious change of economic and social policy would require new people, a new leadership team. Neither Yeltsin and Chernomyrdin, nor Chubais and Lifshitz, nor Potanin and Ilyushin could introduce and carry out new reforms that would avoid either a return to the stagnation of the administrative-command economy or a continuation of the present policy of unrestrained market madness (*bespredel*) and the semi-colonial plundering of Russia. There are also many doubts about the ability of the CPRF's shadow cabinet to do what is needed in this regard. The CPRF cabinet consists almost entirely of people who were active in the Soviet political and economic system as early as the 1980s but failed to distinguish themselves.

A change of economic policy, then, will require a change of leadership. It is hardly likely that such changes will happen automatically. Political pressure from the population will be needed. It exists and is growing, but slowly. Several times boundaries have been crossed that many observers thought would result in a social explosion, but—to the surprise even of those in power—there has been no such explosion. Of course no one desires a blind, undirected social outburst. Any political or social cataclysm could lead to unpredictable and serious consequences. But there do exist in our country social and political mechanisms through which the people can rather clearly express their discontent, their desires, their demands.

Why has this not happened? How has the Yeltsin regime succeeded in winning most of the elections so far? I have already indicated some of the reasons, having to do with our past totalitarian heritage. In addition to those, however, some other considerations having to do with the real situation today need to be taken into account. Below I list some that are evident on the surface.

The Unevenness of Economic Development and Depression

The deterioration of the economic situation in the 1990s occurred everywhere, but to different degrees in different areas. It all depended on such factors as the economy of a city or region, the policies and prestige of local authorities, and the geographic location of a region. Instability in Vladivostok and the Pacific maritime region was combined with relative stability in the neighboring Khabarovsk region; life proceeded more calmly in Lipetsk than in Bryansk; the food situation was better in Ulyanovsk province than in Sverdlovsk; in Tataria things were more stable than in the Komi region.

The general opinion is that things are better now in Moscow than in St. Petersburg. In 1991 the situation in Moscow was very bad, which contributed to the downfall of Gorbachev. They remained bad during 1992, which sharpened the conflict between the Yeltsin-Gaidar government and the Russian Supreme Soviet in 1993. There had been an unwritten law—observed even under Stalin—to keep the material situation as favorable as possible for the population of Moscow and the Moscow region.

Revolutions have often begun in capital cities. We think of Petrograd in 1917, Paris in 1789, Budapest in 1956, East Berlin in 1953 and 1989, and Prague in 1968. Control of the capital usually means control of the country. In the absence of a strong revolutionary movement in the capital, radical movements in other cities find it difficult to succeed. Peasant wars have followed a different pattern, but in industrially developed countries the role of rural regions and the rural population cannot be very great.

The Absence of Inspiring Ideas and Slogans

In early 1996 Yeltsin called on politicians and scholars to come up with an idea that would be unifying for all of Russia. There were many suggestions, and the pro-government newspaper *Rossiiskaya Gazeta* announced a contest with a prize of $2,000 for the best slogan (not very much for such an important item). A true "national idea" could hardly be produced by such a contest. On the other hand, if the government had no unifying idea, neither did the opposition, then or now. Various opposition groups proclaim their own ideas and call for the defense of "sacred values." But calling for a return to the "rosy past" is no more inspiring than appeals based on the prospect of a "rosy future."

Mass protest actions have occurred around such relatively limited ideas and slogans as "Give us back our savings," "Pay us on time," "Pay us our pensions." But these are not slogans than can unite an entire nation.

Politically Active Retirees and Politically Passive Youth

Older people have taken the most active part in mass opposition demonstrations; youth have hardly participated at all. Political passivity is also typical of university students today. There are many ways, none too burdensome on the budget, to distract young people from politics, and the Yeltsin regime has used all of them. In comparison to the totalitarian era, young people today feel relatively free. Russia's material difficulties are more easily overcome by those who are young and strong. But revolutions have historically been the work of the youth. Without participation by the young neither the left nor the nationalist opposition can expect success.

The Rural Population: Primary Support of the Opposition

In the 1996 elections the rural population was more active than the urban working class, and those working on the land supported the CPRF opposition more than did those in the major industrial centers. This can be explained only in part by the economic situation, which was worse in the countryside than in the cities. There is a greater differentiation of the population in the cities, and more distractions from politics; also, government propaganda seems to have more of an impact there. Attractive imported goods flow mainly to the cities. Urban residents are more dependent on a complex life-support system that could be disrupted by mass upheavals—public transportation, municipal heating systems, water supply, gas, electricity, shopping. The structure of modern urban life is quite fragile: millions of city residents depend on elevators, buses, telephones, the subway. Under such conditions, the capture or destruction of government buildings would solve nothing, and the anarchy that would accompany any revolution in its early stages frightens urban dwellers much more than rural inhabitants.

The Absence of a Political Vanguard

In Russia today there are many opposition parties, but the positions held by most of them are relatively moderate. This is true of the CPRF as well. The radical parties have very little influence. There are no firm ties between any party and the masses of workers. Ideas about changing the existing system by force, once so popular, have now lost their attraction for most people in the advanced industrial countries. Other political ways of changing the nature of power have only begun to take shape in Russia. Real political parties, whose policies and tactics could prove adequate to the situation, are also only in their formative stages.

Social Safety Valves for Public Discontent

The enormous potential of social discontent and the great energy of protest have been dissipated to a large extent by a multitude of social

269

safety valves. Most of these have come into existence of their own accord, but some have been supported by the Yeltsin government, which quickly recognized the role that such safety valves could play.

One of the main safety valves has been *the freedom to trade*. In 1992 Yeltsin issued a decree making it possible to sell or buy whatever one wished wherever one wished. Official control over buying and selling was temporarily suspended. Later, some regulations were reimposed on commerce, but only partially. Even today one is permitted to sell things at a bazaar or on the street or at a subway entrance. Impoverished members of the intelligentsia sell their books and belongings, pensioners at subway stations sell cigarettes, vodka, canned goods, and in general everything that could be bought at the store right next to them. The huge number of sidewalk booths and vendors bring goods more directly to the consumer and provide employment for many. Millions of Russian, mostly between the ages of 30 and 50, are engaged in this form of commerce.

A second safety valve is *cheap alcohol*. Today a bottle of vodka costs no more than the equivalent of three loaves of white bread, whereas in 1970–1980 it would have cost the equivalent of 25 loaves. For the price of a kilogram of meat today one can buy two or three bottles of vodka.

Another important safety valve has been *private gardening*. The slogan "land to those who work it" has been carried out in truncated fashion. All restrictions on gardening and fruit growing have been lifted in the last few years, with the land used for gardens and orchards becoming the property of those who work it. Tens of millions of people provide a substantial part of their own diet from such gardens and orchards.

Freedom of Travel and Freedom of Emigration

These also function as social safety valves. The possibility of finding work in other countries exists for a significant section of the socially and intellectually active part of the population, especially the scientific and technical intelligentsia. Thousands of scientists and engineers are working under contract now in China and other countries, including Iran and South Africa. They remain citizens of Russia. Hundreds of thousands of others have left Russia permanently. Their preferred destinations are the United States and Israel, after that Germany. But many former Russian or Soviet citizens can be found in Spain, Italy, Austria, and the Scandinavian countries.

Relative Freedom of Speech

When you can speak, write, or shout if you wish about a difficult situation, it no longer seems so difficult. One does not feel squeezed to the breaking point. Dissidence is no longer persecuted. The press publishes a great deal of critical material, and this gives a certain outlet for feelings of protest and dissatisfaction.

Relatively Democratic Elections

Participation in elections that are conducted according to fairly democratic rules reduces the level of protest and restrains the impulse of many to take to the streets. "After all, we elected this government," some say. Others say, "Wait till the next election. Then we'll show them."

The Role of the Opposition in Parliament

By moving debate from the open streets and squares to within the walls of parliament, the opposition's presence and activity in the Duma reduces the level of discontent by providing an avenue for its expression.

The Role of Television

"Bread and circuses," Ancient Rome's way of keeping the plebeians happy, has been adopted by ruling groups in the modern world. Television of course is not just an information medium but a source of entertainment and distraction for all strata of the population. It also provides unparalleled opportunities for manipulating public opinion. Most television time is devoted to entertainment and sports. The vast number of videos on the market, including pornographic ones, serve the same function—to distract people from real problems. To this may be added the proliferation of computer games and other entertainments inexpensive for both the public and the regime. So much for circuses. Bread, on the other hand, in Russia is still in short supply.

The Marginalization of Protest

In contemporary democratic society ethnic and class differences now play a different role. Children of workers, peasants, and poor people, if they are talented or strong-willed or have exceptional abilities, can rise into higher social circles or make careers for themselves. They can even be successful in business, although this is more difficult in the capitalist economy now taking shape. Nevertheless, capable and energetic people from the lower classes or from groups suffering national discrimination can find advancement and accomplishment in society and therefore do not join or stay in opposition movements. Thus, a substantial number of those who have been impoverished in the last few years are marginal types, people who are not very capable or energetic, and this significantly reduces the potential for an active and effective opposition movement. It is enough to compare the top leadership of the Russian Communist Party in 1917–1918 with the Communist leaders today. Zyuganov is no Lenin and Anpilov is no Trotsky.

The social safety valves enumerated above—and there are others—have undoubtedly reduced the level of social protest and left few prospects for radical opposition. But they have not removed the basic causes of discontent, which, in the absence of any real change for the better, is bound to grow. Pressure from the population will surely increase, although more slowly than the more impatient among us might like. Change is inevitable, difficult though it may be to say how long we must wait before it comes. The most successful opposition will be the one that can combine firmness and moderation, that can engage in massive, but nonviolent forms of protest and political pressure.

The regime has reached the limits of its possibilities, but its crisis may be drawn out for a fairly long time.

The year 1996 did not turn out to be the year of great change that many expected. Nevertheless, even those who today remain in power realize that the decline in production and in the standard of living must be stopped, the growth of crime and of dangerous illnesses must be stopped, the disintegration of our army, the plundering of our national resources, the collapse of science and culture must be stopped, as must the moral degradation of society. The first green shoots of healthy initiatives for change are to be encountered everywhere. They must be supported.

Russia's problems cannot be solved while disregarding its particular features and age-old traditions. On the other hand, our country's problems cannot be solved outside the context of current world events and trends, which are by no means as stable as one might wish. On the whole, in the mid-1980s the gross domestic product of the Soviet Union held second place in the world, after the United States. Today Russia's GDP lags behind that of Japan and China, Germany and France, Italy and England, even behind Brazil's. In per capita production of the most important items every country of Europe and many Asian countries now surpass Russia. Many other indices of economic development show Russia far behind the most advanced counties, and quite a few economists now call it "a great power of the second rank."

The latter definition is true only in part. In territory Russia remains the largest country in the world. Its resources are enormous, and a country's wealth cannot be defined only in terms of its current production. Reunification of Russia with Belarus and Kazakhstan is only a matter of time. This reintegration will inevitably include other countries of the former Soviet Union as well. Russia's special geographic position allows it to play a considerable role in the East as well as the West. In the production of the most advanced kinds of weaponry and space technology it maintains a level close to that of the Untied States, and it has accumulated great potential in many other scientific fields. Under intelligent leadership Russia could double and triple its industrial and agricultural production in a short time. To do so, Russia needs to free itself from the chimera of military supremacy in favor of a policy of reasonable military sufficiency and to build relations with other great powers on the basis of cooperation, not competition. Even without destructive confrontation between the great powers, the world is full of problems and conflicts that could destroy humanity.

The end of the century, the end of the millennium, is a time for prognoses. But making predictions is not a rewarding business, because they hardly ever come true. Various scenarios for the coming century could be sketched out, from the very worst, the destruction of humanity, to the most pleasing—abundance, prosperity, and cooperation among all countries and civilizations. All such scenarios could be based on existing trends and contradictions. Neither individuals nor countries can change their pasts, but they can make changes in the present that will have a positive effect on the future.

For Russia itself, many different kinds of predictions are being made. Some speak of the possible disintegration of the Russian Federation, the possibility of a military dictatorship or another Communist dictatorship, or the development of a colonial-type economy and the persistence of a disastrous stagnation, prolonging the power and privileges of a new oligarchy. Others speak of the progress of democratic institutions and values within the framework of a new kind of socialism and a new ideology. In my opinion, the idea of socialism will not disappear so easily from the Russian consciousness and existence.

The causes and conditions that produced the socialist aspirations of the nineteenth century are well known. What people had hoped for from the socialist movement was that it would overcome economic anarchy and crises, cruel exploitation and poverty, oppression and disease; that the simplest needs, for food, clothing, and shelter, would be met for all; that wealth be distributed more fairly; that the contradiction between city and country, and between manual and mental labor be eliminated; and that the production of goods be faster and better regulated. In addition, it was believed that the free development of society as a whole could be guaranteed by increasing the productivity of labor, eliminating all forms of alienation, establishing equality for all, and ensuring the free development of each individual. Since the beginning of the twentieth century, hopes of freeing humanity from world wars and colonial dependency, from militarism and fascism, have also been linked with hope for the victory of socialism.

The kind of "actually existing socialism" that we had in the USSR, however, was unable to solve many of these problems. Yet for most countries and populations today, these remain burning issues. Many new problems have been added, the kind we call "global," the kind whose solution is hardly possible in a society where the chief motive for production remains maximization of profit and where the contradiction between social production and private appropriation persists in very harsh forms.

The insane arms race, especially the making of weapons of mass destruction, which continues even though the Cold War has ended, must be stopped. In our nuclear age such weapons remain a mortal danger. Terrorism, with the advance of science and technology, takes on new, more dangerous forms; it must also be stopped. The most crucial environmental problems—those of pollution of the world's oceans, destruction of the ozone layer, soil erosion, deforestation, desertification, air and water pollution—can be solved only within the framework of humanity as a whole, through international cooperation, rational regulation, and self-limitation.

Global solutions are also required so that the world's limited natural resources and food resources can be used intelligently. One of the most difficult global problems is that of uncontrolled population growth. New diseases and epidemics, and the spreading drug trade, also represent global problems that are a threat to all. The contradiction between wealthy and poor countries, between the North and the South, is a continuing problem that must be solved. There are many new kinds of technology whose operations or effects cannot be limited to individual countries—nuclear power, genetic engineering, communications and information technology, space research, and new forms of air and sea transport. For all these problems to be solved, what is required is an atmosphere of good will and cooperation, fairness, social justice, and international planning—qualities that have been linked above all with the values of socialism.

Nationalism and xenophobia, religious and ideological fanaticism, imperialism, class or caste egoism—these can only hinder solution of the world's problems today. The moral ideas of socialism, of achieving a social ideal, of providing all people with access to a socially creative life are far more constructive. Many people today are saying that Russia can be made a prosperous country occupying its rightful place in the world only with new ideas that would bring the universal values of the Russian spiritual tradition together with the modern world in all its complexity, its many differing trends and perspectives.

The basic national idea for Russia cannot differ essentially from the ideas that are meaningful in the lives of other countries and nations. Russia's greatness is not such an idea, although we have nothing against Russia being great. If our understanding of such an idea can be expressed in one word it would be prosperity. Prosperity for all citizens, for our country, and for all the world. The most effective way to achieve that is through a new, humane, and democratic socialism.

In the late 1970s the Nobel prize winning economist Jan Tinbergen wrote: "A just social order can best be described as a humanist socialism, because its goal would be the establishment of equal possibilities within and between all countries, and at its base would lie universal human values" (Jan Tinbergen, *Reexamining the International Order*, Moscow: Progress Publishers, 1980).

A few years ago the former socialist premier of France, Michel Rocard, wrote along similar lines: "Four ideologies have left their mark on Europe in this century. Fascism lost the world war. Communism lost the cold war. But socialism and liberalism, which were born before this century began, will also outlive it. With the affirmation of moral values in practice and the new understanding of democracy, the inhabitants of Europe will undoubtedly vote in favor of the socialist project for the next century" (*Socialism of the Future* [Moscow-Madrid], no. 2, 1990–1992, p. 8).

I am convinced that in the coming century not only the nations of Europe but also those of all other continents will vote for socialism.

PART 3

1998: A YEAR OF UPHEAVAL

9

"War on the Rails"

A government crisis in Russia in March–April 1998 was followed in May by a wave of social protest on an unprecedented scale. The decline in living standards (which began in 1990–91 and has continued to the present day), the constantly delayed payment of wages, and the growing threat of unemployment brought millions of industrial and office workers in Russia's many different economic regions to the point of extreme desperation. The "war on the rails"—that is, the blocking of rail lines by protesting workers—which broke out in the coal-mining regions of the country, proved to be a powerful and effective way of pressuring the government.

It was also a profoundly symbolic action. Back in 1991, when Boris Yeltsin was elected president of Russia, he made a promise —to "lay his head on the rails" if his government were ever to allow living standards in the country to fall. What we have seen "on the rails" has not been Yeltsin's head, but hungry miners, with their wives and children. And other working people, teachers and students, doctors and retired people, scientists and farmers, have been speaking out more and more loudly about their difficulties.

Many economists called the situation in Russia not so much a "crisis" as a "catastrophe." Even UN reports referred to Russia and Ukraine as "countries with ruined economies," like Iraq or Yugoslavia.

The miners' protests were a surprise not only to the authorities but to the leaders of the unions themselves. One of the new officials of the Russian government stated that a nationwide labor organization like Poland's Solidarnosc would be a good thing for Russia because, as things stood, it was necessary to negotiate separately with the workers at each mine.

CHUBAIS'S BLUFF

In early 1997 the progovernment press in Russia was full of optimistic predictions and upbeat pronouncements. "The economy is entering a period of growth and the situation is being normalized," wrote Sergei Pavlenko, director of the Russian government's Working Center on Economic Reforms. After a long illness Yeltsin returned to work. One of his first actions was to appoint three vice premiers and to place them in charge of Russia's economy. The three were Anatoly Chubais, Boris Nemtsov, and Oleg Sysuyev. Commentators spoke of a "second liberal revolution." Western experts referred to the threesome as a "dream team." Chubais declared, "We are convinced we will be able to realize the goals we first set for ourselves in 1991."

But there was no revolution. By draining the government budget, this "new" administration was able to reduce the backlog of unpaid wages a little. Inflation was held down to only 11 percent for 1997. For the first time in seven years, a rise in the GDP was announced, though it was only 0.4 percent; average per capita income increased by 0.8 percent; and the number of people below the poverty line was reduced by 0.7 percent. However, these improvements were barely noticeable in the daily lives of ordinary citizens.

On the other hand, the deeper, more fundamental economic processes showed no positive gains in 1997. Instead, they continued to evolve in a direction quite dangerous for Russia. Investments in actual production, which were already insignificant, declined by a further 6 percent. Unemployment rose 3 percent. Total profits for industrial enterprises fell by 15 percent, but losses increased by 140 percent.

Foreign debt went up by \$5–6 billion, reaching a total of nearly \$140 billion. The government's domestic debt rose even more quickly during 1997, increasing from 330 to 530 billion "denominated" rubles. When Russia's currency was "denominated" in 1997 the last three zeros were removed from all bank notes. Thus, one million (1,000,000) rubles became one thousand (1,000).

Vitaly Tretyakov, editor in chief of *Nezavisimaya Gazeta*, wrote:

> I consider 1997 the greatest year in modern Russian history. It was great in that during this year all the internal, material, and intellectual reserves of the present regime were exhausted completely. Yes, it is true that not a single question was given a constructive answer. Yes, as before, Russia may fall apart. Yes, the economy is in a state of stable stagnation and the government is completely bankrupt. But 1997 was good in that now, by all indications, the authorities, the ruling elites, have themselves become aware of this.
>
> (*Nezavisimaya Gazeta*, December 31, 1997)

In fact, neither the government authorities nor the "ruling elites" understood anything. An article by an adviser to Chubais, the economist Andrei Illarionov (*Izvestia*, December 30, 1997), contained the following assertions: Yeltsin has enjoyed "successes of a kind that have not existed in all the years of his presidency"; 1997 was "the best year of the past decade"; "the results of the government's activities during the year just expired" had been "magnificent" and there were "brilliant possibilities" ahead.

An article by the economist Mikhail Delyagin, an adviser to Vice Premier Boris Nemtsov, declared that "Russia has overcome its downward slide and is gathering its strength for the upward pull. Our country is heading uphill, and not toward Golgotha." Aleksandr Frolov, a doctor of political science, wrote: "Exerting all their strength and exhausting themselves in the struggle for survival, overcoming fear and despair, the people of Russia have literally carried our country on their backs out of the abyss of economic crisis" (*Novoye Vremya*, 1998, no. 1, pp. 14, 15).

Chubais outdid all the others in professions of optimism:

> In our country the decline of production has ended and a turnaround has begun, which can be seen quite well by people who

analyze seriously. It seems to me that nothing can stop Russia from a long, steep, powerful upward trajectory of growth, constantly gaining in strength. This will be evident not only to specialists in economics and statistics but will also be felt within the family of every Russian breadwinner: from his wages, from his income, from his ability to buy a new car and go on a full-fledged summer vacation

(*Argumenty i Fakty*, 1997, no. 47. p. 3)

All these assertions turned out to be nothing but bluff.

TWO STEPS BACK

In January 1998 the cautious and concerned predictions of more objective observers were drowned out by the chorus of optimistic official commentary. Even a confidential World Bank report predicted that the Russian economy would have a 6 percent growth rate in 1998 because 70 percent of GDP was being produced by private firms. The Organization for Economic Cooperation and Development foresaw a growth rate for Russia of 3 percent in 1998 and 5 percent in 1999. Russia's Central Bank promised a growth rate of 1–2 percent, with investment increasing by 6–7 percent and inflation dropping to 5–8 percent for the year.

The first months of 1998, however, gave Russians nothing to cheer about. Capital investment in the economy shrank by 7.1 percent compared to the early months of 1997. Industrial production was 0.3 percent less than in the first quarter of 1997. The consumer price index rose 3.1 percent, and real income declined by 6.8 percent. The total indebtedness of industry, construction, agriculture, and transport reached the level of 1.5 trillion denominated rubles. (These figures were reported by the government's Economic Conjuncture Center and other institutions engaged in economic analysis.)

Budget revenue was reduced, and once again the government could not promptly meet its obligations for the payment of wages and pensions to millions of Russian citizens. Wage payments were widely delayed in the private sector as well. The government of Chernomyrdin and Chubais had exerted itself greatly to try to integrate Russia into the world economic and financial system, and as a result not only had Russia been formally recognized as a country with a market economy but also Russia's president was included on a nominally equal basis at a summit of leaders of the most developed countries (the so-called Group of Eight). Integration into the global system, however, also resulted in some heavy blows to the weakened Russian economy.

While capitalism today has little resemblance to what it was a century ago, the inner nature of "post-industrial" capitalism has not changed fundamentally. Such features as competition and the anarchy of production, the constant striving for the maximization of profits, periodic crises of overproduction(with accompanying financial crashes and massive unemployment) have all persisted, although in different form.

Sometimes these economic and financial crises affect the entire world. The first signs of a new global crisis appeared in Asia during 1997. A chain of seemingly unrelated events in Thailand, Malaysia, Indonesia, the Philippines, and South Korea culminated in financial upheavals and stock-market disasters in September–October 1997. For a decade or more these countries had demonstrated steady and rapid economic growth, earning them the nickname "the Asian Tigers." Western investment in the region was nearly $100 billion per year.

But in the fall of 1997, the Hong Kong and Japanese stock markets were hit by the biggest drop in prices in recent years. Stock exchanges all over the world, not just in Singapore or New Zealand, but also New York, were affected.

In December 1997 it also became evident that there was a worldwide glut of oil and of some other raw materials, a crisis of overproduction. The price for a barrel of oil had fallen since the late 1970s, when it stood at $40, to around $17–20 in the period 1991–1997. But in January 1998 the price per barrel fell to $11. And in some cases, only $8–10 was being paid.

For Western industrial countries, lower oil prices made up in part for losses as a result of the downturn in Asia. But the big losses experienced by the oil-producing countries were bound to be reflected in the state of the world economy. Western consumers, out of caution if nothing else, began to buy less, especially in the case of luxury goods. A number of jewelry firms and tourist agencies experienced difficulties, including some bankruptcies. Reduced commodity circulation led to greater unemployment, especially in Germany and France.

Russian officials reassured the public that the Asian crisis would not become a threat to Russia. Deputy Finance Minister Kudrin declared that the crises in the financial markets were "no cause for concern." Russia's Central Bank promised to maintain stability on the Russian securities market.

Again, Chubais outdid all others in his professions of optimism. He asserted that Russia could win, rather than lose, from the Asian crisis "because Russia today is the most attractive of the emerging markets. It is entirely possible that we will again create a situation in which Russia, in comparison to other developing markets, will prove to be the most stable and profitable" (*Obzor Mezhdunarodnoi i Rossiyskoi Informatsii. Yezhenedelny Byulleten* [Review of International and Russian Information: Weekly Bulletin], 1997, no. 48, p. 17).

Several experts predicted heightened interest in Russian securities among foreign investors, but these expectations proved unfounded. In late October 1997 prices on Russian stock markets began to fall. In November and December foreign investors, to whom Russia's capital market had been opened hastily and without any restrictions, began to withdraw their funds just as hastily. At first they turned to the more profitable and reliable Russian market in short-term government bonds, but many soon pulled out of Russia altogether.

The Central Bank, in order to avoid devaluation of the ruble so soon after its "denomination," was forced to make substantial outlays from its foreign currency and gold reserves, which fell from $25 billion in the early fall of 1997 to $18 billion in January 1998. Russia's central savings bank also suffered substantial losses.

Falling world market prices for raw materials also had a painful effect on the Russian economy. In the years 1995–97 Russia exported 100–110 million tons of oil annually, earning substantial profits, with 40–50 percent of those profits in the form of hard currency. "For now, oil and gas are feeding Russia," wrote *Novoye Vremya* in July 1997.

This was nothing new. Petrodollars had also nourished the Brezhnev regime, and to many politicians this cash flow seemed inexhaustible. But everything changed quickly and, it seems, will remain changed for a long time to come. In Russia the prime cost, or production cost, of oil is not just $2–$3 per barrel, as in the Persian Gulf countries, but $13–$14. Oil exports were suddenly bringing not profit but loss.

Russia cannot abruptly curtail its production and export of oil, for that would leave hundreds of thousands of people in its northern and eastern regions without jobs. For such "oil cities" as Surgut, Noyabrsk, and Nefteyugansk, the social consequences of stopping production would be worse than the already serious crisis in the more habitable coal-mining regions.

There is another reason why Russia cannot stop producing and selling oil, even though at a loss. It would be unwise to risk losing the traditional customers that Russia supplies. Almost all the energy needs of the Baltic region are met by exports from Russia; for Ukraine, the figure is 80 percent; for Eastern Europe, 50 percent; for Germany, 15–20 percent. Besides, with oil production you can't just close a valve on a pipeline and wait for better times, as you can with natural gas.

Thus it was necessary to start planning for ongoing losses from oil sales. From January through March 1998, because of the fall in world oil prices, the Russian treasury lost $1.5 billion, according to the State Duma's budget committee. Thus, the many hopes for a quick upward flight of the Russian economy had been dashed as early as the first quarter of 1998. All attention was now focused on trying to maintain economic and social stability against the threat of a new wave of difficulties.

THE FALL OF CHERNOMYRDIN

The new problems in the economy, already troubling the top politicians and government officials, aroused the dissatisfaction of Russia's business elite, those who are called "the oligarchs." The orientation toward the raw materials sector, which had been the basis of economic policy for many years, now proved to have been mistaken. Huge parcels of state property, now in the hands of a few private owners, had stopped bringing in the earnings they had previously brought. With the ruble more stabilized, commercial banks were making less profit from currency speculation in general and from operations involving foreign currency in particular. Disputes among the various oligarchical groups, or "clans," intensified. The question of governmental continuity troubled everyone. Only two years remained until the next presidential elections, and only a year and a half until the elections for a new Duma.

During January and February 1998 Yeltsin seemed little concerned with the new problems that had arisen. He postponed several times his administration's report to the Duma, and when the report was finally given, he walked out of the proceedings at the end of the first hour. In early March he came down with a cold. To his entourage the president's new illness seemed more of a problem than the deepening ills of the Russian economy.

At the same time Chernomyrdin began to display signs of unaccustomed independence. In previous years the premier had hardly ever interfered in the activities of the vice premiers, allowing them to decide matters in direct consultation with the president. It was this passivity that enabled Chernomyrdin to observe the fifth anniversary of his premiership in December 1997, while Yeltsin might well have ousted a more combative individual long before. The average stay in office for *vice* premiers had been no more than one year.

In early 1998, however, Chernomyrdin began issuing statements that the press viewed as rather "daring." He also reorganized the duties of the three vice premiers, reducing the powers of Chubais, Nemtsov, and Sysuyev while increasing his own. When talks were held in the United States within the framework of the Gore-Chernomyrdin Commission the Russian premier conducted himself as though he expected in the near future to be the president of his country. Within the "party of power" and among "the oligarchs" there were many who had linked their fortunes with a Chernomyrdin victory in the elections scheduled for 2000.

Several Russian newspapers ran special features on Chernomyrdin as the candidate of the party in power. In one interview in mid-March Chernomyrdin not only acknowledged a qualitative rise in his authority in the government but actually declared that the political situation in Russia, as he saw it, had reached an adequate level of stability and would probably not change essentially before the elections (*Mir. Ekonomika i Politika* [The World: Economics and Politics], 1998, no. 10, p. 23). People got the hint.

In the first weeks of March 1998, Chubais was active in the public eye to an unprecedented extent, observing with much fanfare the first anniversary of his appointment as vice premier. Many observers agreed that, as one publication stated, this was a "precise and reliable indication that the political process has passed through a period of great strain and has returned to normal, stable channels and will flow smoothly without whirlpools or blockages into the straight-line phase of the election campaign" (*Politicheskaya Nedelya v Rossii. Informatsionno-Analitichesky Monitoring* [The Political Week in Russia: Informational-Analytical Monitoring], March 11–18, 1998, p. 12).

In mid-March, Georgy Kleiner, a doctor of economic sciences, wrote: "The political situation in Russia has taken on new features of predictability, and international politics in relation to Russia have lost their menacing character" (*Nezavisimaya Gazeta*, March 31, 1998). Only a few days after these observations were written Yeltsin showed how little the assessments of such learned experts were worth.

On Monday, March 23, having recovered from his illness and returned to work at his office in the Kremlin, Yeltsin made an early morning announcement that Chernomyrdin, Chubais, and the interior minister, Anatoly Kulikov, were being retired. Under Russian law this meant the resignation of the entire cabinet. Yeltsin gave no reason for this sudden decision. Not until later did he make explanations of some sort. Two months afterward he said he had retired Chernomyrdin "not because he was a poor prime minister or had made any mistakes. It's just that times had changed, and after five, six, seven years society had begun to get tired of this particular leader . . . . It was necessary to seize the time, release him from his duties, and make a change" (*Rossiyskiye Vesti*, May 27, 1998).

Yeltsin's action was a complete surprise to Chernomyrdin, especially because under a new law such action required a statement by the prime minister himself. It was as much a surprise to Chubais, who was getting ready to act as Russia's representative to a meeting of the International Monetary Fund in New York. Kulikov refused to comment about being retired. Of the generals heading the "power ministries" he was considered the one most devoted to Yeltsin.

At noon on March 23 Yeltsin announced that a previously little-known official, Sergei Kiriyenko, would become acting prime minister. It had been only a few months, since November 1997, that this 35-year-old businessman from Nizhny Novgorod had occupied the post of minister for fuel and energy, and he had not distinguished himself in any way.

Hardly anyone could explain or even comment intelligently on Yeltsin's action. A few journalists and "expert commentators" who are generally considered to be in the pay of Yeltsin's administrative apparatus tried to portray this sudden move as part of a carefully considered plan of action, intended to speed up the pace of reform. Most observers, however, agreed that Yeltsin's action was not thought out, but was an emotional decision guided by a single desire and a single aim—to show everyone in Russia and beyond its borders "who was really the boss."

The government crisis continued for more than a month and did considerable damage not only to the participants in this artificially provoked conflict but also to Russia as a whole. Uncertainty in regard to the government probably resulted in several billion dollars worth of harm to the economy. The "party of power" obviously suffered from the crisis, for no major political figures remained in it besides Yeltsin. As *Nezavisimaya Gazeta* observed on March 24, "with a single blow Boris Yeltsin has removed three of the most powerful political figures from the game."

NO WINNERS

For more than a month economists and political experts wrote about the negative consequences of the sudden change of government. The new cabinet, which was finally formed in mid-May, came out of the crisis greatly weakened, although more than half of the cabinet ministers retained the positions they had held in the previous government. Several promising younger politicians refused to enter the new administration, which looked transient and unstable to them. "I don't want to find a paper grave for myself in the White House," said Vladimir Ryzhkov, vice speaker of the Duma, in reply to a proposal that he take a position in the new cabinet.

Two provincial governors, Konstantin Titov and Mikhail Prusak, were even more emphatic in declining positions as cabinet ministers or vice premiers. Top-ranking officials in several different ministries chose this moment to leave the Russian White House rather hurriedly to take jobs in private business. They didn't wish to wait for further "reductions in staff."

No one knew much about the new vice premier, Sergei Khristenko, or such new cabinet ministers as Sergei Generalov, Ilya Yuzhanov, Sergei Frank, Viktor Semyonov, and Pavel Krashennikov. Some described the new government as one of "professionals with a pragmatic orientation"; others spoke of the "revolution of unknown middle-level managers."

In Russia today a government minister needs not just professional expertise but also political and practical experience. This was shown by the events of mid-May when the negotiations with protesting miners in the Kuzbass and Shakhty regions were headed by the "retired" leaders Nemtsov and Sysuyev, who were well known in those troubled regions, having held important political positions there in earlier times.

Within a few weeks Sergei Kiriyenko had become well known, but he had not gained respect. His complete dependence on President Yeltsin was obvious to all, and he himself did not try to hide it. His inexperience and lack of preparation for the high responsibilities of the premier's job were flagrantly obvious.

Where, after all, could he have gained the kind of experience needed for his new job? He had graduated in 1984 from the Gorky Institute of Water Transport Engineering and had worked for a short time as a foreman at the Krasnoye Sormovo shipyard in the city of Gorky (which has retaken its pre-Soviet name of Nizhny Novgorod). At the Gorky Institute, he had been active in the Communist Party and the Komsomol (the Communist Youth organization), and at the shipyard he was elected Komsomol organizer, first for his shop and then for the workplace as a whole. Soon after that we find him as a member of the Central Committee of the nationwide Komsomol organization and first secretary of the Nizhny Novgorod regional committee of the Komsomol.

It was through the "Komsomol economy" that Kiriyenko entered the oil business and joined the board of directors of the Garantiya commercial bank. Boris Nemtsov, whose career had also begun in Nizhny Novgorod, invited the young "banker" Kiriyenko to go to work for the government at the Russian White House.

Such was Kiriyenko's entire biography in a nutshell. An analytical memorandum distributed to government offices and the press in mid-May had this to say about him: "He is ambitious, arrogant, and capricious. Not stupid, but superficial in his opinions and actions. He knows how to avoid responsibility by moving to a new position at the right time. He will take on any job at all, even if he doesn't understand a thing about it. He will consult endlessly with everyone, especially those of equal rank or in positions above him, which allows him to place the blame on them if things go wrong." The people of Russia soon had ample opportunity to judge the accuracy of this characterization.

The change of government meant an especially heavy political and moral loss for Chernomyrdin. In front of the TV cameras on March

23 he was unable to hide that he felt both dismayed and offended. Booted out of his lofty position by a swift kick from the president, Chernomyrdin within two weeks was accepting a medal "For Services to the Fatherland" from that same president. Instead of a triumphal celebration of his sixtieth birthday, he received this honor on the occasion of his retirement from office.

Soon after that Chernomyrdin announced quite loudly that he would be running for president in 2000. But his ratings as a potential presidential candidate were quite low in January and February 1998, and they did not rise any higher in May and June. His status as an influential politician fell very quickly: in a May 1998 listing of Russia's top political figures, instead of his usual position as third or fourth, the place he held was No. 34 (as reported by *Nezavisimaya Gazeta*, June 2, 1998).

Chernomyrdin's political party, Our Home Is Russia (which uses the initials NDR, for Nash Dom—Rossiya), held a "renewal congress" at the end of April, endorsing Chernomyrdin as its candidate for the presidential elections in 2000. But this party had been built as the "party of power" under his protective wing while he was premier and with Yeltsin's support. After Chernomyrdin's ouster, this party's prospects were not at all clear. Instead of a "renewal," there was an intensification of internal conflict and intrigue within the party's top leadership. The NDR sought in vain to obtain some important posts in the new cabinet formed after March 1998. Its regional structures were weak, and in all local elections during the preceding year it had gone down to defeat. "Regionally we are still being taken into account only because of inertia," one of the party's analysts commented. "Regional governors have not yet gotten used to the fact that Chernomyrdin is no longer premier. He no longer has much influence on the economy. . . . Our movement may not survive up to the 1999 Duma elections" (*Itogi*, May 5, 1998, p. 21).

Chernomyrdin did not have many possibilities for strengthening his political movement, or for financing and organizing an election campaign. He has a strong personality, but at the same time he is passive; he does not typically express emotions vividly. He was always more of a businessman than a politician and kept his distance from the play of political passions. It is difficult for a person like him to perform in public. Even his indirect way of speaking, which the Russian press has often joked about, becomes a hindrance for him, because the ability to speak effectively and to sway an audience is one of the main qualities required of a public political figure today.

It was difficult for Chernomyrdin to seek sympathy as a leader who had been mistreated and wrongly cast aside. He bore a large share of the responsibility for all the difficulties Russians have experienced in recent years, and outside of his native Orenburg province he was not likely to win much support from impoverished voters. Although he was no longer leader of "the party of power," he could hardly join the ranks of the opposition. The ex-premier defined his position in relation to the government as one of "critical solidarity."

His slogan was, "I am running for president in order to be No. 1 in the government." But what does the voter gain by that? In what way would the "new" Chernomyrdin differ from the premier of yesterday? Chernomyrdin and the NDR were likely to suffer the same fate as Gaidar and his party with their very poor showing in the polls.

The government crisis also dealt a substantial blow to the authority of the Duma and the left-wing parties who held a majority in it. Twice the Duma rejected Kiriyenko as a candidate for premier, but in the end it approved his nomination. If it had voted a third time to reject Kiriyenko's candidacy, the lower house of the Duma would have been dissolved and new elections held. Most deputies feared the possibility of losing their relatively privileged positions as Duma members in the event of new elections, and therefore voted for Kiriyenko the third time around. Many deputies joked, "Better to have a degraded Duma, than a dissolved one."

The supposedly oppositional character of the left-wing parties, in particular the Communist Party of the Russian Federation (CPRF), turned out to be quite toothless. The "oppositional" Duma deputies apparently hoped that by retaining their relatively comfortable positions as incumbents, they would have an advantage in the 1999 Duma elections.

Another group that gained nothing from the government crisis was the one usually referred to as "the oligarchs." The feuding among them rose while profits fell. Many banks, including some of the largest, found themselves in straitened circumstances. One, which goes by the name Tokobank, had enjoyed great confidence among Western investors and held ninth place among Russian banks in amount of capital owned. But during the government crisis, it was placed under temporary receivership and a new management was brought in from the outside. The credit ratings of other Russian banks

291

were lowered. Some banks, fearing a loss of clientele, raised their interest rates on deposits. But the cost of credit also went up. The "oligarchs" were feeling the need for stability, for government regulation, for the game to be played by fixed rules. The Kiriyenko government, however, was too new and weak to be of much help in solving these problems. Russia's banking and financial crisis continued.

It was Boris Yeltsin who lost the most in the first half of 1998. In December 1992, as we recall, Yeltsin had accepted Chernomyrdin as premier in place of his first choice, Gaidar. Yeltsin came to appreciate the advantages of this compromise. For years he was able to distance himself from the not very successful activities of the government. By retaining Chernomyrdin as premier while changing vice premiers and ministers as he pleased, Yeltsin could let the premier take much of the blame for failed policies.

As for Chernomyrdin, he had agreed, perhaps not fully consciously, to play along with this game. He did not make the main decisions, but took upon himself, at least in part, responsibility for all the disastrous "reforms" of recent years.

Now the situation had changed. Yeltsin could no longer so easily distance himself from the actions of the cabinet. To be sure, Yeltsin requested that Kiriyenko resolve virtually all problems of government, including the appointment of personnel, without submitting his decisions to the executive branch for approval. In 1995 many cabinet decisions and decrees had been endorsed or authorized by the president's administrative apparatus. In 1996, when Chubais joined the presidential apparatus, all documents from the cabinet began to be submitted to him as the head of the president's staff. The head of the presidential apparatus acquired powers and responsibilities that were almost equal to those of the premier. Later this procedure was eliminated by a special decree of the president—except in the case of documents concerning national security and defense. "Let the cabinet answer for its own actions," said Yeltsin. "Let Kiriyenko make the decisions."

The cabinet, however, did not have political authority commensurate with its powers and responsibilities. At the end of May 1998, public confidence in the Kiriyenko-led cabinet was only about 10 percent. On the other hand, in December 1997 confidence in the Chernomyrdin cabinet had been only 9 percent (*Argumenty i Fakty*, 1998, no. 23, p. 6).

During May and June 1998 Yeltsin felt obliged several times to place his own authority on the line in support of decisions made by Kiriyenko. The new premier could not assume all responsibility for the situation in the country, nor was he inclined to do so.

Yeltsin's relations with "the oligarchs" deteriorated significantly. Vladimir Gusinsky, head of the influential MOST Bank and the information conglomerate Media-MOST, stated bluntly that Yeltsin could no longer count on support from the newspapers and television companies belonging to his conglomerate. The most complete coverage about the coal miners' protests was provided to Russia's viewing audience by the NTV channel, which placed the strikers' political demands in the forefront. Every evening Russians heard and saw the striking miners demanding Yeltsin's resignation. Some officials accused the television companies not just of giving excessive coverage to the "war on the rails" but of actually *organizing* it.

During April, many observers commented with good reason that Yeltsin himself had become a chief source of instability in Russia. For example, the political scientist Pavel Tsepura wrote at the end of April:

> On March 23, Yeltsin killed the party of power. Without stopping to consider, he thus lost a considerable part of his electorate. Even wealthy people, who own something in Russia and have something to lose here, are less and less inclined to link their future with our homeland, and still less with Yeltsin and his present team. . . . Yeltsin's "revolution" of March 23 destroyed the objective prerequisites for the establishment of some sort of national harmony or concord. Virtually the entire population has ceased to believe in the reliability or stability of the political regime established by Yeltsin. Fear of the president's unpredictability, his dependence on opinions inside his own family, has spread since March 23 to all regions and all strata of our society. . . . It is beside the point now to say that no one believes in the president's ability to make adequate decisions and be guided by the national interest. He has swept from the political scene a group of political figures who could have ensured the stability of the political system and the democratic continuity of power through the presidential elections of the year 2000.

(*NG-Stsenarii*, April 1998, no. 4, p. 1.)

293

Many people in Russia and the West were wondering who would be able to maintain government authority in the event of mass disturbances. As Yeltsin had lost the remnants of his former government team, without having acquired a new one, only a few people could still be regarded as team members. Among them were Valentin Yumashev, a former journalist; Sergei Yastrzhembsky, a former Interior Ministry official; and Yeltsin's own daughter, Tatyana Dyachenko, a specialist in computer mathematics. None of these people had experience in administering governmental and economic structures. True, a more experienced figure, Sergei Stepashin, had returned to the government. And then there was Sergei Kiriyenko, who could also be counted as part of the team, although not a very valuable addition.

Criticism of Yeltsin rose sharply in both volume and intensity in almost all the mass media during April and May 1998. Even Yeltsin's former press secretary, Vyacheslav Kostikov, published a major article in the popular weekly *Moskovskiye Novosti* ("Moscow News," 1998, no. 23, p. 6), in which he called his former boss a "buffoon."

GROWING THREAT OF CHAOS

Several groups of economists and political scientists, including a group at Gaidar's Institute of Economic Problems, drafted a program for Kiriyenko of renewed economic reforms, which he then presented to the Duma. There is no point in analyzing this program, because the heated events of May quickly rendered it obsolete. The Russian White House at the end of May resembled a major fire department that had to hastily deal with the outbreak of more and more new blazes. Dangerous political and economic complications kept arising and had to be overcome. Besides the coal miners' protests, there were disasters in the northern regions of the country and armed clashes in Dagestan and Abkhazia and on the border between Dagestan and Chechnya. The downfall of the Suharto regime in Indonesia indicated the kind of social upheavals that could result from the spreading "Asian crisis." All these events increased the uneasiness of Western investors and hastened their flight from Russian financial markets and the Russian economy.

More doubts about the stability of the Yeltsin regime arose after the victory of Gen. Aleksandr Lebed in elections for governor of the

Krasnoyarsk region in east-central Siberia, an event which drew favorable commentary in much of the Russian and Western press. I personally was confident that Lebed would win and considered his victory preferable. But I did not expect the incumbent governor, V. Zubov, to be so soundly defeated, especially when Zubov had been endorsed by many prominent political figures, such as the mayor of Moscow, Yuri Luzhkov; the journalist Alla Pugachova; the head of the Communist Party of the Russian Federation (CPRF), Gennady Zyuganov; and the speaker of the lower house of the Duma, Gennady Seleznyov. In spite of these endorsements, Lebed was able to rally behind his banner the entire protest vote in the Krasnoyarsk region, including those who had voted for the CPRF in the first round. Lebed's political opponents in Moscow, it seems, had been too preoccupied with their own governmental crisis.

Lebed's victory resounded throughout Russia and further weakened the standing of the CPRF, which had claimed to be the chief oppositional force. Lebed's overall political influence increased substantially. He was again ranked among the ten most influential politicians in Russia, and his chances as a candidate in the 2000 presidential elections were much higher. In all opinion polls on this question in early June 1998, Lebed's ratings put him right up next to Zyuganov and were twice as high as Yuri Luzhkov's.

Nervousness in Russia's financial markets persisted throughout May. Hundreds of Western investors withdrew from the Russian market during that month, and experts estimated the losses to the market at $12–15 billion. Not everyone mourned the loss of foreign-currency speculators and other sharp operators of dubious merit who had already made a lot of money out of Russia's economic woes. There were signs, however, that large amounts of native capital, including profits from the shadow economy, were flowing out of the country at a significantly higher rate. For example, at the end of May Vladimir Gusinsky, who we mentioned above as owner of the Media-MOST conglomerate, bought a 25 percent share in the second largest newspaper . . . in Israel! Gusinsky offered $85 million for this purchase, twice as much as anyone else bidding for shares in the newspaper *Ma'ariv*. This kind of money could have helped a dozen different operations run more successfully in the depressed coal-mining regions of Russia. Gusinsky's business deal was indicative. It showed not only that there were large amounts of capital in Russia, but also that the owners considered it unwise to invest in the unstable domestic economy.

So great was the economic instability that when the state-owned oil company Rosneft was put up for auction in May, no bidders came forward. Preparations for this auction had been under way for eight months, and the government had hoped to add no less than $2 billion to the budget, with its looming deficit of as much as $12 billion.

PANIC ON THE MOSCOW STOCK EXCHANGE

News of the difficulties at Tokobank, the failure to auction off Rosneft, and a variety of alarming predictions and rumors led to a fall in prices on the Moscow stock exchange on May 27 that turned into a panic. The *Washington Post* reported on May 28: "What happened was reminiscent of Wall Street in 1929, but this time the crash was on the Moscow stock exchange. During the day prices fell another 11 percent, which meant they had lost half their value since the beginning of the year. Russia's inability to restore order in its economy has forced foreign investors to take their money and head for the exit . . . Nervous investors are fleeing the Russian securities markets partly out of fear of an Asian-type crisis and partly out of fear of investing in Russia's capitalist jungle, where lawlessness reigns."

It was impossible without big losses to get out of the situation that had developed in Russia's financial markets. The only question was, Who would have to pay for those losses? Many economists were proposing a 15–20 percent devaluation of the ruble. This would ease the situation for the main Russian banks, for exporters of oil and other raw materials, and for foreign investors. It would also help the government by artificially reducing the value of its domestic debt. But it would be a hard blow to the population as a whole. Inflation would inevitably take a new upward leap that would be hard to stop at just 15–20 percent. Moreover, the value of people's savings would again be slashed. Devaluation would render pointless the whole fiscal policy of Russia's Central Bank during the preceding year, including denomination of the ruble. Also among the sufferers would be importers, as well as Russian businessmen who depended on Western technology and equipment for the conduct of their business inside Russia.

Most of the press in Moscow was calling for a "soft devaluation." The advantages of this move, as presented in the press, did not seem convincing to the nonspecialist. *Nezavisimaya Gazeta*, May 27, 1998, for example, urged Kiriyenko to move ahead with devaluation even though its consequences might be comparable to those of the "shock therapy" of 1991–92. Among specialists, Yegor Gaidar, Russia's chief expert in "shock therapy," rejected the idea. "Only semi-literates could imagine our having a 'controlled devaluation,' that today the exchange rate could be 6.2 rubles to the dollar and tomorrow, 7.3. In fact, tomorrow the rate would be 25 rubles to the dollar. That is, there would be an uncontrollable fall in the value of the ruble, exhaustion of all the Central Bank's reserves, a very harsh blow to the whole banking system, and general panic" (*Moskovskiye Novosti*, 1998, no. 21, p. 3).

Newspaper commentators favoring a "controlled devaluation" of the ruble as a solution to the crisis angrily declared that Yeltsin was the only one preventing this operation from being carried out. And sure enough, the man whose surprise action of March 23 really provoked the crisis of spring 1998 made no attempt to bring it under control. Perhaps for the first time since 1992 Yeltsin was refusing to go further down the road of "shock therapy."

Even Western observers took an understanding attitude. A CBS correspondent reported from Moscow that for Yeltsin "the worst nightmare would be the collapse of Russia's ruble. That would send the Russian economy, which has barely been staying afloat, plunging to the bottom and bring on the danger of political chaos. The Kremlin had a whiff of what that would be like last week when thousands of miners who hadn't been paid blocked rail lines as a sign of protest. The government succeeded in turning them back, but just imagine what they would be capable of if it suddenly became clear that the miserably few rubles they did have were worth nothing." (This report was printed in the Moscow publication *Mir. Ekonomika i Politika* [The World: Economics and Politics], 1998, no. 21, p. 5.)

With Yeltsin's support the Russian government and Central Bank made the decision to raise interest rates on short-term government refinancing bonds up to 150 percent annually! This decision, which was rather incomprehensible to the man in the street, succeeded in stopping the panic on the Moscow stock market. With such high rates, however, the banking system was unable to conduct even ordinary credit transactions let alone engage in large-scale speculative operations.

Everyone began holding onto money whose value had so greatly increased, and the market froze at the low level it had fallen to. By May 28 and 29 it was obvious that the ruble had survived only for the time being.

At the same time a decision was made to introduce harsher tax policies—with the rich generally being favored over the poor once again, except for some taxes that were imposed on highly profitable banking operations and on gambling. These measures were condemned by newspapers of the most varied orientation, from the strongly pro-market *Kommersant* and *Moskovsky Komsomolets* to the formerly Communist *Pravda-Pyat.* "The Bleeding Has Been Stopped—All the Patient's Blood Has Been Drained," declared a headline in *Moskovsky Komsomolets.* And *Nezavisimaya Gazeta* proclaimed, "The Hunt for Speculators Is a Witch Hunt."

The population remained calm despite the outcry in the press, because for the time being prices of everyday consumer goods remained the same. There was a sharp increase in the demand for gold, the free sale of which had been legalized in Russia only two years earlier. The purchase of foreign currency also rose markedly at the end of May and in early June.

A LULL

The first week of June in Russia passed more calmly than the last weeks of May. The crisis, while not overcome, had been brought within acceptable limits. It was generally understood, though, that changed tax policies and financial regulation by themselves would not overcome the crisis. In order to surmount it, the real, underlying causes had to be understood. All economists and politicians of a left persuasion were agreed that the crisis was one of the political system itself and that only a change of social and economic policies could overcome it.

Kiriyenko, who in late May and early June had been showered with praise by President Yeltsin and the Western press, declared that the crisis had been artificially provoked by a group of financial speculators and sharp operators. Such figures were known to exist, although no one named them by name. Deputy Finance Minister Oleg Vyugin said that four major foreign players on the Russian stock market were specifically to blame. They were supported, he said, by some Russian commercial banks that had accumulated a lot of foreign currency and wanted to sell it at a higher price. They wanted to "push through" a devaluation, from which they could profit handsomely (*Argumenty i Fakty*, 1998, no. 3, p. 7).

The events of May 1998 showed rather clearly that there are predatory operators who have played and will continue to play a ruthless game against the Russian ruble and against Russia's economy, whose growth and development is not to their advantage. This is no new discovery, for predators live not only in the forests but also in the jungle of the market economy, wherever it may be. The weak and the unhealthy are their usual prey. The real question, however, is this: Why is Russia now so weak economically, and who made it that way?

Big-time speculators themselves rarely panic. When others panic, selling off their stocks and bonds at low prices, the speculators clean up. The new director of Russia's tax collection agency was Boris Fyodorov. He had taken quite a lenient attitude toward the speculators. "How can you blame people who are playing the market for wanting to save their endangered money?" (*Izvestia*, May 29, 1998). It is true that the stock market is a form of gambling, and no one wants to lose. But the game should be played according to rules, and cheaters should be penalized and ousted.

On June 2, in an attempt to restore his good standing with "the oligarchs," Yeltsin invited Russia's wealthiest businessmen to meet with him in the Kremlin. He did not ask anything of his guests, let alone accuse them of anything. He asked for their political support and complained that Russian bankers had been investing very little in the domestic economy. The oligarchs signed a general declaration on this point, although it did not oblige them to take any action. The weekly *Nezavisimaya Gazeta* reported (June 6, 1998) that one of "the oligarchs" commented quite agreeably: "We have all made so much money that it is time to think about our country." Andrei Bagrov wrote in the daily paper *Kommersant* (June 3, 1998): "Yeltsin finds himself in political isolation. Both politicians and financiers had already been rather contemptuous of the head of state, but during the current financial crisis they became completely disillusioned with him. The meaning of yesterday's meeting, therefore, was that Yeltsin was appealing to the oligarchs for political support at a time that for him was especially difficult."

Many proposals were being made on how to strengthen and develop Russia's economy and finances, and some of them deserved to be adopted. The bureaucratic machinery of state, which had swollen out of all proportion, needed to be cut back. Tighter control was needed over foreign trade and the sale of alcohol. And the tax system needed to be reformed. But current problems could not be solved by reducing government spending on science and education, as some economists were proposing with the argument that there were "too many instructors and professors" in Russia. It is true that investment in the system of science and education does not produce immediately tangible profits. But this system is one of Russia's most important acquisitions, no less than its natural resources. Support for science and education would help assure the prosperity of Russia in the twenty-first century.

Even Western experts were expressing the desire for greater government regulation of the Russian economy and for the development of a real economy (not just speculation or raw materials export). In the final analysis this would improve prospects for cooperation between Russia and the West as well as for increased strategic investment.

Many financiers, stock brokers, and financial analysts were sure that Russia could not overcome the difficulties of spring 1998 without major new loans from the West. "Only Bill Clinton and Helmut Kohl can stop the financial crisis in Russia," wrote Andrei Serov and Yelena Stanova in *Russky Telegraf* (June 2, 1998). Anatoly Chubais was sent to Washington to talk with his "personal friends" at the IMF (as he himself phrased it). Russian newspapers carried such headlines as "Help Is on the Way," "The West Will Help Us," "Chubais Will Bring New Credits from the U.S.," and "Chubais Is Close to Bringing It Home."

One newspaper wrote: "Again the role of savior of the Russian economy has been assigned to Chubais. If he brings home new credits from the U.S., the Kremlin will have a breathing space" (*Delovoi Vtornik* [Business Tuesday], 1998, no. 21, p. 1). The commentator Konstantin Sorokin, writing in the newspaper *Tribuna* (June 2, 1998), observed that without IMF aid the Finance Ministry and Central Bank could keep the situation under control only until mid-June. "After that the bankruptcy of the government will become more and more obvious. The only salvation is to obtain major stabilizing credits from abroad, a loan on the order of $10–15 billion."

Yeltsin, too, gave in to these fears and warnings and personally requested help from Clinton and Kohl. It must be said in Kiriyenko's favor that at first he did not take this road. In April and May he refrained from asking the West for new credits and said repeatedly that Russia should "live within its means." (Once the credits were obtained, however, Kiryenko spoke in favor of them and claimed them as a success for his administration.)

Actually the new loans and credits created a greater problem. Russia's debt to Western governments and financial institutions was already quite large. In 1997 approximately 20 percent of the budget went to servicing the foreign debt. It was expected that in 1998 no less than 30 percent of the budget would go for the same purpose. Russia's debts are structured in such a way that the biggest payments don't even begin until 2002! If present trends continue, the government will be paying as much as 70 percent of its budget just to service the foreign debt. On top of that, there is internal debt, which by some estimates is even larger than the foreign debt.

The only way out of this situation is for actual production, the "real economy," to grow. Most likely, however, 1998 represented another year lost on the way to achieving that goal.

It seemed that by the summer of 1998 the acute phase of the latest crisis in Russia had passed. Once again, though, the autumn would become a difficult time. A group of political analysts of the Gorbachev Foundation had worked out four different scenarios for possible developments in Russia for the period from 1996 through 2000. Not even the most pessimistic of those scenarios envisaged such a sharp and stormy crisis as Russia had experienced from March through May 1998. The general conclusion of the Gorbachev Foundation experts was that a fundamental change for the better was unlikely before the 2000 elections.

10

Financial Collapse and Another

Change of Government

The Kiriyenko government, which had been formed only with great difficulty in May, soon discovered that the chief problem facing the Russian economy was financial. The country in fact did not have a budget and was unable to pay wages and pensions because all the financial reserves of the Central Bank and all taxes then being collected went to pay for foreign and domestic debt. As we have seen, the export of oil, gas, and metals, far from bringing in a profit, was actually increasing the size of the debt. In June 1998 spending on imports began to exceed income from exports, so that for the first time since 1992 Russia faced a negative balance of trade. The volume of industrial production in June 1998 was 9.4 percent lower than in June 1997. The real income of the population declined by almost 10 percent. Under these conditions devaluation of the ruble and postponement of debt repayment were inevitable. This was temporarily avoided only thanks to a credit of $4 billion granted by the International Monetary Fund.

Yeltsin appointed Chubais as his personal representative to talks with the IMF, hoping to demonstrate to these Western creditors that the "chief reformer" of the Russian economy, in whom the Western economists seemed to have virtually unlimited confidence, was still directing the work of the Russian government. Chubais's trip to IMF headquarters in Washington, it seemed, had been successful, and dollars began to flow into the Russian Central Bank to be used immediately for budget expenses. Optimists began to talk about a six or seven month breathing spell during which measures could be taken to save the country from the oncoming crisis. Pessimists thought the new credits would be exhausted within three or four months. Yeltsin flew off to Karelia for a vacation after declaring that "there was no crisis in the country."

That was in June 1998. Actually, the IMF credits made it possible to stabilize the situation only for five or six weeks. By the middle of July substantial sums of foreign currency and gold reserves were once again being spent to maintain the exchange rate at six rubles to the dollar. By the beginning of August these reserves were nearly exhausted. This caused a panic primarily among the hundreds of Russian commercial banks, most of them headquartered in Moscow.

On August 10, the banks began feverishly selling off the government securities they owned, above all the short-term government bonds which were the main form of domestic debt. These bonds, which ordinarily had a two-year maturity date, paid a guaranteed 60 percent interest rate annually. But with a crisis obviously coming on, the banks converted their securities to rubles and hastily began buying up foreign currency at the most advantageous rate, doing so not only on the foreign currency market in Russia but in neighboring former Soviet countries as well. In a single day these banks bought $100 million worth of foreign currency.

That was on August 11. By August 13 the demand for dollars had increased twenty times over. On August 14 the Central Bank sold $500 million to support the ruble, but it could not continue selling foreign currency at that rate. At the same time the Finance Ministry had exhausted its ruble reserves in paying for short-term government bonds and other securities that were being returned to it. A budget disaster was in the making.

Yeltsin cut short his vacation and returned to Moscow, but he announced there would be "no devaluation of the ruble." On August 15 and 16, Kiriyenko held continuous talks with Chubais, Dubinin, director of the Central Bank, and Zadornov, minister of finance, in an attempt to find a solution. But there was no way out of the impasse. Devaluation of the ruble had become unavoidable. That was not the worst thing, though. The government's inability to pay its debts, not only for short-term bonds but also the interest on so-called sovereign credits, the main form of foreign debt, meant bankruptcy.

On August 17 the Kiriyenko government made an announcement that caused shock and panic not only in Russia but also in Western and Asian financial markets. As it turned out, many banks and financial institutions in the United States, Britain, Switzerland, Germany, Japan, and even South Korea had been buying Russian short-term government bonds and other securities as a source of "super profits." George Soros's Quantum Investment Fund in 1997 had acquired $2 billion worth of these bonds.

Devaluation

A statement by the government of the Russian Federation and the Central Bank announced that on August 17, 1998, a new "floating exchange rate" would be introduced, with the ruble ranging from 6 to 9.5 to the dollar. The previous foreign exchange "corridor"—a range of 5.25 to 7.15 rubles to the dollar—was being eliminated. For the first few days the government refused to call this action a devaluation, speaking instead of a "new" foreign exchange policy and defense of the ruble. The government employed various professional and terminological subtleties, and declared that "primitive assessments" of the move were unacceptable.

For several months of course President Yeltsin, Prime Minister Kiriyenko, and Chairman Dubinin of the Central Bank had all vowed that they would not permit devaluation. They now felt it was necessary to try to save face.

What happened in fact was not just a devaluation, but the worst possible kind—an uncontrolled free fall of the ruble. The government and the Central Bank had no reserves left with which to defend the ruble, to maintain its value within the previous "corridor," or to uphold the new "floating rate." In the first half of August the Central Bank had spent $3.8 billion trying to maintain the value of the ruble and could do so no longer. It did not want to end up with no foreign currency at all.

As many specialists had predicted, the exchange rate of the ruble could not be held within the limits announced by the government. As early as August 19 the official rate had fallen below 7 rubles to the dollar. Within a few weeks it was down to 9.5 rubles to the dollar. For several weeks the Central Bank failed to establish any official exchange rate and stopped all trading in the ruble on currency markets. Dollars continued to be bought through other channels and on the black market, and the value of the dollar relative to the ruble rose precipitously. During the first week of September the rate rose to 20 rubles to the dollar, even 25 rubles to the dollar in unofficial dealings, and the value of the ruble continued to plummet.

The Short-Term Bond Pyramid

The Russian government and Central Bank made another decision, one perhaps even more important than devaluation—refusal to honor short-term bond obligations. The official statement on this matter said: "Government securities maturing up to December 31, 1999, inclusively, will be recertified as new securities. . . . Until the recertification of government securities is completed trade in short-term government bonds will be stopped." This resulted in at least the partial ruin of many holders of government bonds (aside from the Central Bank and the Savings Bank, the Sberbank). This was a de facto declaration of bankruptcy by the government. The resulting loss of confidence in government securities brought the activity of many other government and commercial financial institutions to a halt.

During August and September, when explaining the reasons for the financial collapse—an incomprehensible event to most people—responsible officials tried to avoid the question of whether there had been a short-term bond pyramid. The mechanism by which financial pyramids operate is fairly well known, however, and such pyramids usually all end up the same way. There is really only one incomprehensible aspect to the whole affair—why the government itself decided to organize a pyramid scheme and why this operation was not stopped sooner.

The formula "short-term government bond" is rather a cloudy one. Short-term obligations are a normal feature of the financial market, but they should not be the main source for borrowing capital on the internal market. In addition, any loan should be backed by a specific system of guarantees and insurance, nor should any system of domestic borrowing be constructed on the basis of a pyramid in which the first wave of loans is paid for by money borrowed from a second round of creditors. After all, a loan does not represent real income. Finally, the terms under which money is borrowed should correspond to the real possibilities for repayment of those loans. All of these conditions for an intelligent borrowing policy were violated in regard to short-term government bonds.

The collapse of this pyramid scheme was unavoidable. It was sure to collapse sooner or later. Kiriyenko's part of the blame is relatively small, but there is no question that Chernomyrdin and those responsible for financial policy in earlier years were mainly to blame.

The short-term government bond system arose in 1993. The government established this system in order to attract savings from Russian commercial banks and profitable enterprises in order to finance urgent budgetary needs. In 1993 Russia was in the midst of a constant political crisis. Government spending was many times greater than government income. People were thinking in terms of months or at best a year or a year and a half. Their expectation was that things would straighten out, that the situation would become stabilized, and then the debts could be repaid.

In 1993 operations involving the purchase and sale of foreign currency were highly profitable for the banks. In order to put the short-term government bond system into operation, it was necessary to make these government securities more profitable—that is, to pay higher rates of interest. Government income from short-term bonds in 1993 and 1994 was fairly substantial, but the earnings made by holders of those bonds were even greater. The government paid the holders of bonds not out of its own income or from any kind of profitable operations but by borrowing from a new set of investors, lured by the high interest rates. It was not difficult to calculate when this pyramid scheme would cease to be a source of income and would instead become a headache for the government budget.

At first only Russian citizens were allowed to hold government short-term bonds. Those who were serious about the banking business could not have failed to understand that this short-term bond system was a pyramid scheme. But the Russian banks themselves were constantly encountering urgent problems. Their plan apparently was to get rid of these bonds at the right moment by selling them to others. Those involved in this risky game were obviously speculating.

Information now appearing in the Russian press indicates that 40, 50, even 70 percent of the assets of many banks were invested in these short-term government bonds. A huge portion of the assets of the Central Russian Savings Bank, the Sberbank, consisted of these bonds. Investments in actual production earned very little income, if any.

By 1995 the short-term bond system was beginning to flounder. Government income from the sale of these bonds declined, and the hour was approaching when spending to repay holders of these bonds would exceed income from those who were buying new bonds. The social and political situation in the country remained difficult. Elections to the State Duma were about to be held, with presidential elections soon to follow in 1996. The solution was to allow foreigners to buy the short-term government bonds. The enormously high interest rates paid for them did not attract only financial speculators. By early 1998 no less than one-quarter of the total number of Russian short-term government bonds were in the hands of foreign investors. Tens of billions of dollars were involved.

By the end of 1997 it no longer made any sense for the government to issue these types of bonds. Whereas during the first half of 1996 income from the sale of these bonds brought the Ministry of Finance 25 billion new rubles, in the second half of 1997 only 12 billion rubles came in from this source, and taking into account various other expenditures for the repayment of short-term obligations, the income was even less. During the first several months of 1998 a negative balance developed between earnings from the sale of short-term government bonds and expenditures to repay holders of those bonds. The losses suffered by the government on this score rapidly increased.

According to some estimates, if the entire system had remained unchanged, the government would have had to repay the enormous sum of 126 billion rubles in 1998 (*Vlast*, 1998, no. 33, p. 21). There was no provision in the government budget for such an enormous sum.

The enthusiastic promoters of short-term bonds began to make plans for extending the system to all citizens of Russia, not just to corporations or banks. But rapidly developing events intervened. In July payments from the budget to meet the short-term obligations amounted to 7 billion rubles per week, or 35 billion rubles per month. Yet for May and June the total budgetary income was only 20–25 billion rubles per month. (*Itogi*, August 25, 1998, p. 13.) Even if the government stopped all other payments from the budget, it could not settle its accounts with holders of short-term bonds. The pyramid was bound to collapse, and it did.

Moratorium on Foreign Currency Credits

A third major decision of the government was the 90-day moratorium in regard to foreign currency credits previously obtained by Russian banks on Western foreign currency markets. The government decree stated: "In accordance with the bylaws of the International Monetary Fund, a temporary restriction is being imposed for residents of the Russian Federation in the conduct of foreign currency operations." Thus, banks and corporations could not take on new credits or pay on old ones until November 17, 1998. This decision was highly injurious to Western creditors.

In May 1998, shortly after becoming prime minister, Sergei Kiriyenko expressed alarm about Russia's growing indebtedness to foreign creditors. Russia was obliged during 1998 to spend as much as 30 percent of its budget on the repayment of foreign loans. This did not prevent Kiriyenko and Chubais from taking on new loans. The Russian government insistently requested and received from the International Monetary Fund a large new loan, with the first payment being delivered in June and July. As a result the gold and foreign currency reserves of the Central Bank increased to nearly $20 billion.

During August, however, the Central Bank had to spend $3.8 billion to support the ruble, money which in fact was simply poured down the drain. Another $2 billion went to repay foreign holders of short-term bonds. By mid-August the Central Bank's reserves had fallen to between $12 and $13 billion. This obliged the bank to stop foreign currency operations and allow the short-term bond pyramid to collapse. Almost all Russian commercial banks and large businesses, such as Gazprom, had borrowed foreign currency during their last several years on relatively unfavorable terms. In July 1998 the total amount of these debts approached $35–40 billion and continued to grow. Many of these obligations were short-term.

However, almost all of Russia's commercial banks lost a substantial portion of their assets when the short-term bond pyramid collapsed. They had no means of repaying the credits they had borrowed earlier. It became known that several banks had asked their creditors to reschedule payments that were coming due. In almost all cases these requests were refused. The Russian banks for various reasons could not reschedule these payments on their own authority. The credits they had obtained were in the form of fairly solid securities, unlike the Russian short-term government bonds—securities such as Eurobonds. Also, many Russian banks had their own foreign currency reserves in foreign banks. The largest Russian commercial banks had branches in the West. The bankers themselves had individual foreign currency accounts in the West. If bankruptcy were declared, these assets might be confiscated. Thus the Russian government was coming to the aid of the Russian banks by prohibiting them from repaying foreign investors for a period of three months. What would happen after those three months, no one knew: no new money was coming into the banks; to the contrary, they continued to lose clients, and within Russia deposits were being withdrawn from the banks.

OUSTER OF THE KIRIYENKO GOVERNMENT

The government statement of August 17 contained several other points indicating that the authorities did not clearly understand the situation in the country or the reaction that would result from the first three points. The statement spoke, for example, of the formation of a pool of the twelve largest banks in Russian in order to "ensure uninterrupted dealings with clients and with one another." It was not possible to put this decision into effect under the conditions of a collapsing financial system. Some banks did try to pool their resources, but they did not succeed in establishing stable mergers.

Another government decision was completely utopian—"in the immediate future to issue short-term government securities maturing in one or two weeks, and to expand the range of securities issued to the population." Banks and the public would only buy securities that they had confidence in. Under the conditions of complete loss of confidence in the government and the financial institutions of Russia it was impossible to issue any more government securities. In early September the Central Bank did in fact issue a new series of short-term securities, none of which sold on the market.

We need not review in detail the chaotic activity of the Kiriyenko government from August 18 to 23. If the Chernomyrdin government had not been retired in March 1998, there is no question that it would have faced the same financial problems that arose to confront Kiriyenko. Chernomyrdin, however, would undoubtedly have acted more cautiously, keeping both the president and the citizenry in the dark. Chernomyrdin and Chubais together might have been able to issue one more round of short-term bonds and bring in another round of foreign loans in order to stretch things out until the elections to the Duma and, if they were lucky, even until the presidential elections. The collapse might have come later, but it would have been even more disastrous.

Actual production had not grown in the previous few years, but that kind of growth was the only key to solving the problems. During the financial disaster of late August 1998 Chernomyrdin was not at the wheel. But it was Chernomyrdin who had driven the country into this blind alley.

For several days Kiriyenko, along with Chubais and Nemtsov, tried to explain their decisions to the public. They expressed no sympathy for the holders of short-term bonds, who, they pointed out, had been earning no less than 30–35 percent profit for the last several years. Kiriyenko said it wouldn't be a bad thing for them to count up the colossal earnings they had made on the Russian securities market. An earnings rate of 5–7 percent is normal in the world economy. Investments that earn 25 percent annually face a risk up to 50 percent. Those who invest in such a way as to earn 50–60 percent annually increase their risk up to 80–90 percent. These observations were no consolation to those who had just suffered huge losses. Moreover, tens of millions of Russian citizens who had not made any investments also suffered.

On August 22, Yeltsin decided to retire the Kiriyenko government. In his search for a new prime minister he was very reluctant to bring back Chernomyrdin. In the spring Yeltsin had spent an entire month pushing Kiriyenko's candidacy through the Duma. Now he faced the same kind of difficult task in relation to Chernomyrdin. It is hard to imagine a situation more painful to Yeltsin's pride and prestige. Other alternatives existed, and they would have been preferable for Russia, but not for Yeltsin and his "family." On Monday, August 24, Russia learned that Kiriyenko had been retired and Chernomyrdin had been appointed acting prime minister.

RUSSIA'S POLITICIANS: TESTED BY THE CRISIS

The Collapse of Political Careers

The economic crash brought down not only the exchange rate of the ruble but also the careers of many political figures and prominent government officials. Among the 100 leading politicians of Russia in August, in a list published by *Nesavisimaya Gazeta* on September 9, 1998, we see at the top of the list not only Anatoly Chubais and Sergei Kiriyenko but also Boris Nemtsov and Viktor Khristenko, as well as Sergei Dubinin and Aleksandr Livshits. All of these figures have now lost their government posts and virtually all of their influence. Yevgeny Yasin and Oleg Sysuyev are two other figures whose political careers have reached their end. In late September experts would no longer have numbered certain bankers—such as Vladimir Potanin, Aleksandr Smolensky, and Mikhail Khodorkovsky—among the "leading politicians."

There is no point discussing Kiriyenko's fate in detail. As we have said, he was virtually unknown before March 1998. After being appointed acting prime minister by Yeltsin, Kiriyenko said many times that he did not consider himself a politician and would form a government of managers and professionals. When social protests broke out in the mining regions in May, followed by panic on the stock exchange at the end of that month, Kiriyenko was forced to act as a politician but did not do so very successfully. While he did not provoke the same kind of indignation as Burbulis or Gaidar, he was unable to win respect or sympathy from ordinary citizens or from government officials.

Some publications began referring to Kiriyenko in a derogatory way. One described him as "the ever so correct, clean, clever little politician whom Yeltsin adores." In September the newspaper *Tribuna* called Kiriyenko "a little boy whom the grown-ups for some reason gave permission to play with matches." One magazine called the former prime minister a Don Quixote. The day after his ouster Kiriyenko himself commented on his retirement: "I understood that I would not be allowed to stay in this post for long. Still, I didn't think the end would come so quickly" (*Itogi*, September 1, 1998, p. 19).

Kiriyenko did have some admirers. Tatyana Kamazova wrote in the magazine *Novoye Vremya* [*New Times*]: "The execution of Kiriyenko was organized quickly and carried through with swift and severe methods like those of the Cheka. There was no procurator in the case, let alone lawyers. . . . But there should have been. Because Kiriyenko—without exaggeration—was the salvation of Russia, and now we have lost him" (*Novoye Vremya*, 1998, no. 34, p. 5). There were many who tended to regard Kiriyenko as a scapegoat, but after all he did make the disastrous decisions of August 17 with the complete agreement of vice premiers left over from the Chernomyrdin era and with Vice Premier Sergei Dubinin. Kiriyenko's decisions were also approved by President Yeltsin.

Kiriyenko's main fault was excessive self-confidence. He was a weak person, and not only physically. Unable to lift the designated weight, he dropped the bar and it crashed to the ground. But who was it that sent this lightweight politician out onto the playing field, where the going was rough and wrong decisions had disastrous consequences?

Among Russia's politicians of recent times Boris Nemtsov most closely resembled Khlestakov, that outstanding charlatan portrayed in Gogol's novel *Dead Souls*. From a modest career as a research assistant at a scientific institution, he rose on a wave of protests against the construction of nuclear power plants to become the governor of Nizhny Novgorod and a favorite of Yeltsin's. A playboy who scorned convention and protocol, Nemtsov was able to win the sympathy of many Russian citizens for a short time. For about half a year he ranked second in the public opinion ratings as a potential candidate for president of the Russian Federation. He also spoke out against the "oligarchs" and their "robber baron form of capitalism" in favor of so-called people's capitalism. But even his first initiative—an attempt to have all public officials in Moscow drive cars of domestic manufacture instead of foreign automobiles—ended in complete failure. He undertook many new projects, but he never brought a single serious matter to completion. The sympathy many felt for him has long since disappeared, and I neither heard nor read any regrets about his retirement.

Not long ago, Nemtsov spoke at a meeting of Japanese businessmen in Tokyo, urging them to invest their capital in Russia. He promised any Japanese businessman who would put at least $100 million into the Russian economy a great reward—receipt of Boris Nemtsov's own calling card. The card had his personal telephone number, which he revealed only to his most trusted friends. Nemtsov will probably now have more than one telephone: he was offered the presidency of the Svyazinvest Corporation, the value of whose shares have fallen just as low as Nemtsov's political stock.

Anatoly Chubais lost his government position in March 1998, but was restored to it in June. In August he was relieved of the post of vice premier for the third time. I will not repeat here what I have said about him earlier in this book. At the beginning of 1998 he spoke at a congress of the party Russia's Democratic Choice, urging his co-thinkers to be not only more insistent but also more *insolent* in their actions and demands. These words were quoted by all the newspapers of Russia on the next day. In his insolence and shamelessness, in his ability to bluff, or simply his card sharp's skill at changing the cards he was holding, no other Russian politician in recent years can compare with Chubais. And we have seen quite a few insolent and cynical political figures on our political Mount Olympus in the last seven or eight years. Chubais's career both as a politician and as an economic manager seemed at an end. Many suggested that Chubais would probably feel obliged to leave the country if he didn't want things to go worse for him.

End of the Yeltsin Era

Quite a few books have been written about Boris Yeltsin and the Yeltsin phenomenon and there will surely be more to come. Within the framework of this analysis we can only say that although Yeltsin in 1998 retained his post as president, his era had come to an end. Not all the newspapers in Russia described this as his political downfall. At the height of the political and social crisis in the spring of 1998, in fact, a special newspaper began publication in Moscow. It was entitled *Our Beloved President*, and all the materials published in it were devoted to this man "chosen by God," a man about whom "the stars sing," "the source of all our victories," "a man of honor and a man of his word," "Russia's chief genius," "the most progressive man on earth."

But in fact, Yeltsin had exhausted all his resources. He no longer had a large team of people to work with, and signs of lack of confidence in him on the part of the power structure kept multiplying. He did not respond adequately to the critical developments in Russia and was unable to alter the negative course of events. When he removed Chernomyrdin, Kulikov, and Chubais in the spring of 1998, he wished to show that he was the boss. He obviously intended to run for a third term in 2000. In the fall of 1998, when he proposed to return Chernomyrdin to the White House, investing him with powers comparable to those of the president himself, this was an act of total capitulation by Yeltsin. He was simply unable to understand what was going on in Russia and was thinking not so much about holding onto power as guaranteeing his own personal security.

Arguments to the effect that Yeltsin was no longer capable of carrying out the duties of president in August and September 1998 were quite well grounded, and facts documenting these arguments were published by the dozens in the Russian press. Yeltsin's representative Yastrzhembsky (and according to some reports, his daughter Tatyana Dyachenko as well) held talks with Zyuganov for the provision of guarantees to the family of the president if he were to resign. This fact needs no commentary.

The disastrous political and financial crisis in Russia coincided with an obvious turn for the worse in Yeltsin's health. But who would take power if Yeltsin's health rendered him unable to rule any longer? It was obvious that Kiriyenko could not manage the situation. Under these conditions, both for the oligarchs and for the Yeltsin circle, Viktor Chernomyrdin began to look like the only hope of salvation. It seemed that he was the only one who could reach an agreement between Yeltsin's circle and the Duma. One magazine wrote: "Boris Yelsin is no longer able to control the situation in the country. Many guessed at this before, but only a hundred or two hundred people knew for sure. Now it has ceased to be a secret. The financial crisis that has broken out in our country has proved to be a litmus test answering the question of whether the president is really capable of acting and influencing the course of events. The removal of Kiriyenko and the return of Chernomyrdin to the White House have shown that Yeltsin is no longer capable of taking really strong and decisive action at this time of crisis for our country" (*Vlast*, 1998, no. 33, p. 9).

An analytical research center in Moscow drew up a chronology of all Yeltsin's official meetings and evident political activity from August 23 to September 7. This information showed that Yeltsin was working only about three or four hours a day, and that during a period of

15 days he made six brief visits to his office. For example, on August 25 his only activity was to receive the president of Vietnam at the Kremlin. After that he simply disappeared for two days. No one knew at which of his many suburban residences he was staying. Yet the financial and currency crisis was unfolding at full speed with only an acting cabinet, which had not been approved by the Duma. Yeltsin was obviously demoralized and could no longer function as a guarantor of stability in Russia.

"In Russia there is not only no government; there is not even a president," wrote one newspaper. "The president's weeklong silence at the height of the crisis has shown that he is unable to assume the responsibilities necessary for bringing our country out of the crisis. . . . Yeltsin has become president in name only—he signs documents and reads statements to the public, but has no control over the situation" (*Kommersant*, August 25, 1998).

On August 28, after three days of silence, Russians saw Yeltsin on television, speaking not about the situation in the country but only about himself: "I wish to say I am not going anywhere. I am not going to retire. I am going to work as provided for by my constitutional term in office. In the year 2000 there will be elections for a new president, and I will not participate."

Yeltsin's decision not to propose Chernomyrdin for a third time as a candidate for premier was a surprise to many. It amounted to a capitulation to Russian society. In Russia today, as in the past several years, there has been no official party of power. There has been a disjointed or loosely united coalition of social and political forces which in fact has functioned as a party of power, but in 1998 it was seriously weakened and virtually destroyed by the collapse of the Russian economy and financial system. A general realignment of social and political forces in the country took place.

Chernomyrdin and His Path to Nowhere

On August 24 Yeltsin announced that he had made a "difficult decision." He was nominating Chernomyrdin once again to head the government. Yeltsin said that Chernomyrdin was a political heavyweight and in Russia's critical circumstances it needed not only experience but also the kind of weight Chernomyrdin could provide. Yeltsin added that there was "another important consideration—to ensure continuity of power in the year 2000." In other words, Yeltsin was not only appointing Chernomyrdin as acting prime minister but also proposing him as the sole candidate for the party of power in the presidential elections. Yeltsin explained that Chernomyrdin's personal qualities—thoroughness, honesty, decency, and respectability "would be a decisive argument in the presidential elections; neither power nor retirement has corrupted him." Chernomyrdin confidently returned to his office in the White House and held the first meeting of his cabinet, all the ministers in which were acting ministers only.

Returning Chernomyrdin to the premiership was not in keeping with Yeltsin's own character or desires. Chernomyrdin had never been part of Yeltsin's inner circle, and although he was loyal to Yeltsin, he was not "part of the team." They were allies, even partners, but their interests and aims were far from the same. After Chernomyrdin's sudden removal from the White House in March 1998 a crack appeared in the relationship between the president and the ex-premier and it deepened substantially. Chernomyrdin began in an indirect way to oppose the policies of Kiriyenko and Yeltsin. This was the result not so much of Chernomyrdin's personal bitterness as a product of the interests of a certain financial-economic grouping which in fact had pushed Chernomyrdin forward in 1992 and had supported him as prime minister.

Interest groups emerged in the Soviet period, and they became a stable feature of life as early as the 1970s. In the Brezhnev era the interest group connected with the military-industrial complex dominated. But another group connected with the oil and energy complex was given due consideration as well, because it brought in a large share of the foreign currency needed for the development of the military-industrial complex.

The destruction of the Soviet Union changed this situation abruptly. A new group, the financial oligarchy, rose to the number one position in the country. All the raw material sectors of the economy, including the fuel and energy sector, retained and even increased their influence. Chernomyrdin became the representative and protector of those sectors. Unfortunately, as prime minister he did not expand his horizons, but continued to serve that relatively narrow interest group. Not a particularly well-educated man, he was inflexible and rather halting in his speech.

From 1993 to 1997 Chernomyrdin continued to serve the interests primarily of the gas industry, leaving it to his deputies or to the assistant prime ministers to manage other branches of industry and the financial system. Those officials consulted directly with Yeltsin in their decisionmaking. Although Chernomyrdin often claimed that no questions were decided by the government without his participation, in fact that was not so. From 1994 to 1996 all fundamental questions in regard to the military-industrial complex and metallurgical industry were decided by Oleg Soskovets. In 1997 Chubais and Nemtsov had the final word on all sectors of the economy except the oil and gas industry.

The replacement of Chernomyrdin by Kiriyenko changed things. Despite all his shortcomings the "lightweight" Kiriyenko was not the tool of any clearly defined interest group. Nor was he part of the oligarchy. The vice premiers, such as Nemtsov and Khristenko, were not the servants of any of the oligarchical groups, and neither was the new director of taxes, Boris Fyodorov. The actions taken by these "technocrats" during the spring and summer of 1998 alarmed and angered the oligarchs, and after August 17, when the financial system began to collapse, the oligarchical groups forgot about their former differences and categorically demanded that Yeltsin put Chernomyrdin back in office. Yeltsin's entourage was frightened by the fast-breaking crisis, and Yeltsin felt obliged to give in.

Chernomyrdin took his place at the wheel with confidence, but the storm raging in the Russian economy and financial system was so powerful that he was unable to deal with it. There is no point going into all of his contradictory actions and statements at the end of August. We will just take one or two examples. In his first statement to the press after his renewed appointment Chernomyrdin said: "I know how to work. . . . This has not been an easy decision for me. . . . I will devote all my energy. . . . We need a stable banking system, and if someone wants to retire I will not stand in the way." His speech before the State Duma when his candidacy was voted on consisted of an equally empty conglomeration of phrases. That speech was also shown on television. It is not surprising that when viewers were polled, only 7 percent expressed support for Chernomyrdin and 90 percent distinctly expressed lack of confidence in this proposed prime minister.

The magazine *Itogi*, in commenting on Chernomyrdin's statements and actions at the end of August, featured the following headline on its front page for September 1: "Filled with Unbelievable Self-Confidence, Chernomyrdin Is Bravely Heading . . . No One Knows Where." In the Duma debates on Chernomyrdin's candidacy, Yavlinsky declared, not without sarcasm: "Everyone today is talking about a new Chernomyrdin. But as we see it, this new Chernomyrdin is worse than the old one."

Only a small number of newspapers and magazines supported Chernomyrdin. For example, *Segodnya* wrote the following: "Chernomyrdin has returned to power not only because he is a tested fighter but more importantly because his months in retirement have shown that he is the only really solid political figure in the country. . . . He has agreed to become prime minister at the height of the crisis only because he now expects to be given full power and to in fact become the ruler of the country and potentially to be chosen as president in the near future" (*Segodnya*, August 25, 1998).

Most of Russia's newspapers and weekly magazines expressed lack of confidence in Chernomyrdin. *Moskovsky Komsomolets* wrote, for example: "It is precisely Chernomyrdin who is responsible for the financial crisis. It was with his blessing that the short-term bond pyramid was created" (August 25, 1998). This kind of statement of course reflected the political orientation of the publication and of the financial interests behind it. *Segodnya* is owned by the MOST-Media holding company belonging to Vladimir Gusinsky. *Moskovsky Komsomolets*, as well as *Moscow News*, are part of the sphere of influence of the Moscow mayor's office. The Communist and nationalist patriotic newspapers were simply furious. *Sovetskaya Rossiya* wrote: "It was Chernomyrdin who brought our country's economy to ruin and our people to a state of impoverishment."

In the first vote taken on Chernomyrdin's candidacy in the Duma only 94 out of 450 voted for him. There were 251 opposed and the rest either abstained or were not voting. This session of the Duma was broadcast live. Many of the speeches made during this session were clumsy or cynical, but as many newspapers commented, Chernomyrdin's was the clumsiest speech of all. It lacked any specific facts or proposals. After Chernomyrdin's candidacy was rejected Yeltsin sent a letter proposing that Chernomyrdin be considered a second time. If the Duma refused his candidacy three times in a row, Yeltsin would then have had to dissolve the Duma and call for a new elections.

During the eight days between the first and second votes on Chernomyrdin's candidacy the acting prime minister engaged in a great flurry of activity. The main television channel, ORT, and a section of the Russian press openly and self-interestedly promoted his candidacy. Enormous pressure was placed on a group of governors from the provinces, who were invited to meet with Chernomyrdin ten or twenty at a time at his office in the White House. Chernomyrdin spoke at a session of the Council of the Federation, whose decisions on questions of personnel served as recommendations for the Duma as a whole. He made public the main points in his program. This was a hastily thrown together fusion of the worst aspects of extreme monetarism on the South American model and the worst aspects of the administrative-command system based on the inflationary printing of paper money as practiced in the final years of the Soviet Union.

Even the newspaper *Segodnya*, which supported Chernomyrdin, called his program "a second edition of shock therapy," which could never be put into effect. Almost all publications condemned Chernomyrdin's proposal for "economic dictatorship." The magazine *Dengi* [Money] wrote that "Chernomyrdin had the audacity to proclaim himself dictator while the president was still alive. Zero hour is set for January 1, 1999. From that day forth Chernomyrdin promises to make the dollar the national currency of Russia, to increase our country's gold and foreign currency reserves, and to eliminate the nonpayment of wages. Any companies that disagree will be nationalized" (*Dengi*, 1998, no. 34, p. 17).

The main argument of those favoring Chernomyrdin's candidacy was that there was no time to lose. That was true. It was also obvious, however, that his appointment as prime minister, especially with increased powers, would be an entirely unforgivable waste of time, and worse, a journey to nowhere.

The Council of the Federation was unable to withstand the powerful pressure from the interest groups backing Chernomyrdin. They brought all kinds of threats and promises to bear. But the Duma stood firm and rejected Chernomyrdin's candidacy for a second time, even though three out of seven factions in the Duma supported him. That evening, contrary to expectations, no new envelope was submitted to the Duma proposing Chernomyrdin for the third time. President Yeltsin had decided to take a break to think things over.

Chernomyrdin's actions on September 8 and 9 were chaotic; he had clearly lost his self-assurance. Pressure was being applied to Yeltsin through various channels. He had an agreement with Chernomyrdin to go all the way even if the Duma had to be dissolved. But social discontent had risen to such proportions that for Yeltsin Chernomyrdin was transformed into a stumbling block. If the Duma was dissolved, that could result in a deepening of the political and economic crisis and also to paralysis of the government, which was hardly doing anything as things were. Under the Russian constitution all major financial questions, including changes in the tax system and adoption of a budget, came under the exclusive jurisdiction of the Duma. Without its support any changes in the financial sector would be illegal, which would not contribute to restoring confidence in Russia among Western financial institutions. With considerable difficulty Yeltsin managed to arrange for Chernomyrdin himself to withdraw his candidacy from consideration by the Duma. At this point a new name appeared on the list of possible candidates for the premiership—that of Yevgeny Maksimovich Primakov.

SOME OTHER POLITICIANS WHO PLAYED A ROLE

Yavlinsky

During 1998 an obvious change in political mood took place among broad sections of the population in Russia. The disposition of forces on the political arena changed accordingly. But the political prospects for Grigory Yavlinsky did not change. The groups supporting him and his movement, the Yabloko party, and the kind of support he enjoyed saw little alteration. In the big cities Yavlinsky, as a candidate for president, maintained a fairly stable level of support at between 10 and 12 percent of the electorate.

Yavlinksy had been a determined opponent of Chernomyrdin since long before the crisis of 1998. Speaking live over television at the end of August, Yavlinsky declared that his party was entirely ready to take on responsibility for the situation in the country. This suggestion was generally viewed as merely a propaganda stunt. But it was Yavlinsky who in early September first proposed the candidacy of Yevgeny Primakov.

Zyuganov

Another presidential candidate, Gennady Zyuganov, head of the Communist Party of the Russian Federation (CPRF), continued to enjoy the support mainly of rural residents and retired people. During the last three or four years not a single new figure has appeared in this party's leadership, and there are hardly any young people in the CPRF. Zyuganov took an active part in the Duma debates. In April 1998 the parliamentary group of the CPRF had surrendered and voted for Kiriyenko on the third round, but in August and September that kind of behavior would have meant political death for Zyuganov and a split in the CPRF.

Lebed and Luzhkov

A large number of potential voters supported either the mayor of Moscow, Yuri Luzhkov, or the governor of Krasnoyarsk, General Aleksandr Lebed. Luzhkov's support came from Moscow and a number of other large cities. Lebed's support lay mainly in the provinces, in the medium-sized and small cities, and in the industrial regions of the Urals and eastern Siberia. Luzhkov was considered a good economic manager and a patriot who would be capable of ensuring the economic prosperity of the country, especially the capital city. Lebed was considered capable of keeping "order" in the country and reining in not only the gangsters and thieves, but also the bribetakers, whose numbers in Moscow were rather large. If these two figures were able to unite it would have been a great benefit to Russia, comparable to the alliance between the merchant Minin and the military leader Pozharsky, who saved the country during the "Time of Troubles" at the beginning of the seventeenth century.

However, the rivalry between the two was rather obvious. The candidacies of both men were proposed at the beginning of the crisis and again in its final stages, during August and September. Chernomyrdin also met with both of them, because they did support him although not very actively. Neither Luzhkov nor Lebed would speak openly about his aspirations or ambitions. When the parliamentary group of the CPRF presented Yeltsin with a list of possible candidates for prime minister, Luzhkov was on that list, too.

Luzhkov would not have had any serious problems obtaining support within the Duma. He was not the head of any party, but maintained contact with many different parties, movements, and political groups of left-center orientation. He had good relations with Generals A. Nikolaev and B. Gromov, as well as with General Lev Rokhlin, before the latter was killed in July 1998.

In contrast, Lebed's relations with almost all the groups in the Duma were poor. He had often referred to them contemptuously. The Duma as then constituted would never have approved him as a candidate for prime minister, a post in which Lebed himself would have felt rather uncomfortable. Lebed obviously aspired to the presidency. As a leader he is considered "not part of the system." And he could only come to power as a result of a national election, not a vote in parliament. His aim was to make visible progress in Krasnoyarsk, whose problems were the same as those of Russia as a whole, though on a smaller scale. Both Luzhkov and Lebed, like Yavlinsky and Zyuganov, would be key figures in Russia's political life during the next year or two.

The "Yeltsin era" was coming to an end, but no one could say with certainty what kind of era would follow it.

THREE WEEKS WITHOUT A GOVERNMENT

In March-April 1998 Russia went without a government for a whole month. It was undergoing a political and governmental crisis that did considerable harm to the country without seriously altering the general course of events.

From August 23 and lasting through the first two weeks of September, Russia was again without a government, but this time it experienced not only a political but also a very harsh financial and economic crisis. Powerful financial-political groups and the various political movements and parties ended up in a harsh confrontation with one another: none of them could overcome their opponents, but neither would they retreat. Under these conditions Chernomyrdin could not and would never have been able to form an effective government. The greater part of his time and effort was spent negotiating with various groups in the Duma and individual politicians, as well as defending his own position.

Meanwhile, the economic and financial crisis developed according to its own logic.

The Duma had rejected the proposed candidacy of Chernomyrdin as prime minister for the second time. Rather than propose him for a third time, Yeltsin took a break. The pressure on Yeltsin and on all the officials in his administration greatly increased. According to press reports, two officials of Yeltsin's administration proposed their own candidate instead of Chernomyrdin. The secretary of Yeltsin's security council, Andrei Kokoshin, and Yeltsin's press secretary, Sergei Yastrzhembsky, were running ahead of events a little. They proposed the mayor of Moscow, Yuri Luzhkov, as premier. The result was a split in Yeltsin's administration and the firing of Kokoshin and Yastrzhembsky.

At that point a new name was loudly pronounced in the Duma—that of Foreign Minister Yevgeny Primakov. The most persuasive speech along these lines was that of Grigory Yavlinsky. But the list of candidates proposed by the Communist Party of the Russian Federation included Primakov's name along with those of Maslyukov, Luzhkov, and Stroyev. Primakov was invited to the Kremlin to see Yeltsin twice. At first he refused, but at the end of the day on Wednesday, September 9, he gave his consent to be nominated and almost immediately was proposed in the name of President Yeltsin for approval by the Duma. Yeltsin accepted all the conditions that Primakov insisted on. These included first of all the candidacy of Viktor Gerashchenko as chairman of the Central Bank and of Yuri Maslyukov as first deputy prime minister in charge of economic affairs.

Discussion of the new candidate was scheduled for 3:00 p.m. on September 11, and by about 7:00 p.m. a constitutional majority of 315 votes approved Primakov as prime minister. The governmental crisis had ended.

YEVGENY PRIMAKOV—POLITICIAN AND DIPLOMAT

On September 12 all the Russian newspapers commented on Primakov's success. In an article entitled "Primakov's Triumph in the Duma" one newspaper wrote: "Yevgeny Primakov's speech in the Duma yesterday was brilliant. He is truly the most skilled diplomat of post-Soviet Russia. In just a few minutes he contrived to say everything that the different factions wanted to hear—both the left and the right, the patriots and the pro-Western elements. Primakov satisfied everyone except Zhirinovsky. . . . Even the prolonged applause was insufficient to convey a full impression of the brilliance of his speech."

The newspaper in which this was written, *Nezavisimaya Gazeta*, was not happy about Primakov's success. In the opinion of many people, this newspaper expresses the views of the "oligarch" Boris Berezovsky, who acquired ownership of the paper in 1996. "The conclusion to be drawn from what happened is a sad one," the authors of the article continued.

> The threat of a Communist comeback once again hangs over a Russia which has been lacerated by the economic crisis. Once again, as in 1917, intelligent, well-spoken, and educated parliamentary representatives are leading the country toward a dictatorship. Once again the people are taking no part in deciding their own destiny. . . . Soon it may happen that the demand for democracy will be silenced by hunger and traded off for sausage at the price of 2 rubles, 20 kopeks. This is something that Russia obviously does not deserve.
>
> (*Nezavisimaya Gazeta*, September 12, 1998)

Another newspaper wrote:

> Yevgeny Primakov, whose candidacy the president has proposed to the Duma, is a smokescreen. The main question is who is standing behind him? Primakov does not have his own program for solving the crisis, but to make up for it he has the support of the Kremlin and almost the entire Duma. What can be expected from his cabinet remains unknown.
>
> (*Kommersant-Daily*, September 11, 1998)

Under a headline "Reds in the White House" a third newspaper wrote: "The Communists are riding into the government on the shoulders of the non-party member Primakov" (*Segodnya*, September 11, 1998). According to a fourth newspaper,

> It is hard to imagine more of a compromise figure suitable to all factions than Primakov. . . . Of all the possible solutions today to the problem of choosing top government personnel this is the most

sensible and pertinent. . . . There's a great temptation to imagine that the political corpse which everyone considers the president to be as a result of the vain efforts of the head of his own administration, that this corpse suddenly pronounced the words "raise my eyelids!"—and then with trembling forefinger pointed out the true direction that the country must take. However, the near future will depend on the answer to the question whether this gesture was a sign of revival or, to the contrary, the last glimmer of consciousness of an aging president.

(*Russkii Telegraf*, September 12, 1998)

The last-named newspaper was by no means a voice of the left opposition, and the way it was writing about Yeltsin was a symptom of the definitely negative attitude toward him held by a substantial number of people in highly influential circles. Many newspapers observed that a member of the Academy of Sciences for the first time in Russian history had now become head of government. Primakov had indeed been elected a member of the Soviet Academy of Sciences in 1979. As a member of the Academy he served in its division on problems of the world economy and international relations.

Yevgeny Primakov took the post of prime minister at an extremely difficult time for Russia. He assumed responsibility for solving problems of such great difficulty, and the powers entrusted to him were so great that the interest shown in him as an individual was entirely justified. As I survey all the political leaders of today's Russia, and not just the leaders, but all the noteworthy individuals both in the camp of the government and in the opposition, there is not a single person I could name who would be more suitable for the job of prime minister than Primakov. This is true despite the fact that all political observers, including myself, until quite recently didn't even consider Primakov as a possible candidate for this post. In all the years of his presidency Yeltsin did not make a single appointment to a high position that was so exactly appropriate—aside from the appointment of Primakov himself as foreign minister of the Russian Federation in 1996.

Primakov: A Brief Biographical Sketch

Primakov was born in Kiev on October 29, 1929. His mother was a pediatrician. He spent his childhood and school years in the city of

Tbilisi in the Soviet republic of Georgia in the Caucasus. In the 1930s Tbilisi was a multinational city of great diversity with its own special atmosphere, and everyone who spent even a few years of their youth in this city felt the influence of this atmosphere. In this respect Tbilisi was similar to Odessa, the cosmopolitan port city on the Black Sea, and to Baku, the oil industry port on the Caspian, although of course the spirit and tradition of those cities differ from one another.

In Tbilisi there was a warm and friendly atmosphere. The city did not produce extreme individualists, but the influence of the Soviet central government was not so great there. Primakov fully experienced and imbibed the city's special atmosphere. His school friends and neighborhood friends remain part of his circle to this very day, and they often gather to commemorate his major birthdays. Among them is the heart surgeon Burakovsky, also a member of the Academy of Sciences; the film director and artist Lev Kulidzhanov; and Lev Onikov, a former Central Committee official of the Soviet Communist Party. Primakov and his friends often gather around a table with the distinct foods of the Caucasus, with Primakov himself often playing the role of witty master of ceremonies.

The young Primakov, after graduating from school, went to Moscow where he entered the Arab studies division of the Institute of Oriental Studies. During his student years he married. His wife Laura also came from Tbilisi. After graduating from this institute, Primakov attended Moscow State University as a graduate student for three years, then worked for the government agency in charge of television and radio. Primakov's position in that agency was a fairly high one— editor-in-chief of the main administration for radio broadcasts to foreign countries. To hold such a post one had to be a member of the *nomenklatura*, a list of party officials enjoying a high degree of confidence from the top party authorities, including the state security agency (the KGB). It was from this post that he later transferred to work on the party press, joining the staff of *Pravda*, the Communist Party's main newspaper.

At the Moscow editorial offices of *Pravda* Primakov soon took the post of assistant editor for the department dealing with Asia and Africa. In 1966 he was sent to the Middle East to serve as *Pravda's* special correspondent for that region. The newspaper's Egyptian bureau was located in Cairo, from where its reporters traveled to other countries of the region. This was a time when the Middle East was considered a highly important focal point for Soviet interests. It is enough to say that 1967 was the year of the "Six Day War," which changed the balance of forces in the region. In view of the Soviet Union's great involvement in Middle Eastern affairs, it is not surprising that the role of *Pravda's* correspondents there rose accordingly. Primakov developed virtually into a representative of the Soviet Communist Party's Central Committee in the Middle East. Through his newspaper reports he was able to act as an intermediary in resolving a great many important problems, and many missions of various kinds were entrusted to him.

A major feature of Soviet foreign policy at that time was support for the Arab countries, and Primakov was obliged to develop very extensive connections. An intelligent, calm, and good-natured person, who knew Arabic very well, Primakov operated with the highest degree of effectiveness, and this was noticed. I know of no other case in which a *Pravda* correspondent after four years of work outside the Soviet Union returned to Moscow to assume the very high post of deputy director of the Institute of the World Economy and International Relations, part of the Soviet Academy of Sciences system. This was one of five research institutes that directly served the party Central Committee and was also considered part of the system of scientific and scholarly research institutions under that Central Committee.

While director of the institute in the early 1970s Primakov defended his doctoral dissertation, and in 1974 at the age of 45 he was elected a corresponding member of the Academy of Sciences. The chief director of the institute was Academician Nikolai Inozemtsev, with whom Primakov had collaborated for many years. In the 1970s Inozemtsev was not only the director of the Institute of the World Economy and International Relations (Russian initials, IMEMO) and a member of the Academy of Sciences; he was also, in effect, an official adviser to Brezhnev on international affairs. This gave Inozemtsev and his institute a great deal of influence both in determining Soviet foreign policy and in Soviet academic affairs.

It was in this period, with Primakov's active participation, that the IMEMO built a large new building, very attractively designed for that time, on a street in Moscow called Profsoyuznaya Ulitsa (Trade Union Street). To this day the IMEMO occupies the same location, but only memories remain of its former influence in government. The institute now rents some of its facilities to various other organizations in order to earn the means to pay for continuing research as well as the salaries of its research staff.

In 1977 Primakov became head of the Institute of Oriental Studies (from which he had graduated). This was also a very influential scientific and academic institution, which helped work out Soviet foreign policy in Asia, and in particular in the Far East. There was a whole system or chain of such institutes in the Soviet Union—the U.S.-Canada Institute, the Latin America Institute, the Africa Institute. Other institutes of a closed, or confidential, top-security type also existed, for example, one on problems having to do with China.

Primakov was a rather strict director, according to his former colleagues. He insisted that they come to work four times a week, instead of the two times a week required by his predecessor. In his dealings with staff members he insisted that meetings begin and end at strictly scheduled times.

In 1979 Primakov, at age 50, was elected a full member of the Academy of Sciences. It was quite an accomplishment. Most academicians were in their 60s or 70s. Younger ones were usually found only among mathematicians and physicists, hardly ever among historians or economists.

In 1985 Primakov returned to the IMEMO, but this time as director. Within the system of academic institutes this was quite a significant advancement, and it is no accident that in 1988 Primakov was elected a member of the Presidium of the Academy of Sciences while remaining director of the institute and became the secretary in charge of the Academy's division dealing with the world economy and international relations. All institutes dealing with area studies and international relations came under his jurisdiction. When Primakov was appointed prime minister in September 1998 many people wrote that he didn't know much about economics. This is not true. He holds a doctoral degree in economic sciences, and because of his past work in the Academy of Sciences, he has a close acquaintance with and a solid understanding of problems of the world economy and the specific economic characteristics of various countries and regions of the world.

In the 1980s Primakov served as a consultant to politicians but was not a politician himself. He wrote a great deal and spoke at many academic conferences but apparently gave no thought to any political career for himself. It was Gorbachev who began to involve him in politics. He met Primakov during the summit with Ronald Reagan in Rejkyavik, Iceland in 1986. Primakov was not a member of the official Soviet delegation. He had traveled to the Icelandic capital as an adviser to the Soviet delegation and participated in conferences involving its leaders. At one of these discussions Primakov rather emphatically disputed a proposal made by Foreign Minister Eduard Shevardnadze and Marshall Sergei Akhromeyev, head of the Soviet General Staff. Gorbachev did not support Primakov in that disagreement, but he noticed him and soon established a close working relationship with him.

There is no question that Primakov supported Gorbachev, but he was never a "professional promoter of perestroika." Nor did he ever claim, like Aleksandr Yakovlev, to have helped elaborate the fundamental ideas of the so-called new thinking. From 1986 to 1988 Primakov occupied a rather modest place in the hierarchy of power. At the Twenty-Seventh Congress of the CPSU Primakov was elected to the Central Committee, but only as a candidate member, and not until 1989 did he become a full member of the Central Committee.

In February 1989 Primakov was elected to the newly established Congress of People's Deputies as one of the 100 representatives from the Communist Party. At that First Congress of People's Deputies he was elected a member of the Presidium of the Supreme Soviet of the USSR, and later was elected chairman of one of the chambers of the Supreme Soviet—the Union Council. At that time I, too, was a People's Deputy and a member of the Union Council and in that capacity made my first acquaintance with Primakov. I participated several times in discussions with him while I was chairing a commission of the Congress (on problems of corruption), and I worked with him at several meetings or sessions of a more restricted nature.

I must say that Primakov rarely spoke at sessions of the Union Council and almost never at the Congress of People's Deputies. He chaired sessions of the Union Council in a very calm way. (When the two chambers of the Supreme Soviet met jointly it was under the chairmanship of Gorbachev and later of Lukyanov.) As a chairman Gorbachev was very active, often interrupting other speakers, commenting on their remarks or correcting them. His own speeches were quite lengthy and not always as logical as they might have been. Lukyanov chaired sessions skillfully, but often in a rather rigid way, seeking to direct the discussion along a desired channel. The chairman of the Council of Nationalities, Rafik Nishanov, directed the sessions of his chamber in a very emotional way and sometimes chaired the sessions of the Supreme Soviet as a whole in the same way. Primakov showed virtually no emotion as a chairperson. I cannot recall a single case in which Primakov lost his self-control or spoke rudely or harshly. He managed to maintain his calm and even an appearance of indifference in very complicated circumstances. He was chairman of the commission of the Supreme Soviet on the question of privileges. The excessive privileges of the party and government bureaucracy were one of the questions that troubled public opinion the most in 1989–1990.

Primakov was entirely loyal to Gorbachev, but he did not rush to express his support everywhere and on all occasions, as many people did—nor did he speak out against Gorbachev, which many people also did in the period leading up to the Twenty-Eighth CPSU Congress (in 1990) and during that Congress. Primakov was not asked to give a report at that Congress, although he had become a candidate member of the Politburo in 1989. After Gorbachev was elected as the first president of the Soviet Union, Primakov became a member of the President's Council. It was at that time that Primakov made several trips outside the country as a chairperson of the Soviet parliamentary group. He also became a member of the Security Council of the USSR, which was founded in early 1991.

Primakov played no noticeable role in the events of August 1991 (the attempted coup) either on the side of the coup makers or on the side of Yeltsin and the Russian government. After the failure of the August coup he did not speak out either for or against Gorbachev, nor did he rush to swear allegiance to anyone else. When Vadim Bakatin was appointed as the new chairperson of the KGB, Primakov agreed to take the post of first deputy chair, also taking charge of the so-called First Main Administration of the KGB—that is, foreign intelligence. In the fall of 1991 Yeltsin and Bakatin, with Gorbachev's tacit consent or connivance, began to break up the KGB as a unitary organization. The foreign intelligence service was set apart as a distinct agency directly subordinate to the president. A decree signed by Gorbachev made Primakov director of this agency, the so-called Central Foreign Intelligence Service of the USSR. In December 1991, when the USSR was dissolved, Yeltsin appointed Primakov director of the Foreign Intelligence Service of Russia. Primakov spent four years in this post (1992–1996).

The Soviet Foreign Intelligence Service was considered justifiably to be virtually the best special service in the world. In the scale of its activities and the number of employees it apparently exceeded even the United States. For the Russian Federation an intelligence service on such a scale was insupportable. Of all the former departments of the KGB, however, the Foreign Intelligence Service held together better than the others. It retained most of its former personnel.

The interests of the Russian Federation are of course not as global as those of the former USSR. Therefore many departments of the Intelligence Service were reduced in size. Staff cuts occurred at the main administration at Yasenevo. The lack of resources tangibly affected the special services of Russia, but in spite of everything salaries were paid regularly. Various fringe benefits for intelligence personnel were maintained, because it was difficult for such people to earn money on the side. According to some employees of the Intelligence Service, many people working there had serious doubts about the appointment of Primakov in 1991. They called him "the academician." But skepticism was soon replaced by sincere respect. Wherever Primakov worked, sooner or later he was always able to win the support and confidence of his subordinates and colleagues. The Intelligence Service was no exception. They soon began to call him endearingly by his Russian middle name, Maksimych. [Russian middle names are based on the father's name; Primakov's father was Maksim; "Maksimych" of course means "son of Maksim."] They referred to Primakov as "our protector." At any rate he was able to keep many professionals on the staff and prevented the so-called democrats from tearing down the foreign intelligence agency completely.

In the mid-1990s hardly anyone spoke or wrote about Primakov. His appointment was viewed with a certain irony. Several newspapers wrote that he always had been a KGB agent. There is no question that any leading Soviet journalist in the Middle East or any director of a major institute concerned with international relations could not do his job in the Soviet Union without collaborating with or maintaining contacts with the KGB. But this does not mean that he worked as an intelligence agent. Primakov was directly subordinate to the Central Committee of the Soviet Communist Party, but that was true for any and all officials, journalists, diplomats, or directors of institutes of the Soviet Academy of Sciences.

In late 1995 Boris Yeltsin came to the conclusion that he simply could not win the presidential elections in 1996 if he kept Andrei Kozyrev as foreign minister. Kozyrev had conducted a foreign policy that was obviously pro-American; he was simply incapable of behaving in a dignified way on the international arena. Kozyrev's policies had humiliated Russia as a great power, and he had forced many outstanding diplomats to leave the Foreign Ministry.

Kozyrev possessed neither the knowledge nor the experience for work in such a high post. From 1974 to 1989 he had been simply one of many bureaucrats in the Soviet Foreign Ministry. He had never distinguished himself aside from his firm adherence to Yeltsin and the so-called democrats, which he began to display only in early 1991—not so much as a result of inner conviction, in my opinion, but to make up for his own inadequacy.

Yeltsin appointed Kozyrev foreign minister of Russia in 1990, when the Soviet Union still existed. The Russian Foreign Ministry did not have its own apparatus; it had no agencies or staff; it was a ministry with symbolic importance only. After the dissolution of the USSR the enormous apparatus of the Soviet Foreign Ministry came under the jurisdiction of this tiny Russian Foreign Ministry, in which there was not a single person worthy of the role which fell to their lot as the result of the destruction of the Soviet Union.

As Russia's foreign minister, Primakov immediately changed both the style and the character of Russia's foreign policy. He was many times more competent than Kozyrev. Primakov had decades of experience working on and resolving highly complex problems in foreign affairs. In 1990 not long before the conflict between the United Nations and Iraq, Primakov was sent to Baghdad as an intermediary. He was personally acquainted with Saddam Hussein, having known him since the mid-1960s, when Primakov had acted as an intermediary between the rebel Kurds in northern Iraq and the Iraqi government. Saddam Hussein singled Primakov out from among all the diplomats he had known and commented on Primakov's new assignment: "He can be received as a friend even when he is sent by the enemy." Hussein refused to make concessions in 1990 and 1991, and as a consequence suffered a stinging defeat during the "Desert Storm" Gulf War, although he managed to hold on to power.

Primakov for his part, while remaining almost a friend of Hussein also became a friend of Madeleine Albright. He won the respect of all Western leaders and foreign ministers. Many observers number him among the most influential foreign ministers in the world. He is known and respected in China, in Japan, and in Western Europe. What is important in this respect is that he is highly regarded not only as a representative of Russia but as an individual. He is calm, but he is tirelessly persistent. I would estimate that during his lifetime he has visited more than 100 different countries. The Western press has long since acknowledged Primakov's success, never ceasing to express amazement that this "experienced Cold Warrior" could so effortlessly and with such dignity direct the new foreign policy of the new Russia.

Some politicians and political observers as early as 1997 began to say that Primakov had managed to carry out his own kind of diplomatic revolution. One newspaper wrote: "He presents Russia's position on all questions in quite a definite way. Often it turns out that he's holding very poor cards, but he always plays them very well." Primakov changed the priorities of Russia's foreign policy, to focus first of all on the former Soviet countries and Russia's other close neighbors. He was an intermediary in talks between Armenia and Azerbaijan, between Georgia and Abkhazia, in talks between factions in Tajikistan, in the Middle East, and in Yugoslavia. Western newspapers have commented that under Primakov relations between Moscow and Beijing seem to have become warmer than at any time in the entire history of their relationship. Primakov has put forward and defends the idea of a multipolar world in which no one country ought to dominate.

Primakov never sought the position of prime minister. He declined it several times when it was offered to him. Once he had accepted the position, however, he showed very definitely that he would defend his own conception of the tasks and policies that the government of Russia ought to pursue. When Primakov speaks he likes to quote a saying by the Roman philosopher and poet Seneca: "When a man doesn't know in which direction to set his course, no wind will ever be favorable for him." He cited these words in describing Russia's policy in the economic sphere. Primakov knows which way to turn the rudder in order to have favorable winds both within the country and in foreign affairs. He is fully determined to steer in the necessary direction. Primakov's views on the tasks and direction Russia must take on domestic policy have not been formed just in the last few weeks. He has expressed his views for a long time and in many public settings both as foreign minister and as a patriotic statesman. In the spring and summer of 1998 he spoke several times in front of Russian and foreign audiences on problems of both foreign and domestic policy. The main points he made in these speeches were as follows:

- Russia must make its way smoothly into the world economy, to become a part of it, not just as a supplier of raw materials but as an equal partner. The Foreign Ministry must support Russian business, using the resources of foreign policy.
- Russia has become excessively dependent on imports from foreign countries, both capital and goods.
- The government has proved incapable of accumulating internally in order to strengthen the budget and to ensure ongoing spending to move the country forward in a more serious way along the path of industrial reconstruction. Excessive emphasis has been placed in Russia on macroeconomic stabilization without the necessary attention to increased production, especially the creation of an industry that would be competitive on the world market.
- The taxation policies practiced in Russia have proved to be ineffective.
- As a result of mistaken financial and industrial policy no less than $20 billion are leaving Russia every year. In this way Russia has been providing credits for the whole world.
- Loans and credits are necessary, but this is not the chief path.
- The role of government in the economy must be significantly increased, and it must pay more attention to the sphere of production and not just fiscal questions.
- The Asian crisis is not the main reason for the crisis in Russia; it has simply been superimposed on Russia's domestic mistakes and difficulties. The government's main mistake was to focus its attention primarily on financial stabilization on the macroeconomic level in line with the recommendations of the International Monetary Fund rather than the development and growth of our own industrial capacity. As a result foreign capital has invested not in Russian industry, from which it would find withdrawal much more complicated than from the financial sphere and from portfolio investments and investments in government securities.

Primakov said all of these things long before the beginning of the August–September crisis, and as prime minister he acted in the spirit of these policy pronouncements.

The problems facing Primakov and his government were immeasurably more complex and difficult than those he had faced in the past. One of the most difficult was to create a team, to establish a competent and businesslike government that could work as a single unit. In reviewing the Russian governments of the 1990s—from Gorbachev's last government to the recent ones of Chernomyrdin and Kiriyenko—one can only be amazed by how insignificant and even uneducated and intellectually weak the people who constituted those governments were. Yeltsin bears a large part of the blame for this, but not only he. It was Einstein who said that a totalitarian dictatorship leaves a moral vacuum behind it. We might add that the decades of totalitarian dictatorship and authoritarianism created not only a moral but also an intellectual vacuum in the upper echelons of the Soviet Union. The exceptions were very few: Aleksei Kosygin and Yuri Andropov. But even they had to function within the framework of a rigid party discipline, ideology, and hierarchy. Primakov came to power under exceptional circumstances. He did not have to submit his actions for approval to a Central Committee or Politburo members. He could steer the Russian ship of state, which had suffered a great deal of damage, in the proper direction and begin to fix it up and put it in order. Along with many others, I wished Yevgeny Primakov favorable winds.

VIKTOR GERASHCHENKO AND YURI MASLYUKOV

The appointment of these two men, Gerashchenko to head the Central Bank of Russia and Maslyukov to be the first deputy prime minister in charge of economic affairs and industry, was the chief condition Primakov set for becoming prime minister. These terms were accepted by Yeltsin and by the Duma. Thus the main parameters for government policy in the economic and financial field were established. Neither Gerashchenko nor Maslyukov was a newcomer to the government or economic affairs, and their views were well known. Primakov himself knew these two men quite well.

Viktor Gerashchenko was born in 1937 and graduated from the

Moscow Financial Institute in 1960. He immediately began work as an accountant at the State Bank of the USSR, and five years later took charge of a department at the USSR Bank of Foreign Trade. In 1965 the 28-year-old Gerashchenko was sent to London as the director of the Moscow People's Bank in that city. The Soviet Union had several banks in foreign countries which operated under market economy conditions, and therefore their experience was unique. Western financial and business publications as early as the 1960s wrote about Gerashchenko as a banker and financier worth paying attention to, a figure who was unusual for that time.

After London, Gerashchenko worked for five years as assistant manager of the Moscow People's Bank in Lebanon, and during those years, Primakov, then special correspondent for *Pravda* in the Middle East, made Gerashchenko's acquaintance. In 1972 Primakov was back in Moscow, and Gerashchenko after a brief stint at the Soviet Bank of Foreign Trade took charge of the Soviet Bank in West Germany and then another Soviet Bank in Singapore. After returning to Moscow, Gerashchenko became deputy chair of the Soviet Bank of Foreign Trade, which changed its name and some of its functions several times. There was probably no more experienced banker in the Soviet Union, and in 1989 Gerashchenko was appointed to head the State Bank of the USSR. At that time the bank was not an independent financial institution but was subordinated to the Ministry of Finance of the USSR, which in turn followed the orders of the Central Committee of the CPSU. The main decisions on financial questions were taken not by Gerashchenko but by Mikhail Gorbachev.

After the collapse of the Soviet Union Gerashchenko worked for several months at one of the numerous foundations that arose at that time, the so-called Reform Foundation. But the liberalization of prices carried out by the Yeltsin-Burbulis-Gaidar government caused such a painful collapse of Russia's financial system that Yeltsin had no alternative but to call on Gerashchenko for help. In late 1992 Gerashchenko became chairman of the Central Bank of Russia and headed that bank until the end of 1994.

Gerashchenko was an obstacle for many people. He was too independent a figure, and his primary concern was for the good of Russia and the good of Russia's financial system. Moreover, under the new Russian constitution of 1993 the Central Bank was granted extensive powers. Article 75 of that constitution states the following:

"Defending the ruble and ensuring its stability are the main functions of the Central Bank of the Russian Federation, functions which it carries out independently of other government bodies. . . . The issuing of new currency is done only and exclusively by the Central Bank." The Duma can appoint or remove the chairman of the Central Bank, but only when this is proposed in writing by the president of the country.

After the financial crisis in October 1994 referred to as Black Tuesday, Gerashchenko was obliged to leave his position as head of the Central Bank. After that he changed jobs several times but ended up in 1996 as chairman of the board of the Moscow International Bank. This bank did not get swept up in the craze to buy short-term government bonds, and consequently suffered to a lesser degree than others from the financial disaster of August 1998.

Gerashchenko returned to the Central Bank in September 1998 with his own team for the third time. He made no secret of his views or of what he proposes to do. In his opinion, the reason for the financial crash lay in the defective economic policy which failed to support real production in the Russian economy. He believed that what was needed was a carefully weighed and intelligent industrial policy. While taking a very cautious attitude toward the printing of more money, he felt that Russian could not get by without issuing new currency on a controlled basis. He favored a more flexible approach to the problem of the government's indebtedness in relation to short-term bonds. He believes that a new series of negotiations should be held with foreign and domestic investors in this regard. But he warned that there was simply no easy or quick solution to this problem, because the government had become indebted to private creditors to the tune of $125 billion. Moreover, foreign financial institutions were holding a total of $14 billion in Russian short-term government bonds. These debts were too large for a nearly impoverished Russia.

In the new Russian government the responsibility for implementing an intelligent industrial policy, as advocated by both Primakov and Gerashchenko, fell to Yuri Maslyukov. He was less well known in Russia and abroad than Primakov or Gerashchenko, but as we have said, he was no newcomer to economic and industrial management. He had an enormous amount of experience, and had drafted programs for extricating Russia from various crisis situations several times in the past—programs drafted both for the government and for the opposition Communist Party of the Russian Federation. He was even invited to join Kiriyenko's government and in fact took charge of the Ministry of Industry and Trade in July 1998, but had no time to even draw up a plan for work before the August crisis. Maslyukov had taken charge of that ministry in spite of the objections of his party comrades, who were getting ready to expel him from the CPRF. These disagreements later faded away.

Yuri Maslyukov was born in 1937. By profession he was a mechanical engineer. He first worked as an engineer in 1962, and later took various management positions in defense industry operations in the city of Izhevsk. In 1974 the 37-year-old Maslyukov transferred to the USSR Ministry of the Defense Industry and after several years was appointed deputy minister. In the 1980s he served as deputy chairman of the State Planning Commission of the USSR and later was deputy chairman of the Council of Ministers of the USSR. From 1988 to 1991 he headed the State Planning Commission. Maslyukov became a member of the Central Committee of the CPSU in 1986 and a member of the Politburo in 1989. From 1992 to 1998 despite his unique experience Maslyukov remained in effect without a job.

In September 1998 he returned to a position of leadership in the economy. His priorities were not difficult to specify. Here is what he said in one of his first interviews:

> The government invested more than 30 years in making me a specialist in heavy engineering. I know our military and defense industry as perhaps few others do in Russia today. I know heavy engineering and I'm familiar with the fundamentals of foreign trade. . . . A Russia that does not have a powerful industry is not a great power. Raw materials alone, the prices for which are constantly falling, cannot serve as the backbone for our economy. There needs to be a very strong balancing factor. This factor is industry. . . . No matter what the government places its bets on, investment is the fundamental basis for developing Russia. Without investments there will be no Russia. And if the investment component of our budget remains as miserly as it has been in the past and is now, very little time will be left before the ultimate degradation of Russia. . . . The Bacchanalia must be stopped. The situation on the financial markets must become

stable. Everything that can constitute income in spite of inflation must be spent in a sensible and intelligent way, above all by compensating the most needy families and investing in the most ailing sectors of our economy. . . . The government must remember that it functions as a serious, significant, and rational economic directing agency in the market which Russia today constitutes. The government is a full equal partner [in the economy]; the government has a managerial role in the situation; it manages state-owned property and does not abandon this property to the whims of fate.

(*Tribuna*, September 15, 1998)

Maslyukov was an excellent partner for Gerashchenko. Together with Primakov they constituted the core of a government which had great potential.

POSTSCRIPT

YELTSIN'S LAST YEAR

11

Why the Dismissal of Primakov?

On the morning of May 12, 1999, Prime Minister Yevgeny Primakov was summoned to the Kremlin to report to President Yeltsin on the economic situation in Russia. But the president didn't want to hear what the premier had to say, and swept aside all the documents he presented. After several angry reproaches Yeltsin declared he had decided to dismiss Primakov, although he was exceedingly grateful to him for his courageous and helpful efforts. "You did the necessary tactical job well. But to tackle the strategic problems I've decided to appoint someone else as premier."

In a televised speech to the nation Yeltsin stated: "It was Primakov who eight months ago, in a white-hot political situation and a terrible economic crisis, demonstrated his masterful art as a diplomat: he displayed caution and circumspection. The confidence the government has to its credit is great, as in earlier times, but this is primarily because of the personal qualities of the premier, who has shown amazing self-possession, composure, and cool-headedness in the most difficult circumstances."

However, in recent months, said Yeltsin, the government had been making no headway. It did not wish to take unpopular measures that could move things forward more quickly. For that reason, Yeltsin said, he had made "a difficult but necessary decision," to appoint a younger and more energetic man as premier, the 47-year-old colonel-general in charge of the Ministry of Internal Affairs, Sergei Vadimovich Stepashin.

Primakov made no attempt to argue with the president. Within an hour he was at the Russian White House addressing an emergency session of the cabinet. He was brief and to the point. He read aloud the president's decree dismissing himself as prime minister, and presented to the cabinet members their new leader. Primakov made his remarks with great dignity and twice was interrupted by bursts of applause. Almost all the cabinet members had smiles on their faces. Only on Stepashin's face—and on that of his new chief deputy premier, Nikolai Aksyonenko, head of the Ministry of Roads and Railways—was there a worried look, even a look of dismay. After wishing everyone success and making a humorous remark, Primakov left the room.

Politics, in the view of many, is similar to the theater, where you have to know not only how to step forward into the lights, but also how to leave the stage properly. In their next day's reports even the newspapers that were demanding Primakov's retirement had to admit that "Primakov made his exit gracefully."

A SURPRISE THAT WAS EXPECTED

Primakov was prepared for dismissal as early as mid-April. At the end of January materials aimed at discrediting the prime minister and his cabinet began to appear in the press and on television. News commentators on two popular private TV channels—Sergei Dorenko and Mikhail Leontyev—were especially zealous in their denunciations. They blamed Primakov for the collapse of the economy and accused him of trying to organize a "surreptitious coup d'etat." Some newspapers kept repeating the charge that Primakov was a do-nothing premier, and had been since the previous autumn, that he was afraid to take responsibility and avoided making decisions. Others argued that he was doing a lot, but that it was all intended to undermine the market economy, which he simply didn't understand, since he was a "mastodon trained in the school of Andropov." (Yuri Andropov had headed the Soviet government in 1982–84.) The newspaper *Kommersant* declared that Primakov was "not only betraying but selling out the interests of Russia."

Besides trying to discredit the premier, the media tried to create a conflict between him and the president. Headlines such as the following were common: "Yeltsin is no longer Number One in the country," "Primakov wants the president's job," "Yeltsin is ready for rough measures," "The president is going to say goodbye to Primakov."

The Western press was more friendly toward the Russian premier. The French paper *Le Figaro* wrote on February 28: "The situation in Russia is stable, and the author of this surprising stability is Primakov. His public image is of one who rejects confrontation and works quietly. This has calmed and reassured his compatriots. Russian society is beginning to dream of wisdom like Primakov's becoming dominant in the government." Similarly, the *Economist* of London reported on February 9 that "Yevgeny Primakov has done remarkably well. Unimaginable though it seemed when he took office in the chaotic days after the rouble fell out of bed last August, political stability has broken out." Still, said the *Economist*, there was not "any great applause" for Primakov.

Primakov's own reaction to the media campaign was, I would say, rather mild; he took it in stride. The president was more emotional. "There's no use trying to drive a wedge between me and Primakov," Yeltsin told journalists. "No one has yet invented such a wedge." Other comments by Yeltsin included: "Primakov and I have agreed to work together until the year 2000"; and "Don't go trying to make me butt heads with the premier, I beg of you; that is very dangerous." No one listened to Yeltsin's plea, but the effect of the continuing campaign was to lower public confidence not so much in Primakov as in the media themselves.

By mid-April 1999 it was obvious that Yeltsin was being influenced by the stage directors in the anti-Primakov camp and others of similar opinion within his own circle. Still, he had no convincing pretext for dismissing Primakov. Possible scenarios for accomplishing this kept changing from week to week. It was thought that failure in negotiations with the International Monetary Fund and World Bank could be used as a pretext, but these negotiations proceeded successfully despite difficulties.

Then there was an attempt to involve Primakov in the outcome of impeachment proceedings in the Duma. The Kremlin made statements along these lines: "The Duma better stop making preparations for impeachment of Yeltsin, or else Primakov will be dismissed." But Primakov had nothing to do with the impeachment preparations, which had been under way in the inner recesses of the Duma for over a year. The premier spoke out publicly against impeachment several times. Besides, any serious analysis would have shown that none of the various charges being brought against Yeltsin had a chance of winning the 300 votes needed by Yeltsin's accusers. The left-wing Duma politicians made the mistake of presenting too many different charges all at once.

The press claimed that it was the Duma's insistence on impeachment that provoked Yeltsin into firing Primakov, but this argument was not convincing, and Yeltsin himself made no such statement. The impeachment controversy masked the real underlying causes of the conflict.

THE MAIN REASON FOR PRIMAKOV'S OUSTER

In his earlier post as director of intelligence for the Federal Security Service, Primakov had already learned a good deal about the enormous scale of corruption in Russia and the way capital was flowing out of the country. As premier he learned quite a few additional details, but, more importantly, he now had not just information but government power as well. He declared war on corruption and promised to jail all those found guilty of economic crimes.

Thousands of criminal cases were begun, at first in the port cities and the provinces, later in Moscow as well. Boris Berezovsky was not the chief object of these trials, although the papers wrote about him more than others. Bigger targets than he were mentioned. Lists of the twelve richest *families* in Russia, not just the richest individuals, were circulating. It was hinted that these lists were drawn up with assistance from the Swiss attorney general's office. Reports spoke of tens of billions of dollars whose trail could be followed by bank account records. When billions are involved, there are no secret paths, not even for "dirty" money.

As these reports came out bankers and financial speculators began to feel uncomfortable, as did big shots in advertising, major importers and exporters, customs officials, people prominent in the arms industry, and influential government bureaucrats. It was people like this, especially those with media connections, who now found Primakov quite unsuitable as premier. Thus, it was the campaign against corruption that sparked the intrigues against him. Although Primakov did not personally conduct investigations or bring cases to court, he allowed free rein to the considerable number of honest staff members within the Russian Prosecutor General's Office, the Federal Security Service, and the Ministry of Internal Affairs who were willing to take such initiatives.

How would Sergei Stepashin conduct himself in this area? That was a question that concerned people as much as the exchange rate of the ruble. Initially he made some significant statements: "The economy must be kept going, but not swindling," and "Fighting against corruption and gangsterism—those are our priorities."

YELTSIN'S POWERS AND RUSSIA'S GOVERNMENT SYSTEM

It would have been hard to find a worse time for Primakov's dismissal. The economy was slowly coming out of crisis, and industry had grown relative to the previous year. Earnings from exports had increased, and $6 billion of debt had been repaid to Western creditors. The exchange rate of the ruble had begun to improve. In 1999, for the first time in many years, there were no major strikes in the spring. Back wages were paid up, and salaries and pensions increased.

On the other hand, Yeltsin's relations with parliament and with the Prosecutor General's Office had worsened dramatically. In public opinion polls only 2 percent expressed confidence in the president, but 70 percent had confidence in Primakov as premier. Primakov was completely loyal to Yeltsin. In fact, his was the only solid support Yeltsin had. The new premier, Stepashin, did not have the knowledge, experience, wisdom, and charm that Primakov demonstrated. Yeltsin, although he acted within his poswers under the constitution, made a major mistake in dismissing Primakov.

The president of Russia has greater powers than the president of France or the United States. Yeltsin could keep a cabinet in power even if the Duma passed a motion of no confidence. On the other hand, he could dismiss a government that the parliament and the people had confidence in.

This defect in the Russian constitution is the result not just of faulty legislation but of conditions in Russia in general, for democracy is only taking its first steps and no mature, responsible political parties have yet grown up. The Communist Party of the Russian Federation (CPRF) is the only organization that fits the definition of a political party. All the others are still embryonic or in their infancy. But the CPRF is a surviving fragment of the Communist Party of the Soviet Union, which crashed and fell apart in 1991. Could such a party, with rural residents and pensioners as its main support, really run the country? Does the CPRF draw sustenance from society's soil through young roots, or are its the dying roots of a felled tree? In conditions where the only serious political party is one like this, a strong presidency remains necessary for Russia for the time being.

At the height of fame and success, during the Potsdam Conference, Winston Churchill suffered a crushing defeat in the British elections of 1945. His place was taken at Potsdam by the new premier, Clement Attlee. In Stalin's entourage scornful remarks were made: "That's what you get with democracy!" When Churchill first heard about the election results he was dumbfounded and spoke of the ingratitude of the British public. Later he had a more profound comment: "democracy is the worst form of government—except for all those other forms that have been tried. . . ."

In Russia we have become convinced of the accuracy of the first part of this observation. But in the end, who other than we ourselves will be able to demonstrate the true value and full potential of Russian democracy?

12

The Dismissal of Stepashin

On August 10, 1999, less than three months after making Sergei Stepashin prime minister, Yeltsin dismissed him. In announcing that the new premier, Vladimir Putin, director of the security police, would also be Yeltsin's candidate as his successor to the presidency, Yeltsin made it clear to Russian politicians that he was preparing to take early retirement. Putin, who was then so little known that his name had not figured at all in the election campaign, seemed at first to have very little chance of being elected president.

Yeltsin's personal support did not seem likely to add to Putin's popularity. But there was another possibility. If Yeltsin gave up his post before the end of his term, the new prime minister would automatically become acting president. Under the Russian constitution, if the president resigns, presidential power goes to the prime minister for three months, during which time new elections must be held. It was obvious that in such a three-month period Putin, with the combined posts of prime minister and president, would have almost unlimited power. Yeltsin and his immediate circle hoped apparently that this power would give Putin a jumping-off point for making a leap into the Kremlin through democratic elections.

It was clear that Putin could play the same role for Yeltsin, his family, and his inner circle that Gerald Ford played for Richard Nixon after the latter's resignation in 1974. On September 8, 1974, President Ford granted a full pardon to Nixon for any laws he might have broken. In this way he guaranteed that the investigations which had been launched against Nixon would cease. Yeltsin and a rather large number of people in his administration needed a similar amnesty. Sure enough, this scenario was played out. After Yeltsin's surprise resignation on New Year's Eve, Putin soon granted Yeltsin and "the family" immunity from prosecution. He also was quick to remove many of Yeltsin's entourage from key positions in the Kremlin.

But between the August 10 appointment of Putin and his New Year's accession to the acting presidency other significant developments occurred.

Before looking at those, let us pause for a moment to review what we know about the man who suddenly emerged as the likely new president of Russia—Vladimir Vladimirovich Putin.

13

Who Is Putin?

Little was known about Putin before August 10, 1999. He apparently preferred to remain in the shadows, especially after Yeltsin appointed him director of the Federal Security Service (Russian initials, FSB; the successor organization in Russia to the KGB of the Soviet Union). This occurred as part of the government reshuffling in the summer of 1998. In March 1999 Yeltsin also made Putin secretary of the Security Council of the Russian Federation, although he had worked in Kremlin posts only since 1996. Over a period of three years he held six different positions successively—not enough time to reveal very prominently his abilities as a politician or administrator.

[Translator's Note: The London *Financial Times* of January 1, 2000, and other Western newspapers since then, reported the following information about Putin: Born in Leningrad (now St. Petersburg) in 1952, he earned a law degree at Leningrad State University, graduating in 1975 and then working for the KGB in Leningrad for nine years. From 1984 to 1990 he served as a KGB officer in East Germany, where he became fluent in German and acquired an admiration for German efficiency and discipline. In 1989, as pressures for change in

East Germany built up in response to perestroika in the Soviet Union, he is said to have sought out East German reformers during the final crisis of the East German Communist regime. Returning to St. Petersburg, he joined the administration of Anatoly Sobchak, the market-reform "democrat" elected mayor there in 1990. (Sobchak had been one of Putin's law professors at Leningrad State University.) By 1994, Putin was deputy head of the St. Petersburg municipal government, under Sobchak. In 1996, Anatoly Chubais brought Putin to Moscow.] As author of the present book and other books on Soviet and Russian history, I had the occasion to meet Putin personally. This happened only once, but it was a remarkable occasion. Putin asked me to give a presentation about my new book *The Unknown Andropov* to the Collegium, the governing body of the FSB. On June 15, the anniversary of Andropov's birth, I made my presentation to a Collegium session enlarged to include veterans of the KGB. I told the assembled officers about my research work in preparing the book and shared my views on Andropov's place in Soviet and Russian history. (Andropov, of course, had headed the Soviet government in 1982–84 after the death of Leonid Brezhnev, and previously had headebook, *The Unknown Andropov*, to the Collegium, the governing body of the FSB. On June 15, the anniversary of Andropov's birth, I made the presentation to a Collegium session that had been enlarged to include veterans of the KGB. I told the assembled officers about my research work in preparing the book and shared my views on Andropov's place in Soviet and Russian history. (Andropov, of course, had headed the Soviet government in 1982–84 after the death of Leonid Brezhnev, and previously had headed the KGB.) Before the presentation I met with Putin briefly, and I also observed how he handled himself in this assemblage of top officials of the FSB and former KGB. He struck me as serious, calm, and intelligent. He listens more than he talks and is undoubtedly steadier and less vain than the previous prime minister, Sergei Stepashin. Discussions about Putin's relations with Sobchak, with Boris Berezovsky, or with Yeltsin and "the family" make little sense. Whenever a political leader becomes head of government his circle of advisers and the considerations that motivate him inevitably change. A prime minister cannot simply be a pawn in someone else's game.

The military conflict in Dagestan and Chechnya was Putin's first real test. It was he who proposed that combat pay for all Russian troops involved in these operations be raised to $1,000 per month, an amount equal to that paid to Russian peacekeepers in Kosovo.

Sergei Stepashin has referred to himself as a "mere boy" who was thrust into high politics by Yeltsin. In contrast, Putin has never seemed "boyish," not even when he first came to Moscow in 1996. He steers clear of off-the-cuff remarks or actions. A journalist for *Izvestia* described him this way: "Putin's rare television appearances are striking for their extremely laconic quality. His rather acerbic manner, the toughness of an organization man, is rather pleasing in its own way, although this is overridden by the coldly intelligent, impenetrable look in his eyes. He abides strictly by the wise old rule—that language exists to conceal one's thoughts, and facial expressions, to hide one's feelings."

The events around Kosovo revealed that there has now come to the fore in the Russian army a group of 40–50 relatively young generals who command Russia's main military districts and Defense Ministry departments. These are men of unquestionable patriotism and strong determination. They constitute a new power center in Moscow, one that is disconcerting to certain "democrats" in Russia and influential circles in the West. The operations directed by these men in Dagestan and Chechnya are more professional and more politically astute, with tighter control of information, than during the Chechnya war of 1994–96. Putin is clearly working in tandem with these generals.

PRIMAKOV, ZYUGANOV, AND OTHERS

Objective conditions had arisen by the summer of 1999 that could potentially have helped the Communists return to power by democratic means. Russians perceived NATO's war against Yugoslavia in the first half of 1999 as a show of force directed mainly against Russia. In May, the unexpected and unfounded dismissal of Yevgeny Primakov, the most popular prime minister in Russia since Aleksei Kosygin, was perceived to be the result of a plot by "oligarchs," bankers, and other big property owners, who had become anxious about the campaign against corruption. The anti-corruption investigations, as we have said, were reaching close to "the family" around Yeltsin.

Although Primakov did not belong to a political party, his government was considered "left of center." After Sergei Stepashin's appointment, government policy seemed to take a turn to the right. As a result, left-wing forces became more active and the position of CPRF leader Gennady Zyuganov was strengthened. He emerged in first place in public opinion polls on the presidential candidates. The leftward shift in public opinion was intensified by a continued poor showing of key economic indicators in the first half of the year and a rise in food prices caused by a severe drought and very poor harvest in 1998. In the Communist past the price of bread had been kept low by government subsidies and did not depend on the harvest.

In these circumstances a plan was formulated to ban the CPRF. The Communists were to be provoked into demonstrations of protest against the closing of the Mausoleum on Red Square and the reburying of Lenin's body in a cemetery in St. Petersburg. However, this plan was called off because the political and economic elites realized that demonstrations might not occur, and respect for the government might simply fall still further.

There was only one remaining way to prevent a Communist victory—uniting the center-left political groups and small democratic organizations with the regional governors, leaders of national republics, and mayors of large cities. This plan was put into operation at the beginning of August 1999, when the "Fatherland" and "All Russia" political movements formed a coalition. It put the upper house of the Russian parliament, the Federal Council, consisting of governors, leaders of national republics, and the mayors of Moscow and St. Petersburg, in opposition to the president.

This new political coalition seemed to ensure that the right wing would be defeated in the December parliamentary elections, but it did not guarantee victory over Zyuganov and the CPRF. To achieve that aim, the new bloc needed a genuinely popular leader. The only possible candidate was Primakov, who stood outside parties and blocs.

THE RETURN OF PRIMAKOV

When Primakov was dismissed in May 1999, he announced that he was leaving politics and would write his memoirs. He would be seventy years old that October. But his publishing plans were interrupted. He was called to "save the fatherland," literally and figuratively, by becoming leader of the Fatherland-All Russia bloc and putting his name forward as a candidate for president in the elections then scheduled for June 2000. The mayor of Moscow, Yuri Luzhkov, who had frequently announced his intention of contesting the presidential elections and who had established the Fatherland bloc, agreed to take the post of prime minister. As a talented organizer but mediocre politician, this role suited Luzhkov better than the presidency.

The duumvirate of Primakov and Luzhkov seemed to herald a Primakov victory in the 2000 presidential elections, but hopes for a big victory by the new bloc in the Duma elections of December 1999 were not well founded. The Fatherland-All Russia bloc was not a political party, but a coalition of elites. It opposed Yeltsin but was based, not on the mass of the people, and not even on the middle class (which, as we have seen, does not yet exist on any substantial basis in Russia), but on governors and mayors. It was a revolt of the boyars against the tsar. However, this boyar revolt had the potential to be more dangerous for "Tsar Boris" than a popular uprising.

That is why Yeltsin began to prepare his departure from the throne in favor of a personally selected successor, Putin. He hoped to win the end game, or at least end with a draw. The "Putin move" took everyone by surprise. But the "Primakov move" also looked like a very strong one, with the highest popularity ratings as of August 1999. Opinion polls at that time suggested that the Fatherland-All Russia bloc would win 30–35 percent of the vote.

14

The Second Chechnya War

This whole picture changed, however, as the result of Putin's decisive, even ruthless, prosecution of the Chechnya war. Government-controlled television discredited Luzhkov and Primakov, and boosted Putin and his successes in reasserting Russian control of Chechnya, with the result that the Fatherland-All Russia bloc did poorly in the December Duma elections, winning only 12 percent. A new political formation, the Unity bloc, backed by Putin, did surprisingly well, using the advantages of incumbency and riding on Putin's war-related popularity. In January 2000, after becoming acting president, Putin made another surprise move. His hastily created Unity bloc, which had won 24 percent of the vote, formed a parliamentary alliance with the Communists and their allies, who had won more than 25 percent, thus creating a pro-government bloc controlling a majority of votes in parliament.

At first three prominent, democratic-minded leaders, Primakov, Yavlinsky, and Kiriyenko, protested this move and walked out of the Duma. Within a few weeks, after discussions with Putin, they returned and seemed to accept their role as a parliamentary minority. Primakov also abandoned his intention to run for president. To be sure, three major candidates were still competing with Putin—the CPRF leader Zyuganov, the "democrat" Yavlinsky, and the maverick Zhirinovsky —not to mention eight other minor figures. But a fairly solid victory for Putin as Russia's new president in the elections rescheduled for March 26, 2000, seemed virtually assured.

15

The December 1999 Elections

In general, the December voting testified to a more experienced electorate for whom radical sentiments held little appeal. The previous Duma had a large left wing, made up of the CPRF and its allies. The right wing was fragmented, and there was no influential center party or bloc. In 1995, only four parties—representing 50.5 percent of the electorate—had won more than 5 percent of the vote, allowing them to have representation in parliament. Those were the CPRF, on the left, and on the right, the Nash Dom Rossiya party, or NDR, of Chernomyrdin, the Yabloko party of Grigory Yavlinksy, and the so-called Liberal Democratic Party of Vladimir Zhirinovsky. Relations between parliament and president had been hostile, and only the government of Yevgeny Primakov had enjoyed support in the Duma.

The elections of December 19, 1999, fundamentally changed the situation. This time six political organizations—representing 80 percent of the electorate—passed the 5 percent barrier. The CPRF continued to have a large parliamentary group, but it was weaker because many of its allies failed to win reelection. On the right, the Unity bloc, which everyone recognized as the party of President Putin, replaced the NDR. (Chernomyrdin's party, not unexpectedly, suffered a crushing electoral defeat, with only about 1 percent of the vote, and is no longer represented in parliament, although Chernomyrdin himself won an individual seat.) A new party, the Union of Right Forces, headed by Sergei Kiriyenko, the former prime minister, and backed by "democrats" like Anatoly Chubais, also won representation in the Duma. The parties of Yavlinksy and Zhirinovsky remain on the right wing as well, although both suffered heavy losses and were barely able to pass the 5 percent mark. In the center was the new formation, the Fatherland-All Russia bloc of Primakov and Luzhkov, which, as we have said, won only 12 percent instead of the expected 30–35 percent.

The surprise parliamentary alliance between the Unity bloc and the CPRF called into question the characterization of Unity as part of the right wing. It suggested either that Putin had made a shift to the left— or that most of the political parties in Russia were lining up loyally behind the Putin regime, regardless of whether its policies could be characterized as "right" or "left."

It seemed almost certain that the two most influential politicians in Russia would continue to be Putin and Primakov. This is not at all surprising or puzzling. The countless number of political aspirants who have appeared on the Russian stage in the last ten years failed to understand that politics is not just a profession but an art. In order to succeed in politics, it is not enough to have professional training and high ambitions. Real intellect and native leadership abilities are also required. During 1999, only Primakov and Putin demonstrated these qualities. For others mere ambition seemed to suffice.

16

A Change Without a Coup or Revolution

The end of the year, century, and millennium also marked the end of the Yeltsin era, which had lasted for most of the decade and which culminated in his voluntary resignation. This major change occurred without revolution or bloodshed, without a palace coup or plot of any kind. Russia entered the new century with a new leader, Acting President Putin, and almost all the population perceived this, not as cause for alarm, but as a providential New Year's gift..

Yeltsin's resignation was no surprise. Only the timing of it, sprung upon the world on the last day of the year, caught people unprepared. It is true that Yeltsin did not want to leave his post. Yet he had thought and even spoken about his possible resignation ever since the summer of 1996, when heart trouble rendered him practically unable to perform his duties. In the fall of 1996, when he underwent a complex bypass operation, he was forced to consider all possible outcomes, including the one even worse than resignation. In 1997–98 the state of his health continued to be troublesome. In September 1998, U.S. President Clinton and his advisers, during a meeting with Yeltsin, were astounded by his inappropriate behavior. In October, during a visit by

Yeltsin to Tashkent and Alma-Ata, hundreds of people directly witnessed his incapacitation. That same month nearly half the members of the Federation Council called for the "immediate voluntary resignation of the president."

During 1999 Yeltsin was sidelined by illness virtually every month. His ability to snap back after each crisis, firmly grasping the helm of power again, was a constant surprise. For example, in December 1998, after a long stay in the hospital, he had returned to the Kremlin and suddenly fired a number of top people in his administration. Likewise, in May 1999 his dismissal of Primakov occurred without warning. In November 1999, at the Istanbul summit meeting of the Organization for Security and Cooperation in Europe, he impressed diplomats and journalists as being strong, healthy, and self-confident. "Yeltsin didn't pound the rostrum with his shoe," one diplomat commented, "but he had untied his shoelaces. I don't know what pills he's taking, but they certainly seem to help." Such bursts of activity were, however, increasingly rare—and risky for Yeltsin's health. Meanwhile, Russia sorely needed a competent president who could steadily remain at his post, not in the hospital. And it seemed that Russia would soon have such a leader.

Over the preceding hundred years only ten men have stood at the head of the Russian or Soviet state, some for many years, others for only a few months. They were Tsar Nicholas II, Alexander Kerensky, Vladimir Lenin, Joseph Stalin, Nikita Khrushchev, Leonid Brezhnev, Yuri Andropov, Konstantin Chernenko, Mikhail Gorbachev, and Boris Yeltsin. These men differed widely in their political views and individual personalities. Only one of them, Boris Yeltsin, was actually elected by the voters of Russia. The others came to power as the result of revolutions, closed-door decisions by the ruling party, palace coups, or other intrigues behind the scenes. These men had generally come to power against the wishes of their predecessors, and frequently condemned the previous ruler's policies, proclaiming their intention to establish a new and better system.

Kerensky was certainly not about to continue the legacy of Nicholas II, nor Lenin that of Kerensky. For good reason Lenin was apprehensive about Stalin's growing power, and for his part, Stalin praised Lenin in words but turned against much that Lenin had sought to achieve in the early 1920s. Khrushchev made the struggle against the "personality cult of Stalin" one of his prime objectives, while

Brezhnev declared war on the "subjectivism and voluntarism" of Khrushchev. Andropov did not want Chernenko to succeed him, nor did Chernenko want Gorbachev as his successor. Once in power, Gorbachev denounced the preceding "era of stagnation."

There was no natural or normal system for the transfer of power in Russia or the Soviet Union in the twentieth century, and that was one of the most important causes of our country's many difficulties and failures. Five of the leaders listed above remained in power to the last days of their lives. Three were removed by revolutions, one by a palace coup. Yeltsin was the only one to leave office voluntarily before the end of his term, and he transferred power to a successor whom he himself had selected. Still, this is progress. It is to be hoped that this kind of orderly and constitutional procedure will become the norm in Russia. There has arisen the real possibility of creating a democratic system of succession from one leader to another, and we do not have the right to fumble this opportunity.

There is no question that many disorderly practices, habits, and ways of doing things have taken root in Russia in the past ten years, and they need to be reexamined and changed. Some measures need to be taken right away, even before the presidential elections. Let us hope, however, that these inevitable changes will not take the form of a new struggle against a "cult of personality." Our country and people are weary of revolutions, upheavals, and sharp about-faces of the kind that abounded in the twentieth century. The breakthrough that Russia needs can be accomplished without excessive strain, simply by making use of the substantial resources and favorable conditions that, even today, Russia still enjoys. These resources have not been used rationally in past years, or they have been used to the detriment of Russia and its people. We saw no exception to this pattern of wastefulness during the Yeltsin era, which has now passed into history.

Index

Index Prepared by Fred Leise

Chubais, Anatoly *(continued)*
Third Congress of Democratic
Russia, 32; popular opinion of,
91, 95; public activity, 286;
reduction in power of, 286;
remaining in cabinet, 137; resignation, reasons for, 153; responsibility for government decision-
making, 317; return to Yeltsin
government, 84, 153; trip to
Washington, 300, 303; Western
views of, 15; Yeltsin's retirement
of, 287
Chubais, Igor, 88
Chubais government, 146
Church-state separation, 1
Churchill, Winston, 348
Cirrhosis of the liver, 164
Cities, support for Yeltsin government in, 269
Civic Alliance (political party), 132
Civil war in Moscow, 103–130:
bombardment of White House,
123–125; casualties of, 128–129;
end of, 126–127; mass beatings,
127–128; police withdrawal,
120–123; post-confrontation
repression, 129–130; rooftop fir-
ing, 125–126; as test for
Communist Party of the Russian
Federation, 235; writings on,
104; Zyuganov's appearance on
television, 235–236
Civil war in Moscow, chronology;
September 22–23, 109–110;
September 24, 110–111;
September 25, 111–112;
September 26, 112–113;
September 27, 113–114;
September 28, 114–115;
September 29, 115–116;
September 30, 116–117; October
1, 117–118; October 2,
118–119; October 3, 119–120
Civilian consumer economy, 58
Class struggle, 256

Classes. *See* Authorized property
owners; New Russians
Climate, obstacle to capitalist devel-
opment, 63
CNN, 124
Coal miners' protests, 279, 280,
293
Coalitions, 239–240
Collective farms, 73
Collectivism, 65
Collegium of the Defense Ministry,
107–108, 124
Colombia, 166
Comecon (Council of Mutual
Economic Assistance), 72, 266
Commercial banks: losses in short-
term bond pyramid, 308–309;
panic, August 1998, 303; role of
Komsomol in creation of, 172;
service of debts to, 159. *See also*
Banks; Central Bank
Commercial trade, 145
Committee for Economic Reform,
66
Commonwealth of Independent
States, 39
Communism, 276
Communist parties, 196, 233
Communist Party of the Russian
Federation (CPRF): conservatism,
226; effects of Lebed's victory on,
295; election results, 212–213,
236, 358; importance of creation
of, 230; as inheritor of good element of former CPSU, 254; leadership of, 321; Ligachev's views
on, 224; participation in State
Duma elections, 132; plan to
ban, 354; as political party, 348;
program of, 254; proposed candidates for premiership, 323;
quandary as to actions, early
1990s, 228; rise in political influence, 236; small business support
for, 197; strength, 235, 354; sus-
pension of operations, 129;